The Prosody-Morphology Interface

In many languages, word formation is restricted by principles of prosody that organize speech into larger units such as the syllable. Written by an international team of leading linguists in the field of Prosodic Morphology, this book examines a range of key issues in the interaction of word-formation and prosody. It provides an explanation for nonconcatenative morphology which occurs in different forms (such as reduplication) in many languages, by an interaction of independent general principles of prosodic and morphological well-formedness. Surveying developments in the field from the 1970s, the book describes the general transition in linguistic theory from rule-based approaches into constraint-based ones, and most of the contributions are written from the perspective of Optimality Theory, a rapidly developing theory of constraint interaction in generative grammar.

René Kager is a Fellow of the Royal Dutch Academy of Sciences and a researcher at the Research Institute for Language and Speech, Universiteit Utrecht. Harry van der Hulst is Associate Professor of General Linguistics, Universiteit Leiden, and Director of the Holland Institute of Generative Linguistics. Wim Zonneveld is Professor of English Language Studies and Phonology and a researcher at the Research Institute for Language and Speech, Universiteit Utrecht.

The prosody-morphology interface

Edited by

René Kager, Harry van der Hulst, and Wim Zonneveld

CAMBRIDGE
UNIVERSITY PRESS

Published by the Press Syndicate of the University of Cambridge
The Pitt Building, Trumpington Street, Cambridge, United Kingdom

Cambridge University Press
The Edinburgh Building, Cambridge CB2 2RU, UK
http://www.cup.cam.ac.uk
40th West 20th Street, New York, NY10011-4211, USA
http://www.cup.org
10 Stamford Road, Oakleigh, Melbourne 3166, Australia

First published 1999

Printed in the United Kingdom at the University Press, Cambridge

Typeset in 9.25/13.75 pt Concorde BQ Regular   [GC]

A catalogue reference for this book is available from the British Library

Library of Congress cataloguing in publication data

The Prosody-Morphology Interface / edited by René Kager, Harry van
der Hulst, and Wim Zonneveld
     p   cm
  Includes indexes.
  ISBN 0 521 62108 9 (hardback)
     1. Prosodic analysis (Linguistics)   2. Grammar, Comparative and
general–Morphology.   I. Kager, René.   II. Hulst, Harry van der.
III. Zonneveld, Wim.
  P224.P767   1999
  414'.6–dc21   98–35819   CIP
  ISBN   0 521 62108 9 hardback

Contents

Contributors

Stuart Davis
Department of Linguistics, Indiana University, Bloomington

Laura J. Downing
Department of Linguistics, University of California, Berkeley

Harry van der Hulst
Department of General Linguistics, Leiden University

Larry M. Hyman
Department of Linguistics, University of California, Berkeley

Sharon Inkelas
Department of Linguistics, University of California, Berkeley

Junko Itô
Department of Linguistics, University of California, Santa Cruz

René Kager
Department of English, Utrecht University

John J. McCarthy
Department of Linguistics, University of Massachusetts, Amherst

R. Armin Mester
Department of Linguistics, University of California, Santa Cruz

Al Mtenje
Center for Language Studies, University of Malawi

Joe Pater
Department of Linguistics, University of Alberta

Alan S. Prince
Department of Linguistics, Rutgers University

Sam Rosenthall
Department of Linguistics, Ohio State University, Columbus

Grażyna Rowicka
Department of General Linguistics, Leiden University

Suzanne Urbanczyk
Department of Linguistics, University of British Columbia, Vancouver

Wim Zonneveld
Department of English, Utrecht University

Preface

A workshop on Prosodic Morphology took place on 22–24 June 1994 at the Research Institute for Language and Speech at Utrecht University. The workshop was funded by the Dutch L.O.T.-program (*Landelijke Onderzoekschool Taalwetenschap*, Netherlands Graduate School of Linguistics), and the organizers were the three editors of this volume: René Kager and Wim Zonneveld of Utrecht University and Harry van der Hulst of Leiden University.

In the first half of the 1990s, the idea of a workshop focusing on Prosodic Morphology was among those perhaps least in need of a motivation: there appears to be a consensus in both the literature and the field of phonology and its relation to morphology that this is typically one of the areas of linguistics which combines two highly recommendable characteristics – theoretical advancement is rapid, and often novel empirical data, especially from less well-known languages, are brought to bear on theoretical proposals and ideas. Rather than with the comparatively uneventful morpheme concatenations of the languages traditionally familiar to us, Prosodic Morphology deals with the exciting world of *binyanim*, reduplications and even double reduplications, infixes, templates and minimal words. This was reflected in the workshop's attendance figures: funding was based on an expected attendance of some forty people; well over a hundred actually turned up, to listen, to be informed about the latest research results, and to join in the often very lively question and discussion periods. A total of sixteen talks were presented and this volume contains ten of them. The introduction presents a brief background sketch of the research area of Prosodic Morphology.

We would like to express our gratitude to L.O.T. for funding the meeting, to the Utrecht Faculty of Arts and Letters and the Research Institute for Language and Speech for providing logistic facilities, and to staff and students for their help and support.

1 Introduction

René Kager and Wim Zonneveld

1. Prosodic Morphology before the 1990s[1]

One who consults Chomsky and Halle's (1968) Subject Index for entries beginning with *pros* is referred exclusively to passages discussing *prosodic features*. This is just one manifestation of this book's explicit claim that hierarchy has no direct role in the study of sound phenomena. Even though the input to the phonological component (a separate morphological component, including a lexicon, became available only later[2]) includes rich hierarchical structures, in that it is the output of the grammar's syntactic component, these structures are flattened out in a so-called intermediate readjustment component, resulting in completely non-hierarchical, flat strings. These strings are sequences of sound-segments and non-segments. The individual sound-segments represent the "sounds" of a given morpheme or word in an abstract sense, through binary-valued phonological features. These features include the ones traditionally called "prosodic," such as [stress], [pitch] and [tone] (376–77), but they have no special status *vis-à-vis* other features, just as for instance "cavity features" ([anterior], [coronal], [back], etc.) have no special status. Non-segments are the boundary symbols and the syntactic brackets, such as those occurring between a stem and an affix, between two words, between two phrases, and so on. Roughly speaking the number of boundary symbols and/or brackets between two morphemes reflects their degree of "coherence" (or, conversely, their comparative degree of embedding in the syntactic tree), but this not a hard-and-fast rule: not only is it the task of the readjustment component to flatten out hierarchical structure, but some of the rules of this component are also allowed to manipulate (segments and) non-segments,

1

resulting in derived representations from which the original syntactic structure cannot any longer be automatically read off.[3]

In sum, two aspects of *SPE*'s position on the linear nature of a phonological representation are relevant here. First, with respect to sound segments: these are sequences of bundles of unstructured phonological features; this is what Goldsmith (1976a) has called the Absolute Slicing Hypothesis. Second, with respect to non-segments: these are part of the flat string, and they can be manipulated (by readjustment rules) and contextually referred to by the rules of the phonology. These two aspects are what Liberman and Prince (1977: 333) have called the *linear* nature of this account.

Nonlinear phonology of the 1970s is a reaction to these claims of the standard theory.[4] *Prosodic* phonology can be seen as a subbranch of nonlinear phonology, specifically that branch dealing with prosodic categories (although this narrowing down is not always maintained). In the research area of Prosodic Morphology, some of the interesting results of the study of prosodic phonology are applied to the study of morphology, in areas where the two appear to interact. Since morphology, in the sense of *word* formation, is now standardly assumed to be situated in the lexicon (cf. note 2), the prosodic categories typically employed in Prosodic Morphology are those from the word-level down, i.e. the mora, the syllable (and possibly some of its constituents, such as onset, nucleus, and coda), the foot, and the prosodic morpheme, and word.[5] Let us consider some examples.

Two major research areas within nonlinear phonology are *autosegmental* phonology and *metrical* phonology. Although both are hierarchical or three-dimensional, they differ with respect to the empirical material they focus on. Although there is no *a priori* or principled strict division of tasks between the two, autosegmental theory traditionally deals with phenomena such as tone (spreading) and various types of assimilation (prominently including vowel harmony), whereas metrical theory deals with syllable structure, stress, and rhythm. The first work to turn doubts about absolute slicing into a theoretical framework of spreading and assimilation phenomena is Goldsmith (1976b):[6] it introduces autosegmental phonology as a reaction to the linear *SPE* theory. As an illustration of the basic tenets of this framework, consider the following brief description of Igbo vowel harmony, comparing the *SPE* treatment with the autosegmental one by Clements (1976).

In a vowel-harmony system characteristically all vowels within a word have the same value for a "harmonic feature." Usually, there can be identified within a word a source or trigger of the harmony, and there are two ways in which the pertinent feature value can spread throughout the word from this source. First, the feature can spread from the stem to all the affixes in a word; this is called symmetric or root-controlled vowel harmony. Second, the feature can spread from a fixed position (the leftmost or rightmost vowel of a certain quality) in one particular direction; this is called directional harmony. The West-African Igbo language has symmetric harmony, and the *SPE* account assumes a relatively complicated set of three separate ordered rules to capture it (Chomsky and Halle 1968: 378–79). On the other hand, Clements's account looks (at worst) like this:

(1) Associate

The question is how autosegmental phonology enables one to accomplish this extreme descriptive reduction. Some simple Igbo facts:

(2) e-ke-le   "don't share"   a-zu-la   "don't buy"
     i-vu   "to carry"   i-lu   "to marry"

The property of Igbo harmony any analysis aspires to account for is that vowels in a word are either [+ATR] or [−ATR], i.e. they have or they have not an "advanced tongue root" (the underlined vowels in the lefthand words are all [+ATR]; this property is lacking ([−ATR]) from the vowels in the righthand words). An *SPE*-type derivational analysis with rules distinguishes three steps in this procedure. First, all affix vowels are specified [−H]. This is a completely arbitrary "diacritic" specification, which will have a phonological function only later in the derivation. Stems can be underlyingly specified either [+H] or [−H]. When the stem is intrinsically [−H] and all affixes are [−H] following the first step, we have already come a large part of the way towards accounting for harmony. When the stem is intrinsically [+H], however, a second rule specifies all vowels to the left and to the right of the stem (so: all affix vowels again) as [+H] as well. Finally, a third rule gives a phonological interpretation to the arbitrary feature [H]: it says that the feature actually means [ATR], and that [+H] corresponds to [+ATR] and [−H] to [−ATR]. Reconsider the data in (2), the righthand words first, since the state of affairs in these words is simple: the stems -zu- and -lu- are [−H] underlyingly, all affix vowels become [–H], and at the final stage the [–ATR] interpretation is provided. The lefthand words are rather where the action is: three consecutive operations ([–H] on affixes, spreading of [–H], and phonetic interpretation) result in words that have [+ATR] vowels only.

One interesting type of data Chomsky and Halle apparently did not have the opportunity to have a look at is the phenomenon of *opacity* in vowel-harmony systems. This means that certain vowels or certain affixes may block the spreading of the harmonic feature throughout the word: they interrupt the wave. In (3) below are some Igbo data (nonopaque vowels are in italics):

(3) a. ...-bho-wa-ghi   "put-begin-emph."
    b. vu-si   "distr.-carry"
    c. ...-bho-si-ghi   "put-carry-emph."

(3a) is a case of perfect harmony, involving the suffixes *-wa* and *-ghi*. The second example, (3b), shows that the suffix *-si* exceptionally does not take part in harmony. The bottom form shows that the harmonic wave cannot reach the rightmost suffix *-ghi* across the exceptional suffix *-si*: it is as if, as well as being an exception, *-si* automatically has the property of inducing its own harmony, to the right. There is nothing in the linear account of (1) that hints at how this may come about, although opacity is a very common phenomenon in harmony languages.

What happens in an autosegmental account of these data? The crucial step in an autosegmental analysis can be compared to solving the puzzle of having to make three triangles with six matches: one is required to introduce hierarchy or multi-dimensionality. More specifically, we observe the "autosegmentalization," or "setting apart" of the harmony feature on a separate level or "tier." Autosegmental representations of regular cases of Igbo harmony look as in (4):

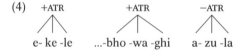

(4)   +ATR   +ATR   −ATR
       /|\   /|\   /|\
    e- ke -le   ...-bho -wa -ghi   a- zu -la

Such representations are derived from underlying forms in which the autosegment, as it were, floats over the vowel of the stem, and affix vowels are unspecified for the harmony feature, i.e., representations such as (4) without any "association lines" whatsoever, the latter being drawn as a result of the so-called Well-Formedness Condition (WFC) on autosegmental representations. This WFC is a universal, and has the following form:

(5) a. all vowels are associated to at least one autosegment
 b. all autosegments are associated to at least one vowel
 c. association lines may not cross
 d. association of unassociated autosegments precedes drawing lines from associated autosegments

The WFC derives (2) and (3) from (4), through (5a–b). The role of (5c–d) becomes clear from the way it allows opacity to be treated. An exceptional affix is underlyingly preassociated with its own harmony feature: in this way, [+ATR] can never reach vowels outside (to the left or to the right of) exceptional vowels, as association lines may not cross.

(6)   +ATR   −ATR   +ATR   −ATR

...-bho -si -ghi   e- vu -te -si -ghi

The correct direction of spreading (the dotted lines in (6)) follows from (5d). The language-specific information needed to trigger the procedure is that -si is an opaque (preassociated) suffix, and [ATR] is an autosegmental feature. All else simply follows from the universal WFC.

   Then consider the next event, of crucial importance to this introduction. McCarthy (1979) applies the principles of autosegmental phonology to morphology, effectively establishing the field of Prosodic Morphology. He discusses the phenomenon of discontinuous affixation in Semitic morphological systems, specifically that of Arabic; in data such as those in (7) below, consonants play the role of stems (or *binyanim*) and vowels play the role of affixes.

(7)	katab	I	Perfective Active
	kaatab	III	Perfective Active
	ktabab	IX	Perfective Active
	ukaatab	III	Imperfective Passive
	kuutib	III	Perfective Passive
	ktanbab	XIV	Perfective Active
	aktanbib	XIV	Imperfective Active

McCarthy first shows how a linear account, more specifically that of Chomsky (1951) (but all others have the same relevant formal properties), deals with the discontinuities in such output forms. Given consonantal stem patterns (C_1-C_2-C_3) and affixal vowel patterns (V_1-V_2), a transformational rule of the following sort is required in order to derive the linear sequence of consonants and vowels in the output, for the first form of (7):

(8) C_1-C_2-C_3 + V_1-V_2 → $C_1V_1C_2V_2C_3$

Similar rules will be required for the other forms. But transformational rules are an extremely powerful device for morphology to incorporate (McCarthy 1979: 358):

> (9) Morphological transformations potentially allow any arbitrary operation on a segmental string. For example, transformational morphological rules of this sort can freely move particular segments an unbounded distance within the word, copy all and only the vowels in a word, or reverse strings of finite length.

This is a strong incentive to look for alternatives, and one such alternative lies in the strategy of seeking an analogy between autosegmental phonological phenomena and the morphological one under discussion.

Thus, just considering the top two forms of (7), the stem consonants and affix vowels can be seen to be exactly the same (and in exactly the same order), with only a single difference residing in the number of vowels occurring in the forms. McCarthy proposes to deal with these two cases in the following fashion. In so far as the mix of vowels and consonants in a given *binyan* is unpredictable, the shape of the *binyan* is specified in a so-called "syllabic skeleton" or "template"; for the two forms under discussion these templates look as in (11b) below. Then, in an autosegmental manner, stem and affix "melodies" are each specified on separate tiers ((11a) and (11c), respectively), which in this case clearly have a morphological function. The WFC variant employed in order to establish the correct associations between template and melodies is that of (10). Notice the high degree of similarity between (10) and (5), which makes it desirable to assume a theoretical common denominator.

> (10) a. each slot in the skeleton must be linked with at least one segment in the melody
>   b. linking lines must never cross

c. (unless otherwise stipulated) segments in the melody and slots in the skeleton are linked one-to-one from left-to-right

d. when a melody contains both linked and unlinked units, it is the latter that are spread to unfilled slots

Immediately including the next two cases of (9), representations for the first four forms look as in (11), after application of the WFC of (10):

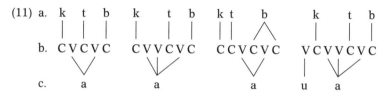

(11) a.

b.

c.

We have seen that in vowel harmony, (vowels of) affixes may be pre-specified as opaque, by prelinking them. Exactly the same technique is a useful device in the remaining cases of (7), which either have an unpredictable vowel pattern or a consonantal infix in an unpredictable position, or both at the same time:

(12)

Without prelinking, the infix could go anywhere with respect to the stem consonants; and left-to-right association predicts that similar vowels will cooccur on the righthand side rather than the (in these cases empirically correct) lefthand side. There are many more intricacies to these Semitic morphological systems (see the remainder of chapter 4 of McCarthy's dissertation, and example (23) below), but the claim seems justified that Prosodic Morphology, leaning heavily on the earlier results of nonlinear phonology, allows for both much more insightful and theoretically less powerful accounts.

As pointed out above, metrical phonology is a reaction to the analyses of the standard theory in the realm of stress, rhythm, and syllable structure. The earliest work in the nonlinear approach in these areas is represented by the mid-1970s Ph.D. theses by Liberman (1975) and Kahn (1976). Taking a syllable structure example from the latter, in fact one that has a classical structure: generalizations are lost when syllable structure is not directly available in phonological analyses (the position of the *SPE* theory is of course the reverse: there is no need for fear that generalizations are lost by not directly representing syllable structure). The argument for the syllable is two-pronged. First, in standard phonological analyses a rule like that in (13a) below expresses a generalization via the curly bracket notation which two separate rules would fail to capture. Second, however, the fact that an equally general, abbreviated rule pair such as that in (13b) does not occur very frequently (if at all), argues against the bracket notation as the correct generalizing device for these cases.

(13) a. $/r/ \rightarrow \Phi \ / \ \_\_\_ \begin{Bmatrix} C \\ \# \end{Bmatrix}$ b. $/r/ \rightarrow \Phi \ / \ \_\_\_ \begin{Bmatrix} V \\ \# \end{Bmatrix}$

If this is so, we need something to replace these curly brackets. In fact, cases of type (13a) remind one strongly of the traditional notion of "syllable"; consider data such as those in (14) regarding the process of *r*-loss in many varieties of English:

(14) /r/ lost:
        b a r k   b a r k e r   b a r (# is...)
     /r/ retained:
        r e d   M a r y   c o r r e c t   b a r⌢ i s

In *SPE* terminology, *r* is lost before a consonant or a word boundary (but the latter not in relatively fast speech). Such a statement implies curly brackets; however, these can be eliminated when we say directly that *r* is lost when tautosyllabic with a preceding vowel.[7]

Once we assume, on the basis of a phenomenon such as English *r*-loss, and others like it, that the syllable is part of the basic linguistic vocabulary, one of the questions that arises is whether perhaps, just as segments (insofar as the notion of "segment" survives an articulated theory of autosegmental phenomena[8]) are organized into syllables, syllables themselves are organized into higher units. The answer to this question has turned out to be an affirmative one, the relevant unit of organization one level up being the "foot." The earliest arguments for this unit can be found in Selkirk (1978, 1980) and Vergnaud and Halle (1978). This time consider the phenomenon of French *e-muet*: in this process, schwas are optionally deleted, as long as the output does not contain a triliteral consonant cluster.

(15) a. souv(ə)nir   pass(ə)ra

   b. parvənir   souffləra   *pa[rv-n]ir   *sou[fl-r]a

   c. (tu) dəvənais, dəv-nais, d-vənais   *[d-v-n]ais

The linear analysis of Dell (1973) mentions exactly the required condition as a constraint on the possible outputs of the rule, but such an addition (i.e., a "derivational constraint") functions as a "violation of the otherwise Markovian character of phonological deviations [sic]" (Vergnaud and Halle, 1978: 32). A nonlinear account may run as follows. First, assume that full vowels have that property represented by a branching structure over them; second, assume that *schwas* count as full after two consonants, and optionally as full (or nonbranching) otherwise. Finally, a nonbranching syllable must be accommodated by its left neighbor into superordinate structure. One can easily make out that four structures will thus become available for the phrase *tu devenais*:

(16)   ∧   ∧   ∧
         ∧ | | ∧   ∧ | ∧ ∧   ∧ ∧ | ∧   ∧ ∧ ∧ ∧
         tu dəvənais   tu dəvənais   tu dəvənais   tu dəvənais

It is equally easy to see that the rule of *schwa* deletion can now be formulated, Markovianly, as in (17):

(17)   F

                   /∧
    ə → ø / / ⎯⎯⎯

So much is clear: the name of the superordinate structure cannot be "syllable"; it is, rather, a sequence of syllables, organized in a particular fashion; it is the foot.[9]

Syllable and foot are now known as "prosodic categories," and the study of prosodic categories is a separate branch of (metrical) phonology. Lexical prosodic categories that have been added more recently are the mora (a unit of phonological "weight," especially in systems of stress and length) at a level lower than the syllable, and the (prosodic) word, as a unit in which feet are commonly organized. It may furthermore be useful to divide the syllable into the constituents of "Onset" and "Rhyme" (and the "Rhyme" into "Nucleus" and "Coda").

An extremely interesting phenomenon in which notions from autosegmental and metrical theory have been argued to team up, is that of "reduplication," i.e., the type of morphology in which affixation takes place by repeating either the whole stem or part of the stem in the derived form. Influential in this area has been Marantz (1982). Consider from that article reduplication data from Agta (a Philippine language) such as those in (18):

(18) bari   "body"   bar-bari...   "my whole body"
     saddu   "to leak"   ...sad-saddu "to leak in many places"
     wakay   "lost"   ...wak-wakay "many things lost"
     takki   "leg"   tak-takki   "legs"
     uffu   "thigh"   uf-uffu   "thighs"
     ulu   "head"   ul-ulu   "heads"

Referring to McCarthy's analysis of Semitic *binyanim*, Marantz argues that the reduplicative affix is a complete melodic copy of the stem, but the shape of the copy is ultimately constrained by a (morphological) templatic condition on CV-sequences. In the case at hand, this template has the shape CVC. Association takes place from left to right (for prefixes and in the mirror image fashion for suffixes):

(19)

An example in which the prosodic category of the syllable plays a role in a reduplication process is that of Yidinʸ (Dixon 1977, Nash 1980, Marantz 1982: 453–56):

(20) ḍimurU   "house"   ḍimu-ḍimurU   "houses"
     ḍaḍaman   "to jump"   ḍaḍa-ḍaḍaman   "to jump a lot"
     gindalba "lizard"   gindal-gindalba "lizards"
     ḍugarban "to have an   ḍugar-ḍugarban "to have an
               unsettled mind"   unsettled mind
                                               for a long
                                               period"

Two observations are in order here. First, the reduplicative morpheme of Yidinʸ is disyllabic, and second, this morpheme does not necessarily use a consonant to close the final syllable, even if the opportunity arises (*dimur-dimurU). This is where Yidinʸ also differs from Agta:

(21)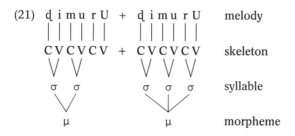

Developments so far may be characterized as the application of autosegmental and metrical principles, both originally motivated in the domain of "phonology proper," to the new domain of nonconcatenative morphology. The central concept involved in this kind of morphology is the "template": a skeletal morpheme that is segmentally unspecified except for information on the positions of consonants and vowels.

In the early eighties an increasing recognition arose of the key role of prosodic templates in syllabification (cf. Vergnaud and Halle 1978, Selkirk 1980, 1982, Itô 1986). Central in this "prosodic-template-matching" approach was the idea that languages draw their syllable shapes from a narrow pool of universal possibilities. For example, languages may select the option "onsets are obligatory," thereby imposing this as a well-formedness criterion on the outputs of all phonological processes that affect syllable structure. In their unpublished paper called "Prosodic Morphology" dating from 1986, McCarthy and Prince argued that this *prosodic*-template approach should be extended to the domain of nonconcatenative morphology, which had previously been analyzed in terms of *segmental* templates and autosegmental association (McCarthy 1979, Marantz 1982). The landmark contribution of this 1986 paper was the elimination of segmental templates by prosodic templates, defined in terms of universal prosodic units such as the mora, syllable, and foot. This idea was stated as follows by McCarthy and Prince (1986: 6):

Patterns of obligatoriness and optionality will follow in general from independent characterization of the prosodic units, both universally and language-specifically....The fact that the templates are bounded by a language's prosody follows from their being literally built from that prosody.

The endpoint of this initial stage of the study of Prosodic Morphology can be found in McCarthy and Prince (1990). This paper is a combination of parts of the earlier unpublished paper, and original work on Arabic "broken" plurals and diminutive formation. In it, the authors present "three fundamental theses" of the theory of Prosodic Morphology:[10]

(22) a. Prosodic Morphology Hypothesis
    Templates are defined in terms of the authentic units of prosody: mora, syllable, foot, prosodic word, and so on.
b. Template Satisfaction Condition
    Satisfaction of templatic constraints is obligatory and is determined by the principles of prosody, both universal and language-specific.
c. Prosodic Circumscription of Domains
    The domain to which morphological operations apply may be circumscribed by prosodic criteria as well as by the more familiar morphological ones. In particular, the "minimal word" within a domain may be selected as the locus of morphological transformation in lieu of the whole domain.

In this framework, Agta reduplication above is a case where the CVC reduplicative prefix is redefined as a heavy syllable ($\sigma_{\mu\mu}$). The analysis of Yidin^y is slightly more complicated. The authors start by noting that the unqualified notion of "syllable" does not appear to be involved in cases of reduplication: "The curious property of Yidin^y reduplication is the way that the syllabification of the base is carried over, as if the initial disyllabic sequence were copied whole. A large amount of descriptive research has failed to turn up a reduplicative process that unambiguously *copies* a single syllable…Why then should reduplication appear to copy *two* syllables but never just one?" (p. 233). Within the theory of Prosodic Morphology in (22), the answer runs as follows. The first step is to select from the base (by a process called "prosodic circumscription") the so-called minimal word: in Yidin^y this is the bisyllabic – initial – foot (no stem may be monosyllabic). Then, on this minimal word, reduplication is simply complete.

Some relevant Arabic "broken" plurals can be found in (23) below.

(23) Sg. jundub   "locust"   Pl. janaadib
        sultaan   "sultan"   salaatin
        xaatam   "signet ring"   xawaatim
        haluub(-at) "milch camel"   halaa?ib

We get from singulars to plurals by the following route. First, the minimal word is used in circumscription, and its content is the bimoraic foot: thus, it contains either one heavy syllable or two light ones. Second, the minimal word is associated to an "affixal" template, which is the unmarked iambic foot: $\sigma_\mu\sigma_\mu$ (light-heavy). Third, the residue of phonological material outside the minimal word is maintained. Fourth, the vowels of the singular are overwritten by an *a-i* melody: *-a-* within the iambic foot, *-i-* outside it. Finally, default insertion consonants may appear at the verge between vowels. Consider the following displays resulting from this analysis.

(24)

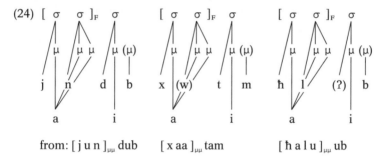

from: [j u n]$_{\mu\mu}$ dub   [x aa]$_{\mu\mu}$ tam   [ħ a l u]$_{\mu\mu}$ ub

McCarthy and Prince support the prosodic-morphological subparts of this analysis with a considerable amount of language-internal evidence. Moreover, they support the theory of Prosodic Morphology with an enormous amount of evidence from reduplication and other affixational phenomena from a wide range of natural languages.

The overriding force of prosodic factors in templatic and reduplicative morphology was emphasised by Steriade (1988: 80), in the form of a major cross-linguistic observation that would become a focus of attention in later years: templates tend to have *unmarked syllable structure*:[11]

Prosodic templates frequently eliminate certain marked options from their syllabic structures. Although the language may in general allow complex onsets or consonantal nuclei, the template might specifically revoke these options.

We observe the following range of syllabic simplification in prosodic templates: onset simplification (Tagalog *ta-trabaho*, *bo-bloaut* from McCarthy and Prince 1986: 16); coda simplification (Sanskrit intensive *kan-i-krand...*); coda drop (cf. the French hypocoristics *zabe*, *mini* from (*i*)*zabel*, (*do*)*minik*); elimination of consonantal nuclei (Sanskrit perfect *va-vṛma*).

Steriade proposed that prosodically marked properties were *literally* cancelled from the reduplicant, which is in its initial state a *full copy* of the base – including its prosody. This full-copy-plus-cancellation model explains certain properties of reduplication that pose problems to Marantzian "melody-copy-plus-association" models (assumed by McCarthy and Prince 1990). In particular it explains why syllabic roles of segments can be transferred under reduplication. Steriade's proposal also raised new questions: why are cancellations of prosodic marked-ness limited to reduplicants and truncations, both morphemes whose segmental content is dependent upon a basic stem form?[12] Why does reduplication never (unambiguously) *copy* a single syllable? We will return to these questions in sections 2.2 and 2.5.

Summarizing the developments in the late 1980s, we find that researchers came to recognize the major role played by prosodic well-formedness in what became appropriately known as Prosodic Morphology. Although Prosodic Morphology was now firmly integrated with prosodic theory, questions remained with respect to the prosody-morphology *interface*. Most work published in the 1970s and 1980s assumed a strict division of labor between morphology and phonology.[13] In reduplication this was reflected as the *serial ordering* of a morphological operation (the affixation of a reduplicative template) before its construction-specific phonology: the full copying (and cancellation of marked properties in Steriade's model). As we will see in the next section, precisely this serial grammatical organization came under fire by developments in the 1990s.

2. Prosodic Morphology in the 1990s

In this section, we briefly discuss recent developments in Prosodic Morphology, those that have taken place in the 1990s, and especially those in the recent framework of Optimality Theory. Recall from the previous section that the main goal of the theory of Prosodic Morphology is an explanation of morphological patterns of reduplication, root-and-pattern morphology, etc., as these occur in different forms in a large number of languages, by the interaction of independent general principles. To state it, provocatively, the field is ultimately self-destructive in the sense that morphology-specific properties are eliminated in favor of more general principles of phonological and morphological well-formedness. To the extent that such a reduction is successful, the field of prosodic morphology will be assimilated into the fields of "prosody" and "morphology."

2.1 General ideas

Optimality Theory (Prince and Smolensky 1993, McCarthy and Prince 1993a, b) adopts a view of the prosody-morphology interface that is radically different from its rule-based ancestors. According to this view prosodic well-formedness requirements *directly interact* with morphological requirements. Interaction takes the form of *constraint domination*, the setting of priorities among conflicting constraints, which make general requirements about output forms. This new idea of the prosody-morphology interface is embedded in a theory of language as a whole, which has the following characteristics.

The central idea of Optimality Theory (OT) is that language is the domain of conflicting requirements. Grammars are language-specific ways to resolve such conflicts, on the basis of a hierarchy of constraints. Constraints are violable, but violation must be minimal. The well-formedness of an output form is a relative notion: it only means to convey that no other output forms are possible that are better-formed as evaluated by the set of ranked output constraints. The *optimal* output form is the one that minimally violates high-ranked constraints, possibly at the expense of violations of lower-ranked constraints. The ranking of two constraints is demonstrated by comparing two (or any number of) candidate output forms, taking into account their violations of each constraint. This demonstration takes the form of a *tableau*: this lists all the candidates vertically, and the constraints horizontally, in a descending ranking from left to right, while the cells contain violation marks incurred by each candidate for a constraint:

(25)

	C_1	C_2
a. ☞ *candidate 1*		**
b. *candidate 2*	*!	

The optimal candidate ☞ is (25a) since this has no violations of the highest-ranked constraint C_1, while its competitor (25b) has one. (This violation is fatal to (25b), hence the exclamation mark accompanying it.) Observe that the optimal candidate (25a) is far from impeccable: it has two violations of C_2, but this factor is insignificant, given that no candidate occurs that has no violations on either constraint. This shows that domination is strict: a candidate that incurs violations of some high-ranking constraint (on which another candidate incurs no viola-tions) is mercilessly excluded, regardless of its relative well-formedness with respect to lower-ranked constraints.

Constraints fall into different types. *Well-formedness* constraints enforce prosodic or segmental markedness, such as "syllables must have onsets," or "syllables must not have codas." *Faithfulness* constraints militate against any divergences between an output form and its basic (underlying) form, such as "input segments must be preserved in the output." Well-formedness constraints provide the pressure for changes; they inherently conflict with faithfulness constraints, which inhibit any changes. Other constraint types enforce morpheme-specific require-ments, mostly referring to the matching of morphological and prosodic edges. Among the morphological constraints are also those enforcing the identity between the reduplicant and the base, which is otherwise captured by the copying rules of Marantz (1982) and Steriade (1988).

A crucial property of the OT model, when it comes to the interface of phonology and morphology, is *parallelism*: constraints of different modalities interact in a single hierarchy. Parallelism predicts that mor-phological requirements may (in principle at least) be violated under pressure of dominating prosodic requirements, which is precisely what seems to be required in cases discussed so far. This constitutes an essen-tial difference from the derivational model, which assumes a strict divi-sion of labor between morphology and prosody. Let us now find out how Prosodic Morphology can be construed under the OT model.

2.2 Prosodic Morphology as constraint interaction: P ≫ M

The OT model of Prosodic Morphology shares with its derivational ancestor the driving idea that the patterns of reduplication, truncation, or infixation, as observed in different languages, result from a com-bination of independent and general principles. The central idea of this model is that *prosodic* well-formedness constraints have priority over *morphological* requirements. The major change in perspective that became possible as a result of OT concerns the interaction between the independent and general principles, principles alluded to above, an interaction which now takes the form of a competition between violable constraints, ranked in language-specific hierarchies.

For example, consider the cross-linguistically common situation of a reduplicant that is less prosodically marked than the basic form from which it copies segments, as discussed by Steriade (1988). In Optimality Theory, this situation is analyzed as a ranking of *prosodic well-formedness* constraints over morphological constraints which enforce the *identity* between the reduplicant and its base. Precisely this situation occurs in the pattern of reduplication of the Peruvian language Axininca Campa (Payne 1981, Spring 1990, McCarthy and Prince 1993a, b). Reduplication copies the entire root (26a), except in the case of a root starting with a vowel, which is left uncopied (26b).

(26) Axininca Campa reduplication
    a. /kawosi + RED/kawosi-<u>kawosi</u>   "bathe"
    b. /osampi + RED/osampi-<u>sampi</u>   "ask" *not* *osampi-<u>osampi</u>

A partial reduplicant -<u>sampi</u> that has an onset (an unmarked prosodic structure) is chosen instead of a full reduplicant -<u>osampi</u> that lacks an onset (a marked prosodic structure). McCarthy and Prince (1993b) analyze the pattern as an interaction between a morphological constraint requiring reduplication to be total,[14] dominated by a prosodic constraint, requiring syllables to have onsets:

(27) MAX
    Reduplicant = Base

(28) ONSET
    Syllables must have onsets.

The interaction of these constraints is captured by a simple ranking statement in (29):

(29) ONSET ≫ MAX

This interaction is shown in tableau (30):

(30)

Input: /osampi-RED/	ONSET	MAX
a. ☞ osampi-<u>sampi</u>	*	o
b. osampi-<u>osampi</u>	**!	

The optimal reduplicant in (30a) may be imperfect in terms of completeness of copying, but it enjoys the important advantage of being prosodically unmarked. The grammar of Axininca assigns more importance to the latter (prosodic) factor than to the former (morphological) factor. This ranking of prosody over morphology, P $\gg$ M, is, according to McCarthy and Prince (1993b), the true hallmark of Prosodic Morphology.

A preliminary explanation can now be given of Steriade's important finding that "cancellation" of marked prosody is typical of templatic morphology. This explanation is based on the interaction of the configuration ONSET $\gg$ MAX with a third constraint, PARSE, a *faithfulness* constraint which militates against the loss of segments from the input:

(31) PARSE
      Input segments must appear in the output.

When ONSET ranks above PARSE, vowels may be deleted in order to create unmarked syllables with onsets. But when PARSE is ranked above ONSET, as is the case in Axininca Campa, then no vowel is deletable from a root's input form in order to avoid an onsetless syllable in the output. In tableau (32) this is shown in the form of fatal violation marks in the cells of candidates c and d in the column headed by PARSE:

(32)

Input: /osampi-RED/	PARSE	ONSET	MAX
a. ☞ osampi-<u>sampi</u>		*	o
b. osampi-<u>osampi</u>		**!	
c. sampi-<u>sampi</u>	o!		
d. sampi-<u>osampi</u>	o!	*	

Note that no logically possible ranking of these three constraints will produce the effect that the reduplicant retains the input /o/, while the base drops it. That is, candidate (32d) is necessarily suboptimal to any of the other candidates, regardless of constraint ranking. This explains why a difference in prosodic markedness between the base and reduplicant is *always in favor of the reduplicant*: only the base, not the reduplicant, is subject to faithfulness to the input. Observe that this explanation is based on a minimal assumption about reduplication that has to be made under any theory, which is that the reduplicant morpheme has no input segments affiliated with it in its input form. Segmental emptiness of the input is what exempts the reduplicant from faithfulness constraints (e.g., PARSE).[15]

This interaction of input faithfulness (PARSE), prosodic well-formedness (ONSET) and reduplicative identity (MAX) is what McCarthy and Prince (1994) have referred to as an *"emergence of the unmarked."* Well-formedness constraints may seem to be "inactive" in a language, but in fact they are only "hidden" behind higher-ranking faithfulness constraints. Well-formedness suddenly jumps into activity in situations where faithfulness has no grip. In Axininca Campa PARSE (a faithfulness constraint) dominates ONSET (a well-formedness constraint), ruling out deletion of input vowels as a strategy to avoid onsetless syllables. But in reduplicants, where input faithfulness plays no role (as reduplicants have no input segments), ONSET takes effect (even at the expense of reduplicative identity). This result is typical of OT since the "hide-and-emerge" effect is predicted by constraint domination.

Next consider the pattern of *um*-infixation in Tagalog (French 1988), which serves as a further illustration of the domination of prosodic constraints over morphological ones. The generalization is that *-um-* is infixed directly after the onset of the word (cf. (33b) and (33c), if it has one; if the word has no onset, *-um-* becomes a prefix, cf. (33a):

(33) Tagalog prefixal infixation
     a. um+aral   →   <u>um</u>-aral   "teach"
     b. um+salat   →   s-<u>um</u>-alat   "write"
     c. um+gradwet →   gr-<u>um</u>-adwet "graduate"

The prefix skips over the initial onset, settling itself between a consonant and vowel in the base, with which it integrates into a well-formed sequence of syllables. What is avoided is an output form in which the vowel of *-um-* lacks an onset, while its consonant syllabifies as a coda, as in **um-tawag*. In sum, the creation of well-formed syllables is what drives *-um-*infixation: we observe a dependence of morphology on the prosody of the output.

The analysis by Prince and Smolensky (1993) of this pattern is strikingly simple, since it directly encodes the dominance of prosody over morphological requirements. The constraint that comes into play here is stated in (34), and it militates against codas:

(34) No-Coda
Syllables do not have codas.

This prosodic well-formedness constraint interacts with a morphological constraint that expresses the status of *-um-* as an affix which must be as close as possible to the left edge of the word:

(35) Edgemost (*um*; L)
The item *um* is situated at the left edge of the word

In fact, this is nothing but the requirement that "*-um-* is a prefix." Like other constraints, this morphological constraint is in principle violable. And in Tagalog, it actually is violated in cases where *-um-* is adjoined in a position that is not strictly at the beginning of the word.

The constraint ranking producing the mixed effect of "infixation" in some contexts, and of "prefixation" in other contexts, is stated in (36):

(36) P-constraint ≫ M-constraint
No-Coda ≫ Edgemost (*um*; L)

That is, Tagalog assigns more importance to the avoidance of codas than to the prefixal status of the affix *-um-*. However, the prefixal status of *-um-* still asserts itself maximally in the sense that it stands *as close as possible* to the left edge of the word, respecting the superordinate requirements of prosody. This analysis is illustrated by the tableau of *gr-um-adwet*:

(37)

Input: {um, gradwet}	No-Coda	Edgemost (*um*; L)
a. <u>um</u>.grad.wet	***!	#
b. g<u>um</u>.rad.wet	***!	# g
c. ☞ gr<u>u</u>.<u>m</u>ad.wet	**	# g r
d. gra.<u>um</u>.dwet	**	# g r a!
e. gra.d<u>um</u>.wet	**	# g r a! d
f. grad.w<u>u</u>.<u>m</u>et	**	# g r a! d w
g. grad.we.<u>um</u>t	**	# g r a! d w e
h. grad.we.t<u>um</u>	**	# g r a! d w e t

Observe that the prefixational candidate (37a) violates No-Coda more than is necessary (for a base of the skeletal type *gradwet* this amounts to two violations). No improvement with respect to No-Coda is reached in candidate (37b), which infixes *-um-* between the first and second consonants of the base. Each of the remaining candidates (37c)–(37h) incurs two violations of No-Coda. From these the one is selected that minimally violates the next constraint down the hierarchy, which is Edgemost (*um*; L). Violations of Edgemost are marked by segments lying between the left word edge and the affix *-um-*. The optimal output is (37c), since this has the smallest number of violations of this constraint, and it can be said to maximally respect the prefixal status of *-um-*. All remaining infixational candidates (37c)–(37e) violate Edgemost (*um*; L) to a larger degree than is strictly necessary. (Recall one of the basic principles of OT: constraint violation is minimal.) This analysis is based on the *parallel* evaluation of prosodic and morphological constraints.

Now compare the way in which *serial* theory might deal with the Tagalog pattern. This would involve "prosodic circumscription," a device proposed by McCarthy and Prince (1990), which was briefly mentioned in section 1. The first step would be the circumscription of the word onset (on the assumption that this is a prosodic unit). Next, *-um-* is prefixed to the residue of circumscription (the base minus the word onset), which begins with a vowel. Finally, the word onset is put back in its place, producing the effect of *um*-infixation. But this analysis leaves unexpressed the relation between the prosodic shape of the affix *-um-* (VC), and its surface distribution, directly after the word onset. Circumscription theory is unable to make this connection, as it separates circumscription from the morphological operation that it potentiates. In retrospect, circumscription was a mechanism without a cause.[16]

2.3 The notion of "template" in OT Prosodic Morphology

The key idea that Prosodic Morphology involves the domination of prosodic constraints over morphological constraints was elaborated in McCarthy and Prince (1993b). This 184-page manuscript deals mainly with aspects of the prosodic morphology of Axininca Campa, of which we have already seen an example above. A recurrent theme of this manuscript is that templatic requirements are only satisfied maximally, within the limits imposed by the superordinate requirements of the language. Violability of templatic constraints is in fact predicted by OT, given the assumption of *parallelism*, according to which morphological constraints are ranked in a single hierarchy together with universal prosodic constraints.

As a second modification of the notion of "template" McCarthy and Prince (1993b: 82) argue that templates are *constraints on the Prosody-Morphology interface*, which assert the coincidence of morphological and prosodic constituents:

the classical notion of template and template-satisfaction needs to be generalized. Optimality Theory provides a means of dealing effectively with the violability of the constraint; this is entirely expected behavior, in the general context of the theory...The place to look for generalization of the notion of "template," we propose, is in the family of constraints on the prosody/ morphology interface, such as ALIGN. The idea is that the Reduplicant must be in a particular alignment with prosodic structure. The strictest such alignments will amount to classical templates.

The notion of "template" is integrated with the notion of "alignment" of morphological and prosodic edges (McCarthy and Prince 1993a):

(38) Constraint schema for classical templates

MCAT=PCAT

where MCAT ≡ Morphological Category ≡ Prefix, Suffix, RED, Root, Stem, LexWd, etc.

and PCAT ≡ Prosodic Category ≡ Mora, Syllable (type), Foot (type), PrWd (type), etc.

A related change is the decomposition of the "template" into different constraints, each having its own position in the ranking. Earlier work, starting with McCarthy (1979) and Marantz (1982), assumed that the template is a segmentally empty morpheme combining in it the full set of properties defining prosodic "shape invariance." McCarthy and Prince (1993b: 82) argue instead that the template is not a monolithic entity, and that it is in fact not a theoretical primitive at all. What was formerly attributed to a template now follows from the interaction of multiple constraints on the size, shape, and position of morphemes.

In Axininca Campa, for example, four constraints are responsible for defining the reduplicant's shape. These four constraints are stated in pretheoretical terminology below.

(39) a. DISYLL "The Reduplicant is at least disyllabic."
     b. R=SFX "The Reduplicant is a suffix – not an independent PrWd."
     c. R≤ROOT "The Reduplicant consists of material drawn from the root alone."
     d. MAX "Reduplication is total."

Each of these constraints is known to govern absolutely properties of reduplication in other languages. But in Axininca Campa all of these templatic constraints are literally untrue, that is, dominated by other constraints. See, for example, the following tableaux, each of which demonstrates the dominated status of a templatic constraint.

A monosyllabic reduplicant that has no epenthetic segments is preferred over a disyllabic reduplicant with epenthetic segments (indicated by "TA"):

(40)

Input: /naa-RED/	FILL	DISYLL
a. ☞ naa-<u>naa</u>		*
b. naaTA-<u>naaTA</u>	*!***	

A disyllabic reduplicant containing non-root material (the prefix *no-*) is preferred over a monosyllabic reduplicant containing only root material:

(41)

Input: /no-naa-RED/	DISYLL	R≤ROOT
a. ☞ no-naa-<u>nonaa</u>		*
b. no-naa-<u>naa</u>	*!	

A partial reduplicant containing only root material is preferred over a full reduplicant containing non-root material (the prefix *noŋ-*):

(42)

Input: /noŋ-kawosi-RED/	R≤ROOT	MAX
a. ☞ noŋ-kawosi-<u>kawosi</u>		noŋ-
b. noŋ-kawosi-<u>noŋ-kawosi</u>	*!	

Both modifications of the 1986 theory (violability of templatic requirements, and a compositional, alignment-based, notion of template) are integrated into the revised version of the principles of Prosodic Morphology:

(43) New Prosodic Morphology (McCarthy and Prince 1993b: 138)
   a. Prosodic Morphology Hypothesis
      Templates are constraints on the Prosody-Morphology inter-
      face, asserting the coincidence of morphological and prosodic
      constituents.
   b. Template Satisfaction Condition
      Templatic constraints may be undominated, in which case
      they are satisfied fully, or they may be dominated, in which
      case they are violated minimally, in accordance with general
      principles of Optimality Theory.
   c. Ranking Schema:
      P ≫ M

2.4 Correspondence theory

A major change which the OT framework underwent was towards
"Correspondence Theory" (CT, McCarthy and Prince 1995 and this volume). Its general claim is that *faithfulness to the input* and *reduplicant-
base identity* are two instantiations of a similar kind of requirement:
that a pair of representations must be *identical*. In the case of input
faithfulness, the requirement of identity is imposed on the input and
output, while in the case of reduplication, the base and reduplicant are
required to be identical.

An example of an identity requirement which is expressed by both a
faithfulness constraint and a base-reduplicant identity constraint is
MAXIMALITY.

(44) MAXIMALITY
     Every element in S_1 must have a correspondent in S_2.

In reduplication this constraint enforces *total* reduplication. (Then the
string S_1 represents the base, while the string S_2 is the reduplicant.) A
similar requirement, that every element in a basic string must be
matched by some element in a derived string, also holds for the relationship between input and output. If S_1 is an input string, and S_2 an output
string, then MAX boils down to the requirement that no element of
the input may be deleted. We see that faithfulness constraints which
enforce identity of the input and output are related (in their format) to

constraints which enforce base–reduplicant identity. The notion both share is correspondence.

Correspondence Theory is not restricted to MAXIMALITY. It encompasses a set of correspondence constraints, each of which is responsible for checking a specific aspect of identity between representations, for example in the presence of segments, their featural composition, linear order, etc. All correspondence constraints are generalized versions of constraints that were previously part of the theory of reduplication (stated informally):

(45) MAXIMALITY   Elements in S_1 must have correspondents in S_2.
DEPENDENCE   Elements in S_2 must have correspondents in S_1.
IDENTITY[ξF]   Corresponding elements must have identical values for [F].
ANCHORING   Corresponding elements have identical positions relative to edges.
LINEARITY   Linear order of sets of corresponding elements are preserved.
CONTIGUITY   Adjacency between sets of corresponding elements is preserved.

Correspondence is a highly general relation between elements in two strings. Two elements are correspondents when one element is part of S_1, while the other is part of S_2, and both elements are coindexed: one element is the *image* of the other. The generator component of the grammar, Gen, supplies different output candidates including relations of correspondences. The evaluation of these correspondence relations is implemented by constraints, for example:

(46)

S_1	S_2	MAX	DEP	IDENT[high]	LINEARITY
a. $a_1 b_2 i_3$	$a_1 b_2 i_3$				
b. $a_1 b_2 i$	$a_1 b_2$	*			
c. $a_1 b_2 i_3$	$a_1 b_2 i_3 \underline{m}$		*		
d. $a_1 b_2 \underline{i}_3$	$a_1 b_2 \underline{e}_3$			*	
e. $a_1 \underline{b}_2 i_3$	$a_1 i_3 \underline{b}_2$				*

Like other constraints, correspondence constraints are violable – but violation is minimal.

By conceiving of faithfulness as a set of constraints on correspondence relations between elements in the input and the output, Correspondence

Theory abandons the notion of "containment" that was part of the original model (Prince and Smolensky 1993):

(47) Containment
     No input element may be literally removed.

Potential arguments against containment are based on patterns of epenthesis and deletion. First, it has been observed that *epenthetic elements* may be phonologically active, in the sense that their feature content participates in phonological patterns (of vowel harmony, Obligatory Contour Principle [OCP], etc.). This argues for a featurally fully fledged representation of epenthetic segments, and against a containment theory which considers them to be mere phonetic spell-outs of empty prosodic positions.[17] With respect to deletion, CT holds analogous consequences: elements are genuinely removed from the output, rather than represented in the output as prosodically underparsed. It follows from this that deleted segments are phonologically inactive. Whether or not this prediction should be counted as an argument in favor of CT depends on the relative success by which this theory will be able to reanalyze cases that were known in derivational theory as "counter-bleeding" rule ordering: where an input segment triggering some structural change is lost from the output.

2.5 Unresolved issues

Here we will identify some unresolved issues which we (and other authors, judging from the literature) consider important. Both issues are related to the Prosody-Morphology interface, hence to Prosodic Morphology.

First, the stratal organization of the grammar. A strong non-derivational version of Optimality Theory would say that grammars are strictly mono-stratal, and hence allow no feeding of output forms into Gen. However, this position is not shared by McCarthy and Prince (1993b), whose analysis of Axininca Campa involves a bifurcation of the grammar into two levels, as in Lexical Phonology (Kiparsky 1982). The interface between levels is defined as "bracket erasure" (Pesetsky 1979, Inkelas 1989). Do the important results about reduplication (such as the emergence of the unmarked, or reduplicative identity as surface correspondence) still follow from a model that allows this multi-stratal organization?

Second, morphological and prosodic limitations on the correspondence relation. In what morphological relationship must a pair of representations stand for a correspondence relation between their composing elements to be possible? Recently Correspondence Theory has been extended to relationships between separate words, for example a truncated form and its morphological base, or an affixed form and its base (Burzio 1994, Benua 1995, McCarthy 1995). Left unconstrained, "output-to-output" correspondence is a very powerful instrument that allows an output form to be affected by phonological properties of any morphologically related word. Similarly, are there limitations on elements of phonological structure that are in a relation of correspondence? It seems clear that to account for the full array of phenomena that previous autosegmental theories covered, correspondence must be allowed between units that cannot be identified as segments. Correspondence of features is required for stability phenomena involving floating features (Zoll 1996); correspondence of moras for stability phenomena involving quantity, such as compensatory lengthening (Hayes 1989). Indeed vowel length and syllable weight may be copied under reduplication (Clements 1985; McCarthy and Prince 1986, 1988; Steriade 1988). This suggests that other prosodic units, such as the syllable and the foot, similarly participate in correspondence relations. Yet, there is a remarkable lack of evidence for the transfer of syllables and feet in reduplication (Moravcsik 1978, Marantz 1982). From the viewpoint of Correspondence Theory, there is an interesting parallel here with faithfulness: no languages are known to have distinctive syllabification; that is, the syllable is remarkably absent in correspondence relations between the input and output.[18]

3. The contributions to this volume

Using the text of the previous two subsections as a background, we present summaries[19] of the contributions to this volume below, arranged in their order of appearance.

Stuart Davis: *On the moraic representation of underlying geminates*
Davis discusses the role that geminates play in determining syllable weight, bringing new evidence to bear on this issue both from phonology proper and from Prosodic Morphology. He shows that situations

occur in which syllables closed by the left half of a geminate are heavy, while other closed syllables are not. The point of departure is Hayes's (1989) proposal that geminate consonants are underlyingly moraic. This indeed predicts that there should be languages in which a syllable closed by the first part of a geminate (henceforth CVG) behaves as heavy, like a CVV syllable, but other types of closed syllables (henceforth CVC) behave as light, like a CV syllable. Several linguists (Selkirk, Koreman, Lahiri, and Tranel) have argued that this prediction is problematic since it is not so clear that stress systems exist which treat CVG syllables as heavy while treating other types of closed syllables as light.

To support the prediction of Hayes's proposal, Davis presents phonological evidence from such phenomena as umlaut blocking, closed-syllable shortening, and stress. He also presents Prosodic Morphological evidence from Hausa and Sinhala supporting the predicted distinction. In a certain class of plurals in Hausa, roots with CVV or CVG (where G stands for left half of geminate) syllables take one type of plural affix while roots with CV or CVC syllables require another. In Sinhala, both genitive allomorphy and inanimate plural formation distinguish CVG and CVV syllable types from CV and CVC. Davis also discusses the behavior of syllables closed by nasal consonants that are homorganic with a following obstruent. He concludes that the evidence presented does support the view that geminate consonants are underlyingly moraic.

Laura Downing: *Verbal reduplication in three Bantu languages*
Downing proposes a combination of Prosodic Morphology and Optimality Theory. The article challenges the Prosodic Morphology Hypothesis (22a) by showing that the templatic shape of reduplicants may be defined in terms of nonmetrical constituents; thus Downing proposes that the inventory of constituents which are active in Prosodic Morphology must include morphoprosodic constituents like "canonical stem" and "prosodic stem." The second contribution of this article is that it demonstrates that infixing reduplications with vowel-initial bases can be analyzed in terms of a familiar constraint that syllables must have onsets, cf. (28). This account generalizes earlier work on infixation by McCarthy and Prince, and eliminates template-specific vowel extra-prosodicity which is now understood as prosodic misalignment.

The empirical basis for the discussion is formed by reduplication patterns of Seswati, Kinande and Kikuyu. In all three languages, the reduplicant is a disyllabic prefix to the verb stem, but there are differences in the treatment of monosyllabic stems and vowel hiatus before vowel-initial stems that she shows can be accounted straightforwardly for by the factorial typology predicted by OT. Reranking the same small set of constraints predicts the observed variation for these properties across the three languages. However, she also argues that some of the variation among the three languages can only be accounted for by modifying some claims of OT. Kikuyu and Kinande are best analyzed by assuming that a morphoprosodic constituent, the canonical verb stem, is the reduplicative template, since this accounts for why the reduplicant always ends in the vowel /a/, which is identical to the theme vowel of the canonical verb stem. For Seswati and Kinande Downing argues that defining a morphoprosodic constituent, the prosodic stem, as the base for reduplication is the most straightforward way to account for infixation of the reduplicant before longer vowel-initial stems. Requiring the left edge of the prosodic stem to be aligned with the left edge of an optimal, onsetful syllable makes the stem-initial vowels extraprosodic.

Larry M. Hyman and Al Mtenje: *Prosodic morphology and tone: the case of Chichewa*
This chapter addresses the interaction of verbal reduplication and tonal transfer in Bantu languages, more specifically two dialects of Chichewa. It is argued that these data cannot be satisfactorily analyzed within a cyclic level-ordered model of the morphology-phonology interface, and instead require a model in which inner domains (stems) and outer domains (prefixed stems) are accessible in parallel. The analysis takes the form of a "direct mapping" model, which is motivated in two ways. First, reduplication only copies segmental material from the inner domain, and crucially never from the outer one. And second, the effects of tonal rules applying to the outer domain tend to be copied along in the reduplicant. More specifically, base-reduplicant indentity cannot be established until word-level prefixes have interacted with the base tones. The need to refer to larger domains before or simultaneously with reference to smaller domains is compatible with a constraint-based model such as OT.

Sharon Inkelas: *Exceptional stress-attracting suffixes in Turkish: representations versus the grammar*
Inkelas offers a detailed analysis of certain aspects of Turkish stress. The analysis is presented in the context of a discussion on the proper way of representing exceptional behaviour of stems and affixes in the OT model. Inkelas contrasts an approach using templatic metrical structure with one that states morpheme-specific alignment constraints, ultimately arguing in favor of the former. Both accounts reach descriptive adequacy. The prespecification account, however, is argued to be superior because it is both more economical and more explanatory: it reveals the naturalness of the set of exceptions whose members form a natural class. In addition, the prespecification uniformly appeals to a binary trochaic foot. On the methodological side, this study shows the importance of taking exceptional cases into account.

Junko Itô and R. Armin Mester: *Realignment*
This chapter deals with syllable theory. It pursues two independent but interrelated lines of inquiry into Alignment Theory. First, it shows that a small extension of the theory of alignment results in the subsumption of a significant part of traditional syllable theory, including various conditions on syllabic complexity (such as conditions on codas, complex onsets, complex nuclei, and complex codas). More specifically, it offers some speculations regarding an alignment-theoretic approach to classical sonority theory in terms of grid alignment. This move allows Itô and Mester to unite several seemingly unrelated constraints. The second half of the chapter, then, discusses a modification of the theory of alignment. Here, the article takes up a problem arising for the concept of "alignment" (as defined in McCarthy and Prince 1993a) in connection with the multiple-linked structures that are the hallmark of nonlinear phonological representations. The central idea is that, different from the standard view, alignment *per se* must be decoupled from the requirement that prosodic categories need sharp edges, not blurred by double linking. This requires a formal notion "CrispEdge" for prosodic categories and concomitantly a revised definition of alignment.

John J. McCarthy and Alan S. Prince: *Faithfulness and identity in Prosodic Morphology*
The goal of the theory of Prosodic Morphology is to provide independent, general explanations for the properties of phenomena like

reduplication, infixation, root-and-pattern morphology, observed word minima, and other restrictions on canonical form. This chapter contributes to the realization of that goal in the domain of base-reduplicant identity. It specifically addresses the well-known issues of underapplication and overapplication in cases of reduplication. The proposal is that base-reduplicant identity is connected with input–output faithfulness through Correspondence Theory (McCarthy and Prince, 1995), which provides a general means of capturing similarity between linguistic representations within Optimality Theory. In particular, so-called constraints of faithfulness (PARSE/FILL) are replaced with a more general notion of "correspondence," potentially holding between linguistic representations, including base and reduplicant, but also others.

Joe Pater: *Austronesian nasal substitution and other NÇ effects*
The framework of this article is that of Optimality Theory, and the subtheories of correspondence and of morphology-phonology interaction play a central role. Phenomena of Prosodic Morphology are characterized by McCarthy and Prince (1993b) as involving the crucial domination of a morphological constraint by a prosodic one. Pater argues that this characterization of the interaction between morphology and phonology is not in any way limited to the prosodic domain, however: any phonotactic constraint could potentially affect the shape of affixes. He examines a set of morphophonological and phonological processes that are driven by a sequential constraint against nasal/voiceless obstruent sequences, *NÇ. These processes, all well attested in a number of language families, include nasal substitution, postnasal voicing, nasal deletion, and denasalization. In OT, these "NÇ effects" can be generated by varying the ranking of *NÇ relative to the faithfulness constraints of McCarthy and Prince (1995); morphophonological processes are captured by the introduction of morpheme-specific faithfulness constraints. In examining these data, however, we find that the original formulation of identity constraints must be amended, so as to differentiate between input-to-output and output-to-input faithfulness.

Sam Rosenthall: *The prosodic base of the Hausa plural*
Rosenthall discusses root augmentation in Hausa. The analysis combines elements from two theoretical domains. The first, Prosodic Morphology, hypothesizes that morphological templates can be defined in

terms of prosodic categories. In Hausa, this is instantiated by the base of the plural, which must be an iambic foot. The second, Optimality Theory, asserts that the surface form is the best possible output, given a hierarchy of conflicting constraints. Rosenthall shows that the various augmented forms of the Hausa plural (e.g., consonant gemination, breaking up of consonant clusters in the root by long vowels) arise as a consequence of constraints that cannot be simultaneously satisfied. The conclusion is that templatic requirements can be violated under duress of higher-ranking requirements. Hausa plural formation has associated with it a number of phonological phenomena called "root augmenta-tion" (Newman 1972). Root augmentation in the different plural classes is shown here to follow from the satisfaction of prosodic requirements on the base for the plural morpheme. The prosodic requirement in Hausa plural formation is that the plural must attach to a base that is equal to an iambic foot, but, as will be shown, the particular expansion of the iamb is subject to variation. The prosodic requirement is one of a number of constraints on the base of the Hausa plural.

Grażyna Rowicka: *Prosodic optimality and prefixation in Polish*
Rowicka proposes an Optimality Theory analysis of *yer*, surfacing in prefixed words in Polish. The chapter puts forward a prosodic inter-pretation of *yers* as "weightless nuclei." To account for the fact that *yers* surface only if there is a sequence of them within one prosodic word, and that a surface *yer* must always be followed by a nonsurfacing one, it is proposed that *yers* are weight-insensitive bisyllabic feet. Heads of such feet surface and participate together with proper vowels in moraic foot structure.

Prefixed verbs are argued to have a different prosodic structure, de-pending on whether their root does or does not contain a *yer*. If it does, the prefixed verb is parsed as a single prosodic word, as evidenced by *yer* surfacing in the prefix. If it does not, the prefix is parsed separately from the root, as evidenced by (the blockage of) palatal assimilation. It is argued that the selection of different parsings follows from the inter-action of various requirements on the alignment between prosodic and morphological categories (specifically, root to prosodic word and pro-sodic word to foot). Sequences of *yers* are parsed into feet of their own and the nuclei in foot-head positions surface. The location of *yer*-feet can also be affected by the prosodic alignment constraints. This is the case in doubly prefixed verbs with *yer*-containing roots. There a *yer*-foot is formed on the first two *yers*, rather than the last two, so that the whole sequence begins with a pedifiable syllable.

Suzanne Urbanczyk: *Double reduplications in parallel*
The chapter examines words formed with two reduplicative morphemes in Lushootseed (Central Coast Salish). Double reduplications raise the issue of whether these are evaluated by constraints in parallel, or serially, assuming a cyclic derivation. Irregularities in the shape and segmental content of one set of stems are shown to follow automatically from assuming that each doubly reduplicated stem is formed in parallel, that is, nonserially. The main argument for parallellism is that the outer layer of reduplication may affect the inner layer, an overapplication effect that is difficult to model under serial evaluation. In parallel Optimality Theory, the adjacency of reduplicant and base in the output obviates the need for cyclicity. This contrasts with other models of reduplication, in which the formation of doubly reduplicated words requires cyclic copying (cf. Broselow 1983). Furthermore, the interest of the Lushootseed data is that there is a phonological irregularity in the shape and segmental content of one set of doubly reduplicated stems. These irregularities are explained as instances of antigemination and overapplication.

Notes

1 We are grateful to Jan Don and Mieke Trommelen for elaborate comments on an earlier version of this section.
2 Cf. Halle (1973).
3 As in the well-known example *This is the cat that caught the rat that stole the cheese*, cf. Chomsky and Halle (1968: 372 and 365–70). This work is referred to henceforth as *SPE*.
4 In 1979, Van der Hulst co-organized and Zonneveld attended a lecture by Jean-Roger Vergnaud (then University of Massachusetts at Amherst) at the Linguistics Department of the University of Amsterdam on Semitic *binyanim* (cf. Halle and Vergnaud 1980). Right in the middle of what at least part of the audience perceived as an extremely exciting but highly technical account, the speaker added a clarification on the blackboard: "CV." "Three Dimensional Phonology" had arrived in the Old World.

5 The prosodic hierarchy continues above the post-lexical word level, including categories such as (possibly) the clitic phrase, the phonological and intonation phrases, and the Utterance. These, however, are not usually targeted by prosodic morphological studies. For discussion, see Selkirk (1984), Nespor and Vogel (1986), and the papers in Inkelas and Zec (1990).

6 Early generative predecessors are Harms (1978), Williams (1976), Leben (1973), and Anderson (1976).

7 Or: lost if /r/ is at the end of a syllable, assuming an additional consonant such as the *k* of *bark* is "extrametrical", i.e. not part of the syllable proper (cf. Hayes 1983); or: lost from a coda, if the consonant(s) following the vowel in a syllable are allowed to go by that common denominator.

8 For a lucid discussion, cf. Kaye (1989), chapter 5.

9 For an overview of later analyses of French *e-muet*, cf. Charette (1991) and references cited there.

10 Of these, principles (22a) and (22b) were stated earlier in the McCarthy and Prince (1986) manuscript.

11 For the notion of syllabic markedness, see Jakobson (1962), Kaye and Lowenstamm (1981), among others. Similar observations on templates, less explicitly, were made in work preceding Steriade's paper, e.g., Yip (1982: 647).

12 However, Steriade's footnote 10 makes a very interesting suggestion, which has later been elaborated on by various researchers: "This cancellation of marked syllabic options may be more generally a property of affixes. For instance, the Sanskrit affixal syllables are, with very few exceptions, of the form CV(C), in contrast with the stem morphemes, which frequently allow up to three consonants in the onset and extra-heavy rhymes of VVC or VCC shapes."

13 There were some notable deviations from this view of the interface; see for example Anderson (1975).

14 The constraint dubbed MAX was originally part of the set of universal principles of association in the template-plus-association theory (McCarthy 1979, Marantz 1982, McCarthy and Prince 1986) discussed in section 1, together with a predecessor of the constraint LINEARITY (both have their origins in autosegmental phonology: Goldsmith 1976b).

15 This result must be relativized somewhat, however, since cases of reduplication occur in which the reduplicant contains segments which do not occur in the base, yet which can be shown to be morphologically sponsored by the input. An example is the interaction of reduplication and syncope in Southeastern Tepehuan (Kager 1997).

16 Under this analysis the fact that the infix has the skeletal shape VC is an arbitrary property, and this shape might just as well have been different. For example, such an analysis equally easily handles hypothetical data

based on a (hypothetical) infix *-mu-*, as in *mu-abot, t-mu-awag, gr-mu-adwet*. One might argue that such outputs never arise because they would seriously violate the phonotactic principles of the language (more specifically, the requirements that onsets be maximally binary, and that hiatus be ill-formed). However, this is precisely the point that can be made against the circumscriptional analysis: it fails to express the overall contribution of prosodic well-formedness to the distribution of the infix *-um-*.

17 The observation that epenthetic segments tend to be segmentally unmarked (in underspecification terminology: maximally underspecified) is attributed to featural markedness constraints. Epenthetic segments are unmarked as a consequence of the fact that they are morphologically unsponsored, hence lack input correspondents. That is, unlike morphologically sponsored segments epenthetic segments are outside the scope of faithfulness constraints such as IDENTITY[ξF].

18 Following the same line of thought, it has been argued by McCarthy and Prince (1988) that only distinctive properties (such as length, but crucially not syllabification) may be transferred under reduplication. However, this hypothesis has been falsified by cases of reduplication which involve the transfer of "allophonic" phonology, as was observed by Kiparsky (1986) and Steriade (1988).

19 In preparing the summaries in this section we received help from Harry van der Hulst and the contributors, but we take responsibility for the text presented here.

References

Anderson, Stephen R. 1975. On the interaction of phonological rules of various types, *Journal of Linguistics* 11: 39–62.

    1976. Nasal consonants and the internal structure of segments, *Language* 52 (1976): 326–44. [1975 prepublication version in Ch. A. Ferguson, L. M. Hyman and J. J. Chala (eds.), *Nasálfest: papers from a symposium on nasals and nasalization*. Language Universals Project, Department of Linguistics, Stanford University, CA.]

Benua, Laura. 1995. Identity effects in morphological truncation, in J. Beckman, S. Urbanczyk, and L. Walsh Dickey (eds.), *University of Massachusetts Occasional Papers in Linguistics* 18: *Papers in Optimality Theory*, Amherst, MA: Graduate Linguistic Student Association.

Broselow, Ellen. 1983. Subjacency in morphology: Salish double reduplication, *Natural Language and Linguistic Theory* 1: 317–46.

Burzio, Luigi. 1994. *Principles of English Stress*, Cambridge University Press.

Charette, Monik. 1991. *Conditions on Phonological Government*, Cambridge University Press.

Chomsky, Noam. 1951. Morphophonemics of Modern Hebrew. MA dissertation, University of Pennsylvania, Philadelphia.

Chomsky, Noam, and Morris Halle. 1968. *The Sound Pattern of English*, New York, NY: Harper & Row.

Clements, George N. 1976. Vowel harmony in nonlinear generative phonology: an autosegmental model. [Distributed in 1980 by Indiana University Linguistics Club.]

    1985. The problem of transfer in nonlinear morphology, *Cornell Working Papers in Linguistics* 7: 38–73.

Dell, François. 1973. *Les Règles et les Sons: Introduction à la Phonologie Générative*, Paris: Hermann.

Dixon, Robert M. W. 1977. *A Grammar of Yidiny*, Cambridge University Press.

French, Koleen M. 1988. *Insights into Tagalog Reduplication, Infixation, and Stress from Nonlinear Phonology*, Dallas, TX: Summer Institute of Linguistics and University of Texas, Arlington.

Goldsmith, John. 1976a. An overview of autosegmental phonology, *Linguistic Analysis* 2: 23–68.

    1976b. Autosegmental phonology, Ph.D. dissertation, Massachusetts Institute of Technology. [Published later, 1979. New York, NY: Garland Press.]

Halle, Morris. 1973. Prolegomena to a theory of word formation, *Linguistic Inquiry* 4: 3–16.

Halle, Morris, and Jean-Roger Vergnaud. 1980. Three-dimensional phonology, *Journal of Linguistic Research* 1: 83–105.

Harms, Robert T. 1973. Some nonrules of English, in M. A. Jazayery, E. C. Polemé, and W. Winter (eds.), *Linguistic and Literary Studies in Honor of Archibald A. Hill*, vol. 2: *Descriptive Linguistics*, The Hague: Mouton, 39–52. [Originally distributed by Indiana University Linguistics Club.]

Hayes, Bruce. 1989. Compensatory lengthening in moraic phonology, *Linguistic Inquiry* 20: 253–306.

Inkelas, Sharon 1989. Prosodic constituency in the lexicon, Ph.D. dissertation, Stanford University, CA. [Published later, 1990. New York, NY: Garland.]

Inkelas, Sharon and Draga Zec (eds.). 1990. *The Phonology-Syntax Connection*, University of Chicago Press.

Itô, Junko. 1986. Syllable theory in prosodic phonology, Ph.D. dissertation, University of Massachusetts, Amherst, MA. [Published later 1988. New York, NY: Garland Press.]

Jakobson, Roman. 1962. *Selected Writings*, 8 vols., vol. I: *Phonological Studies*, The Hague: Mouton.

Kager, René. 1997. Rhythmic vowel deletion in Optimality Theory, in I. Roca (ed.), *Derivations and Constraints in Phonology*, Oxford University Press, 463–99.

Kahn, Daniel. 1976. Syllable-based generalizations in English phonology, Ph.D. dissertation, Massachusetts Institute of Technology, Cambridge, MA. [Published later, 1980. New York, NY: Garland Press.]

Kaye, Jonathan. 1989. *Phonology: a Cognitive View*, Hillsdale, NJ: Lawrence Erlbaum.

Kaye, Jonathan, and Jean Lowenstamm. 1981. Syllable structure and markedness theory, in A. Belletti, L. Brandi, and L. Rizzi (eds.), *Theory of Markedness in Generative Grammar*, Pisa: Scuola Normale Superiore di Pisa, 287–315.

Kiparsky, Paul. 1982. From cyclic phonology to lexical phonology, in H. van der Hulst and N. S. H. Smith (eds.), *The Structure of Phonological Representations*, vol. 2, Dordrecht: Foris, 131–75.

1986. The phonology of reduplication, ms. Stanford University, CA.

Leben, William. 1973. Suprasegmental phonology, Ph.D. dissertation, Massachusetts Institute of Technology, Cambridge, MA. [Published later, 1980. New York, NY: Garland Press.]

Liberman, Mark. 1975. The intonational system of English, Ph.D. dissertation, Massachusetts Institute of Technology, Cambridge, MA. [Also distributed by Indiana University Linguistics Club and Published later, 1979. New York, NY: Garland Press.]

Liberman, Mark and Alan S. Prince. 1977. On stress and linguistic rhythm, *Linguistic Inquiry* 8: 249–336.

Marantz, Alec. 1982. Re reduplication, *Linguistic Inquiry* 13: 483–545.

McCarthy, John J. 1979. Formal problems in Semitic phonology and morphology, Ph.D. dissertation, Massachusetts Institute of Technology.

1995. Extensions of faithfulness: Rotuman revisited, ms. University of Massachusetts, Amherst, MA.

McCarthy, John J., and Alan S. Prince. 1986. Prosodic morphology, ms. University of Massachusetts, Amherst, MA and Brandeis University, Waltham, MA.

1988. Quantitative transfer in reduplicative and templatic morphology, in Linguistic Society of Korea (ed.), *Linguistics in the Morning Calm*, vol. 2, Seoul: Hanshin Publishing Company, 3–35.

1990. Foot and word in Prosodic Morphology: the Arabic broken plural, *Natural Language and Linguistic Theory* 8: 209–83.

1993a. Generalized alignment, in G. E. Booij and J. van Marle (eds.), *Yearbook of Morphology 1993*, Dordrecht: Kluwer, 79–153.

1993b. Prosodic Morphology I: constraint interaction and satisfaction, ms. University of Massachusetts, Amherst, MA and Rutgers University, New Brunswick, NJ.

1994. The emergence of the unmarked: Optimality in Prosodic Morphology, in M. Gonzàlez (ed.), *Proceedings of the North East Linguistic Society* 24, Amherst, MA: Graduate Linguistic Student Association, University of Massachusetts, 333–79.

1995. Faithfulness and reduplicative identity, in J. Beckman, S. Urbanczyk, and L. Walsh Dickey (eds.), *University of Massachusetts Occasional Papers in Linguistics* 18: *Papers in Optimality Theory*, Amherst, MA: Graduate Linguistic Student Association, 249–384.

Moravcsik, Edith. 1978. Reduplicative constructions, in J. Greenberg (ed.), *Universals of Human Language*, vol. 3: *Word Structure*, Stanford University Press, CA, 297–334.

Nash, David. 1980. Topics in Warlpiri grammar, Ph.D. dissertation, Massachusetts Institute of Technology. [Published later, 1986. New York, NY: Garland Press.]

Nespor, Marina, and Irene Vogel. 1986. *Prosodic Phonology*, Dordrecht: Foris.

Newman, Paul. 1972. Syllable weight as a phonological variable, *Studies in African Linguistics* 3: 301–23.

Payne, David L. 1981. *The Phonology and Morphology of Axininca Campa*, University of Texas, Arlington: Summer Institute of Linguistics Publications in Linguistics.

Pesetsky, David. 1979. Russian morphology and lexical theory, ms. Massachusetts Institute of Technology, Cambridge, MA.

Prince, Alan, and Paul Smolensky. 1993. Optimality Theory: constraint interaction in generative grammar, ms. Rutgers University, New Brunswick, NJ and University of Colorado, Boulder, CO.

Selkirk, Elisabeth O. 1978. The French foot: on the status of mute *e*, *Studies in French Linguistics* 1: 141–50.

1980. The role of prosodic categories in English word stress, *Linguistic Inquiry* 11: 563–605.

1982. Syllables, in H. van der Hulst and N. S. H. Smith (eds.), *The Structure of Phonological Representations*, vol. 2, Dordrecht: Foris, 337–83.

1984. *Phonology and Syntax: the Relation between Sound and Structure*, Cambridge, MA: MIT Press.

Spring, Cari. 1990. Implications of Axininca Campa for Prosodic Morphology and reduplication, Ph.D. dissertation, University of Arizona, Tucson, AZ.

Steriade, Donca. 1988. Reduplication and syllable transfer in Sanskrit and elsewhere, *Phonology* 5: 73–155.

Vergnaud, Jean-Roger, and Morris Halle. 1978. Metrical structures in phonology: a fragment of a draft, ms. Massachusetts Institute of Technology, Cambridge, MA.

Williams, Edwin S. 1976. Underlying tone in Margi and Igbo, *Linguistic Inquiry* 7: 463–84. [Note: first written in 1971.]

Yip, Moira. 1982. Reduplication and C-V skeleta in Chinese secret languages, *Linguistic Inquiry* 13: 637–61.

Zoll, Cheryl C. 1996. Parsing below the segment in a constraint-based framework, Ph.D. dissertation, University of California, Berkeley, CA.

2 On the moraic representation of underlying geminates: evidence from Prosodic Morphology

Stuart Davis

1. Introduction

In the versions of moraic phonology[1] put forward in McCarthy and Prince (1986) and Hayes (1989) geminate consonants are underlyingly moraic. Selkirk (1990) and Tranel (1991) independently point out that this view of geminate consonants predicts the existence of languages where a syllable closed by the first part of the geminate (henceforth CVG) behaves as heavy, like a CVV syllable, but other types of closed syllables (henceforth, CVC) behave as light, like a CV syllable. Thus the groupings shown in (1) and (2) are predicted to occur.

(1) a. CVV syllable   b. CVG syllable (syllable closed by a geminate)

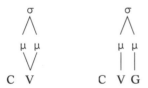

The syllable types in (1) should act as bimoraic while those in (2) should pattern as monomoraic.

(2) a. CV syllable   b. CVC syllable (syllable closed by a nongeminate)

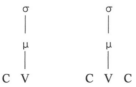

The division between the bimoraic syllable types in (1) and the mono-moraic syllable types in (2) follows from Hayes's (1989) theory of moraic phonology, given his posited language-specific rule of Weight-by-Position shown in (3).

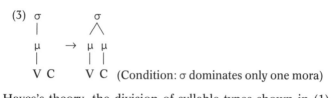

(3) σ   σ
     | ∧
     μ   →   μ μ
     | | |
     V C   V C   (Condition: σ dominates only one mora)

In Hayes's theory, the division of syllable types shown in (1) and (2) arises in languages where Weight-by-Position does not apply and where there are geminate consonants; the two syllable types in (1) would be the only bimoraic syllables.[2]

Given the division shown in (1) and (2), we would expect to find evidence for it from stress, vowel shortening, and other phonological and morphophonological phenomena. Both Selkirk (1990) and Tranel (1991) are doubtful about the existence of phenomena showing this division. Specifically, neither of these researchers is able to find cases where the two syllable types in (1) pattern together. They each refer to problematic cases for the division. Most problematic are languages with geminates in which syllables containing long vowels are stressed but closed syllables in general are not stressed (including those closed by a geminate). If stress is sensitive to syllable weight or moraic structure, it is predicted that bimoraic CVG syllables should be just as stressable as bimoraic CVV syllables. CVG syllables should not be ignored by such stress rules since they are bimoraic.

There are several languages that can be cited to show that the predicted division of syllable types in (1) and (2) is problematic. The specific example cited by Tranel (1991) is the Paleo-Siberian language Selkup based on the data in Halle and Clements (1983). In Selkup, stress falls on the rightmost heavy syllable, or if there are no heavy syllables, stress falls on the initial syllable. The relevant data from Halle & Clements (1983) are shown in (4).

(4) Selkup
    a. qumó:qi   "two human beings"
    b. ú:cɨqo   "to work"
    c. qumo:qlilf: "your two friends"
    d. ú:cɨkkak   "I am working"
    e. u:cómɨt   "we work"
    f. qúmɨnɨk   "human being"
    g. ámɨrna   "eats"

Under the assumption that the Selkup stress rule picks out the rightmost heavy (or bimoraic) syllable of a word, the lack of second syllable stress in (4d) is unexpected since the CVG second syllable should act as bimoraic, attracting the stress.

To show that Selkup is not an isolated example, one can point to the same phenomena in Chuvash, an Altaic language of the Turkic group. According to the description of stress in Krueger (1961), primary stress falls on the rightmost syllable with a full vowel or else on the initial syllable. (I follow Hayes 1981 in assuming that the difference between a full versus reduced vowel is equivalent to long versus short.) Chuvash has geminates but a CVG syllable is not treated as heavy by the stress rule. As in Selkup, they are skipped in the determination of stress. Some relevant examples are given in (5).

(5) Chuvash (Krueger 1961)

a.	lăšá	"horse"	b.	ĕné	"cow"
c.	kămaká	"stove"	d.	sarlaká	"window"
e.	álăk	"door"	f.	yĕnérčĕk	"saddle"
g.	kálăttămăr	"we would say"			

The key piece of data is (5g) where stress falls on the first syllable of the word even though the second syllable is closed by a geminate. Thus in both Chuvash and Selkup CVG syllables do not seem to function like bimoraic CVV syllables but rather like monomoraic CV and CVC syllables.

Based on evidence like that seen in Chuvash and Selkup, Tranel (1991) and Selkirk (1990) contend that geminate consonants are not underlyingly moraic. However, they each make a different proposal on how to account for this. Tranel proposes that the reason why stress rules do not distinguish CVG syllables from CVC syllables derives from the Principle of Equal Weight for Codas. Under this principle, geminates are not special; a syllable closed by a geminate is treated like any other closed syllable in the language. If a language treats closed syllables as heavy then CVG syllables are heavy, but if a language treats closed syllables as light then CVG syllables are light. Thus, on Tranel's account, in languages like Selkup and Chuvash all coda consonants are weightless, even if they are part of a geminate; neither CVC nor CVG syllables are heavy.

On the other hand, Selkirk (1990) argues that geminates are represented underlyingly as having two root nodes that share stricture and place features as shown in (6). (RN = root node)

(6)

RN   RN

[±cont]

Place

On Selkirk's account, a geminate is not underlyingly moraic. The implication of this is that if Weight-by-Position (3) applies in a language assigning a mora to a coda consonant it would assign a mora to the initial root node of a geminate. But since in Selkup and Chuvash, Weight-by-Position does not apply, a geminate does not make a syllable heavy.

Given the work of Selkirk (1990) and Tranel (1991) it seems that a Hayes-type moraic theory makes wrong predictions in treating the syllable types in (1) as patterning together as bimoraic. Nonetheless, recent work done independently by Davis (1994) and Sherer (1994), based on a variety of phonological phenomena, provide strong evidence that, contrary to the claims of Tranel (1991), there are languages that instantiate the division of syllable types shown in (1) and (2). In section 2 of this chapter I briefly review some of this phonological evidence. Now, if Davis and Sherer are correct in the contention that within one language CVG syllables are treated as bimoraic while other CVC syllables are treated as monomoraic, then there should be cases to support the contention from Prosodic Morphology. (See McCarthy and Prince 1986, 1990, and 1993 for the development of Prosodic Morphology.) Such evidence is presented in section 3 from Prosodic Morphological phenomena in Hausa and Sinhala. I conclude in section 4 by discussing the implications for moraic theory of the division shown in (1) and (2) and by discussing why in languages such as Selkup and Chuvash geminates do not seem to pattern as bimoraic.

2. Phonological evidence for the distinction between CVG and CVC

Both Sherer (1994) and Davis (1994) provide a variety of phonological evidence for the syllable types in (1) and (2). While Davis (1994) cites stress in the Hindi dialect described in Gupta (1987, 1988) as evidence for this division, here we focus on vowel shortening and umlaut phenomena that support the division.

One type of evidence for bimoraic CVVG syllables versus monomoraic CVVC syllables comes from languages in which vowel shortening occurs in the former but not in the latter. The implication is that a potential CVVG syllable would have three moras so should be disallowed while CVVC syllables would just have two moras and so should occur. One language displaying this pattern of shortening is the Dravidian language Koya discussed by Sherer (1994) based on Tyler (1969). Koya has long vowels, consonant clusters, and geminate consonants. Sherer notes that there are words in Koya like those in (7) where a long vowel can occur before a consonant cluster. However, there are no words in which a long vowel occurs before a geminate.

(7) a. leːŋga   "calf"   b. aːnd   "female power"
     c. daːlguddan   "red cloths"   d. goːtra   "lineage"
     e. guːnji   "post"

Moreover, Sherer notes cases where a stem-final long vowel shortens before a suffix beginning with a geminate, as the examples in (8) show.

(8) a. keː + tt + oːnḍa   [kettonḍa]   "he told"
     b. oː + tt + oːnḍa   [ottoːnḍa]   "he bought"

This shortening does not occur before a nongeminate consonant cluster as the examples in (9) show.

(9) a. tuŋg + anaː + n + ki   [tuŋganaːŋki]   "for doing"
     b. koːy + si   [koːysi]   "having cut"

Furthermore, long vowels surface as short when before a syllable containing a long vowel or when before a syllable closed by a geminate. A rule formulation is given in (10) with the examples from Tyler (1969) in (11).

(10)   V: → V / __ CV:
               CVG

(11) a. taːt + aːl + oːru   [taːtaloːru]   "mother's fathers"
     b. tung + aːni + addu   [tunganaddu]   "which does"

The data in (7) to (11) are consistent with the division of syllable types in (1) and (2). A potential CVVG syllable would be trimoraic and so surfaces with a short vowel whereas a CVVC syllable is bimoraic and so can surface as such.

The Koya example is not an isolated one. Another example comes from Hindi where Ohala (1983) notes that CVVC syllables are common but CVVG syllables do not occur. Also, Sherer (1994) observes languages that have surface CVVC syllables but potentially occurring CVVG syllables surface without the geminate consonant.

In addition to the interaction between a long vowel and a following geminate just discussed, another phonological phenomenon that can provide evidence for the division of syllable types shown in (1) and (2) is umlaut. Typologically, in languages that have umlaut, it is not uncommon for back vowels in certain syllable types to fail to undergo umlaut. In particular, in a variety of languages a target back vowel in a heavy syllable fails to undergo umlaut. For example, Hahn (1991) notes that in Spoken Uyghur (an Altaic language of China), long vowels as well as short vowels in closed syllables fail to undergo umlaut. Since both long vowels and closed syllables attract stress in the quantity-sensitive stress system of the language, it would seem reasonable to maintain that only vowels in monomoraic syllables undergo umlaut. Davis (1994) proposes a similar constraint on umlaut in Seoul Korean. Typical data showing Korean umlaut are found in (12) and come from Lee (1993). (The umlauted forms are for the most part nonprescriptive, frequently having a pejorative connotation.)

(12) a. /aki/   → [agi] or [ægi]   "baby"
     b. /əmi/   → [əmi] or [emi]   "mother"
     c. /ak'i/   → [ak'i] or [æk'i]   "to hold dear"
     d. /soncapi/ → [sonjabi] or [sonjæbi] "handle"
     e. /s'ili/   → [s'iri] or [s'iri]   "to be sick"
     f. /tani/   → [tani] or [tæni]   "to go to and from"

In all the examples in (12) the target back vowel is in a CV syllable. Umlaut, though, also applies over an intervening consonant cluster where the target vowel would be in a CVC syllable. This is shown in (13).

(13) a. /nampi/   → [nambi] or [næmbi]   "kettle"
     b. /əŋki/   → [əŋgi] or [eŋgi]   "to be curdled"
     c. /namki/   → [naŋgi] or [næŋgi]   "to leave behind"
     d. /anki/   → [aŋgi] or [æŋgi]   "to be embraced"
     e. /palk + hi/ → [palkʰi] or [pælkʰi]   "to brighten"

These data show that the presence of a coda consonant does not block umlaut. However, Lee (1993) makes the interesting observation that umlaut fails to apply over an intervening geminate consonant in the Seoul dialect. Relevant data are in (14).

(14) Umlaut does not occur over an intervening geminate
  a. /ənni/   → [ənni]   *[enni]   "sister"
  b. /al+li/   → [alli]   *[ælli]   "to inform"
  c. /kəl+li/   → [kəlli] *[kelli]   "to be hung"
  d. /p'al+li/   → [p'alli] *[pælli]   "to be sucked"
  e. /mal+li/   → [malli] *[mælli]   "to dry"
  f. /ak+ki/   → [akk'i] *[ækk'i]   "instrument"
  g. /kammi (lop-ta)/ → [kammi] *[kæmmi]   "to be sweet"

Based on data like those in (12) to (14) Davis (1994) proposes that umlaut in Seoul Korean only occurs if the target vowel is in a mono-moraic syllable. Evidence for this comes from the additional data in (15) where it is shown that umlaut fails to occur if the target vowel is long.

(15) a. /saːlm + ki/ → [saːmgi] *[sæːmgi]   "to be boiled"
     b. /pəːli/   → [pəːri] *[peːri]   "earning"

Thus we observe that umlaut fails to occur in CVV and CVG syllables but occurs in CV and CVC syllables. Given that other languages (such as Spoken Uyghur) display weight restrictions on umlaut, it is not surprising to find them in Korean. The Seoul Korean pattern is interesting because it groups together CVV and CVG syllables. This can be taken as instantiating the division of syllable types shown in (1) and (2).[3]

3. The evidence from Prosodic Morphology

Given the phonological evidence for the division of syllable types shown in (1) and (2), it would be expected that there would be corroborating evidence from the Prosodic Morphology of particular languages where CVV and CVG syllables would be treated as bimoraic while CV and CVC syllables would be treated as monomoraic. In this section I present such evidence from Hausa and Sinhala.

3.1 Hausa

Nouns in Hausa fall into one (or more) of several possible plural patterns. The different plural patterns are referred to as classes by Kraft and Kraft (1973). In this subsection I focus on the pattern they call Class 3. I will show that plurals of this type treat CVG and CVV root syllables as distinct from CV and CVC syllables. The Class 3 plurals have been discussed previously in the works of Leben (1980) and Newman (1992), but neither of these works considered the full range of data or noted the implications for the moraic view of syllable weight.[4]

Class 3 plurals are formed by the addition of a bisyllabic suffix to the nominal root. Within this class there are two allomorphs. These are given in (16) (where the C-slot in (16a) is realized as a consonant identical to the last root consonant).

(16) a. -aaCee   b. -aayee

I will maintain that the choice between these two allomorphs involves partial-mode prosodic circumscription (or prosodic delimitation) which defines a morphological operation over a prosodically delimited subset, as discussed in McCarthy and Prince (1990) as well as in the nonderivational approach of McCarthy and Prince (1993). The formal analysis within McCarthy and Prince's (1990) prosodic circumscription theory is given in (17).

(17) $O:\Phi'<\sigma_\mu>$,   O = suffixing -aaCee   (elsewhere: suffix -aayee)

The analysis in (17) states that the allomorph in (16a) only suffixes onto a (nominal) root that consists of a light syllable; otherwise, the allomorph in (16b) is the suffix. The focus of the discussion will be on which syllable types are treated as light. I will show that the Hausa plural pattern provides support for the division given in (1) and (2).

First, consider examples illustrating the allomorph in (16a). These are exemplified by the data in (18) and (19). In these data the onset consonant of the suffix's second syllable is identical to the root-final consonant of the noun. The data in (18) show nouns whose roots end in a single consonant while the data in (19) show nouns whose roots end in a consonant cluster. (As shown in the data, most singular nouns in Hausa end in a final long vowel extension that is not part of the root. Tones are not indicated in the data, but the affixation is accompanied by a HLH tone pattern over the whole plural form.)

(18)   Singular   Plural   Gloss
       a. dam-oo   dam-aamee   "monitor"
       b. wur-ii   wur-aaree   "place"
       c. kaf-aa   kaf-aafee   "small hole"

(19)   Singular   Plural   Gloss
       a. gulb-ii gul-aabee   "stream"
       b. birn-ii bir-aanee   "city"
       c. kask-oo kas-aakee   "bowl"

Now consider examples showing the allomorph in (16b). These are exemplified by the data in (20) and (21), where the suffix's second syllable is realized by the default consonant [y] which Newman (1972) notes is found elsewhere in Hausa as an epenthetic consonant. (20) contains data where the root vowel is long and (21) contains data where the root vowel is a diphthong.

(20)   Singular   Plural   Gloss
       a. zoom-oo   zoom-aayee   "hare"
       b. kiif-ii   kiif-aayee   "fish"
       c. suun-aa   suun-aayee   "name"
       d. jaa (?*jaaj-aa) jaaj-aayee   "red"

(21)   Singular   Plural   Gloss
       a. ɓaun-aa   ɓaun-aayee   "buffalo"
       b. mais-oo   mais-aayee   "disused farm"
       c. gaul-aa   gaul-aayee   "idiot"

Based on the data in (18) to (21) one could posit that if the root syllable contains a short vowel the allomorph *-aaCee* is selected, but if the root syllable contains a long vowel or diphthong then *-aayee* is selected. However, the data in (22) show that this generalization is not quite correct.

(22)   Singular   Plural   Gloss
       a. tukk-uu   tukk-aayee   "bird crest"
       b. tall-ee   tall-aayee   "soup pot"
       c. gamm-oo   gamm-aayee   "heat pad"
       (d. tangaran   tangar-aayee   "chinaware, dish")

The nouns in (22) have short root vowels yet they nonetheless pattern like the nouns containing long vowels in (20) and (21) by taking the plural allomorph shown in (16b). The question that emerges then is what unifies the roots in (20) to (22) that distinguishes them from those in (18) and (19). The answer I propose relates to the weight of these nouns. The root syllables in (20) and (21) have the shape CVV, the root syllables in (22a) to (22c) have the shape CVG, and the noun root in (22d) is polysyllabic (though it should be noted that an example like (22d) in which a polysyllabic noun root takes a Class 3 plural is very unusual). These then are forms where the roots are at least bimoraic. This is clearly seen by the data in (20) and (21), but the data involving CVG root syllables in (22a) to (22c) also pattern with the CVV type. These two types of monosyllables, CVV and CVG, would be initially bimoraic given Hayes's moraification algorithm as reflected in (1). On the other hand, the root syllables in (18) and (19) have the shape CV and CVC; these are the syllable types that would be initially monomoraic as reflected in (2).[5] We see then that the allomorph in (16a) only attaches to a noun root that is monomoraic.[6] The allomorph in (16b) attaches to other types of noun roots. But what is crucial for our discussion is that it is just CV and CVC syllables that are being treated as monomoraic; CVV and CVG syllables are being treated as heavier. This then supports the division shown in (1) and (2).

The Hausa plural pattern illustrated in (18) to (22) is made more interesting by roots ending in a homorganic nasal cluster. Consider the data in (23).

(23)	Singular	Plural	Gloss
a.	kund-ii	kund-aayee	"notebook"
b.	gunt-uu	gunt-aayee	"stub"
c.	dumɓ-uu	dumɓ-aayee	"old tool"
d.	gwank-ii	gwank-aayee	"roan antelope"

These data are like those found in (19) where the noun roots end in a sequence of consonants, yet the data in (23) form their plurals like roots with geminates as in (22). I would like to suggest that the partial place geminates in the noun roots in (23) are inherently or lexically moraic. In this way, the CVN root syllable of these words is bimoraic. By having a bimoraic root syllable they then form the plural like the words in (20) to (22) by taking the allomorph in (16b).[7]

In support of this proposal it should be pointed out that there are languages that do treat partial place geminates as inherently moraic. For example, Downing (1991) argues convincingly based on compensatory lengthening evidence that the homorganic nasal clusters of Jita are underlyingly moraic. However, it probably is a language-specific issue as to whether partial place geminates are treated as moraic since the lack of umlaut blocking by the partial place geminates in the Korean data in (13a) to (13d) suggests that such clusters are not inherently moraic.

In this subsection I have maintained that the factor determining the selection of the plural allomorph of the data in (18) to (23) is the weight of the root syllables. Monomoraic roots take the allomorph in (16a) as exemplified by the data in (18) to (19) while roots containing more weight take the allomorph in (16b). That a CV and CVC monosyllable is being treated as light while CVV and CVG monosyllables are being treated as heavy supports the division shown in (1) and (2).

3.2 Sinhala

In this section I consider Prosodic Morphological evidence from Sinhala (or Sinhalese), an Indo-European language primarily spoken in Sri Lanka, that provides additional support for the syllable division shown in (1) and (2). Specifically, I will consider evidence from the pattern of allomorph selection found with the genitive and then I will consider the plural formation pattern found with inanimate nouns. The Sinhalese data that I will discuss come from Feinstein (1977, 1979), Reynolds (1980), Pyatt (1993), Steriade (1993) and Letterman (1994). The analysis I offer here is for the most part different and independent of these previous works in that I examine the various types of affixation through the perspective of Prosodic Morphology. I will conclude that the Sinhalese morphological phenomena to be discussed are consistent with the division of syllable types given in (1) and (2).

The data in (24) show genitive formation in Sinhala and come from Pyatt (1993) and Pyatt (personal communication).

(24)	Noun roots	Genitive	Gloss
	a. mudəl-	mudəl-e	"the fund's"
	b. mal-	mal-ee	"the flower's"
	c. pot-	pot-ee	"the book's"
	d. paar-	paar-e	"the street's"
	e. pawl-	pawl-e	"the family's"
	f. pætt-	pætt-e	"the side's"
	g. pott-	pott-e	"the core's"

The genitive ending exhibits two allomorphs: one allomorph is [ee] found in words like those exemplified in (24b) and (24c), and the other allomorph is [e] as exemplified by the remaining words of (24). The question arises as to what factor determines the choice of allomorphs. First, consider the item in (24a). This form is representative of noun roots that are two syllables or longer. With such nouns the genitive is always [e]. Next, consider the roots in (24b) and (24c). These roots take [ee] for the genitive. Based on the first three words one might posit that monosyllabic roots like (24b) and (24c) take [ee] while polysyllabic roots take [e]. But an examination of the monosyllabic roots in (24d) to (24g) shows that this is not correct. The roots in (24d) to (24g) pattern like that in (24a) though they are monosyllabic. However, note that the monosyllabic roots in (24d) to (24g) can be considered bimoraic given the presence of a long vowel, a diphthong, or a geminate. Given that the root syllables in (24b) and (24c) are monomoraic,[8] the generalization that emerges is that the genitive is realized as [ee] if the noun is monomoraic otherwise the genitive surfaces as [e]. Both CVG and CVV syllable types are being treated as bimoraic which is consistent with the moraification in (1).

An interesting complication to the genitive pattern is observed from the data in (25):

(25)	Noun roots	Genitive	Gloss
a.	kand-	kand-e	"the hill's"
b.	kand-	kand-ee	"the trunk's"

The form in (25a) patterns as a bimoraic noun in that it takes [e] while the form in (25b) patterns as a monomoraic noun in that it takes [ee]. My analysis of these forms closely follows Steriade (1993). She posits that the nasal closure in (25a) is moraic while in a form like (25b) it is not. As evidence for this Steriade (1993: 456) cites Maddieson and Ladefoged's (1993) study of Sinhala nasal-plus-stop sequences and observes "Their interpretation is that even on a purely phonetic basis, the contrast in Sinhala appears more appropriately described as a contrast of single versus geminate nasals followed by stops, that is [mb, nd] versus [mmb, nnd], and so on." In other words, the nasal cluster in (25a) is lexically moraic like a geminate while that in (25b) is nonmoraic. Their phonetic differences as noted by Maddieson and Ladefoged as well as Feinstein (1977, 1979) follow from the moraic versus nonmoraic property of the nasal closure. The implication is that the root syllable in (25a) is bimoraic and so selects [e] while the root syllable in (25b) is monomoraic and so selects [ee]. Thus monosyllabic noun stems are divided into two types by the genitive allomorphy. These are the bimoraic syllables CVV and CVG and the monomoraic syllable CV. The CVN type can be either bimoraic or monomoraic depending on whether the nasal closure is lexically moraic. This division of monomoraic versus bimoraic syllables is thus consistent with the division shown in (1) and (2).

Further evidence for the moraic analysis of geminates and certain nasals in homorganic nasal-plus-stop sequences comes from the plural formation of inanimate nouns. Consider the data in (26) and (27). (In (27), a glide shown in parentheses means that it predictably occurs in hiatus.)

(26)	Singular noun	Plural	Gloss
a.	mull-ə	mulu	"corner"
b.	pætt-ə	pæti	"area"
c.	awurudd-ə	awurudu	"year"
d.	baDəginn-ə	baDəgini	"hunger"
e.	watt-ə	watu	"estate"
f.	kææll-ə	kææli	"piece"
g.	wæss-ə	wæsi	"rain"
h.	ginn-ə	gini	"fire"
i.	redd-ə	redi	"cloth"
j.	hatt-ə	hatu	"mushroom"
k.	bell-ə	beli	"neck"
l.	pott-ə	potu	"core"

(27)	Singular noun	Plural	Gloss
a.	mal-ə	mal	"flower"
b.	mænik-ə	mænik	"gem"
c.	pot-ə	pot	"book"
d.	rææ	rææ	"dark, night"
e.	dawas-ə	dawas	"day"
f.	gal-ə	gal	"stone"
g.	olu-(w)ə	olu	"head"
h.	kaasi-(y)ə	kaasi	"coin"
i.	putu-(w)ə	putu	"chair"
j.	toppi-(y)ə	toppi	"hat"
k.	ispaasu-(w)ə	ispaasu	"peace, rest"
l.	bim-ə	biŋ	"ground"
m.	ayin-ə	ayiŋ	"edge, bank"
n.	igænniim-ə	igænniiŋ	"teaching"

In (27) the plural is the same as the bare noun root, though the last three examples reflect a general condition in the language that a word-final nasal is always realized as [ŋ]. That is, nothing happens with the words in (27) in forming the plurals. Descriptively, in (26), in forming the plural noun from the corresponding singular, a root-final geminate consonant degeminates and a default high vowel is added after it whose backness value matches that of the last root vowel. The high vowel can be considered as the default vowel given that Feinstein (1977) shows that it is the high vowel which is generally inserted to break up impermissible consonant clusters created by morpheme concatenation.

The difference between the data in (26) and (27) is that the noun stems in (26) end in a moraic consonant. Given this observation, I offer the analysis in (28) involving partial-mode prosodic circumscription, formalized within the theory of McCarthy and Prince (1990).

(28) Sinhala Inanimate Noun Plural

$$O{:}\Phi' \quad <\mu>]_{root,} \quad O = delink \quad <\mu>]_{root}$$

$$[+cons] \qquad\qquad\qquad [+cons]$$

Specifically, if the root of an inanimate noun ends in a moraic consonant, then that mora delinks in forming the plural. This results in degemination as is seen in (26). If the root does not end in a final moraic (or geminate) consonant then nothing happens in forming the plural and the plural is realized simply as the bare root, as seen in (27).

While the plural process essentially involves the demoraification of a root-final geminate as formalized in (28), we still need to account for the presence of a final high vowel after the degeminated consonant in (26). This can be accounted for serially if after the demoraification of the root-final (geminate) consonant the delinked floating mora projects a syllable of its own. A default high vowel then surfaces as the nucleus of this added syllable, with the onset being realized with the degeminated consonant. In this way, the mora count of the singular stem is always identical to the mora count of the corresponding plural. In (29), I show a procedural illustration of the derivation of the plural in (26l), from the singular stem.

(29) a.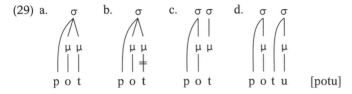

The form in (29a) is the singular. (29b) shows the delinking of the stem-final consonantal mora that occurs in forming the plural; (29c) shows the projection of the new syllable; and (29d) shows the final form with the default high vowel which takes on the backness value of the last root vowel. A potential monosyllabic output for (29) like that in (30) would be ruled out independently since Sinhala does not seem to allow for final CVVC syllables (though such syllables occur nonfinally).

(30)

The plural forms in (27) are identical to the bare noun root since they do not meet the input requirement of having a final mora consonant, and so they do not have a unique plural form.

Evidence that the plural involves the delinking of a moraic consonant comes from the data involving nasal-plus-stop clusters in (31) and (32).

(31)	Singular Noun	Plural	Gloss
a.	kand-ə	kandu	"hill"
b.	homb-ə	hombu	"chin"
c.	ænd-ə	ændi	"fence"

(32)	Singular Noun	Plural	Gloss
a.	kand-ə	kaŋ	"trunk"
b.	lind-ə	liŋ	"well"
c.	amb-ə	aŋ	"mango"
d.	huləng-ə	hulaŋ	"wind"

The forms in (31) pattern like those in (26). Even though the final root syllable of (31) does not seem to end in a geminate consonant, the appearance of a final high vowel in the plural suggests that they do undergo plural formation. On the other hand, the forms in (32) pattern like (27), especially (27l) to (27n), in that the plural forms are equivalent to the bare noun roots. The implication is that the nasal closure of the root meaning "hill" in (31a) is moraic whereas the nasal closure for the root meaning "trunk" in (32a) is nonmoraic. This is supported by the genitive data in (25a) and (25b) where "hill" acts as bimoraic in taking [e] for the genitive, whereas "trunk" acts as monomoraic in taking [ee] for the genitive. Thus the moraification required for the genitive allomorphy is supported by inanimate noun plural formation as seen by the data and analysis in (26) to (32).

While I have maintained that plural formation involves the delinking of a root-final moraic consonant as formalized in (28), the standard view in the literature of the Sinhala inanimate plural is that the singular is derived from the plural by a gemination process. This was specifically argued for by Feinstein (1977, 1979) and has been generally assumed in works such as Rosenthall (1988), Steriade (1993) and Letterman (1994). Feinstein's proposal is that for data like that in (26) the noun roots underlyingly have a single consonant as reflected in the plural form and then the formation of the singular involves the gemination of the root-final consonant. There are two shortcomings of Feinstein's gemination analysis. The first shortcoming that I will mention but not discuss is the oddity of deriving the singular from the plural. This seems highly unusual and, if all else is equal, an analysis in which the plural is formed from the singular would seem preferable. The second shortcoming has to do with distinguishing the roots in (26) from (27). To be specific, why does the root-final /l/ undergo gemination in the formation of the singular in (26a) but not in (27a)? Feinstein (1977) deals with this question and rejects the idea that the stems in (27) are lexically marked as exceptions. Rather, he proposes that neither the noun roots in (26) nor the ones in (27) have underlying geminates; instead, he proposes that the roots in (26) all end in a glide. Thus on Feinstein's analysis the underlying root of (26a) is given in (33a) while that in (27a) is given in (33b)

(33) a. /mulw/ = (26a)   b. /mal/ = (27a)

In Feinstein's analysis, then, there is no process involved in the plural formation. This is clear from the form in (33b) where the posited underlying noun root is the same as the plural shown in (27a). It is also clear from (33a). In forming the plural of (33a), the final glide vocalizes and so surfaces as shown in (26a). Thus the underlying noun roots are always equivalent to the plural. In forming the singular of (26a), where suffixes normally appear, the appearance of a suffix triggers a glide assimilation rule where the glide totally assimilates to a preceding consonant. The Feinstein-type derivation for the singular in (26a) is shown in (34a) and that for (26b) is shown in (34b).

(34) Derivation of (26a) and (26b) based on Feinstein (1977, 1979)

a.	UR	/mulw + a/	b.	UR	/pæty + a/
	Glide	mulla		Glide	pætta
	assimilation			assimilation	
	Other rules	mullə		Other rules	pættə
	PR	[mullə]		PR	[pættə]

There are at least two problems with Feinstein's specific analysis. The first problem is that the underlying glide is never realized in any of the surface allomorphs. If a suffix is added it causes gemination and if no suffix is added it vocalizes. If a phoneme is not realized in any surface allomorph it is unlikely that the language learner would posit that phoneme as part of the underlying representation. A second problem has to do with whether the underlying glide in (34) is /w/ or /y/. The pattern that emerges is that if the last root vowel is back then the underlying glide is /w/, as in (34a); but when the last root vowel is front then the underlying glide is /y/, as in (34b). This is the way in which Feinstein accounts for final [u] and final [i] in the plural forms of (26). However, this is not normally true of underlying forms. The appearance of an underlying /w/ or /y/ is not normally restricted by the nature of a preceding vowel. The fact that the nature of the underlying glide as a /w/ or /y/ is predictable (i.e., /w/ after back vowels and /y/ after front vowels as exemplified in (34)) calls into question his analysis of this phenomenon. Under the analysis I offer, reflected derivationally in (29), the final high vowel of the plural is the default realization of a floating mora brought about by the demoraification of the final moraic consonant. The backness value of the default high vowel simply matches that of the last root vowel by spreading.

4. Conclusion

In conclusion, evidence from both phonology and Prosodic Morphology can be gathered to show that there are languages in which CVG

syllables function as bimoraic while CVC syllables function as monomoraic. The phonological evidence supporting this presented in section
2 included vowel shortening patterns in Koya and umlaut blocking in
Korean. The Prosodic Morphological evidence presented came from
Hausa Class 3 plurals and Sinhala genitive formation and inanimate
plurals.

Languages where CVG syllables can function as bimoraic while CVC
syllables function as monomoraic are problematic for Tranel's (1991)
proposed Principle of Equal Weight for Codas since a coda consonant
that is part of a geminate contributes to the weight of the syllable
whereas other coda consonants do not. Moreover, the patterning of CVC
and CVG as heavy is also problematic for Zec's (1988) sonority-based
approach to moraification. Zec's theory predicts that in a language
where an obstruent in a coda contributes to the weight of a syllable, a
sonorant in a coda must also contribute to the weight of a syllable.
However, Hausa data in (22) are problematic for this view since a CVG
syllable closed by the first part of a geminate obstruent (as in (22a)) is
heavier than a CVC syllable closed by a sonorant consonant (as in
(19a)). Such would constitute an example in which a syllable closed
by an obstruent makes a syllable heavy where a syllable closed by a
sonorant is light. Thus the patterning of CVG syllables as heavy and
CVC syllables as light is potentially problematic for Zec's sonority-based
approach.[9]

An interesting issue emerges from this chapter regarding the patterning of a syllable closed by a partial geminate, specifically a nasal that is
homorganic to a following consonant. Do such syllables pattern like
CVG syllables or not? And what are the consequences for the representation of such homorganic clusters? While this specific issue was not
the focus of the chapter, the behavior of syllables closed by a homorganic
nasal arose in the discussion of several of the languages. For example,
such syllables in Hausa patterned like CVG syllables and not like CVC
syllables. As noted independently by both Davis (1994) and Sherer
(1994) this is the predicted behavior with Selkirk's (1990) two-root-
node theory of geminates shown in (6). On the other hand, syllables
closed by a homorganic nasal functioned like any other CVC syllable in
the Korean data and not like a CVG syllable. A third possibility arose
in the Sinhala data where such clusters sometimes added weight to
the syllable and sometimes not. This seems to be exactly the predicted

behavior in Steriade's (1993) representation of homorganic nasal sequences in which the feature [nasal] is linked just to the A_o position of a stop type segment given her aperture node theory. I leave open the issue of weight properties of partial geminates and their implications for future research.

Finally, the question that needs to be addressed is if geminate consonants are underlyingly moraic and contribute weight to the syllable, how is it that there are languages like Selkup and Chuvash in (4) and (5) which have quantity-sensitive stress but ignore the moraic status of geminates? Here I would refer to Steriade (1991) and Hyman (1992) who show that different moraic projections may be required within the same language to account for different weight-sensitive phenomena, what Hyman has termed "moraic mismatches." For example, only a subset of moras may be relevant for stress. Thus, in Selkup and Chuvash, only moras dominating vowels are projected for stress; moras dominating consonants would not be relevant. In discussing the situation in Mongolian where CVC syllables always function as heavy except for stress, Steriade (1991: 275) suggests that some languages may restrict the set of stress-bearing segments so that such segments may also be tone bearing, "for reasons that are clearly related to the fact that pitch is one of the main realizations of metrical prominence." Thus, Steriade concludes that in a language like Mongolian a CVC syllable is bimoraic but may not contain two stress-bearing elements. This is an intriguing idea which makes predictions about the types of moraic mismatches that should be found. Nonetheless, the data presented in this chapter do show that there are languages where syllables closed by geminates act as bimoraic, like CVV syllables, even when syllables closed by non-geminates do not act as such.[10]

Notes

1 I would like to thank Paul Newman and Elizabeth Pyatt for extensive discussion of the Hausa and Sinhala data, respectively, and Daniel Dinnsen for comments on an earlier draft of this paper. None of these researchers should be viewed as necessarily endorsing the analyses that I offer in the paper. I would also like to acknowledge the participants of the Workshop on Prosodic Morphology for their valuable comments. Any errors are my responsibility.

2 Sherer (1994) shows that the division of the syllable types in (1) and (2) can be manifested under Optimality Theory given a specific ranking of various constraints (P_{seg}, $*\sigma_{\mu\mu\mu}$, P_μ, $*L$-V, $*\mu_c$, $*AP$ ranked from high to low as shown) and assuming that geminates are underlyingly moraic.

3 In Korean, long vowels do not normally shorten in closed syllables of any type. Both CVVC syllables and CVVG syllables do occur as exemplified by [kiːl-ta] "be long (declarative)" and [aːn+ni] "do you embrace" respectively. This means that vowel shortening in Korean is generally not sensitive to factors of syllable weight. Nonetheless, there is other evidence for the treatment of CVV and CVG syllables as heavy. The Korean effective suffix /-ɨni/ has the consequence of shortening the stem-final syllable. If the syllable contains a long vowel the vowel shortens and if the syllable ends in a geminate consonant that consonant degeminates. Given this, one can maintain that the effective suffix imposes a prosodic requirement on the syllable to which it attaches in that it must be monomoraic, thus the shortening of a long vowel and the degemination of a final consonant. Examples include /s'iːp-ɨni/ "chew" and /null-ɨni/ "press" which are realized as [s'ipɨni] and [nurɨni], respectively. The fact that the effective suffix shortens CVG stems but not CVCC stems is consistent with bimoraic CVG syllables and monomoraic CVC syllables.

4 Leben (1980) does not consider roots ending in a homorganic nasal cluster and Newman (1992) does not consider roots ending in a geminate.

5 It is assumed that a root-final consonant does not syllabify as part of the root. It normally serves as the onset of the syllable containing the immediately following vowel.

6 I consider the CVC roots in (19) as monomoraic at the stage of the lexical phonology where plural allomorphy would occur. However, there is evidence from vowel shortening in Hausa that CVC syllables are bimoraic. One type of evidence comes from vowel shortening where a long vowel in a potentially occurring CVVC syllable shortens and so surfaces as CVC. This suggests that a nongeminate coda consonant is indeed moraic. In order to account for the monomoraic behavior of a coda consonant with respect to plural allomorphy selection, but its bimoraic behavior with respect to vowel shortening, I propose that Weight-by-Position (3) applies after plural allomorphy selection but before vowel shortening. This proposal is virtually identical to the one made by Archangeli (1991: 241) for Yawelmani syllabification where she states, "the behavior of long vowels motivates two stages of syllabification – an early stage where coda consonants are not moraic and a later stage where coda consonants are moraic. Weight-by-Position mediates between the two stages."

7 There is evidence that a word-final nasal, especially /n/, is also moraic in Hausa. One type of evidence comes from the expressive of contempt,

discussed by Newman (1988, 1992). These expressives are formed by affixing -*oo* to a noun. If a noun ends in a long vowel or diphthong, -*oo* replaces the bimoraic sequence as shown in (i)

(i) ʔàlbasàa "onion"   ʔalbas-oo "onion (expressive)"
     kìbau   "arrow"   kib-oo   "arrow (expressive)"

If a word ends in a single consonant, the -*oo* normally appears after that consonant as shown in (ii) (though words ending in a single consonant are rare, usually loan words or proper nouns).

(ii) teebùr   "table"   teebur-oo   "table (expressive)"
      jaamùs   "Germany" jaamus-oo   "Germany (expressive)"

Newman (1992), however, observes that most words ending in the nasal /n/ pattern like (i), as seen in (iii):

(iii) tàlàatin   "thirty"   talaat-oo   "thirty (expressive)"
       ʔambùlan   "envelope"   ʔambul-oo   "envelope (expressive)"

One can posit that the similarity in the formation of expressives seen between (i) and (iii) results from the stems in both (i) and (iii) ending in a sequence of two moras, whereas the stems in (ii) do not contain a final moraic segment. Under this view, the affix -*oo* replaces a stem-final bimoraic sequence, but is suffixed after a stem-final nonmoraic segment. This suggests that a word-final nasal can be lexically moraic (though see Newman 1992 for a different analysis).

8 As mentioned in note 5 with respect to Hausa, it is assumed that a root-final consonant does not syllabify as the coda of the syllable with the root vowel; rather, it serves as the onset of the syllable containing an immediately following suffix vowel.

9 Zec (1988) does not explicitly discuss the moraic status of geminates, but in her discussion on Italian she seems to assume that geminates are underlyingly nonmoraic.

10 During the discussion of the presented version of this paper at the Workshop, it was suggested by one of the participants that the grouping together of CVG syllables with CVV syllables may not actually reflect on weight. Rather, their similarity can be understood in terms of linked structure. That is both geminates and long vowels entail a melodic segment linked to two slots (be they two root nodes as in (6) or two X-slots on a segmental view of the prosodic tier). However, there are some problematic aspects of this view of relating the grouping of CVV and CVG to linked structure. One problem is that it is unable to account for the fact that diphthongs, which do not involve a linked structure, typically pattern with syllables containing long vowels. This is seen in the Hausa data in (20) and (21). A

second problem has to do with the behavior of syllables closed by partial geminates. In Hausa they pattern with CVG syllables, in Korean they pattern with CVC syllables, and in Sinhala their patterning as CVC or CVG depends on the specific lexical item. This strongly suggests an analysis in which partial geminates are lexically moraic. Their status can vary among languages, and, as in Sinhala, it can vary within a language. This is supportive of the view of prespecification in Inkelas and Cho (1993).

References

Archangeli, Diana. 1991. Syllabification and prosodic templates in Yawelmani, *Natural Language and Linguistic Theory* 9: 231–83.

Davis, Stuart. 1994. Geminate consonants in moraic phonology, *West Coast Conference on Formal Linguistics* 13: 32–45.

Downing, Laura. 1991. The moraic representation of nasal-consonant clusters in Jita, *Afrikanistische Arbeitspapiere* 25: 105–30.

Feinstein, Mark. 1977. The linguistic nature of prenasalization, Ph.D. dissertation, City University of New York, NY.

    1979. Prenasalization and syllable structure, *Linguistic Inquiry* 10: 245–78.

Furniss, Graham, and Philip Jaggar (eds.). 1988. *Studies in Hausa Language and Linguistics in Honour of F. W. Parsons*, London: Kegan Paul International.

Gupta, Abha. 1987. Hindi word stress and the obligatory branching parameter, *Chicago Linguistic Society* 23.2: 134–48.

    1988. Peculiarities of geminates in Hindi, ms. University of Arizona, Tucson.

Hahn, Reinhard. 1991. *Spoken Uyghur*, Seattle, WA: University of Washington Press.

Halle, Morris, and G. N. Clements. 1983. *Problem Book in Phonology*, Cambridge, MA: MIT Press.

Hayes, Bruce. 1981. A metrical theory of stress rules, Ph.D. dissertation, Massachusetts Institute of Technology, Cambridge, MA. [Revised version distributed by Indiana University Linguistics Club.]

    1989. Compensatory lengthening in moraic phonology, *Linguistic Inquiry* 20: 253–306.

Hyman, Larry. 1992. Moraic mismatches in Bantu, *Phonology* 9: 255–65.

Inkelas, Sharon, and Young-mee Yu Cho. 1993. Inalterability as prespecification, *Language* 69: 529–74.

Kraft, K., and M. Kraft. 1973. *Introductory Hausa*, Berkeley, CA: University of California Press.

Krueger, John. 1961. *Chuvash Manual*, Bloomington, IN: Indiana University Publications.

Leben, William. 1980. A metrical analysis of length, *Linguistic Inquiry* 11: 97–509.

Lee, Yongsung. 1993. Topics in the vowel phonology of Korean, Ph.D. dissertation, Indiana University, Bloomington, IN.

Letterman, Rebecca. 1994. Nominal gemination in Sinhala and its implications for the status of prenasalized stops. Paper presented at Annual Meeting of the Linguistic Society of America.

McCarthy, John, and Alan Prince. 1986. Prosodic Morphology, ms. University of Massachusetts, Amherst, MA and Brandeis University, Waltham, MA.

1990. Foot and word in Prosodic Morphology: the Arabic broken plural, *Natural Language and Linguistic Theory* 8: 209–83.

1993. Prosodic Morphology 1: constraint interaction and satisfaction, ms. University of Massachusetts, Amherst, MA and Rutgers University, New Brunswick, NJ.

Newman, Paul. 1972. Syllable weight as a phonological variable, *Studies in African Linguistics* 3: 301–24.

1988. O Shush! An exclamatory construction in Hausa, in Furniss and Jaggar (eds.), 89–98.

1992. The drift from the coda into the syllable nucleus in Hausa, *Diachronica* 9: 227–38.

Ohala, Manjari. 1983. *Aspects of Hindi Phonology*, Delhi: Motilal Banarsidass.

Pyatt, Elizabeth. 1993. Gemination and the Sinhala prenasalized stop, *Harvard Working Papers in Linguistics* 2: 173–90.

Reynolds, Christopher. 1980. *Sinhalese: an Introductory Course*, London: School of Oriental and African Studies, University of London.

Rosenthall, Samuel. 1988. The representation of prenasalized consonants, *West Coast Conference on Formal Linguistics* 8: 277–91.

Selkirk, Elisabeth. 1990. A two root theory of length, *University of Massachusetts Occasional Papers* 14: 123–71.

Sherer, Timothy. 1994. Prosodic phonotactics, Ph.D. dissertation, University of Massachusetts, Amherst, MA.

Steriade, Donca. 1991. Moras and other slots, *Formal Linguistics Society of Midamerica* 1: 254–80.

1993. Closure, release, and nasal contours, in M. K. Huffman and R. A. Krakow (eds.), *Phonetics and Phonology* 5: *Nasals, Nasalization, and the Velum*, San Diego, CA: Academic Press, 401–70.

Tranel, Bernard. 1991. CVC light syllables, geminates and moraic theory, *Phonology* 8: 291–302.

Tyler, Stephen. 1969. *Koya: an Outline Grammar. University of California Publications in Linguistics* 54.

Zec, Draga. 1988. Sonority constraints on prosodic structure, Ph.D. dissertation, Stanford University, CA.

3 Verbal reduplication in three Bantu languages

Laura J. Downing

1. Introduction

The central proposal of Optimality Theory is that phonological outputs are not derived by the interaction of ordered rules. Rather, outputs are freely generated and the actual output for any input within a particular language is the one which is optimal given the ranking of the relevant constraints in that language. While constraints are assumed to be universal, constraint rankings are language particular, so that inter-linguistic variation may be accounted for by ranking the same constraints in different orders. To test this hypothesis, this study[1] compares verbal reduplication in three Bantu languages: SiSwati, Kinande and Kikuyu. These languages were chosen because, as shown in section 2, in all three the reduplicant is realized as a two-syllable prefix to the verb stem. Not surprisingly, these similarities will be accounted for by proposing that the three languages share similar constraints on the shape and position of the reduplicant. More surprisingly, perhaps, differences in the realization of the reduplicant in these languages will also be accounted for by proposing that the languages share similar constraints. Variation results from ranking these constraints differently in the three languages.

While Optimality Theory gives an elegant account for some of the variations in the form of reduplicants in these languages, I will show that there are aspects of the reduplication patterns discussed which pose problems for some claims of the theory. In sections 3 and 4 I argue that these languages provide evidence for Spring's (1990) proposal that non-metrical prosodic constituents, as well as metrical ones, may define bases and templates for reduplication. This analysis thus challenges the proposal current since McCarthy and Prince (1986) that only metrical prosodic constituents play a role in Prosodic Morphology.

In section 4 I discuss the infixing pattern of reduplication found in some vowel-initial stems in SiSwati and Kinande. McCarthy and Prince (1993a, b) discuss a similar reduplication pattern in Timugon Murut and argue that infixation before vowel-initial stems is universally to be accounted for by ranking prosodic constraints against vowel hiatus above the morphological constraint aligning the reduplicant at the left edge of the base. The initial vowel need not be made extraprosodic to derive the infixing pattern. However, I will show that the SiSwati and Kinande infixation patterns are best accounted for by proposing that stem-initial vowels are extraprosodic. Simply misaligning the reduplicative template with the base cannot account for the full range of data.

2. Basic reduplication patterns of SiSwati, Kinande and Kikuyu

2.1 Similarities

SiSwati, Kinande and Kikuyu are Bantu languages spoken in Swaziland, Zaïre, and Kenya, respectively, and all three have a productive process of verbal reduplication used to signify that the action of the verb is done on a small scale, or little by little, or from time to time.[2] As shown by the data in (1) to (3), below, the reduplicant is realized as a prefix (or infixed after a stem-initial vowel) in all three languages and is always two syllables long, no matter how long the stem is. (In all the data, the reduplicant is underlined; vowels in parentheses have undergone coalescence.)

(1) SiSwati verbal reduplication

Stem	Reduplicated Form	Gloss
a. Consonant-initial:		
-bóna	-<u>boná</u>-bona	"see"
-bonísa	-<u>boni</u>-bonísa	"show"
-bonísana	-<u>boni</u>-bonísana	"show each other"
b. Monosyllabic:		
-phá	-<u>phayí</u>-pha	"give"
-wa	-<u>wayi</u>-wa	"fall"
c. Vowel-initial, prefixing:		
-ákha	-<u>akhá</u>-yakha	"build"
-akhéla	-<u>akhe</u>-yakhéla	"build for"

d. Vowel-initial, infixing:
    -engeta   -e-<u>ngeta</u>-ngeta   "increase"
    -engetisa   -e-<u>ngeti</u>-ngetisa   "cause to increase"

(2) Kinande verbal reduplication (Mutaka and Hyman 1990)
    Stem   Reduplicated Form   Gloss
    a. Consonant-initial:
       -huma   -<u>huma</u>-huma   "beat"
       -humira   -<u>huma</u>-humira   "beat for"
       -humirana   -<u>huma</u>-humirana   "beat for each other"
    b. Monosyllabic:
       -swa   -<u>swa.swa</u>-swa   "grind"
       -ta   -<u>ta.ta</u>-ta   "bury"
    c. Vowel-initial, prefixing:
       -esa   -e<u>s(a)</u>e.<u>s(a)</u>-e.sa   "play"
       -oha   -o<u>h(a)</u>o.<u>h(a)</u>-o.ha   "pick"
    d. Vowel-initial, infixing:
       -esera   -e-<u>sera</u>-sera   "play for"
       -ohera   -o-<u>hera</u>-hera   "pick for"

(3) Kikuyu verbal reduplication (consonants in Kikuyu orthography;
    vowels in IPA)
    Stem   Reduplicated Form   Gloss
    a. Consonant-initial:
       -cama   -<u>cama</u>-cama   "taste"
       -thuːra   -<u>thuːra</u>-thuːra   "choose"
       -hetoka   -<u>heta</u>-hetoka   "pass"
       -hetokana   -<u>heta</u>-hetokana   "pass each other"
    b. Monosyllabic:
       -goa   -<u>goːa</u>-goːa   "fall"
       -hea   -<u>heːa</u>-heːa   "be burnt"
    c. Vowel-initial:
       -enja   -ɛ<u>nj(a)</u>-ɛːnja   "dig up"
       -andeka   -<u>and(a)</u>-aːndeka   "write"
       -okera   -<u>ok(a)</u>-oːkera [okɔːkera] "wake up"

All three languages have previously been given insightful analyses –
SiSwati by Kiyomi & Davis (1992); Kinande by Mutaka and Hyman
(1990); and Kikuyu by Peng (1992) – in the McCarthy and Prince
(1986) prosodic framework, and I follow these authors in proposing
that the disyllabic maximum size limit on the reduplicative affix is best

accounted for by requiring the affix to be aligned with a disyllabic foot. In the optimality framework (McCarthy and Prince 1993a, b; Prince and Smolensky 1993) adopted here, this requirement would be accounted for by the constraint in (4a), while the alignment constraint in (4b) accounts for the prefixal position of the reduplicant (RED):

(4) a. RED=FOOT (adapted McCarthy and Prince 1993b):
The left and right edges of RED must coincide, respectively, with the left and right edges of a syllabic trochee.

   b. ALIGN-RED (adapted McCarthy and Prince 1993a, b):
ALIGN-RED, RIGHT; (PROSODIC) STEM, LEFT

The left to right mapping of the base to the reduplicative foot is accounted for by the constraints below (McCarthy and Prince 1993b: 62–63, (110), (111)):

(5) a. CONTIGUITY   RED (R) corresponds to a contiguous substring of BASE (B).

   b. ANCHORING   In R+B, the initial element in R is identical to the initial element in B.

   c. MAX   R=B

As a result of the constraints in (4) and (5), the optimal parse for the reduplicant will contain the leftmost foot of the verb stem which serves as the morphological base for reduplication in all three languages. (For the moment, I shall ignore some obvious problems with the mapping constraints in (5), such as why the final vowel of the RED is always /a/ in Kinande and Kikuyu (instead of the second stem vowel) – this will be discussed in section 3 – and why the RED is sometimes infixed in Kinande and SiSwati – this will be discussed in section 4.)

2.2 Variations

Striking confirmation that the reduplicative template is minimally (as well as maximally) two syllables long in all three languages comes from the monosyllabic stems. In all three languages, monosyllabic stems are expanded to fill the two-syllable reduplicative template, but each language adopts a different strategy for expansion. In SiSwati, an epenthetic /-yi/ fills the second syllable of the template, as shown by the data in (1b). In Kinande, (2b), the monosyllabic stems are expanded by copying them twice. And in Kikuyu, (3b), the monosyllabic stems are expanded by lengthening the root vowel.[3] To account for these variations in how the monosyllabic stems are expanded, I propose that the three languages share the family of FILL constraints cited in (6), but that these constraints are ranked differently in each language, leading to different optimal strategies for satisfying the two-syllable minimum.

(6) FILL constraints

    a. FILL ONSET   Onset position is filled by input segment(s).

    b. FILL-NUCLEUS   Nucleus position is filled by input segment(s).

    c. *COPY-FEATURE   Prosodic positions are not filled by copying input segment(s).

    d. FILL-μ   Moras are not inserted.

As noted by McCarthy and Prince (1993a), the family of FILL constraints, which includes those in (6), limits the abstractness of outputs by allowing structure to be inserted only to fulfill other higher ranked constraints. FILL-ONSET (6a) and FILL-NUCLEUS (6b) militate against epenthesis by requiring that these syllabic positions be filled by segmental material from the input. In order for a syllable to be epenthesized to expand the reduplicant to two syllables in SiSwati, these two FILL constraints (referred to jointly as FILL-σ) must be outranked by RED=FOOT (4a). (Anchoring, (5b), the constraint which requires the first element in the reduplicant to be identical to the first element of the base, accounts for the fact that the epenthetic syllable is the second syllable of the reduplicant.) But since epenthesis is not the optimal way to expand the base to two syllables in Kinande or Kikuyu, these two FILL constraints, (6a) and (6b), must be ranked above RED=FOOT in those languages.

The FILL constraint on copying features, (6c), militates against copying segmental material to fill prosodic positions. (Of course, all reduplication processes violate this constraint, but only violate it once, typically.) In order for the monosyllabic base to be copied twice to fill out the two-syllable reduplicant in Kinande, this constraint must be ranked below RED=FOOT, so that copying features twice becomes the optimal way to fill out the second syllable of the template. The opposite ranking makes copying non-optimal in the other languages.

Finally, the FILL constraint on inserting moras, (6d), militates against vowel lengthening to fill out the two-syllable template. Since long vowels may not syllabify with a following short vowel, and long vowels may not occur stem-finally in Kikuyu, lengthening the first vowel of the monosyllabic base forces the two stem vowels to occupy separate syllables. Ranking FILL-μ (6d) below RED = FOOT in Kikuyu makes vowel lengthening the optimal way to expand monosyllabic stems to two syllables. The opposite ranking makes vowel lengthening non-optimal in the other two languages. These constraint rankings are summarized in (7):

(7) a. RED=FOOT ≫ FILL-ONSET, Fill-NUCLEUS
   (SiSwati ranking optimizing epenthesis)
   b. FILL-ONSET, Fill-NUCLEUS ≫ RED=FOOT
   (Kinande, Kikuyu ranking blocking epenthesis)
   c. FILL-μ ≫ RED=FOOT ≫ *COPYF
   (Kinande ranking optimizing double copy)
   d. *COPYF ≫ RED=FOOT ≫ FILL-μ
   (Kikuyu ranking optimizing vowel lengthening)

The tableaux in (8) to (10) show how these rankings pick out the correct surface form as the most optimal output in each language.[4] (The reduplicant is underlined.)

(8) Evaluation of reduplication candidates for monosyllabic SiSwati stems

Candidates	ONSET	ALIGN	RED= FOOT	FILL- NUCLEUS	FILL- ONSET	PARSE-μ
a. ☞ lwa.YI.lwa				*	*	
b. lwa.I.lwa	*!			*		
c. lwa.lwa			*!			
d. lw<a>I.lwa[lwelwa]			*!	*		*

(9) Evaluation of reduplication candidates for monosyllabic Kinande stems

Candidates	ONSET	ALIGN	FILL- σ	INSERT- μ	RED= FOOT	*COPY- FEATURE	PARSE- μ
a. swa-swa					*!		
b. ☞ swa.swa-swa						*	
c. swaYI-swa			*!				
d. so:a-swa				*!			

(10) Evaluation of reduplication candidates for monosyllabic Kikuyu
stems

Candidates	Onset	Align	Fill-σ	*Copy-Feature	Red=Foot	Insert-μ	Parse-μ
a. goa.-go:a					*!		
b. goa.goa-go:a				*!			
c. goa.YI-go:a			*!				
d. ☞ go:a-go:a						*	

This variation in the ranking of the different FILL constraints also
accounts for another difference in the realization of the reduplicant in
the three languages. In Kinande and Kikuyu (2c; 3c), the final reduplicant vowel and the initial base vowel coalesce, while in SiSwati the final
reduplicant vowel and the initial base vowel are separated by an epenthetic /y/ (1c). The occurrence of the epenthetic /y/ is surprising in
SiSwati since, as shown by the data in (11), other vowel-final prefixes
coalesce or glide before vowel-initial stems.

(11) Vowel hiatus in SiSwati
  a. kú-kála   "to weigh"   versus kw-élusa   "to herd"
                                          k-ósa   "to roast"
  b. u-ya-bala   "you are   versus u-y-elusa "you are herding"
                   counting"
                                          u-y-osa   "you are roasting"
  c. u-ya-li-kála "you are   versus u-ya-l-ósa "you are
                   weighing it"   roasting it"

As work by Kaye (1989) and others (see Downing 1996d and references
cited therein) argues, vowel coalescence and gliding may be motivated
by the Onset Principle (12), since these processes insure that all syllables have onsets (Itô 1989: (3)).

(12) Onset Principle   Avoid σ[V

The problem is to explain why coalescence with an initial stem vowel
fails only in the reduplicative context in SiSwati. What I propose is that
this is predicted by ranking RED=FOOT (4a) above FILL-ONSET, the ranking motivated just above to allow epenthesis to fill the reduplicative

template in the case of monosyllabic stems. Recall that RED=FOOT requires each edge of the reduplicant to be aligned with a syllable edge. If RED=FOOT outranks FILL-ONSET, this alignment may be maintained by epenthesizing a /y/ between the reduplicant and the base.[5] The tableau in (13) illustrates how this ranking makes epenthesis more optimal than coalescence:

(13) Evaluation of reduplication candidates for prefixing V-initial SiSwati stems

Candidates	ONSET	ALIGN	RED=FOOT	FILL-NUCLEUS	FILL-ONSET	PARSE-μ
a. ☞ akha-Yakha					*	
b. akh<a>a.kha			*!			*
c. akha.akha	*!					

In Kinande and Kikuyu, however, FILL-NUCLEUS and FILL-ONSET are ranked above RED=FOOT to block epenthesis as the optimal strategy for filling out the second syllable of the reduplicant in the case of monosyllabic stems. As shown by the tableau in (14), this same ranking also optimizes coalescence between the reduplicant and the base.

(14) Evaluation of reduplication candidates for V-initial Kikuyu stems

Candidates	ONSET	ALIGN	FILL-NUCLEUS	FILL ONSET	RED=FOOT	PARSE-μ
a. oka-Yokera				*!		
b. ☞ ok<a>o:.kera					*	*
c. oka.okera	*!					

To sum up this section, both the similarities and the differences in the reduplication patterns discussed so far find a straightforward treatment within Optimality Theory. The optimality analysis has the benefit that the same constraint rankings which make epenthesis the optimal way to fill out the second syllable of the reduplicant in SiSwati also make epenthesis between the reduplicant and the base the optimal way to avoid an onset violation in that context, even though coalescence occurs between other prefixes and vowel-initial stems. In a derivational account like that of Kiyomi & Davis (1992), these epenthetic processes are unrelated to each other, and no explanation is provided for why epenthesis should be favored over vowel coalescence in the reduplicative context.

3. The canonical stem as template in Kinande and Kikuyu

The mapping constraints in (5) predict that the disyllabic reduplicant should be identical to the first two syllables of the base (in bases of at least two syllables). While this is true for the SiSwati data cited in (1), in Kinande and Kikuyu the second vowel of the reduplicant is always /a/, no matter what the second vowel of the base might be. To account for this pattern we must explain, first, why the second stem vowel does not copy and, second, why the second reduplicant vowel is /a/ rather than some other vowel.

Peng's (1992) analysis of Kikuyu and Mutaka and Hyman's (1990) analysis of Kinande each propose a different account for why the second vowel does not copy. Peng proposes that the base for reduplication is not the entire morphological stem, but rather the canonical root which he defines as the first [σ.C] sequence in the stem. The canonical root is circumscribed from the rest of the stem, and then mapped to the disyllabic reduplicative template, as shown in (15):

(15) Derivation of -heta-hetoka "pass little by little" (adapted, Peng 1992)

    a. Input representation   b. Affixing (trochee) and copying
                                        (canonical root = [σ.C])

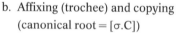

    c. Left to right mapping

As shown, the second stem vowel is not copied, because it is not part of the base for reduplication defined by the canonical root.

In Mutaka and Hyman's (1990) analysis of Kinande, in contrast, the entire stem is the base for reduplication, but only the first [σ.C] may map to the disyllabic template due to the Morpheme Integrity Constraint cited in (16):

(16) *Morpheme Integrity Constraint* (MIC) (Mutaka and Hyman 1990: (22)) Mapping of a melody to a reduplicative template takes place *by morpheme*. If the whole of a morpheme cannot be successfully mapped into the bisyllabic reduplicative template, then none of the morpheme may be mapped.

As shown by the derivation in (17), the second stem vowel may not copy in longer stems, because this would always split up a suffixal morpheme (in (17), this morpheme is the benefactive suffix /-ir-/) in violation of the MIC (hyphens indicate morpheme breaks). The unmapped portion of the copied stem deletes by Stray Erasure (Itô 1986):

(17) Derivation of *-huma-humira* "beat for here and there" (adapted from Mutaka and Hyman 1990: (44))

a. Input representation   b. Affixing (trochee) and copying
                                  (entire stem)

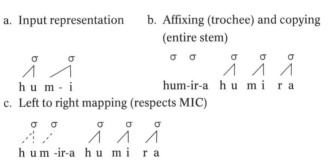

c. Left to right mapping (respects MIC)

Where Peng's analysis of Kikuyu and Mutaka and Hyman's analysis of Kinande agree is in the source of the fixed /a/ in the second syllable of the reduplicant, once the [σ.C] sequence has been mapped to the template. Both propose that /a/ is inserted because it is the phonological default vowel. However, there is good evidence in both languages against this proposal. It is usually assumed that the epenthetic vowel in a particular language is the phonological default vowel in that language (Archangeli 1984, 1988). So if /a/ were the default vowel for Kikuyu, one would expect it to also be the vowel which is inserted in epenthesis contexts. However, as shown in (18), when English words are borrowed in Kikuyu, /i/ is the vowel which is epenthesized to break up English consonant clusters which may not be parsed by Kikuyu's CV(V) syllable template.

(18) English words borrowed into Kikuyu (in Kikuyu orthography, "th" indicates a voiced interdental fricative)
   a. marigiti   "market"
   b. thinoo   "snow"
   c. kirithitia:no   "Christian"
   d. kiraoni   "crown"
   e. gaithimiri   "cashmere"

Likewise, Hyman (1989) notes that /a/ is not the general epenthetic vowel for Kinande. When French words are borrowed into that language, front vowels are usually inserted to syllabify consonants (Kinande, like Kikuyu, only has open syllables):

(19) French words borrowed into Kinande (Larry Hyman, personal communication)
   a. masini   "machine"
   b. kamisere   "magistrate"   (French "commissaire")
   c. soferi   "chauffeur"
   d. e-sosoti   "sock"   (French "chaussette")
   e. olu-supe   "soup"

If the second vowel of the reduplicant is filled by epenthesis in Kikuyu and Kinande, as these authors propose, then /a/ is not predicted to surface, since /a/ is not the usual epenthetic vowel.

If /a/ is not the phonological default vowel in either Kikuyu or Kinande, then some other explanation must be found for the presence of this vowel in the reduplicant. One might propose that the /a/ is phonologically specified to fill the second vowel slot in the template. But then the fact that /a/ and not some other vowel occurs in the second syllable is unpredictable and arbitrary. While the occurrence of /a/ is phonologically arbitrary, morphologically /a/ is the unmarked, predicted verbal ending. Indeed, what is striking about the form of the reduplicant is that it resembles a canonical two-syllable Bantu verb stem, ending with the default final vowel morpheme /a/. I propose that this resemblance may best be accounted for by defining the canonical stem (20) as the template for reduplication in these two languages:

(20) Canonical stem (adapted, Peng 1992)
   a. Prosodic shape: syllabic trochee
   b. Morphological form: verb stem

The canonical stem must still meet a prosodic constraint – it must be a syllabic trochee (20a). But it must also meet a morphological constraint (20b) – it must resemble a verb stem and so must contain the final vowel verb morpheme /a/.[6]

This analysis straightforwardly solves both problems these patterns raised. The second stem vowel of the base does not copy, because the second reduplicant vowel must be identifiable as the final vowel morpheme. The vowel /a/ occurs in the reduplicant because it is the default final vowel morpheme.[7] In proposing that a morphoprosodic constituent, the canonical stem, is the template for reduplication in Kinande and Kikuyu, this analysis contradicts the Prosodic Morphology Hypothesis:

(21) Prosodic Morphology Hypothesis (McCarthy and Prince 1993b: 1)
Templates are defined in terms of the authentic units of prosody: mora, syllable, foot, prosodic word.

However, a growing body of work has challenged the claim that this hierarchy is sufficient to characterize constituents which play a role in Prosodic Morphology. Itô (1990), for example, argues that separate minimality constraints in Japanese define a prosodic stem as well as a prosodic word. Likewise, Peng's analysis of Kikuyu reduplication relies on circumscribing the canonical root as the base for reduplication, even though the canonical root is not a metrical constituent. Inkelas (1989, 1993) and Spring (1990) have argued that other nonmetrical prosodic constituents play a role in the grammar by defining the domains of phonological rules and defining the base for reduplication. The present analysis extends this earlier work by arguing that morphoprosodic constituents like the canonical stem may also provide the template for reduplication.

4. Infixation in SiSwati and Kinande

In both SiSwati and Kinande, we find that the reduplicative prefix occurs in two positions in vowel-initial stems. In some cases, (1c) and (2c), the reduplicant is a prefix. But in some vowel-initial verbs, (1d) and (2d), the initial vowel is ignored for reduplication, and the reduplicant is infixed after this initial vowel. In this section, I first present an analysis of infixation in SiSwati, then show how the same analysis, with minor modification, can be extended to account for infixation in Kinande. I will argue for both languages that McCarthy and Prince's (1993a, b) general analysis of reduplicative infixation fails to account for the data presented.

4.1 SiSwati infixation

As shown by the data in (22), in some SiSwati vowel-initial stems, the reduplicant occurs after the initial vowel of the verb and that initial vowel is not reduplicated.

(22) SiSwati verbal reduplication, infixing V-initial stems

Verb stem	Reduplicated form	Gloss
a. -endlúla	-e-ndlulá-ndlula	"pass by"
b. -endluklána	-e-ndlula-ndlulána	"pass by each other"
c. -enyéla	-e-nyelá-nyela	"be hurt"
d. -etsaméla	-e-tsame-tsaméla	"bask"
e. -engeta	-e-ngeta-ngeta	"increase"
f. -engetisa	-e-ngeti-ngetisa	"cause to increase"

It is a striking coincidence that all the infixing verb stems I have discovered to date begin with [e]. One might, then, propose that the initial [e] is not part of the lexical verb stem in order to account for this predictable quality. However, there is no phonological or morphological motivation for eliminating the [e] from the stems. Phonologically, [e] is not plausibly epenthetic, since [i], not [e], is the epenthetic vowel in SiSwati, as shown by epenthesis in the monosyllabic stems. (See Kiyomi and Davis 1992 for further arguments that [i] is the epenthetic vowel.) Morphologically, [e] may not plausibly be a separate morpheme from the verb stems, because it is included in the imperative form of these verbs, which consists of only the bare verb stem (see Downing 1994). Further, an inspection of the glosses of the stems in (22) shows there is no consistent meaning associated with [e] which might motivate analyzing it as a separate morpheme. Given that the initial vowel is indeed part of the verb stems, there are two problems these data present for an analysis. First, how may the infixed position of the reduplicative affix be accounted for? Secondly, how may we predict which vowel-initial verbs follow the infixing pattern of reduplication and which follow the prefixing pattern? I will address each of these in turn.

Kiyomi and Davis (1992) propose that infixation may be derived by making the initial vowels of the stems in (22) extraprosodic. If these vowels are not part of the base, they are predicted to be ignored for reduplication. But simply stipulating that some initial vowels are extraprosodic does not explain why only vowel-initial stems show the infixing pattern of reduplication while consonant-initial ones do not. As McCarthy and Prince (1993a, b) and Prince and Smolensky (1993) argue, the reason initial vowels may be ignored for reduplication is because onsetless syllables are ill-formed. In their analysis of Timugon Murut reduplication, McCarthy and Prince (1993a, b) propose that the theory of Generalized Alignment may account for the role of the Onset Principle in deriving reduplicative infixation without appealing to extraprosodicity. As shown by the data in (23), in Timugon Murut, as in SiSwati, a reduplicative affix is realized as a prefix to a consonant-initial base but as an infix to a vowel-initial base (except note the form of the reduplicant is a single syllable):

(23) Timugon Murut reduplication (McCarthy and Prince 1993a, b)

a. bulud	<u>bu</u>-bulud	"hill/ridge"
b. limo	<u>li</u>-limo	"five/about five"
c. ulampoy	u-<u>la</u>-lampoy	(no gloss)
d. abalan	a-<u>ba</u>-balan	"bathes/often bathes"
e. ompodon	om-<u>po</u>-podon	"flatter/always flatter"

In McCarthy and Prince's analysis, infixation before vowel-initial stems falls out straightforwardly from ranking the Onset Principle (and other prosodic constraints required in resolving vowel hiatus) above the constraint aligning the reduplicant at the left edge of the stem. As shown by the tableau in (24), infixation is the optimal output, since infixation minimizes violations of prosodic constraints by minimally misaligning the reduplicant.

(24) Evaluation of reduplication candidates for vowel-initial SiSwati stems (<u>kw-</u> is the infinitive prefix)

Candidates	ONSET	RED=FOOT	FILL-ONSET	PARSE-μ	ALIGN
a. ☞ kw-e.<u>lapha</u>.lapha					*
b. kw-<u>ela</u>.e.lapha	*!				
c. kw-<u>ela</u>.Ye.lapha			*!		
d. kw-<u>el<a>e</u>.lapha		*!		*	

McCarthy and Prince argue explicitly against extraprosodicity as an alternative means of excluding onsetless initial vowels from the base for reduplication. First they note that onsetless vowels are not prosodic constituents. Since only constituents may be made extraprosodic, there does not appear to be any nonstipulative way to exclude onsetless vowels from a prosodic domain. However, if we require the base to begin with a well-formed, onsetful syllable which only includes material from the morphological stem, a stem-initial vowel, since it does not begin a well-formed syllable, will be excluded from the base precisely because it is not a well-formed prosodic constituent. The three constraints in (25), along with the Onset Principle, derive this misalignment by requiring that the left edge of the prosodic stem[8] be aligned with the left edge of a syllable within the morphological stem (MStem):[9]

(25) ALIGN PROSODIC STEM (STEM)

    a. STEM1 Every element of the prosodic stem has a correspondent in the morphological stem.

    b. STEM2 Align (Morphological Stem, L; Prosodic Stem, L)

    c. STEM3 Every element of the morphological stem has a correspondent in the prosodic stem.

To derive this result, I assume that morpheme boundaries are indicated in the output candidates and so are available to be referred to by Alignment constraints. It is ranking ONSET above the ALIGN PROSODIC STEM constraints (especially (25b)) which I propose determines that the prosodic stem is ill-aligned if it begins with an onsetless syllable. Ranking (25a) above ONSET and (25b) has the effect of allowing only morphological stem (MStem) material to be included in the prosodic stem. As a result, prefixes may not be included in the prosodic stem even though they may be syllabified with a stem-initial vowel. And (25a) and (25b) must be ranked above (25c) since infixing is only optimal if the prosodic stem need not include all the segments of the morphological stem. Following Inkelas (1989, 1993) and Buckley (1994), then, I propose that extraprosodicity results from a misalignment of prosodic and morphological structure, in this case motivated by syllable well-formedness. Finally, since the reduplicant must be aligned with the left edge of the prosodic stem (ALIGN(RED) (4b)), the reduplicant will be optimally infixed following the extraprosodic vowel. These points are illustrated in the tableau in (26). (Only crucial constraints are listed. Note that

ALIGN is again highly ranked in this analysis, in contrast with (24), because it is never violated.)

(26) Evaluation of reduplication candidates for vowel-initial SiSwati stems ("[" indicates the Prosodic Stem edge; ku- is the infinitival prefix)

Candidates	ALIGN	RED=FOOT	STEM1	ONSET	STEM2	FILL	STEM3
a. ☞ kw-e.lapha.[lapha					*		*
b. kw-ela.[e.lapha				*!			
c. kw-e.l<a>[e.lapha			*!				
d. ku-la.ph<a>e.[lapha	*!				*		*
e. kwela[kwe.lapha			*!		*		
f. kw-e.la[Ye.lapha			*!		*	*	

Another argument McCarthy and Prince (1993b) present against an appeal to extraprosodicity of the initial vowel to account for reduplicative infixation is that independent support for extraprosodicity of the initial vowel is seldom available. However, the prosodic stem defined by the constraints in (25) finds independent support in SiSwati from several tone-association processes. All of these processes are sensitive to the number of syllables in the prosodic stem. Significantly, for all of these processes, initial vowels which are extraprosodic for reduplication are also ignored in counting the number of syllables for tone association.[10]

One tone pattern in SiSwati which is determined by the length of the prosodic stem is the location of the rightmost high-toned syllable in stems with an underlying high tone. As shown by the data in (27), stems with two or three syllables have the rightmost high tone on the penult, while longer stems have the rightmost high tone on the antepenult:

(27) SiSwati high-toned C-initial stems
        Verb stem   Gloss
    a. 2–3 syllable stems:
        -tfútsa   "move house"
        -kála   "weigh"
        -kaléla   "weigh for"
        -khulúma   "talk"
        -hlanyéla   "plant"

b. >3 syllable stems:

-khulumísana   "talk to each other"
-hlanyélela   "plant for"

Space does not permit accounting for these tone patterns, but the interested reader may find detailed analyses in Downing (1990, 1996d) and Kisseberth (1993). The important point to note is that the number of syllables in the stem determines the location of the rightmost high tone. If we turn to vowel-initial stems, the nonreduplicated forms in (28a) and (28b) show that the prefixing vowel-initial stems have the same tone patterns as in (27): two- and three-syllable stems have the rightmost high tone on the penult, while longer stems have the rightmost high tone on the antepenult. However, the infixing vowel-initial stems in (28c) and (28d) have the high tone on the penult even in four-syllable stems. Only in five-syllable stems or longer is the tone found on the antepenult:

(28) SiSwati high-toned V-initial stems

Verb stem	Reduplicated form	Gloss
a. Prefixing 2–3 syllable stems:		
-ókha	-okhá-yokha	"light (a fire)"
-okhéla	-okhe-yokhéla	"light for"
-énya	-enyá-yenya	"soak"
-enyéla	-enye-yenyéla	"soak for"
b. Prefixing >3 syllable stems:		
-onákala	-ona-yonákala	"get spoilt"
-atísana	-ati-yatísana	"introduce each other"
c. Infixing 3–4 syllable stems:		
-enyéla	-e-nyelá-nyela	"be hurt"
-eyáma	-e-yamá-yama	"lean"
-etsaméla	-e-tsame-tsaméla	"bask"
-eyamísa	-e-yami-yamísa	"cause to lean"
d. Infixing >4 syllable stem:		
-ehlukánisa	-e-hluka-hlukánisa	"distinguish"

The tone patterns of the infixing verb stems in (28c) and (28d) may be straightforwardly accounted for, however, if the prosodic stem which is the base for reduplication is also the domain for assigning this tone pattern. If the initial vowel is excluded from the prosodic stem, then these verbs are correctly predicted to have the same tone patterns as prefixing stems which are one syllable shorter.

The tone pattern of high-toned reduplicated forms is also determined by the length of the verb stem. As shown by the data in (29), two-syllable consonant-initial stems have the rightmost high tone on the antepenult, while three-syllable stems have their rightmost high tone on the penult:

(29) SiSwati high-toned C-initial stems

Verb stem	Reduplicate	Gloss
a. 2-syllable stems:		
-tfútsa	-<u>tfutsá</u>-tfutsa	"move house"
-kála	-<u>kalá</u>-kala	"weigh"
b. 3-syllable stems:		
-tfutséla	-<u>tfutse</u>-tfutséla	"move for"
-kaléla	-<u>kale</u>-kaléla	"weigh for"
-khulúma	-<u>khulu</u>-khulúma	"talk"

Space does not permit accounting for these tone patterns, but the interested reader is referred to Hewitt (1992) for an analysis of a similar distinction in Shona verbal reduplication. The important point is that the number of syllables in the stem determines the tone pattern of the reduplicated form. If we turn back to the reduplicated forms of the vowel-initial stems in (28a) and (28b), we see that the prefixing vowel-initial stems follow the same tone pattern shown in (29): two-syllable stems have the rightmost high tone on the antepenult, while three-syllable stems have their rightmost high tone on the penult. In contrast, the infixing vowel-initial verb stems in (28c) and (28d) follow a different pattern: three-syllable stems (if we count the initial vowel as a syllable) have the rightmost high tone on the antepenult, while four-syllable stems have the rightmost high tone on the penult. Again, this is exactly what we predict, if the initial vowel of the infixing stems is extraprosodic, and the length of the prosodic stem is what conditions this tone pattern.

It remains to be explained how we may predict which vowel-initial stems follow the infixing reduplication pattern and which follow the prefixing pattern illustrated in (28a) and (28b). The minimal pair in (30) shows that it is the length of the verb root which correlates with the position of the reduplicant:

(30) a. -enyéla   -e-<u>nyelá</u>-nyela   "be hurt"   (infixing)
      b. -enyéla   -<u>enye</u>-yenyéla   "soak for" (prefixing)
      c. -énya   -<u>enyá</u>-yenya   "soak"

What distinguishes (30a) from (30b) is that (30a) is an underived stem, while (30b) is transparently derived from the two-syllable stem in (30c). What all infixing verb stems have in common, in fact, is that they are underived stems of at least three syllables.[11] Three-syllable stems, or longer, which are derived from shorter verb stems are systematically prefixing.

To account for this, I propose that every prosodic stem must minimally contain one vowel of the verb root:

(31) SiSwati PROSODIC STEM MINIMALITY
At least one root vowel of the morphological stem has a correspondent in the prosodic stem.

That is, the left edge of the prosodic stem may not be aligned at the left edge of the root-final consonant. (Recall that the final vowel of verb stems is a separate morpheme, not part of the root.) MINIMALITY (31) must outrank STEM (25) so that outputs which include the initial vowel of shorter roots in the prosodic stem are optimal. But MINIMALITY is dominated by the FILL-NUCLEUS constraint, since monosyllabic bases like -lwa "fight" are not expanded to avoid MINIMALITY violations. These points are illustrated by the tableaux in (32):

(32) Evaluation of outputs to reduplication ("[" marks left edge of prosodic stem; "+" marks boundary between root and suffixes)

Candidates	ONSET	ALIGN	RED= FOOT	FILL NUCLEUS	MINIMALITY	FILL-ONSET	STEM	PARSE-μ
a. ☞ -elapha[laph+a							*	
b. -ela[Yelaph+a						*!	*	

Candidates	ONSET	ALIGN	RED= FOOT	FILL NUCLEUS	MINIMALITY	FILL-ONSET	STEM	PARSE-μ
c. ☞ -lwaYI[lw+a				*	*	*		
d. -lwaYI[YIlw+a				**!		**	*	

Candidates	ONSET	ALIGN	RED= FOOT	FILL-NUCLEUS	MINIMALITY	FILL-ONSET	STEM	PARSE-μ
e. ☞ -omi[Yom+isa							*	*
f. -o-misa[m+isa					*!		*	

To sum up this section, excluding the initial vowel from the prosodic stem of some vowel-initial verbs not only accounts for the infixing reduplication pattern found in these verbs, it also provides an explanation for why the initial vowel does not count for tone association processes which are conditioned by the length of the stem. In contrast, adapting McCarthy and Prince's (1993a, b) analysis of Timugon Murut would only account for reduplicative infixation in SiSwati. It could not explain why the initial vowel is also ignored for other processes.

4.2 Kinande infixation

In Kinande vowel-initial stems, we find similar patterns to those in SiSwati: only some vowel-initial stems (33d), repeated below, follow the infixing pattern. Similar to SiSwati, it is shorter vowel-initial stems (33c) which do not follow the infixing pattern.

(33) Kinande verbal reduplication (Mutaka and Hyman 1990)

Stem	Reduplicated Form	Gloss
a. Consonant-initial:		
-huma	-<u>huma</u>-huma	"beat"
-humira	-<u>huma</u>-humira	"beat for"
-humirana	-<u>huma</u>-humirana	"beat for each other"
b. Monosyllabic:		
-swa	-<u>swa</u>.<u>swa</u>-swa	"grind"
-ta	-<u>ta</u>.<u>ta</u>-ta	"bury"
c. Vowel-initial, prefixing:		
-esa	-e<u>s(a)</u>.e.<u>s(a)</u>-e.sa	"play"
-oha	-o<u>h(a)</u>.o.<u>h(a)</u>-o.ha	"pick"
d. Vowel-initial, infixing:		
-esera	-e-<u>sera</u>-sera	"play for"
-ohera	-o-<u>hera</u>-hera	"pick for"

These shorter Kinande stems also are interesting in that the initial vowel of the base is copied (notice it is this vowel which surfaces after coalescence), but the initial vowel apparently is not aligned with the reduplicative template since these stems, like monosyllabic stems, trigger double reduplication. These points are highlighted by the derivation in (34):

(34) Derivation of -oh(a)o.h(a)-o.ha "pick here and there" (adapted from Mutaka and Hyman 1990: (39))

a. Input representation

b. Affixing (trochee) and copying (entire stem)

σ
/\
o h - a

σ σ   σ
            /\
oh - a o h - a

c. Second copy and left to right mapping

σ   σ   σ
/\   /\   /\
oh-a oh-a o h- a → [ohohoha] after coalescence

It is exactly this property of shorter stems – that the stem-initial vowel occurs in the reduplicative domain but is not aligned with the reduplicative template – which is problematic to account for if one tries to extend McCarthy and Prince's (1993a, b) analysis of Timugon Murut reduplicative infixation to Kinande. This is because a base for reduplication is not defined by any constraint in the Timugon Murut analysis to derive infixation. Rather, ranking the prosodic requirement that syllables begin with onsets above ALIGN makes infixation the optimal position for the reduplicant in vowel-initial stems. Since no base for reduplication is explicitly defined in the Timugon Murut analysis, it is not possible to force the stem-initial vowel to be included in the base by a minimality constraint on the base like that proposed for SiSwati (31). Instead, the only way the stem-initial vowel may be included in the base – since this would violate the Onset Principle (12) – is by proposing that the minimality constraint in (35) (similar to the one in (31)) is ranked higher than the Onset Principle, and so optimizes outputs which include the initial vowel in the base:

(35) REDUPLICANT MINIMALITY (M-RED)
     At least one stem vowel (excluding the final vowel) of the morphological stem must have a correspondent in the RED.

M-RED (35) requires that the reduplicant include at least one stem vowel of the base. As shown by the tableau in (36), this constraint optimizes including the stem-initial vowel in both the base and the reduplicant, as in (36d).

(36) Evaluation of outputs to Kinande reduplication, VCV stems (parentheses indicate vowels copied but not anchored to RED; angled brackets indicate coalesced vowels; underlined segments are anchored to RED)

Candidates	M-RED	ONSET	RED=CS	*COPY-FEATURE	ANCHORING	PARSE-μ	ALIGN
a. -(o)<u>h\<a\></u>-o.ha	*!		**		*	*	
b. -(o)<u>h\<a\></u>(o.)<u>h\<a\></u>-o.ha			*	*!	*	**	
c. -o-<u>haha</u>-ha	*!		*				*
d. ☞ -<u>o.h\<a\></u>-o.ha			*			*	

But the actual output (36b) would violate this constraint. Notice that even though the initial stem vowel in (36b) is included in the base and is reduplicated, it is not anchored to the left edge of the left syllable of the reduplicant. Instead, the stem-final consonant is. Mutaka & Hyman argue that the initial vowel of the base may not map to the reduplicant because this would violate the Onset Principle: the reduplicant may not begin with an onsetless syllable. But this leaves us with a ranking paradox. M-RED must outrank the Onset Principle in order to force the stem-initial vowel to be included in the base. But the Onset Principle must outrank M-RED in order to explain why the initial vowel of the base may not be anchored to the reduplicant. I conclude, then, that McCarthy and Prince's analysis of Timugon Murut cannot be successfully extended to Kinande.

However, if we adopt the extraprosodicity analysis of SiSwati reduplicative infixation, we may provide a straightforward account both of the infixing pattern found in longer Kinande stems and of the prefixing pattern found in shorter stems. The alignment constraints in (25) which require the base for reduplication in SiSwati to begin with a well-formed syllable will normally exclude the initial vowel from the base in Kinande, too, leading to infixation. The minimality constraint on the base in (36) optimizes including the initial vowel in the base of shorter stems. (Note that in Kinande it is the entire stem, not just the root, which is evaluated for minimality.)

(37) Kinande PROSODIC STEM MINIMALITY (MIN-ST)
       At least one stem vowel (excluding the final vowel) of the morphological stem must have a corresondent in the prosodic stem.

To account for the fact that the initial vowel of the shorter stems is copied, even though it is not mapped to the reduplicative template, I propose that MAX outranks ANCHORING. As a result, it is optimal for as much material from the base to be reduplicated as can be parsed somehow, even if some of the base material may not be anchored in the reduplicant. To account for the fact that the initial vowel of the shorter stems does not align to the reduplicant, I propose that the Onset Principle also outranks ANCHORING. Since the initial vowel cannot begin an onsetful syllable, it is nonoptimal to anchor it in the reduplicant. (It is the violation of ONSET in the reduplicant which rules out candidate (d) in the tableau below.) The base is copied again, then, in order to provide the reduplicant with a second syllable. The following tableau shows how this analysis selects the actual output (38b) as the most optimal.

(38) Evaluation of outputs to Kinande reduplication, VCV stems (parentheses indicate vowels copied but not anchored to the RED template; angled brackets indicate coalesced vowels; underlined segments have been both copied and anchored to the RED template)

Candidates	ONSET	MIN-ST	RED=CS	MAX	ANCHORING	*COPY-FEATURE	STEM	PARSE-μ
a. -(o)h<u>a</u>-o.ha			**!		*			*
b. ☞ -(o)h<u>a</u>(o.)h<u>a</u>-o.ha			*		*	*		**
c. -o.<u>haha</u>-ha		*!					*3	
d. -<u>o.h</u><u>a</u>-o.ha	*!		*					*
e. -<u>hah</u><u>a</u>-o.ha			*	*!	*	*		*

5. Conclusion

In sum, I have shown that some similarities and differences in the verbal reduplication patterns of SiSwati, Kinande and Kikuyu find a straightforward treatment within Optimality Theory. However, I have also shown that an insightful analysis of reduplication in these three Bantu languages forces us to modify some claims of the theory. First, this study argues against the Prosodic Morphology Hypothesis which states that only metrical constituents may be prosodic templates. Instead, for Kikuyu and Kinande I have argued that a morphoprosodic constituent, the canonical verb stem, is the reduplicative template, since this best accounts for why the reduplicant always ends in the vowel /a/. For SiSwati and Kinande I have argued that defining a morphoprosodic constituent, the prosodic stem, as the base for reduplication is the most straightforward way to account for infixation of the reduplicant before longer vowel-initial stems. By requiring the left edge of the prosodic stem to be aligned with the left edge of a syllable, stem-initial vowels may be excluded from the prosodic stem because they do not begin well-formed syllables. This study shows, then, that we must expand the inventory of constituents which are active in Prosodic Morphology and that extraprosodicity, understood as prosodic misalignment, may be required to define these constituents.

Notes

1 I am grateful to Joyce Sukumane and Muroki Mwaura for their friendly, patient cooperation in providing me with the SiSwati data and the Kikuyu data, respectively. I also would like to thank Simon Donnelly, Chuck Kisseberth, and Seok-Chae Rhee for help in collecting SiSwati reduplication data and owe them along with Gene Buckley, Larry Hyman, John McCarthy, Scott Myers, David Odden, Doug Pulleyblank, and audiences at Rutgers, CUNY, Swarthmore, and the University of Pennsylvania my appreciation for helpful comments on various aspects of the analysis. Any errors of fact or interpretation are, of course, my own responsibility.

The analysis presented here adopts the version of Optimality Theory current at the time of the Utrecht Workshop on Prosodic Morphology where this paper was first presented in June 1994. See Downing (1997, 1998a, b) for a recasting of portions of this analysis in a more current version of the theory.

2 The SiSwati data presented here come from my work with Joyce Sukumane, a native speaker of SiSwati from Swaziland. The Kikuyu data presented comes from my work with Muroki Mwaura, a native speaker of Kikuyu from Kenya. The Kinande data are from Mutaka and Hyman (1990).

In these Bantu languages, the verb stem consists of a radical, derivational suffixes, and a final vowel. Stems are bound forms, occurring in isolation only in the imperative, but otherwise are always preceded by some inflectional prefix(es). See Myers (1987) for a detailed motivation of the verb stem as a morphosyntactic constituent in Bantu, as well as arguments that the stem is a subconstituent of the morphosyntactic and phonological word.

3 The root vowel of the base is also lengthened in Kikuyu in the reduplicated form of the verb. I assume this lengthening provides evidence that the base is subject to a two-syllable minimality condition in certain morphological contexts which is distinct from the two-syllable minimality condition on the reduplicant. Under this assumption, the base and reduplicant lengthen independently in order to satisfy these distinct minimality constraints. Alternatively, one might propose that the base vowel has already been lengthened under minimality at the point when reduplication takes place. Nothing special would then need to be said about the form of the reduplicant.

4 In all the constraint tableaux in this paper, "*" in a column under a constraint indicates a violation; "!" indicates a violation which decides between two competing output candidates; the optimal candidate is preceded by ☞; epenthetic segments are capitalized.

5 Prefixes to the reduplicant do coalesce with an initial reduplicant vowel in SiSwati: e.g., *u-ya-l-omi-yomísa* "you are drying it a little" (compare with (11c)). Following a suggestion of John McCarthy (personal communication), one might account for this by breaking RED=FOOT into two constraints, one aligning the left edge of the reduplicant with the left edge of a syllabic trochee (REDL), and the other aligning the right edge of the reduplicant with the right edge of a syllabic trochee (REDR). Only REDR would dominate FILL-ONSET (6a), optimizing epenthesis at the right edge of the base but optimizing coalescence or glide formation at the left edge. (An alternative analysis is presented in Downing (1994).)

6 McCarthy and Prince (1994b) suggest that, in general, phonological properties of templates should fall out from their morphological status. Following this suggestion, the stipulation that the template end in /a/ need not be specified as it falls out once the template is assigned the morphological status of verb stem.

7 I am considering /a/ the default or unmarked final vowel morpheme, because, as noted by Benson (1964), Mutaka and Hyman (1990), and Ziervogel and Mabuza (1976), in these languages it is the most commonly occurring final vowel.

8 In adopting the term "prosodic stem" I am following work like that of Inkelas (1989), among many others, in designating as a prosodic domain a constituent which is constructed based on some morphosyntactic constituent but is not necessarily isomorphic with that constituent.

9 The wording of STEM1 and STEM3 is inspired by McCarthy and Prince's (1994a) formulation of the BASE-DEPENDENCE and MAX constraints respectively, which they propose define the extent of correspondence between the base and reduplicant. In the spirit of recent work on correspondence, I propose that these two constraints may define the correspondence between any two constituents when one constituent determines the form of the other.

10 See Downing (1994) for discussion of a third tone pattern which is sensitive to the length of the prosodic stem.

11 My claim that all the infixing stems are underived is motivated as follows. First, in some cases, the infixing verbs do not end in a productive derivational suffix which might have been added to a shorter verb root (e.g., /-am-/ in /-eyama/ is not a derivational suffix which might have been added to a hypothetical root /-ey-/ to derive a longer verb stem), so there is no plausible morphological derivation for the stem. In cases like (30a), where the verb does end in a sequence which might be a suffix (compare with (30b)), I asked my language consultant whether she knew a verb without that suffix (like (30c)) which was related in meaning to the infixing verb stem. In all cases the response was negative. Finally, I searched Rycroft's (1981) dictionary for two-syllable verb roots from which the infixing verbs might plausibly be derived. Again, results were negative.

References

Archangeli, Diana. 1984. Underspecification in Yawelmani phonology and morphology, Ph.D. dissertation, Massachusetts Institute of Technology, Cambridge, MA.

1988. Aspects of underspecification theory, *Phonology* 5: 183–208.

Benson, T. G. 1964. *Kikuyu-English Dictionary*, Oxford: Oxford University Press.

Buckley, Eugene. 1994. Persistent and cumulative extrametricality in Kashaya, *Natural Language and Linguistic Theory* 12: 423–464.

Downing, Laura J. 1990. Local and metrical tone shift in Nguni, *Studies in African Linguistics* 21: 261–317.

1994. SiSwati verbal reduplication and the theory of Generalized Alignment, in M. Gonzàlez (ed.), *Proceedings of the North East Linguistic Society* 24, Amherst, MA: Graduate Student Linguistic Association, 81–95.

1996. *Problems in Jita Tonology*, Munich: Lincom Europa. [Revised version of 1990 Ph.D. dissertation, University of Illinois at Urbana-Champaign, IL.]

1997. Correspondence effects in SiSwati reduplication, *Studies in the Linguistic Sciences* 25, 17–35.

1998a. Prosodic misalignment and reduplication, in G. E. Booij and J. van Marle (eds.), *Yearbook of Morphology 1997*, Dordrecht: Kluwer, 83–120.

1998b. On the prosodic misalignment of onsetless syllables, *Natural Language and Linguistic Theory* 16, 1–52.

Hewitt, Mark. 1992. Vertical maximization and metrical theory, Ph.D. dissertation, Brandeis University, Waltham, MA.

Hyman, Larry. 1989. Advanced tongue root in Kinande, ms. University of California, Berkeley, CA.

Inkelas, Sharon. 1989. Prosodic constituency in the lexicon, Ph.D. dissertation, Stanford University, CA.

1993. Consonant invisibility in Amele: evidence for domain windows, ms. University of California, Berkeley, CA.

Itô, Junko. 1986. Syllable Theory in Prosodic Morphology, Ph.D. dissertation, University of Massachusetts, Amherst, MA.

1989. A prosodic theory of epenthesis, *Natural Language and Linguistic Theory* 7: 217–60.

1990. Prosodic minimality in Japanese. *Chicago Linguistic Society* 26.2: 213–39.

Kaye, Jonathan. 1989. *Phonology: a cognitive view*. Hillsdale, NJ: Lawrence Erlbaum Associates.

Kisseberth, Charles W. 1993. Optimal domains: a theory of Bantu tone (A case study from IsiXhosa). Presented at the Optimality Workshop I, Rutgers University, 22–24 October 1993.

Kiyomi, S., and S. Davis. 1992. Verb reduplication in Swati. *African Languages and Cultures* 5: 113–24.

McCarthy, John J. and Alan Prince. 1986. Prosodic Morphology, ms. University of Massachusetts, Amherst, MA and Brandeis University, Waltham, Mass.

1993a. Generalized alignment, in G. E. Booij and J. van Marle (eds.), *Yearbook of Morphology 1993*, Dordrecht: Kluwer, 79–153.

1993b. Prosodic Morphology I: constraint interaction and satisfaction, ms. University of Massachusetts, Amherst, MA and Rutgers University, New Brunswick, NS.

1994a. The emergence of the unmarked: Optimality in Prosodic Morphology, *Proceedings of North East Linguistic Society* 24; Amherst, MA: Graduate Linguistic Student Association: University of Massachusetts, 333–79.

1994b. An overview of Prosodic Morphology, Part I. Template form in reduplication. Paper presented at the Workshop on Prosodic Morphology, University of Utrecht, 22–24 June 1994.

Mutaka, Ngessimo, and Larry M. Hyman. 1990. Syllables and morpheme integrity in Kinande reduplication, *Phonology* 7: 73–120.

Myers, Scott. 1987. Tone and the structure of words in Shona, Ph.D. dissertation, University of Massachusetts, Amherst, MA.

Peng, Long (Bruce). 1992. Prosodic preservation and loss in Kikuyu reduplication, ms. University of Arizona, Tucson, AZ.

Prince, Alan, and Paul Smolensky. 1993. Optimality Theory: constraint interaction in generative grammar, ms. Rutgers University, New Brunswick, NS and University of Colorado, Boulder, CO.

Rycroft, David. 1981. *Concise SiSwati Dictionary*, Pretoria: J. L. van Schaik Ltd.

Spring, Cari. 1990. Implications of Axininca Campa for Prosodic Morphology and Reduplication, Ph.D. dissertation, University of Arizona, Tucson, AZ.

Ziervogel, D., and E. J. Mabuza. 1976. *A grammar of the Swati language (SiSwati)*, Pretoria: J. L. van Schaik Ltd.

4 Prosodic Morphology and tone: the case of Chichewa

Larry M. Hyman and Al Mtenje

1. Introduction

The Bantu languages have provided interesting and important input on at least two major aspects of prosodic morphology. First, numerous Bantu languages such as Shona (Myers 1987), Chichewa (Kanerva 1990), Kinande (Mutaka and Hyman 1990), Ikalanga (Hyman and Mathangwane 1993), Kikuyu (Downing this volume) and SiSwati (Downing this volume) have been cited in support of bisyllabic or bimoraic minimality conditions on morphological operations. Second, in the area of reduplication, an increasing number of studies of Bantu languages have revealed a kind of theme and variations: they all seem to have something in common, but then they are all different. As elsewhere in phonology, the trend has been to reinterpret Bantu minimality and reduplication in nonderivational terms, particularly within Prince and Smolensky's (1993) rapidly developing Optimality Theory (OT). Thus, Carleton and Myers (1993), Downing (this volume), and others have made proposals as to how OT can be applied to basic facts of redu- plication in Bantu languages. The assumption in all of this work is that a constraint-based approach to phonology will be at least as adequate and perhaps more insightful than analyses that might be proposed within a derivational model such as Lexical Phonology (Kiparsky 1982; Mohanan 1986). Of course the strongest kind of evidence in favor of non-derivational phonology would come from cases where the deriva- tional approach runs into serious empirical difficulties. In Hyman (1993) the first author of this chapter showed that complications which arise in derivational models with extrinsic rule ordering do not appear if one adopts instead analyses with a "direct mapping" of one level of repres- entation onto another. In this chapter[1] we turn to another aspect of the derivational/non-derivational debate in phonology. We argue that some rather complex tonal facts from Chichewa, a Bantu language spoken in Malawi and neighboring parts of Mozambique, Zambia, and Zimbabwe, reveal the inadequacy of a level-ordered approach to Chichewa verb stem reduplication, i.e., one where the derivation proceeds in a compositional or "cyclic" manner by lexical level or domain. Tentatively assuming the word structure in (1),

(1) [prefixes   [base]$_{stem}$ [reduplicant]$_{stem}$]$_{word}$

we demonstrate that the stem tone must be identical in both the base and the reduplicant – but that this identity cannot be established until word-level prefixes have interacted with the base tones. Although only stem-level material may be reduplicated, we will show that the analysis runs into serious complications and misses important generalizations if the outer prefixal domain is not referred to at the same time as the inner (reduplicated) stem domain. Instead, we show the need for a "mixed-level" approach to reduplication. The structure of this chapter will be as follows: for the purpose of comparison, we begin in section 2 with a brief illustration of how a level-ordered approach leads to a satisfactory account of prosodic minimality and reduplication in Kinande, a Bantu language spoken in Zaire. We then turn to the quite different facts of Chichewa. We first introduce the tone system and then discuss the morphological assignment of verb tones in section 3. After examining the transfer of tone in verb-stem reduplication in section 4, we demonstrate in section 5 that a nonlevel-ordered account of tonal transfer is required. The conclusion in section 6 is followed by an appendix that deals with relevant differences between the two dialects of Chichewa we have investigated.

2. An example of level-ordered Prosodic Morphology

As indicated in section 1, we shall present data from Chichewa showing that a level-ordered approach to reduplication is problematic in that language. However, for the purpose of comparison, let us first consider Kinande, another Bantu language, where a more traditional derivational approach makes the right predictions. As we shall also see for Chichewa, Kinande requires that a verb consist of at least two surface syllables. One consequence of this requirement is seen in (2).

(2) a. hum-a   "beat!"   lim-a   "cultivate!"   *u-hum-a/*u-lim-a
       bugul-a "find!"   balik-a "jump!"   *u-bugul-a/*u-balik-a
    b. u-sw-a "grind!"   u-y-a   "go!"   *sw-a/*y-a

The examples in (2a) which consist of two or more syllables show that
the imperative is normally expressed in Kinande by the bare verb stem.
However, as seen in (2b), when the verb stem is monosyllabic, the second person singular prefix *u*- must be used. The asterisked forms in (2a)
show that the *u*- prefix is not available for longer stems, and the asterisked forms in (2b) show that the *u*- prefix may not be omitted when the
stem is monosyllabic. Kinande verbal morphology is thus conditioned
by prosodic minimality in just this way (Mutaka and Hyman 1990).[2]

Related to this fact, the data in (3) show that the prefixed reduplicant
(RED) in verb-stem reduplication must consist of exactly two syllables:

(3) a. Bisyllabic verbs in reduplication (base = σ σ)
       hum-a   →   hum-a-hum-a   "to beat
                                          (here and there)"
       túm-a   →   túm-a-tum-a   "to send
                                          (here and there)"
    b. Polysyllabic verbs in reduplication (base > σ σ)
       hum-an-a   →   hum-a-hum-an-a   "to beat each other
                                          (here and there)"
       túm-an-a   →   túm-a-tum-an-a   "to send each other
                                          (here and there)"
    c. Monosyllabic verbs in reduplication (base < σ σ)
       sw-a   →   sw-a-sw-a-sw-a   "to grind
                                          (here and there)"
       tw-á   →   tw-á-tw-a-tw-a   "to cut
                                          (here and there)"

In (3a), where the base is two syllables, RED is identical to it. In (3b)
where the base contains more than two syllables, RED is a trimmed down
version of it. Finally, in (3c), where the base is monosyllabic, the bisyllabic condition on RED requires a double reduplication. Note also that
tone is not copied in Kinande verb reduplication.

The conclusions drawn from the Kinande data in (2) and (3) are, first,
that the RED must consist of exactly two syllables, and, second, that a
verb must consist of at least two syllables. The first generalization is seen
throughout both noun and verb reduplication in Kinande. The effects of

the second generalization, however, are seen only in the imperative, i.e., the one verbal construction where there is no obligatory subject prefix to provide the second syllable needed when the verb stem is mono-syllabic. Now consider the data in (4).

(4) a. swa-swa-swa! $[swa]_s$ → $[swa\text{-}swa]_r [swa]_s$
                          → $[[swaswa]_r [swa]_s]_w$

   b. *u-swa-swa-swa! $[swa]_s$ → $[swa\text{-}swa]_r [swa]_s$
                          → $[u[swaswa]_r [swa]_s]_w$

   c. *u-swa-u-swa! $[swa]_s$ → $[u [swa]_s]_w$
                          → $[u[swa]_s]_r [u [swa]_s]_w$

   d. *u-swa-swa! $[swa]_s$ → $[u[swa]_s]_w$
                          → $[[u[swa]_s]_r [swa]_s]_w$

(4a) shows the correct realization of a reduplicated monosyllabic verb stem (s) in the imperative. As seen in the derivation to the right, redu-plication takes place at the stem level, i.e., "prior" to prefixation, which takes place at word (w) level. Because the reduplicant (r) must be bisyl-labic, the result is double reduplication. (4b) is ruled out because the 2nd person sg. prefix *u-* is grammatical in the imperative only when needed to fill out the bisyllabic template. (4c) is ruled out by the fact that reduplication is at stem level in Kinande: it is never sensitive to what precedes it, nor does any prefix ever participate in the reduplication process. Thus it would not be possible to "first" prefix *u-* and then redu-plicate the resulting bisyllabic structure.

The crucial ungrammatical output for our comparison with Chichewa is (4d), which is ruled out because the stem-level bisyllabic condition on RED cannot be satisfied by the word-level prefix *u-*. What this means is that the facts of Kinande reduplication are consistent with a derivational model of phonology such as Lexical Phonology in which the morpho-logy and phonology are interwoven, and each successive domain (stem, word, etc.) is constructed from the smallest to the largest: reduplication takes place at stem level "followed by" prefixation at word level. We will refer to this as the "level-ordered" view of the morphology-phonology interface. The present chapter argues that Chichewa reduplication pro-vides evidence that such level-ordering can be violated in Prosodic Morphology. Since stem-level reduplication must refer to word-level properties in Chichewa, it is necessary to abandon the level-ordered view and do "everything at once." This is, of course, consistent with recent work on OT and other constraint-based approaches which allow inter-leaving of constraints found at different levels of the grammar.[3]

In this chapter we have two goals. The first is to provide a reasonably complete documentation of the interaction between tone and verb-stem reduplication in Chichewa. The second is to show how this interaction argues against the "strict separation of levels" in Prosodic Morphology. Although we present a partial OT analysis in section 5, most of the discussion will be couched within familiar derivational terms. We shall begin, however, with a necessary introduction to Chichewa verb tonology.

3. Chichewa verb tonology

Chichewa tone has been the subject of extensive study (Trithart 1976; Moto 1983; Mtenje 1986, 1987, 1988; Kanerva 1985, 1986, 1989, 1990; Peterson 1987; Carleton and Myers 1993). There is dialect variation in Chichewa. In this study, data were compared from two tonal dialects, which we label Chichewa-Al (for Al Mtenje) and Chichewa-Sam (for Sam Mchombo, who also graciously worked with us).[4] All data will be from Chichewa-Al unless otherwise noted. Divergent tonal realizations in Chichewa-Sam that are of interest to this study are kept to a minimum in the text, but summarized in the appendix. To produce an extensive database for this study, all of the combinations of the variables listed in (5) were systematically collected in both dialects:

(5) a. clause type (main/relative) (e.g., MCA = main clause affirmative)
   b. polarity (affirmative/negative)
   c. tense/mood (INF, IMP, SUBJUNCTIVE, PROG, F0, FUT, PERF, P1, P2, P3, PRESENTHABITUAL, PASTHABITUAL)
   d. ±aspect (-ka- "motion away from speaker", -dza- "motion towards speaker", -ngo- "just")
   e. ±non-reflexive object prefix -mu- "him/her" (human sg. noun class 1)
   f. ±reflexive object prefix -dzi-
   g. ±high tone intensive suffix -its-

The various markers obtained are realized in the typical Bantu agglutinative fashion shown in (6).

(6) Chichewa verbal complex (SM = subject marker; TM = tense marker;
      OM = object marker)

NEG- SM- NEG- TM-   ASP*   [-OM- [root -EXT* -FV]$_{stem}$]$_{macro\text{-}stem}$
si-   -ti- -sa- -ku- -ka-   -mu-   -its- -a
                  -na- -dza-   -dzi-   -ir-   -e
                  -ma-

The asterisks indicate that there can be more than one aspect marker
(ASP) and more than one derivational suffix or extension (EXT) (see
Hyman and Mchombo 1992). Only the root and final vowel (FV) are
obligatory. As seen, the root, optional extensions, and the FV together
define the stem domain, which is typically preceded by one or more prefixes at word level.

The verb roots used in this study are those in (7).

(7) a. Toneless roots   b. H-tone roots
         -ph-   "kill"   ——[5]
         -meny-   "hit"   -pez-   "find"
         -thandiz-   "help"   -namiz-   "deceive"
         -vundikir-   "cover"   -thamang-   "run"
         -fotokoz-[6] "explain"   -khululukir-   "pardon"

As seen, verb roots vary in size and, as indicated, are either toneless or
have an inherent H tone. All roots must be expanded at least by a FV. As
seen in (8a),

(8) a. i-ph-a   "kill!"   b. ——
         meny-a   "hit!"   pez-á   "find!"
         thandiz-a   "help!"   namiz-á   "deceive!"
         vundikir-a   "cover!"   thamang-á   "run!"
         fotokoz-a   "explain!"   khululukir-á   "pardon!"

the imperative FV -a is toneless and so the whole stem (root + FV) is
toneless.[7] In (8b), on the other hand, where the verb roots are underlying H, we see that this H is realized on the FV. Note that all consonantal
roots such as -ph- "kill" are underlyingly toneless and acquire an epenthetic [i] in the imperative, because verbs must be at least two syllables
long in Chichewa. Now consider the corresponding infinitive forms
in (9).

(9) a. ku-ph-á   "to kill"   b. —
    ku-mény-a   "to hit"   ku-péz-a   "to find"
    ku-thándiz-a   "to help"   ku-námíz-á   "to deceive"
    ku-vúndíkir-a "to cover"   ku-thámáng-á   "to run"
    ku-fótókoz-a   "to explain to" ku-khúlúlukir-á "to pardon"

In the affirmative, the syllable following the infinitive prefix *ku-* is always H. In addition, when the verb stem is long enough, this H is realized double. In order to account for these facts, we recognize representations such as in (10a).

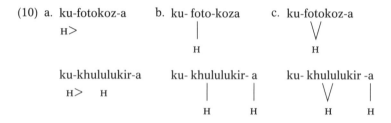

(10) a. ku-fotokoz-a   b. ku- foto-koza   c. ku-fotokoz-a
     H> | \/
                          H   H

     ku-khululukir-a   ku- khululukir- a   ku- khululukir -a
     H>   H | | \/ |
                         H   H   H   H

In (10b) the H> of *ku-* is placed on the next vowel (hence the use of the Symbol "H>") and the H of the H-tone verb root *-khululukir-* is placed on the FV. In (10c) we see that the H following *ku-* can undergo H-tone spreading (HTS, equalling Kanerva's 1989 Nonfinal Doubling) which, as pointed out by Kanerva (1989) and as formalized in (11), spreads a H one syllable to the right, as long as it does not enter one of the last two syllables of the domain:

(11) H-tone spreading (HTS):   σᵢ   σⱼ   (Condition: σⱼ is not in
                                 └ ‑ ‑ ‑ ⸍   prepausal bisyllabic foot)
                                 H

Consider, however, the realization of the bisyllabic stems in (12).

(12) Bisyllabic stems in the infinitive: ku-mény-a / ku-péz-a
     a. ku-meny-a   → ku-meny-a   b. ku-pez-a   → ku- pez-a
        H> | H> H | |
                        H   H H̲

In (12a) the only H is that of the infinitive prefix *ku-*, which is assigned to the first syllable of the toneless verb stem. In (12b), the H of the verb root is linked to the FV and the H of the infinitive prefix is linked again to the first syllable of the verb stem. As seen, this produces a sequence of

H's on two successive syllables. Consequently, Meeussen's Rule, formulated in (13), removes the second H, as indicated:[8]

(13) Meeussen's Rule (MR)

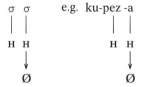

With preliminaries out of the way, we can now address the first generalization in (14), which concerns the fact that no matter how long a verb stem is, it can have only one of three stem-tone patterns (ignoring H> for the moment):

(14) Three stem-tone patterns (cf. Kanerva 1985, 1986, 1990)
    a. No H tone
    b. Final H tone
    c. Penultimate H tone

The first of these was illustrated in (8a), where toneless verb roots surface as toneless in the imperative. The second pattern was seen in (8b), where the underlying H of the verb root was realized on the FV. The second pattern is also observed in (15), where both toneless and H-tone verb roots are realized with a H-tone FV -é in the subjunctive:

(15) a. (ti-) ph-é   "let's kill!"
      (ti-) meny-é   "let's hit!"
      (ti-) thandiz-é   "let's help!"
      (ti-) vundikir-é   "let's cover!"
      (ti-) fotokoz-é   "let's explain!"
    b. —
      (ti-) pez-é   "let's find!"
      (ti-) namiz-é   "let's deceive!"
      (ti-) thamang-é   "let's run!"
      (ti-) khululukir-é   "let's pardon!"

Finally, in the third pattern, seen in (16), both toneless and H-tone roots are realized with penultimate H tone when occurring in the distant past P3 tense:

(16) a. (tí-náa-) ph-á[9]   "we killed"
     (tí-náa-) mény-a   "we hit"
     (tí-náa-) thandíz-a   "we helped"
     (tí-náa-) vundikír-a   "we covered"
     (tí-náa-) fotokóz-a   "we explained"

   b. ——
     (tí-náa-) péz-a   "we found"
     (tí-náa-) namíz-a   "we deceived"
     (tí-náa-) thamáng-a   "we ran"
     (tí-náa-) khululukír-a "we pardoned"

Concerning these three patterns a verb stem will be toneless only if there is no underlying lexical or grammatical H tone assigned. On the other hand, as seen in (17), a H on the FV can be conditioned by one of three factors in Chichewa:

(17) a. Verb roots with underlying H (see (8b))
   b. Subjunctive FV -é, see (15); this is the only tense/mood to assign final H tone
   c. Extensions (-its- "INTENSIVE," -ik- "STATIVE," -uk- "REVERSIVE INTR," versus toneless -ir- "APPLICATIVE," -an- "RECIPROCAL," -its- "CAUSATIVE")[10]

ph-ets-á	"kill a lot!"	ph-ets-a	"cause to kill!"
meny-ets-á	"hit a lot!"	meny-ets-a	"cause to hit!"
thandiz-its-á	"help a lot!"	thandiz-its-a	"cause to help!"
vundikir-its-á	"cover a lot!"	vundikir-its-a	"cause to cover!"
fotokoz-ets-á	"explain a lot!"	fotokoz-ets-a	"cause to explain!"

We have already seen in (8b) that an underlying root H will be realized on the FV, also in (15) that the SUBJUNCTIVE assigns a FV -é with H tone. In (17c) we observe a fact, unusual from the Bantu perspective, that some extensions such as INTENSIVE -its-/-ets- also assign a H on the FV, while other extensions such as the homophonous CAUSATIVE -its-/-ets- do not.

Similarly, as seen in (18), there are several sources of H tone being assigned to the penultimate vowel (PV) in the language:

(18) a. Some affirmative tenses (MCA P3, PRHAB; RCA F0, FUT, PERF, P2, P3, PRHAB)

tí-ma-ph-á	"we kill"	—	
tí-ma-mény-a	"we hit"	tí-ma-péz-a	"we find"
tí-ma-thandíz-a	"we help"	tí-ma-namíz-a	"we deceive"
tí-ma-vundikír-a	"we cover"	tí-ma-thamang-ír-a	"we run to"
tí-ma-fotokoz-ér-a	"we explain to"	tí-ma-khululukír-a	"we pardon"

b. Most negative tenses (INF, IMP, SUBJUNCTIVE, F0, FUT, PAST, PRHAB [opt] – not PROG, PSTHAB)

ku-sa-ph-á	"to not kill"	—	
ku-sa-mény-a	"to not hit"	ku-sa-péz-a	"to not find"
ku-sa-thandíz-a	"to not help"	ku-sa-namíz-a	"to not deceive"
ku-sa-vundikír-a	"to not cover"	ku-sa-thamang-ír-a	"to not run to"
ku-sa-fotokoz-ér-a	"to not explain to"	ku-sa-khululukír-a	"to not pardon"

c. Reflexive object prefix *-dzi-* (☞ = first line of <u>surface</u> penultimate H)

ku-dzí-ph-a	"to kill self"	—	
ku-dzí-mény-á	"to hit self"	ku-dzí-péz-á	"to find self"
ku-dzí-thándiz-á	"to help self"	ku-dzí-námiz-á	"to deceive self"
☞ ku-dzí-vúndikír-a	"to cover self"	ku-dzí-thámang-ír-a	"to run to self"
ku-dzí-fótokoz-ér-a	"to explain to self"	ku-dzí-khúlulukír-a	"to pardon self"

In (18a) we see that certain tenses, such as the PRESENT HABITUAL, require a stem-penultimate H tone. The examples in (18b) show the penultimate H-tone pattern in the NEGATIVE INFI NITIVE Looking at the forms in (18c) from the pointer down, we see that the reflexive prefix *-dzi-* conditions a penultimate H. The bisyllabic and trisyllabic stems above the pointer in (18c) have a final H tone instead of the expected penultimate H. This is due to a process which Kanerva (1989) calls "tone shift" but which we shall refer to as "bumping." As seen in (19), there are two related environments where bumping takes place:

(19) a. Local tone bumping   b. Non-local tone bumping

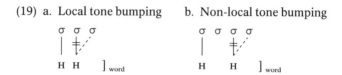

In (19a) local bumping shifts a penultimate H to final position when it is immediately preceded by an antepenultimate H. This apparent OCP effect is illustrated in (20a).

(20) a. ku-dzi-meny-a   →   ku-dzi-meny-a   →   ku-dzi-meny-a

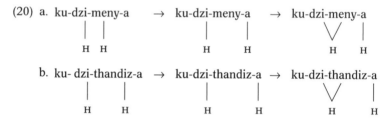

b. ku- dzi-thandiz-a   →   ku-dzi-thandiz-a   →   ku-dzi-thandiz-a

In the input the H tone on the REFL EXIVEprefix -*dzi*- comes from the INFI NITIVEprefix, and the following penultimate H comes from the RE-FL EXIVEAs seen, local tone bumping shifts the penultimate H to the FV. This is followed by HTS. In (20b) the stem -*thandiz-a* has an additional syllable and can undergo non-local tone bumping.[11] The output form is obtained after HTS. What this of course means is that it is necessary to look at sufficiently long verb stems in order to determine whether we have the final H tone pattern or the penultimate H pattern.

Having demonstrated that various morphs or morphological features can require either final or penultimate H tone, we arrive at two important questions: first, what happens if multiple morphs/features assign the same FV or PV tone? And second, what happens if multiple morphs/features assign different tones (FV versus PV)? The answer to the first question is rather straightforward: if multiple morphs or features assign the same tone, we simply get that tone. Some of the examples we have already seen show this. The examples in (15b), for instance, combine H-tone verb roots with a H-tone FV -*é* and, as seen, we simply get one final H tone. As shown in (21), it is possible in principle to get up to four H tones, any one of which would produce a stem-final H:[12]

(21) [ti - [[[[pez] -etsets-] -edw-] -e]]   →   ti-pez-etsets-edw-é
        H   H   H   H   "let's be found a lot"
      find - INTENSIVE - PASSIVE - FV

In (21) the four H tones come from the verb root, the INTENSIVE suffix, the PASSIVE suffix and the SUBJUNCTIVE FV -é. Despite its multiple conditioning, there is only one H tone on the FV of the verb stem, as indicated.

The same result is found with multiple conditioning of a penultimate H. All of the examples in (22) have a penultimate H tone.

(22) a. Neg INFI NITIVE+ REFL EXIVE-*dzi*-

ku-sa-ph-á	"to not kill"	ku-sa-	"to not
		dzí-ph-a	kill self"
ku-sa-	"to not hit"	ku-sa-	"to not
mény-a		dzi-péz-a	find self"
ku-sa-	"to not help"	ku-sa-	"to not
thandíz-a		dzi-namíz-a	deceive self"
ku-sa-	"to not cover"	ku-sa-dzi-	"to not
vundikír-a		thamang-ír-a	run to self"
ku-sa-	"to not explain to"	ku-sa-dzi-	"to not
fotokoz-ér-a		khululukír-a	pardon self"

    b. Neg INFI NITIVE+ ASP -*ka*-, "go &" + REFL EXIVE-*dzi*-

ku-ká-ph-a	"to go and	ku-sa-ka-dzí-	"to not go and
	kill"	ph-a	kill self"
ku-ká-	"to go and	ku-sa-ka-dzi-	"to not go and
mény-á	hit"	mény-a	hit self"
ku-ká-	"to go and	ku-sa-ka-dzi-	"to not go and
thándiz-á	help"	thandíz-a	help self"
☞ ku-ká-	"to go and	ku-sa-ka-dzi-	"to not go and
vúndikír-a	cover"	vundikír-a	cover self"
ku-ká-	"to go and	ku-sa-ka-dzi-	"to not go and
fótokoz-ér-a	explain to"	fotokoz-ér-a	explain to self"

As seen in (22a) the negative INFI NITIVE like almost all negative tenses, requires a penultimate H, as does the REFL EXIVE OM *dzi*-. In (22b) we see in the left column that the ASP marker -*ka*- also conditions a penultimate H. In the right-hand column there are therefore three reasons for the penultimate H: (i) negation; (ii) reflexive -*dzi*-; and (iii) aspectual -*ka*-.[13]

There is an important observation to be made about the penultimate H pattern. As seen in the first example in the left-hand column (22a), the H will be on the FV if the macro-stem is monosyllabic. If the mono-syllabic stem is preceded by an OM such as the reflexive -dzi- in the first example of the right-hand column in (22a), the H goes on the OM. Pre-fixes that precede the OM are never counted for the purpose of penultim-ate H assignment. This includes the PRESENT HABITUAL marker -ma- in (18a) and the negative prefix -sa- in (22a) which condition the penultim-ate H. What we conclude from this is that the penultimate H pattern is a property of the macro-stem, i.e., of the stem + OM, if present.

Given the above facts, the question now is how the morphology deter-mines these final and penultimate H-tone assignments. Consider again the form in (21), where four morphemes were each said to contribute a H which wanders somehow to final position. For the purpose of dis-cussion we have indicated stem-internal brackets in (21). We have also assumed, so far without evidence, that the tones are not prelinked to their respective morpheme. But if they are not prelinked, then how do we even know whether there are multiple Hs present in the underlying representation? One alternative, for example, would be to say that so-called H-tone roots and suffixes subcategorize for a stem H right-aligned to the FV in (23a) or right-misaligned to the PV in (23b).

(23) a. If -pez-, -its-, -e (etc.), then [H]$_{stem}$ (→ FV)
      b. If PRHAB -ma-, NEG -sa- (etc.), then [H] stem + non-alignment
                                                        (→ PV)

However, as we shall now demonstrate, there is a need for both prelinked tones and tones assigned by morphological rule.

In order to show this we need to consider more carefully the assign-ment of tone by OMS and ASP markers such as -ka-. In (18c) we saw that the reflexive OM -dzi- assigns a penultimate H. As seen in (24),

(24) a. ku-mú-ph-a   "to kill him"   —
        ku-mú-   "to hit him"   ku-mú-   "to find him"
        mény-á   péz-á
        ku-mú-   "to help him"   ku-mú-   "to deceive
        thándiz-á   námiz-á   him"
    ☞ ku-mú-   "to cover him"   ku-mú-   "to run to him"
        vúndikír-a   thámang-ír-a
        ku-mú-   "to explain   ku-mú-   "to pardon
        fótokoz-ér-a   to him"   khúlulukír-a   him"

b. ku-ká-ph-a   "to go and kill"   —

   ku-ká-   "to go and   ku-ká-péz-á   "to go and
   mény-á   hit"   find"

   ku-ká-   "to go and   ku-ká-   "to go and
   thándiz-á   help"   námiz-á   deceive"

☞ ku-ká-   "to go and   ku-ká-   "to go and
   vúndikír-a cover"   thámang-ír-a run to"

   ku-ká-   "to go and   ku-ká-   "to go and
   fótokoz-ér-a explain to"   khúlulukír-a pardon"

nonreflexive OMS and ASP markers also condition a penultimate H.[14] What we must consider now is something that has not been pointed out in the literature, but which plays an important role in what we shall have to say about tonal transfer in verb stem reduplication in section 4. As seen in (25),

(25) No H on PV when -*mu*-, -*dzi*- or -*ka*- are preceded by the P2 TM -ná-

a. ti-ná-mú-   "we killed him"   —
   -ph-á[15]

   ti-ná-mú-   "we hit him"   ti-ná-mú-   "we found him"
   meny-a   pez-á

   ti-ná-mú-   "we helped   ti-ná-mú-   "we deceived
   thandiz-a   him"   namiz-á   him"

   ti-ná-mú-   "we covered   ti-ná-mú-   "we ran to him"
   vundikir-a   him"   thamang-ir-á

   ti-ná-mú-   "we explained ti-ná-mú-   "we pardoned
   fotokoz-er-a to him"   khululukir-á him"

b. ti-ná-dzí-   "we killed   —
   ph-á   selves"

   ti-ná-dzí-   "we hit selves" ti-ná-dzí-   "we found
   meny-a   pez-á   selves"

   ti-ná-dzí-   "we helped   ti-ná-dzí-   "we deceived
   thandiz-a   selves"   namiz-á   selves"

   ti-ná-dzí-   "we covered ti-ná-dzí-   "we ran to
   vundikir-a   selves"   thamang-ir-á selves"

   ti-ná-dzí-   "we explained ti-ná-dzí-   "we pardoned
   fotokoz-er-a to selves"   khululukir-á selves"

c. ti-ná-ká-   "we went and   —
   ph-a   killed"
   ti-ná-ká-   "we went and   ti-ná-ká-   "we went and
   meny-a   hit"   pez-á   found"
   ti-ná-ká-   "we went and   ti-ná-ká-   "we went and
   thándiz-a   helped"   námiz-á   deceived"
   ti-ná-ká-   "we went and   ti-ná-ká-   "we went and
   vúndikir-a   covered"   thámang-ir-á   ran to"
   ti-ná-ká-   "we went and   ti-ná-ká-   "we went and
   fótokoz-er-a explained to"   khúlulukir-á   pardoned"

when an OM or ASP marker is preceded by a linked H, e.g., the P2 TM -*ná*-, it fails to condition a penultimate H. Our analysis is as follows. As indicated in (26),

(26)

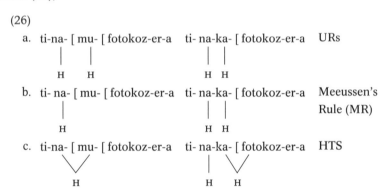

a. ti-na- [mu- [fotokoz-er-a   ti- na-ka- [fotokoz-er-a   URs

       H   H   H   H

b. ti- na- [mu- [fotokoz-er-a   ti- na-ka- [fotokoz-er-a   Meeussen's
                                                               Rule (MR)
       H   H   H

c. ti-na- [mu- [fotokoz-er-a   ti- na-ka- [fotokoz-er-a   HTS

       H   H   H

we propose that H of the OM -*mu*- and ASP marker -*ka*- are prelinked. In (26b) the H of the OM -*mu*- is deleted by MR (13), which however does not affect the ASP marker -*ka*-, because MR applies only within the macro-stem (marked by the outer left bracket). This is followed in (26c) by the postlexical rule of HTS.[16]

In order to predict the final H on the forms in the right-hand columns of (25a) and (25b), we propose the derivations in (27).

(27) a. ti-na- [mu- [khululukir-a   ti-na-ka- [khululukir-a   URs +
                                                                 linking
         H   H   H   H   H   H   of root
                                                                 H to FV

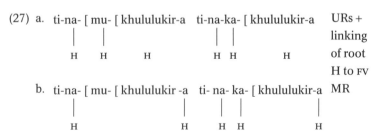

     b. ti-na- [mu- [khululukir -a   ti- na- ka- [khululukir-a   MR

         H   H   H   H   H

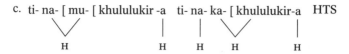

We begin in (27a) by linking the root H to the FV. This is followed by MR in (27b) and HTS in (27c).

By assuming that the H of the OM -*mu*- is prelinked, its loss is directly explained by application of MR, which is already needed in the tonology. Where the H of the OM or ASP marker is not lost by MR, it relinks to the PV of the stem, as seen in (28).

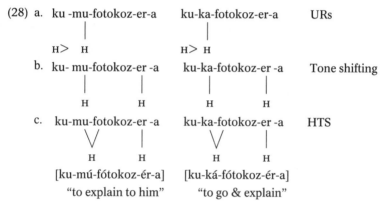

In (28a) the prelinked H of both the OM and ASP marker are preceded by the next-vowel H> tone of the infinitive prefix *ku*-. As seen in (28b), this H does go onto the next vowel, displacing the H of the OM, which relinks to the PV. HTS applies to the first H in (28c). In fact, the term "bumping" seems to apply again, since, we claim, the prelinked H of -*mu*- and -*ka*- does not shift to the PV unless there is a next-vowel H> tone that precedes them.[17]

The importance of these facts for the discussion of verb-stem reduplication in the next section is that the presence versus absence of a H on the FV or PV depends not only on morphological factors, but also on phonological factors that occur outside the stem itself – specifically on whether the above prefixes are themselves preceded by a next-vowel H or by a prelinked H. But before moving on to this discussion, the final tonal issue to be resolved concerns the second question that we raised earlier: what happens if multiple morphs/features assign different tones (FV versus PV)? With the one exception in (32) below, penultimate H overrides final H. We have already seen this in some of the examples, e.g., in (16b), (18) and (22), where the penultimate H of various sources overrides the final H of a H-tone verb root.

How then do we account for this overriding? One conceivable approach would be to say that certain morphological features cause the final syllable to become extrametrical. A serious problem for this proposal is that there is no construction in Chichewa morphology where we get the combined effects in (29):

(29) a. [CVCVCVC-V]   →   [CV- [CVCVCVC] <V>   (FV → PV)
                                          |
           H   H

     b. [CVCVCVC-V]   →   [CV- [CVCVCVC] <V>   (∅ → ∅)

The input in (29a) shows the H of a verb root linking to the FV, which when prefixed in morphological construction, M, becomes penultimate by virtue of extrametricality. The input in (29b) starts with the corresponding toneless stem, which, when prefixed in morphological construction M, undergoes no change. However, in Chichewa every time a morphological feature conditions a penultimate H it also *assigns* a H in case the input form does not have one of its own. The simple addition of extrametricality to the representation thus makes the wrong prediction that we should find the state of affairs in (29). Instead, something more is needed.

Our hypothesis is summarized in (30):

(30) a. Stem H   →   FV
     b. Macro-stem H   →   PV
     c. No H   →   No change

If a H comes in at the stem level, it will go to the FV. If a H comes in at the macro-stem level, it will go to the penult. Where a tense is expressed through a toneless affix, there is no effect on the inherited stem tone. If a macro-stem penultimate H comes in, it will, on the other hand, override the final stem H. Kanerva's explanation for why penultimate H overrides final H is schematized in (31).

(31)
   [CVCVCVCV]   →   [CV- [CVCVCVCV]]   →   [CV- [CVCVCVCV]]
        | | | |
        H   H   H   H

Starting with a final H from the stem, a macro-stem is created with a H that links to the penult, producing a H on both of the last two syllables. This then creates the input for MR, which applies, yielding the output with one H on the penult. While this works, it does not explain how the H gets to the penult, particularly in cases where there is no H at the stem level. Peterson (1987) proposes that this is accomplished by differential prominences: we could say final prominence at the stem level, penultimate prominence at the macro-stem level.

The alternative to (31) is for the new pattern to simply override the old. We have one piece of evidence in its favor. There is exactly one case in the language where final H tone appears to override penult H tone. This is in the subjunctive, which as seen in the examples in (32), requires the H tone FV -*é*:

(32) a. ti-vundikir-é   "let us cover"   ti-thamang-   "let us run"
                                             ir-é

         ti-vundikir-   "let us cover   ti-thamang-   "let us run
         its-é   a lot"   ir-its-é   a lot"

      b. ti-dzi-   "let us cover   ti-dzi-   "let us run for
         vúndíkir-é   ourselves"   thámáng-ir-é   ourselves"

         ti-dzi-   "let us cover   ti-dzi-thámáng- "let us run for
         vúndíkir-its-é   ourselves   ir-its-é   ourselves a lot"
                          a lot"

It just so happens that this is also the only case where the scope of a final H-tone assigner falls outside that of the penultimate H assign: the SUB-JUNCTIVE mood clearly has wider scope than the reflexive OM -*dzi*-.[18] Consequently, the final H of -*é* overrides the penultimate H of -*dzi*-, which must go on the next vowel instead.

This completes our survey of the tonal morphology of the Chichewa verb. We turn now to consider how the above interreacts with reduplication.

4. Reduplication and tone

In section 3 we examined in detail the morphological and phonological factors that determine whether a verb (macro-) stem will acquire a H tone – and, if so, where it will be realized. In this section, we examine how these factors support a nonlevel-ordered view of reduplication.

As pointed out by Mtenje (1988) and Kanerva (1990), Chichewa has extensive verb stem reduplication marking a frequentative or distributive ("here and there") sense. The forms in (33) show how bare verb stems are reduplicated in the IMPERATIVE:

(33) a. i-ph-a   → i-ph-a-i-ph-a   "kill (here and there)!"

        meny-a   → meny-a-meny-a   "hit (here and there)!"

        thandiz-a   → thandiz-a-thandiz-a   "help (here and there)!"

        vundikir-a   → vundikir-a-vundikir-a   "cover (here and there)!"

        fotokoz-er-a   → fotokoz-er-a-fotokoz-er-a   "explain to (here and there)!"

   b. pez-á   → pez-á-péz-á   "find!"

        namiz-á   → namiz-á-namiz-á   "deceive!"

        thamang-ir-á → thamang-ir-á-thamang-ir-á   "run to!"

        khululukir-á   → khululukir-á-khululukir-á   "pardon!"

In the first example in (33a) it is observed that a Chichewa verb must have at least two syllables. Thus, an epenthetic [i] must be added to the verb stem *ph-a* to form the imperative *i-ph-a* "kill!". In (33a) the imperative forms are toneless, whether the stem is reduplicated or not. In (33b), however, where we have underlying H-tone roots, each stem in the reduplication acquires a H on its FV, as indicated. Thus, as pointed out by Mtenje (1988) and Carleton and Myers (1993), we see that tone is *transferred* in verb-stem reduplication.[19]

Further evidence for this is seen in distant past P3 forms in (34).

(34) a. (tí-náa-)   → (tí-náa-)   "we killed
        ph-á   ph-á-í-ph-á   (here and there)"
        (tí-náa-)   → (tí-náa-)   "we hit (here
        mény-a   mény-á-meny-á   and there)"
        (tí-náa-)   → (tí-náa-) thandíz-á-   "we helped
        thandíz-a   thandíz-a   (here and there)"
        (tí-náa-)   → (tí-náa-) vundikír-á- "we covered
        vundikír-a   vundikír-a   (here and there)"
        (tí-náa-)   → (tí-náa-) fotokoz-ér-á- "we explained
        fotokoz-ér-a   fotokoz-ér-a   to (here and there)"

b. (tí-náa-)   → (tí-náa-) péz-á-pez-á   "we found"
   péz-a
   (tí-náa-)   → (tí-náa-) namíz-á-   "we deceived"
   namíz-a   namíz-a
   (tí-náa-)   → (tí-náa-) thamang-ír-á-   "we ran to"
   thamang-ír-a   thamang-ír-a
   (tí-náa-)   → (tí-náa-) khululukír-á-   "we pardoned"
   khululukír-a   khululukír-a

The distant past is one of the two MCA tenses that assign a penultimate
H tone. As seen, this penultimate H is realized on both stems, show-
ing that there has been tonal transfer. Examples such as these can
be multiplied at will: where the BASE STEM has a final H, so does the
REDUPLICANT; where the BASE STEM has a penultimate H, so does the
REDUPLICANT. In some cases, because of tone bumping, the penultimate
H is realized on the FV instead of on the PV. Sample derivations are given
in (35).

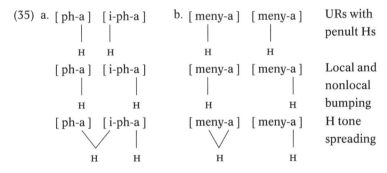

In (35a) we start off with two H tones in sequence. By local bumping,
the second H is shifted to the FV. This is followed by HTS. In (35b) the
two underlying Hs are separated by a toneless syllable. This time it is
non-local bumping that shifts the second H to the FV. Again, HTS
applies.

The representations in (35) presuppose that the REDUPLICANT is
postposed to the BASE. As seen in (35a), the second part is required to
take an epenthetic [i] whenever the stem is monosyllabic. We know
from the imperative forms in (33) that what precedes the reduplicant
must also satisfy bisyllabic minimality. Whenever a prefix is present, no
[i] is inserted – thus only in the imperative will *i-* be obtained on a non-
reduplicated verb form. This fact raises the question of what the correct

structure is of a reduplicated verb. Two possibilities are given in (36) of the structure of a reduplicated monosyllabic stem either preceded by the infinitive prefix *ku-* or unprefixed in the imperative:

(36) a.   b.

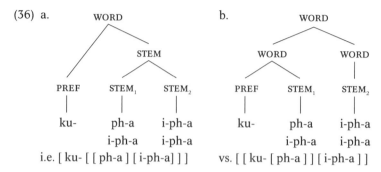

i.e. [ku- [[ph-a] [i-ph-a]]]   vs. [[ku- [ph-a]] [i-ph-a]]

In (36a) reduplication is shown to be a compounding of stems, forming a higher order stem which joins the prefix *ku-* to form a phonological word. In (36b) the reduplicant STEM₂ is not only a stem, but actually a phonological word. The advantage of (36a) is that it represents the reduplicated stem as a constituent, thereby directly predicting that only stem material will be involved in reduplication.[20] Its drawback is that there is no explanation as to why there must be an epenthetic [i] in case STEM₂ would otherwise be monosyllabic. This fact is directly accounted for by the structure in (36b): if we assume that what we have labeled as WORD is a phonological constituent, then it is this constituent that must meet the bisyllabic minimality condition.

We shall present tonal evidence that it is the structure in (36b) that we want. First, consider a simple case in (37) where the lexical H of a H verb root such as *-namiz-* "deceive" is transferred in reduplication:

(37) a. [namiz-a]   b. [namiz-a]   [namiz-a]

H   H   H

The root H links to the FV in (37a) and is then copied along with the segments in verb-stem reduplication. If one were to reduplicate before linking the H tone, as in (38a), an additional mechanism would be needed to copy a H on the second, underlined FV in (38b).

(38) a. [namiz-a]   [namiz-a]   b. [namiz-a]   [namiz-a̲]

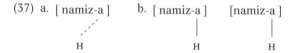

H   H

Finally, there seems to be no advantage to copying the unlinked H in reduplication, as in (39).

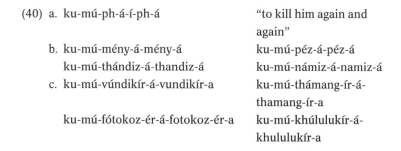

(39) a. [namiz-a] [namiz-a]   b. [namiz-a] [namiz-a]

      H   H   H   H

We shall therefore assume that (37) represents the right way to get transfer of the H of a verb root, also the H of suffixes such as intensive *-its-* and the SUBJUNCTIVE FV *-é*. In sum, if the H originates within the stem, then we expect its automatic transfer.

Let us then turn to cases where a penultimate H is assigned from outside the stem. Recall that the OM *-mu-* has a prelinked H which is realized in one of two ways. First, it may shift to the PV, as seen most clearly in the polysyllabic toneless verb roots in the left hand column of (40c).

(40) a. ku-mú-ph-á-í-ph-á   "to kill him again and
                                       again"

    b. ku-mú-mény-á-mény-á   ku-mú-péz-á-péz-á
        ku-mú-thándiz-á-thandiz-á   ku-mú-námiz-á-namiz-á
    c. ku-mú-vúndikír-á-vundikír-a   ku-mú-thámang-ír-á-
                                        thamang-ír-a
       ku-mú-fótokoz-ér-á-fotokoz-ér-a   ku-mú-khúlulukír-á-
                                          khululukír-a

Since both STEM$_1$ and STEM$_2$ receive the shifted penultimate H tone, the most straightforward derivational analysis is the one in (41).

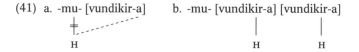

(41) a. -mu- [vundikir-a]   b. -mu- [vundikir-a] [vundikir-a]

      H   H   H

In (41a) the H of the OM shifts to the PV of the nonreduplicated stem. This is followed in (41b) by stem reduplication, which then copies the tone. Now imagine if the stem had first been reduplicated before prefixation, as in (42a).

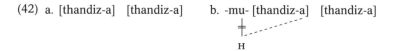

(42) a. [thandiz-a] [thandiz-a]   b. -mu- [thandiz-a] [thandiz-a]

                                          H

We assume in (42b) that the H of the OM -*mu*- would shift to the first PV. It would thus appear to be necessary to assume a rule that copies the H on the PV of STEM₁ onto STEM₂ separate from the reduplication process. If tone shifting precedes reduplication, this rule is not necessary, and all tonal transfers in reduplication are handled by the same mechanism: copy the tones of STEM₁ along with its segments.

What this shows, then, is that reduplication ought not to "precede" prefixation and tone assignment. Two more facts support this conclusion. First, recall from earlier discussion that the H of the OM -*mu*- fails to appear on the PV if it is preceded by a linked H tone. Examples involving reduplication and toneless verb roots are seen in the left hand column of (43b), where we also schematize MR again:

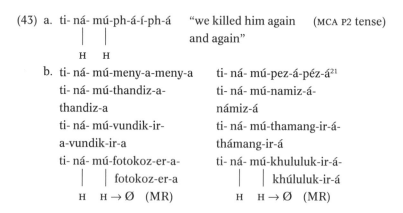

(43) a. ti- ná- mú-ph-á-í-ph-á   "we killed him again   (MCA P2 tense)
         | | and again"
         H   H

     b. ti- ná- mú-meny-a-meny-a   ti- ná- mú-pez-á-péz-á²¹
         ti- ná- mú-thandiz-a-   ti- ná- mú-namiz-á-
         thandiz-a   námiz-á
         ti- ná- mú-vundik-ir-   ti- ná- mú-thamang-ir-á-
         a-vundik-ir-a   thámang-ir-á
         ti- ná- mú-fotokoz-er-a-   ti- ná- mú-khululuk-ir-á-
         | | fotokoz-er-a | | khúluluk-ir-á
         H   H → Ø   (MR)   H   H → Ø   (MR)

As a consequence, when MR removes the H of the OM -*mu*-, both stems must be toneless in reduplication. We have rejected a subcategorization approach, and have insisted that the H of the OM must be prelinked. What this means is that before the H tone shift can take place in (43a), it must be established whether the H of the OM is preceded by a linked H-tone prefix. The picture that is emerging is that we must "first" construct the whole verbal complex, prefixes and all, then do the lexical tonology, and then reduplicate the stem.

An additional piece of evidence concerns the reduplication of monosyllabic verb stems again – this time their tones. Consider the form in (43a) whose underlying tones are indicated. Since the verb stem is underlying toneless, the H on the FV of STEM₁ must come from the OM -*mu*-. But why hasn't this H undergone MR? The answer is seen in the derivation in (44).

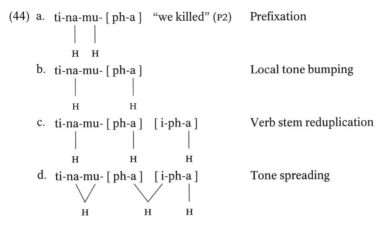

(44) a. ti-na-mu- [ph-a] "we killed" (P2)   Prefixation

b. ti-na-mu- [ph-a]   Local tone bumping

c. ti-na-mu- [ph-a] [i-ph-a]   Verb stem reduplication

d. ti-na-mu- [ph-a] [i-ph-a]   Tone spreading

In (44a) we see that the environment is met for local tone bumping: a final toneless syllable preceded by two linked H syllables. Thus, tone bumping shifts the H of the OM onto the monosyllabic stem in (44b). At this point reduplication can occur in (44c), with automatic copying of the final H. Finally HTS applies in (44d).

Now compare (44) with the alternative derivation in (45), which we reject:

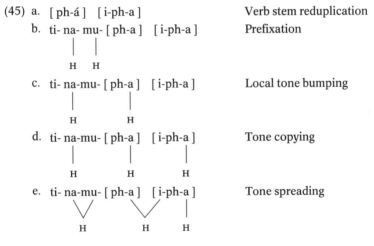

(45) a. [ph-á] [i-ph-a]   Verb stem reduplication

b. ti- na- mu- [ph-a] [i-ph-a]   Prefixation

c. ti- na-mu- [ph-a] [i-ph-a]   Local tone bumping

d. ti- na-mu- [ph-a] [i-ph-a]   Tone copying

e. ti- na-mu- [ph-a] [i-ph-a]   Tone spreading

In this case we begin by reduplicating the toneless verb stem in (45a), followed by prefixation in (45b). Local tone bumping applies in (45c), where we have assumed that STEM₁ still counts as having a right bracket to condition the bumping. In (45d) we again need to invoke an extra tone-copying rule to get a H on the FV of the STEM₂.

Of course, this example is a case of what Marantz (1982) called "rule overapplication" in reduplication, and the derivation in (44) accounts for it in the classical way: one first does a modification on the base (here, STEM$_1$), and then copies the modified STEM$_1$ as STEM$_2$. Although the stem is phonologically well-defined in Chichewa, as elsewhere in Bantu (e.g., for vowel harmony), one crucially cannot do stem reduplication exclusively at stem level. In a nonlevel-ordered account, one would require that the lexical representation of STEM$_1$ and STEM$_2$ be identical in phonological content, i.e., segmentally *and* tonally. However, we have already seen that bumping can cause STEM$_2$ to be tonally distinct from STEM$_1$.[22] In the next section we address this and other tonal discrepancies in nonlevel-ordered terms.

5. Towards a nonlevel-ordered account

In the preceding sections we first considered the effect of prefixes on verb-stem tonology and then saw that this effect is duplicated on the copied stem in reduplication. Unlike Kinande verb-stem reduplication in section 2, the Chichewa facts are not amenable to a level-ordered account: we cannot proceed compositionally by first building the stem, reduplicating it, and then adding word-level prefixes. In this section we will examine additional evidence for a nonlevel-ordered approach to Chichewa prosodic morphology. We begin by presenting a partial OT statement of (some of) the data we have considered thus far.

We are concerned to present an OT alternative of the derivation in (44). The local bumping rule in (19a) stipulates that a penultimate H is "bumped" into final position when immediately preceded by a H. Starting with the input in (44a) we must explain why bumping takes precedence over MR. We also must explain why bumping can only affect a penultimate H. We can get the desired result by recognizing four constraints affecting H tone, presented in ranked order in (46).

(46) a. PRESERVE-LINK (H)   An input pre-macro-stem linked H should remain linked to the same vowel in the output.

b. OCP (H)   A macro-stem H is not immediately preceded by a H.[23]

c. MORPH (H)   A H is assigned according to the widest scope morphology.

d. PARSE (H)   An input H should be realized in the output.

The effect of these constraints is transparent. OCP (H) is responsible both for MR and bumping.[24] As we saw in (26b), prefixes that precede the OM, e.g., the ASP marker -ká-, are not affected by MR. We thus conclude that it is only a macro-stem H that is subject to the OCP, although the preceding H may or may not itself belong to the macro-stem.[25] MORPH (H) states that a H should be assigned according to the prevailing morphology. As discussed in section 3, this means according to widest scope morphology, and usually involves a PV assignment overriding a FV assignment. PARSE (H) says that an input H should be preserved in the output.

With this enumeration of constraints, we can now see in (47) how the input in (44a) successfully surfaces as in (44b).

(47) Input: ti-ná- [-mú-ph-a]

		PRESERVE-LINK (H)	OCP (H)	MORPH (H)	PARSE (H)
a.	ti-ná-mú-ph-a		*!		
b. ☞	ti-ná-mu-ph-á			*	
c.	ti-ná-mu-ph-a			*	*!
d.	ti-ná-mú-ph-á		*!*		
e.	ti-na-mú-ph-á	*!	*	*	*
f.	ti-na-mu-ph-a	*!		*	**
g.	ti-na-mu-ph-á	*!		*	*
h.	ti-na-mú-ph-a	*!			*
i.	tí-na-mú-ph-a	*!			

(47) includes the eight logical combinations of H and Ø on the last three vowels of the form plus one last form in (47i), where the subject marker (SM) *ti-* is H. As seen in (47a), if no change is made to the input, an OCP violation will occur, which, being high ranked, eliminates this output. In (47b) the correct output is obtained by bumping the penultimate H to final position. MORPH (H) is is violated since the penultimate H tone conditioned by the OM -mú- surfaces instead on the FV. The same violation of MORPH (H) is found in (47c), where the H of -mú- fails to surface at all. This output is disfavored over (47b) because of its violation of

PARSE (H). The output in (47d) is put in only to show what happens if we simply add a H tone to the FV. As seen, there are now two violations of OCP (H): stem -*ph-á*, because it is preceded by -*mú*-, and macro-stem -*mú*- because it is preceded by -*ná*-. The next set of candidates in (47e) to (47i) show what happens if the linked H is not preserved on the tense marker -*ná*-. Without PRESERVE-LINK (H), candidates (47e) to (47g) would have been eliminated by either OCP (H) or PARSE (H). The last two candidates, however, show why PRESERVE-LINK (H) is needed. Both realize the morphological penultimate H conditioned by -*mú*-. Without PRESERVE-LINK (H) the output in (47h), which does not parse the H of -*ná*-, or the output in (47i), which "anticipates" the H of -*ná*- onto the SM *ti*-, would have been preferred over the correct candidate in (47b).

In summary, then, the constraints in (46) nicely motivate the preference of bumping over MR, when both can "apply."[26] With this accomplished, we can now return to reduplication. In most cases we have considered, the same tones appear on both stems in reduplication. This is captured by invoking McCarthy and Prince's (1993a) violable constraint MAX in (48).

(48) MAX

     Base = Reduplicant

Unless a higher ranked constraint would be violated, MAX will guarantee that the tones of STEM$_1$ and STEM$_2$ will be identical. The major exception to this was seen in the reduplication of mono- and bisyllabic stems with penultimate tone in (34). Additional forms are seen in (49).

(49) a.	(ti-sa-) thandíz-e	→	(ti-sa-) thandíz-é-thandíz-e	"let's not help (here and there)"
	(ti-sa-) vundikír-e	→	(ti-sa-) vundikír-é-vundikír-e	"let's not cover (here and there)"
	(ti-sa-) fotokoz-ér-e	→	(ti-sa-) fotokoz-ér-é-fotokoz-ér-e	"let's not explain to (here and there)"
	(ti-sa-) namíz-e	→	(ti-sa-) namíz-é-namíz-e	"let's not deceive (here and there)"
	(ti-sa-) thamang-ír-e	→	(ti-sa-) thamang-ír-é-thamang-ír-e	"let's not run to (here and there)"
	(ti-sa-) khululukír-e	→	(ti-sa-) khululukír-é-khululukír-e	"let's not pardon (here and there)"

b. (ti-sa-) ph-é   →   (ti-sa-) ph-é-í-ph-é   "let's not kill
                                                   (here and there)"

    (ti-sa-) mény-e   →   (ti-sa-) mény-é-   "let's not hit
                           meny-é   (here and there)"

    (ti-sa-) péz-e   →   (ti-sa-)   "let's not find
                           péz-é-pez-é   (here and there)"

c. (ti-sa-) ph-é   →   (ti-sa-)   "let's not kill
                           ph-e-í-ph-e   (here and there)"
                                                   (Chichewa-Sam)

    (ti-sa-) mény-e   →   (ti-sa-) meny-e-   "let's not hit
                           mény-e   (here and there)"

    (ti-sa-) péz-e   →   (ti-sa-)   "let's not find
                           pez-e-péz-e   (here and there)"

Like almost all negatives, the negative subjunctive assigns a penultimate
H tone. In the longer forms in (49a), we see that the penultimate H is
assigned to both STEM₁ and STEM₂.[27] In (49b) we see that when the stem is
monosyllabic or bisyllabic, only STEM₁ gets a penultimate H, while STEM₂
gets a final H. This is of course the result of bumping, either local, as
shown in (50a), or nonlocal, as shown in (50b).

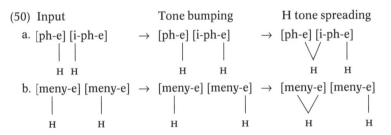

(50) Input   Tone bumping   H tone spreading
a. [ph-e] [i-ph-e]   → [ph-e] [i-ph-e]   → [ph-e] [i-ph-e]

        H H   H   H   H   H

b. [meny-e] [meny-e] → [meny-e] [meny-e] → [meny-e] [meny-e]

        H   H   H   H   H   H

This suggests that MAX is ranked lower than OCP (H).[28] Comparable
data in our second dialect, Chichewa-Sam, in (49c), show an alternative
"repair strategy" at work in avoiding the OCP violation.[29] Here we see
that only a single penultimate tone surfaces on STEM₂. One way to get
this effect is to follow Hewitt's (1992) treatment of comparable data in
Shona and represent the forms in (49c) as a single-stem domain, in
Chichewa-Sam, as in (51).

(51) a. [ph-e-i-ph-e]   b. [meny-e-meny-e]   [pez-e-pez-e]

        H   H   H

However, as pointed out to us by an anonymous reviewer, the single-stem representation in (51a) does not explain why an epenthetic [i] is needed in [ph-e-i-ph-e]. As a single stem, *[ph-e-ph-e] should have met bisyllabic minimality, but does not. Instead, the representations that appear to be needed are those in (52).

(52) a. -ph-e- [i-ph-e]   b. -meny-e- [meny-e]   -pez-e-[pez-e]
         | | |
         H   H   H

Here, a mono- or bisyllabic STEM₁ loses its "stemicity" and is prefixed to STEM₂. What is significant is that the prefixed STEM₁ representation of shorter stems is obligatory in Chichewa-Sam reduplication whenever a penultimate H input contains a "bumpy relationship," whether local, as in (50a), or nonlocal, as in (50b). As seen in (53), "monostemicity" is only optional in Chichewa-Sam, when the bumping H tones are assigned to the FV in the input:

(53) a. ti- [thandiz-é]   → ti- [thandiz-é]   "let's help (here
                                        [thandiz-é]   and there)"
         ti- [vundikir-é]   → ti- [vundikir-é]   "let's cover (here
                                        [vundikir-é]   and there)"
         ti- [fotokoz-er-é]   → ti- [fotokoz-er-é]   "let's explain to
                                        [fotokoz-er-é]   (here and there)"
         ti- [namiz-é]   → ti- [namiz-é]   "let's deceive
                                        [namiz-é]   (here and there)"
         ti- [thamang-ir-é]   → ti- [thamang-ir-é]   "let's run to (here
                                        [thamang-ir-é]   and there)"
         ti- [khululukir-é]   → ti- [khululukir-é]   "let's pardon
                                        [khululukir-é]   (here and there)"
     b. Chichewa-Al/Chichewa-Sam (penult H < HTS)
         ti- [ph-é]   → ti- [ph-é]   "let's kill
                                        [í-ph-é]   (here and there)"
         ti- [meny-é]   → ti- [meny-é]   "let's hit
                                        [mény-é]   (here and there)"
         ti- [pez-é]   → ti- [pez-é]   "let's find
                                        [péz-é]   (here and there)"

c. Chichewa-Sam

ti- [ph-é]	→	ti-ph-e-	"let's kill
		[i-ph-é]	(here and there)"
ti- [meny-é]	→	ti-meny-e-	"let's hit
		[meny-é]	(here and there)"
ti- [pez-é]	→	ti-pez-e-	"let's find
		[pez-é]	(here and there)"

In (53a), where the input stem is three or more syllables long, STEM₁ and STEM₂ each receive a final H. When the input stem is monosyllabic or bisyllabic, STEM₁ and STEM₂ may again each receive a final H, as in (53b) in both dialects. However, Chichewa-Sam has the option in (53c) of prefixing STEM₁ to STEM₂, in which case a final H is found only on STEM₂.[30]

In the preceding examples, MAX is violated on short stems because an OCP violation would otherwise result. A last violation of MAX is pointed out by Mtenje (1988) and Carleton and Myers (1993). Whenever STEM₁ is directly preceded by a prefix which places a H> on its first syllable, this H is not transferred to STEM₂ in reduplication. We have seen numerous examples where the infinitive prefix *ku-* has this effect. As seen in the examples in the left hand column of (54), the H which is thereby placed on the first syllable of STEM₁ does not get copied onto STEM₂:

(54) a. ku-ph-á-i-ph-a   "to kill again and again"
     b. ku-mény-á-meny-a   ku-péz-á-pez-á
        ku-thándíz-a-thandiz-a   ku-námíz-á-namiz-á
        ku-vúndík-ir-a-vúndik-ir-a   ku-thámáng-ir-á-thamang-ir-á
        ku-fótókoz-er-a-fotokoz-er-a ku-khúlúluk-ir-á-khululuk-ir-á

Reduplication thus appears to take place before the assignment of the H of the infinitive prefix *ku-* to STEM₁, as seen in the derivation in (55).

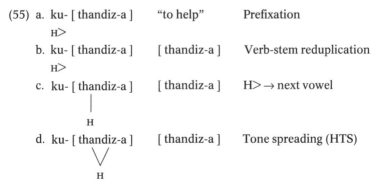

(55) a. ku- [thandiz-a]   "to help"   Prefixation
        H>

     b. ku- [thandiz-a]   [thandiz-a]   Verb-stem reduplication
        H>

     c. ku- [thandiz-a]   [thandiz-a]   H> → next vowel
           |
           H

     d. ku- [thandiz-a]   [thandiz-a]   Tone spreading (HTS)
             \/
             H

However, in examples such as those seen earlier in (40), we have had to assign the H of the infinitive prefix *ku-* to the macro-stem *prior to* reduplication in order to get proper bumping. Consider also the Chichewa-Al forms in (56).

(56) Penultimate H with reflexive *-dzi-* in affirmative infinitive

a. ku-dzí-vúndikír-a   "to cover self"   → ku-dzí-vúndikír-á-
                                                  vundikír-a

   ku-dzí-fótokoz-ér-a   "to explain   → ku-dzí-fótokoz-ér-á-
                           to self"   fotokoz-ér-a

   ku-dzí-thámang-ír-a   "to run to self"   → ku-dzí-thámang-ír-á-
                                                  thamang-ír-a

   ku-dzí-khúlulukír-a   "to pardon self"   → ku-dzí-khúlulukír-á-
                                                  khululukír-a

b. ku-dzí-ph-á   "to kill self"   → ku-dzí-ph-á-i-ph-á

   ku-dzí-mény-a   "to hit self"   → ku-dzí-mény-á-
                                                  mény-á

   ku-dzí-péz-a   "to find self"   → ku-dzí-péz-á-péz-á

c. ku-dzí-thándiz-á   "to help self"   → ku-dzí-thándiz-á-
                                                  thandiz-á

   ku-dzí-námiz-á   "to deceive self"   → ku-dzí-námiz-á-
                                                  namiz-á

In (56a), reduplication is effected with a H assigned to the penult of both STEM₁ and STEM₂. The mono- and bisyllabic STEM₁ and STEM₂ both undergo local tone bumping in (56b), conditioned by the H> of the infinitive prefix *ku-*, which is realized on the reflexive OM *-dzi-*. It is crucially the trisyllabic stems in (56c) that show that assignment of H> must precede tone-bumping and reduplication in a rule-ordered account, as in the derivation in (57).

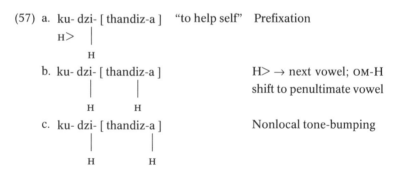

(57) a. ku- dzi- [thandiz-a]   "to help self"   Prefixation
        H> |
            |
            H

    b. ku- dzi- [thandiz-a]   H> → next vowel; OM-H
           | | shift to penultimate vowel
           | |
           H   H

    c. ku- dzi- [thandiz-a]   Nonlocal tone-bumping
           | |
           | |
           H   H

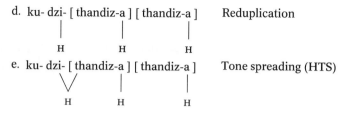

d. ku- dzi- [thandiz-a] [thandiz-a]   Reduplication

e. ku- dzi- [thandiz-a] [thandiz-a]   Tone spreading (HTS)

Since assignment of H> to the next vowel applies before reduplication in (57) but after reduplication in (55), this represents a serious rule-ordering problem – and, we therefore maintain, one more reason to believe that there should be a nonlevel-ordered approach to reduplication in Chichewa.

To capture the non-copying of the H tone in (55), Carleton and Myers (1993) adopt the MAX constraint and further specify that "MAX will only be sensitive to those elements that belong morphologically to the stem, and will ignore material from other morphological domains that happen to be realized on the stem" (17). We have already seen the need to restrict constraints by domain, e.g., only macro-stem Hs are subject to OCP (H), which seems to lend at least some support to the possibility of such a restriction. An alternative account was suggested by John McCarthy at the workshop: starting with the requirement that H> be on the next vowel, if it were to be transferred in reduplication, its second occurrence on the reduplicant would violate the next-vowel requirement on H>. The morpheme-specific next-vowel constraint would have to outrank MAX. In order that H> not simply be deleted (which would avoid all problems, including nontransfer), the next-vowel constraint would itself have to be outranked by a pre-macro-stem version of Parse (H). Assuming then the right set of ranked constraints, it should be possible to account for this one exceptional case of nontransfer.

6. Conclusion

In this brief section, we would like to end by speculating as to why the MAX constraint in (48) is ranked so much higher in Chichewa verb-stem reduplication than in most other Bantu languages, many of which truncate STEM$_1$. In addition, Chichewa is the only Bantu language we know that transfers tone in verb-stem reduplication. Some possible explanations for the transfer versus nontransfer of tone in Bantu reduplication are as follows.

(i) The input domain may be different, e.g., WORD versus STEM (Mutaka and Hyman 1990). In case the reduplication produces a WORD-WORD sequence, there is tonal transfer (e.g., Kinande nouns); in case it produces a STEM-STEM, there is no tonal transfer (e.g., Kinande verbs).

(ii) The output structure may be different, e.g., prefixing versus suffixing versus compounding (Carleton and Myers 1993). Perhaps only compounding structures show tonal transfer.

(iii) The tones may be linked or unlinked to their respective tone-bearing units (Mutaka and Hyman 1990; Hewitt 1992). Unlinked tones are not transferred in reduplication.

(iv) Reduplication may target only certain tiers, e.g., all but tonal tier (Hyman and Byarushengo 1984).

Of these, we prefer the account in (i). Although verb reduplication is limited to the STEM, it is clear that STEM$_2$ is a phonological WORD. Some of the reasons have already been given. We wish now to end with a last piece of evidence, this time coming from the postlexical rule of HTS. Although HTS applies generally in both dialects within the word (subject to the condition expressed in (11)), the following tonal differences are found in the reduplications in (58).

(58)   Chichewa-Al   Chichewa-Sam

a. ti- [thandiz-é] [thandiz-é]   ti- [thandiz-é]
                                                                      [thándiz-é]

   ti- [vundikir-é] [vundikir-é]   ti- [vundukir-é]
                                                                      [vúndikir-é]

   ti- [fotokoz-er-é] [fotokoz-er-é]   ti- [fotokoz-er-é]
                                                                      [fótokoz-er-é]

   ti- [namiz-é] [namiz-é]   ti- [namiz-é] [námiz-é]
   ti- [thamang-ir-é] [thamang-ir-é]   ti- [thamang-ir-é]
                                                                      [thámang-ir-é]

   ti- [khululukir-é] [khululukir-é]   ti- [khululukir-é]
                                                                      [khúlulukir-é]

b. ti- [ph-é] [í-ph-é]   ti- [ph-é] [í-ph-é]
   ti- [meny-é] [mény-é]   ti- [meny-é] [mény-é]
   ti- [pez-é] [péz-é]   ti- [pez-é] [péz-é]

c.   ti- [ph-e-i-ph-é]

                                                              ti- [meny-e-meny-é]

                                                              ti- [pez-e-pez-é]

In (58a) we see that there is no HTS across the STEM₁-STEM₂ boundary in Chichewa-Al versus Chichewa-Sam, where there is. On the other hand, in the shorter forms in (58b), both dialects show HTS. In Chichewa-Al HTS will apply onto STEM₂ only if we have the configuration in (59).

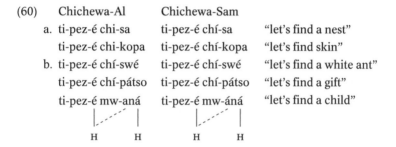

(59)   V] [C V C V   e.g.   [pez-e] [pez-e]

         H   H   H   H

While HTS applies in all environments in Chichewa-Sam, the only time a H spreads onto a following word in Chichewa-Al is if the result is a H tone plateau, as in (59). This is verified also in the following comparison in (60).

(60)   Chichewa-Al   Chichewa-Sam
   a. ti-pez-é chi-sa   ti-pez-é chí-sa   "let's find a nest"
       ti-pez-é chi-kopa   ti-pez-é chí-kopa   "let's find skin"
   b. ti-pez-é chí-swé   ti-pez-é chí-swé   "let's find a white ant"
       ti-pez-é chí-pátso   ti-pez-é chí-pátso   "let's find a gift"
       ti-pez-é mw-aná   ti-pez-é mw-áná   "let's find a child"

            H   H   H   H

In (60a) there is HTS onto the toneless noun prefix *chi-* in Chichewa-Sam, but not in Chichewa-Al. In (60b) there is HTS onto the noun prefix in both dialects. The reason why Chichewa-Al undergoes HTS in (60b) but not in (60a) is because the rule applies only when a H plateau is created. Thus, from the perspective of HTS, the tones in Chichewa-Al are the same in the verb reduplications in (58) as in the verb + noun object sequences in (60). This, then, we take as final evidence that the STEM₂ in verb reduplication is a separate word – and in this respect different from verb-stem reduplication in all other Bantu languages we know.[31]

To summarize, we have shown that the facts from tonal transfer argue that Chichewa reduplication should not be done in the level-ordered fashion described in section 1. Rather than applying at the STEM domain, reduplication is more accurately viewed as a WORD-domain rule whose base is limited to the verb stem. As such we can make cross-domain reference to the tones of prefixes which determine the shape of the stem tones which are to be transferred. In this sense Chichewa offers the phonological analogue to the morphological facts demonstrated for verb reduplication in languages like Kihehe (Odden and Odden 1985). In the latter language a prefix is transferred only if it syllabifies with the stem. While prefixal tones (e.g., H>) do not themselves transfer in Chichewa, they are allowed to exert their influence "prior" to reduplication. It is this property which is hard to capture in a compositional level-ordered framework such as Lexical Phonology. Since constraint-based theories such as OT do not have the property of starting with smaller domains and proceeding outwards to larger ones, the cross-referencing of domains in Chichewa reduplication seems more compatible with this increasingly popular view of phonology.

Appendix

In this section we briefly contrast the tonal properties of a second dialect, Chichewa-Sam, with our principal dialect, Chichewa-Al (cf. note 4). Although most work seems to be on Chichewa-Al, Kanerva's extensive work has been based on Chichewa-Sam. The following discussion should hopefully clarify some of the discrepancies that readers can observe, which also can be exploited to gain a fuller understanding of the issues involved in Chichewa verb tonology and reduplication. We have grouped the tonal differences between the two dialects into five areas, the first four of which have already been encountered:[32]

1. Differences in tone transfer in reduplication. In Chichewa-Al, tonal transfer is completely general: the tones on STEM_2 are identical to those on STEM_1 modulo tone bumping. In Chichewa-Sam, however, when the stem is mono- or bisyllabic, the tone may appear only on STEM_2.[33] A toneless STEM_1 is optional when the tone pattern is final, as we saw in (59b) and (59c), but obligatory when the tone pattern is penultimate, as in (49b). (Cf. note 30, however.)

2. Differences in HTS. As noted in the examples in (58), HTS regularly applies across the $\text{STEM}_1\text{-STEM}_2$ boundary in Chichewa-Sam, but applies in Chichewa-Al only if the result is the plateauing of a H] [Ø H sequence to H] [H H.

3. Differences in final lowering. As pointed out in note 7, Chichewa-Sam does not allow an underlying lexical H to surface on the FV at the end of an intonational phrase, while Chichewa-Al does.

4. Differences in nonlocal bumping. In Chichewa-Sam, a next-vowel H> does not condition nonlocal tone bumping. The H> in the underlying representations in (61a) is part of the INFI NITIVEprefix *ku-*:

(61) a. ku-dzi-thandiz-a   "to help self"   ku-dzi-namiz-a   "to deceive
      H> H   H> H   H   self"
   b. ku-dzí-thándíz-a   ku-dzí-námíz-a
   c. ku-dzí-thándiz-á   ku-dzí-namiz-á

In both dialects the H> of *ku-* links to the following reflexive OM *-dzi-* and undergoes HTS onto the first vowel of the verb stem. The H of *-dzi-* should be assigned to the PV. This is what does in fact happen in Chichewa-Sam in (61b). However, in (61c) we see that the penultimate H is shifted to the FV by nonlocal bumping in Chichewa-Al. This is a consistent difference between the dialects.

5. Differences in OM and ASP tone. In section 3 we indicated two facts about OM tone in Chichewa-Al. First, both the reflexive OM *-dzi-* and all non-reflexive OMS (e.g. *-mu-*) assign a H to the PV. Second, this H will not be realized if the OM is directly preceded by a linked H (e.g. the tense marker *-ná-*). A special situation arose when the stem was monosyllabic. In this case the OM is in penultimate position. Unless preceded by a linked H, it will thus carry the H tone itself. If preceded by a linked H, the penultimate H of the OM is generally deleted by MR. Recall, however, from (44) that if it is followed by a monosyllabic stem, the H of the OM is instead bumped onto the FV. The tableau in (47) showed how bumping results from an interaction of four constraints.

The situation is different in two ways in Chichewa-Sam. First, non-reflexive OMS and ASP markers condition H on the FV, not the PV. Thus, the examples in (62) should be compared with the Chichewa-Al forms seen earlier in (24).

(62) a. ku-mú-ph-a   "to kill him"   —
      ku-mú-   "to hit him"   ku-mú-péz-á   "to find him"
      mény-á
      ku-mú-   "to help him"   ku-mú-   "to deceive him"
      thándiz-á   námiz-á
      ku-mú-   "to cover him"   ku-mú-   "to run to him"
      vúndikir-á   thámang-ir-á
      ku-mú-   "to explain   ku-mú-   "to pardon him"
      fótokoz-er-á   to him"   khúlulukir-á

b. ku-ká-ph-a   "to go   —
                   and kill"
    ku-ká-   "to go   ku-ká-péz-á   "to go and find"
    mény-á   and hit"
    ku-ká-   "to go   ku-ká-   "to go and
    thándiz-á   and help"   námiz-á   deceive"
    ku-ká-   "to go   ku-ká-   "to go and
    vúndikir-á   and cover"   thámang-ir-á   run to"
    ku-ká-   "to go and   ku-ká-   "to go and
    fótokoz-er-á   explain to"   khúlulukir-á   explain to"

As before, in these examples the H on the OM -*mú*- and the ASP marker
-*ká*- comes from the infinitive prefix *ku*- and spreads onto the first vowel
of the stem. There is no H on the monosyllabic stem -*ph-a* because of
MR. As seen, both -*mu*- and -*ka*- condition a H on the FV. As in the case
of our primary dialect, where these markers conditioned a penultimate
H, non-reflexive OMs and ASP markers do not condition a H on the FV if
they are directly preceded by a linked H tone. Thus, Chichewa-Sam forms
in (63) are identical to those seen in Chichewa-Al in (25a) and (25c).[34]

(63) No H on FV when -*mu*- or -*ka*- are preceded by the P2 TM -*ná*-
    a. ti-ná-mú-   "we killed   —
        ph-á   him"
        ti-ná-mú-   "we hit him"   ti-ná-mú-   "we found
        meny-a   pez-á   him"
        ti-ná-mú-   "we helped   ti-ná-mú-   "we deceived
        thandiz-a   him"   namiz-á   him"
        ti-ná-mú-   "we covered   ti-ná-mú-   "we ran to
        vundikir-a   him"   thamang-ir-á   him"
        ti-ná-mú-   "we explained ti-ná-mú-   "we pardoned
        fotokoz-er-a   to him"   khululukir-á   him"
    b. ti-ná-ká-   "we went   —
        ph-a   and killed"
        ti-ná-ká-   "we went   ti-ná-ká-   "we went and
        meny-a   and hit"   pez-á   found"
        ti-ná-ká-   "we went and   ti-ná-ká-   "we went and
        thándiz-a   helped"   námiz-á   deceived"
        ti-ná-ká-   "we went and   ti-ná-ká-   "we went and
        vúndikir-a   covered"   thámang-ir-á   ran to"
        ti-ná-ká-   "we went and   ti-ná-ká-   "we went and
        fótokoz-er-a   explained to" khúlulukir-á   pardoned"

Interestingly, the reflexive OM *-dzi-* still conditions a penultimate H in Chichewa-Sam, as we saw in (61b). Differing from Chichewa-Al, this penultimate H surfaces even if *-dzi-* is preceded by a linked H. The Chichewa-Sam forms in (64) should be contrasted with the Chichewa-Al forms in (25b):

(64)   ti-ná-dzí-ph-á   "we killed
                                                            selves"
        ti-ná-dzí-meny-á   ti-ná-dzí-pez-á   "we hit/found
                                                            selves"
   ☞ ti-ná-dzí-thandíz-a   ti-ná-dzí-námíz-a   "we helped/
                                                            deceived selves"
        ti-ná-dzí-vundikír-a   ti-ná-dzí-thámang-ír-a   "we covered/
                                                            ran to selves"
        ti-ná-dzí-fotokoz-ér-a ti-ná-dzí-khúlulukír-a   "we explained
                                                            to/pardoned
                                                            selves"

These differences are summarized in the table in (65).

(65) Dialectal differences

	Chichewa-Sam		Chichewa-Al	
	After H>	After H	After H>	After H
NON-REFL EXIVE OMS (*-mu-*)	FV	Ø	PV	Ø
REFL EXIVE OM (*-dzi-*)	PV	PV	PV	Ø
ASPECT MARKERS (*-ka-*)	FV	H	PV	H

In order to account for the differential behavior of the reflexive OM with respect to MR we propose that the H of *-dzi-* is not prelinked in Chichewa-Sam, as in (66a).

(66) a. ti-na-dzi-fotokoz-er-a   b. ti-na-dzi-fotokoz-er-a
          | \/ |
          H   H   H   H

As a consequence it escapes MR and is assigned to the penult in (66b).

Notes

1 We wish to thank Sharon Inkelas, an anonymous reviewer, and the participants at the Utrecht Workshop on Prosodic Morphology for valuable comments on an earlier version of this chapter.

2 Note that *u-sw-a* and *u-y-a* are still imperatives rather than subjunctives, in which case the final vowel would be *-e*.

3 A popular form of this concerns the treatment of phonologically conditioned allomorphy, where a phonological constraint can "outrank" a grammatical constraint (cf. McCarthy and Prince 1993b; Mester 1994; Perlmutter 1995; Tranel 1995).

4 Forms of Chichewa-Al are presented as spoken in Ntcheu, while Chichewa-Sam forms are given as spoken in Nkhotakota. We would like to thank Sam Mchombo for his great help in collecting paradigms for this project.

5 All "consonantal" roots such as *-ph-* "kill", *-dy-* "eat", etc. are underlyingly toneless.

6 In some of the examples, *-fotokoz-er-* "explain to" and *-thamang-ir-* "run to" are used with an applicative *-ir-/-er-* extension so that these verbs can take an object.

7 Throughout this chapter we ignore postlexical rules that potentially affect the shape and tone of the final two syllables of a phonological phrase. One of these is penultimate lengthening. Another is the anticipation of a final H onto the second half of the lengthened vowel. In addition, in Chichewa-Sam a lexical H cannot be realized on the FV phrase-finally. Thus, the transcriptions given for the final two syllables of each form can be converted to phrase-final realizations as follows:

meny-a   →   [mèènyà]   meny-á   →   [mèényá] (Chichewa-Al)
                                        [mèényà] (Chichewa-Sam)
mény-a   →   [méènyà]   mény-á   →   [méényá] (Chichewa-Al)
                                        [méényà] (Chichewa-Sam)

8 As further examples will show, the correct generalization is that a macro-stem H is deleted when preceded by another H (which may be in the macro-stem or may precede it).

9 The H goes on the FV when the macro-stem consists of a single syllable, e.g., *ph-á* (cf. 17b, 18a, b).

10 The passive extension *-idw-* is toneless in Chichewa-Al but H in Chichewa-Sam.

11 Interestingly, trisyllabic verb stems do not undergo nonlocal bumping and are hence pronounced with PV H tone in Chichewa-Sam: *ku-dzí-thándíz-a, ku-dzí-námíz-a*.

12 In order to get the fourth H tone on the passive extension *-idw-*, this form is cited from Chichewa-Sam. In both dialects the intensive suffix is doubled when not followed directly by the FV – see Hyman and Mchombo (1992).

13 In Chichewa-Sam, aspect markers such as *-ka-* assign a H to the FV rather than to the PV (see appendix). Note also that the next-vowel H> of the INFI NITIVEprefix *ku-* is found only in the affirmative.

14 This is an area where the two dialects diverge. The discussion of this section pertains only to Chichewa-Al. For comparable details concerning
Chichewa-Sam and additional support for our analysis, see the appendix.

15 For an indication of why the FV of monosyllabic stems is H, see the derivation in (44).

16 The H of -ká- cannot get to the penult unless "pushed" by an immediately
preceding H>. We assume that the next-syllable H> takes precedence,
therefore, over a prelinked H (cf. the derivations in (28)).

17 Note that if the H of -mu- and -ka- were not prelinked, as in (i),

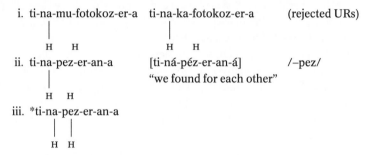

i. ti-na-mu-fotokoz-er-a   ti-na-ka-fotokoz-er-a   (rejected URs)

        H   H   H   H
ii. ti-na-pez-er-an-a   [ti-ná-péz-er-an-á]   /–pez/
                           "we found for each other"

       H   H
iii. *ti-na-pez-er-an-a

        H   H

we would have to say that the unlinked H of the OM is deleted when directly
preceded by a linked H tone. However, since we have seen that the H of a
H verb root is not deleted, it cannot be the case that such forms which
have the parallel representation in (ii) also undergo the rule affecting OMS
and ASPECT MARKERS. We must, therefore, reject intermediate representations such as in (iii), where the root H is linked to the first vowel (the following suffixes being toneless). Instead, the H of a root (or of a H tone
suffix such as intensive -its-) starts out unlinked and becomes linked to the
FV, while the H of an OM starts out as linked and is therefore subject to MR.
Another possibility to be rejected is outward-looking allomorphy: an OM
has an unlinked H unless preceded by a linked H. This analysis would also
fail to relate the alternation to MR, as well as to the realization of -ka-,
which, as seen in (26), must have a prelinked H.

18 Actually, we would prefer to say the "imperative" mood. The FV -é is used
in two cases: (i) in the imperative affirmative if there is an OM; (ii) in the
subjunctive affirmative, if there is no ASPECT MARKER. If either is negative
or there is an aspect marker in the subjunctive affirmative, there will be a
H on the PV.

19 We discuss the (non-) application of HTS across the STEM₁ + STEM₂ boundary
in section 6.

20 Thus we do not obtain *ku-phá-ku-pha either, where the word-level infinitive prefix may not appear within the stem in reduplication.

21 The Hs observed on the FV of the stems in these forms come from the H
tone roots, e.g., -péz-, etc. As discussed in section 6, HTS applies across the

STEM₁ + STEM₂ boundary in Chichewa-Al only if the result is the plateauing of H] [Ø-H to H] [H-H.

22 The only case where the two stems are segmentally distinct is when only STEM₂ requires an epenthetic [i] to meet the bisyllabic requirement. This [i] could of course be considered as segmentally underspecified.

23 For more on the OCP in Optimality Theory, see Myers (1993).

24 At this point we are concerned only with local bumping (19a) and do not address nonlocal bumping (19b) which requires a slightly different statement (and ranking). We assume that the reason why the second H is lost by MR rather than the first is that a word output with a later H will be preferred over one with an earlier H, other things being equal. This presumably can be related to right-alignment.

25 Strictly speaking this is another nonlevel-ordered fact in Chichewa, this time involving the MACRO-STEM versus WORD. The same conclusion can be drawn with respect to bumping. The crucial example is *ti-ná-ká-ph-a* "we went and killed" in (25c). Not only does the H of the ASPECT MARKER *-ká-* fail to undergo MR; it also fails to be bumped to produce **ti-ná-ka-ph-á*. This is because the bumped H must be part of the macro-stem. In this case we follow Kanerva (1989) in recognizing bumping as a foot-related phenomenon: Construction of a binary foot is limited to material in the macro-stem and only a *footed* penultimate H can shift to final position.

26 The constraints do not handle cases in (25a) and (25b) when the verb form is longer and bumping is not applicable. In these cases MR applies instead. In the derivational account we would say that MR precedes shifting of the OM H to the PV. It is not obvious to us how to produce this output in an OT account. The reason is that bumping bleeds MR, but MR bleeds H-shifting to the PV. The problem seems even worse if one were to question our underlying representations, e.g., by denying that the H of OMs is prelinked (for which additional evidence is produced in the appendix). Finally, a solution with tonal allomorphy would also be quite complex: use *-mú-* if preceded by a toneless vowel, or if followed by a monosyllabic stem; otherwise use *-mu-*.

27 As in other forms, the penultimate H spreads to the FV in STEM₁ only.

28 We will assume, following Kanerva (1989), that nonlocal bumping is also OCP-related, even though a single toneless vowel intervenes between the trigger and target Hs.

29 For a general discussion of repair strategies in constraint-based phonology, see Paradis (1984).

30 It is interesting to note that nonlocal bumping is not as generally applicable in the verb paradigm in Chichewa-Sam as it is in Chichewa-Al (cf. note 11 and the appendix). Perhaps the loss of the H on STEM₁ should be related to this fact. For some reason it is not possible to have monostemicity in the

imperative or perfect, e.g. *pez-á-péz-á* (**pez-a-pez-á*) "find here and there!", *t-a-pez-á-péz-á* (**t-a-pez-a-pez-á*) "we have found here and there." The only generalization we have been able to find is that a single stem is not possible if the H on the FV is from the root or from an extension and if there is no H preceding the stem.

31 In fact we are aware of no evidence that clearly establishes that STEM₁ and STEM₂ form a morphological or syntactic constituent – other than that no phonetic material may occur between them.

32 Minor, morphological-restricted differences are ignored, e.g. the fact that the passive suffix *-idz-* is toneless in Chichewa-Al, but introduces a H in Chichewa-Sam.

33 From our Bantu perspective STEM₂ should be the base and STEM₁ the reduplicant. Since it makes little or no difference in Chichewa we have attempted to stick with the STEM₁-STEM₂ terminology.

34 Once again there is a final H on the monosyllabic stem *-ph-á* in (63a) because of tone bumping of the underlying macro-stem H of *-mú-*.

References

Carleton, Troi, and Scott Myers. 1993. On tonal transfer, ms. University of Texas, Austin, TX.

Downing, Laura this volume. Verbal reduplication in three Bantu languages.

Hewitt, Mark. 1992. Vertical maximization and metrical theory, Ph.D. dissertation, Brandeis University, Waltham, MA.

Hyman, Larry M. 1993. Problems in rule ordering in phonology: two Bantu test cases, in J. Goldsmith (ed.), *The Last Phonological Rule*, University of Chicago Press, 195–222.

Hyman, Larry M., and Ernest Rugwa Byarushengo. 1984. A model of Haya tonology, in G. N. Clements and J. Goldsmith (eds.), *Autosegmental Studies in Bantu Tone*, Dordrecht: Foris, 53–103.

Hyman, Larry M., and Joyce Mathangwane. 1993. Tonal domains and depressor consonants in Ikalanga, to appear in L. M. Hyman and C. Kisseberth (eds.), *Theoretical Aspects of Bantu Tone*, Stanford, CA: CSLI Publications, Center for the Study of Language and Information.

Hyman, Larry M., and Sam Mchombo. 1992. Morphotactic constraints in the Chichewa verb stem, *Berkeley Linguistic Society* 18.

Kanerva, Jonni. 1985. A cyclic analysis of tone in Chichewa verbs, ms. Stanford University, CA.

1986. Cyclic tone assignment in Chichewa verbs, ms. Stanford University, CA.

1989. Focus and phrasing in Chichewa phonology, Ph.D. dissertation, Stanford University, CA.

1990. Focusing on phonological phrases in Chichewa, in S. Inkelas and D. Zec (eds.), *The Phonology-Syntax Connection*, University of Chicago Press, 145–61.

Maddieson, Ian, and Peter Ladefoged. 1993. Phonetics of partially nasal consonants, in M. K. Huffman and R. A. Krakow (eds.), *Phonetics and Phonology 5: Nasals, Nasalization, and the Velum*. San Diego, CA: Academic Press, 251–301.

Marantz, Alec. 1982. Re reduplication. *Linguistic Inquiry* 13: 435–82.

McCarthy, John J., and Alan S. Prince. 1993a. Prosodic Morphology I: constraint interaction and satisfaction, ms. University of Massachusetts, Amherst, MA and Rutgers University, New Brunswick, NJ.

1993b. Generalized alignment, in G. E. Booij and J. van Marle (eds.), *Yearbook of Morphology 1993*: Dordrecht: Kluwer, 79–154.

Mester, R. Armin. 1994. The quantitative trochee in Latin, *Natural Language and Linguistic Theory* 12: 1–61.

Mohanan, K. P. 1986. *The Theory of Lexical Phonology*. Dordrecht: D. Reidel Publishing Co.

Moto, Francis. 1983. Aspects of tone assignment in Chichewa, *Journal of Contemporary African Studies* 4: 199–210.

Mtenje, Al. 1986. Issues in the nonlinear phonology of Chichewa, Ph.D. dissertation, University College London.

1987. Tone shift principles in the Chichewa verb: a case for a tone lexicon, *Lingua* 72: 169–209.

1988. On tone and transfer in Chichewa reduplication, *Linguistics* 26: 125–55.

Mutaka, Ngessimo and Larry M. Hyman. 1990. Syllables and morpheme integrity in Kinande reduplication, *Phonology* 7: 73–120.

Myers, Scott. 1987. Tone and the structure of words in Shona, Ph.D. dissertation, University of Massachusetts, Amherst, MA.

1993. OCP effects in Optimality Theory, ms. University of Texas, Austin.

Odden, David, and Mary Odden. 1985. Ordered reduplication in Kíhehe, *Linguistic Inquiry* 16: 497–503.

Paradis, Carole. 1988. On constraints and repair strategies, *Linguistic Review* 6: 71–97.

Perlmutter, David. 1995. Explanation of allomorphy and the architecture of grammars. Paper presented at the Davis Morphology Conference, 6 May 1995.

Peterson, Karen. 1987. Accent in the Chichewa verb, *Chicago Linguistic Society* 23, *Parasession on Autosegmental and Metrical Phonology*, 210–22.

Prince, Alan and Paul Smolensky. 1993. Optimality Theory: constraint interaction in generative grammar, ms. Rutgers University, Amherst, MA and University of Colorado, Boulder, CO.

Tranel, Bernard. 1995. Exceptionality in Optimality Theory and final consonants in French, ms. University of California, Irvine, CA.

Trithart, Lee. 1976. Desyllabified noun class prefixes and depressor consonants in Chichewa, in L. M. Hyman (ed.), *Studies in Bantu Tonology, Southern California Occasional Papers in Linguistics* 3, Los Angeles, CA: University of Southern California, 259–86.

5 Exceptional stress-attracting suffixes in Turkish: representations versus the grammar

Sharon Inkelas

1. Introduction

Generative phonology has wrestled since its inception with the question of whether, for some given phenomenon, that phenomenon should be handled with rules or constraints – i.e., in the grammar – or with pre-specified representations – i.e., in the lexicon. The introduction by Prince and Smolensky (1993) of Optimality Theory provides a fresh outlook on this old question. By fundamentally changing the nature of grammar, Optimality Theory may change the answer to any given question of this kind.

The specific question to be addressed in this chapter,[1] from the view-point of Optimality Theory, is how to handle exceptional patterns in Turkish stress: in the lexicon, with underlying templatic metrical structure, or in the grammar, through morpheme-specific constraints? The question is of particular interest because of work by McCarthy and Prince (1993b) which challenges one of the strongest arguments in favor of underlying metrical structure in phonological theory.

1.1 Doing without templates in Optimality Theory

Since McCarthy and Prince (1986), reduplication has been a major source of evidence for the existence of underlying metrical structure, or templates, in lexical entries. In "classical" reduplication, the phonological representation of a reduplicative morpheme consists virtually entirely of metrical structure (usually a syllable or a foot). However, McCarthy and Prince (1993b, this volume) have argued that Optimality Theory makes templates[2] unnecessary even in the analyses of the very phenomena that originally motivated their existence.

The essential idea is that in Optimality Theory, the work of a template can be taken over by a grammatical constraint determining the type of metrical structure to which a morpheme corresponds in the output. The particular implementation adopted in McCarthy and Prince (1993b) is stated in (1); a morpheme-specific grammatical constraint specifies the exact metrical shape of each reduplicative affix:

(1) a classical template is really nothing more than an assertion about how some morphological category...is to be aligned with some prosodic category, such as a heavy syllable or a trochaic foot. [McCarthy and Prince 1993b: 139]

Consider, for example, a simple case of prefixing reduplication of a light syllable. An analysis along the lines proposed by McCarthy and Prince (1993b) is sketched in (2). In underlying representation, the reduplicative prefix is identified simply as being reduplicative (which any analysis must do in some fashion). The rest of the work is done by grammatical constraints. Constraint (2a) states that the reduplicant is a light syllable. Constraint (2b) states that the reduplicant is a prefix; constraint (2c), that the first segment of the reduplicant is identical to the first segment of the base. Constraints (2d) and (2e) are highly general, holding over every reduplicative morpheme. They ensure that as much of the base is copied as possible and that what is copied is a contiguous substring of the base.

(2) Nontemplatic account of prefixing CV reduplication, following McCarthy and Prince (1993b)

Lexical entry for prefix, X: [RED(uplicative)]

Grammar: a. $X=\sigma_\mu$ Morpheme X is a light syllable (in the output)

b. ALIGN-X   Align(X, R, Base, L), i.e., X is a prefix

c. ANCHOR-X   Leftmost segment in X = leftmost segment in base

d. MAX   A [RED] affix is phonologically identical to the base

e. CONTIGUITY   A [RED] affix is a contiguous subpart of the base

Only constraints (2a) and (2d) directly pertain to the issue of templates. (2a) ($X = \sigma_\mu$) states that the reduplicant consists of exactly a light syllable; by ranking (2a) above above (2d) (MAX), we ensure that the maximal light syllable (but no more than a light syllable) is reduplicated.

(3) Ranking: $X=\sigma_\mu \gg$ MAX   (The reduplicant is exactly one light syllable)

	/kapo-$X_{[\text{RED}]}$/	$X=\sigma_\mu$	MAX
a. ☞	ka̲-kapo		*po
b.	k̲-kapo	*!	*apo
c.	kapo̲-kapo	*!	

In subsequent work, McCarthy and Prince (this volume) propose doing away with morpheme-specific constraints on reduplicant shape (e.g., $X=$FT or $X=\sigma_\mu$), instead invoking much simpler morpheme-specific constraints. One, $X=$STEM, states that the morpheme in question is a morphological stem (which the grammar ensures is minimally a foot, by STEM=PRWD); another, $X=$AFFI x,states that the morpheme is a morphological affix (which the grammar ensures is maximally monosyllabic, by AFFI x≤ σ; the actual shape of X is due to the ranking of $X=$AFFI xin the grammar).[3] Though the mechanics of this approach differ from what is assumed in McCarthy and Prince (1993b), the two proposals share the premise that reduplicant shape is due to the grammar (albeit via morpheme-specific constraints) – and not to the lexicon.

Of course, it is perfectly *possible* to use a template in an optimality analysis. (4) and (5) show how this would work for the same case we have just discussed. The reduplicating prefix in question, X, is associated underlyingly with metrical structure – a monomoraic syllable template. In turn, the grammar is adjusted such that instead of stipulating that X is a light syllable, we now stipulate that underlying structure must be parsed, i.e., must surface. Reduplication is the chosen means of ensuring that the metrical structure dominates actual segmental material, a precondition for being parsed.[4]

(4) A templatic account of the same kind of reduplication
   Lexical entry for prefix, X: $[\sigma_\mu]_{[\text{RED}]}$
   Added to grammar: PARSE   Preserve input structure
                                                     in output
                                   *STRUC   Structure is prohibited
   Removed from grammar: $X=\sigma_\mu$

As shown in (5), PARSE distinguishes winning candidate (a) from losing candidate (b). PARSE outranks *STRUC, which ensures that no *more* than a light syllable is copied. If it were, as in losing candidate (c), additional metrical structure would have to be assigned to the excess material.

(5) Ranking: PARSE ≫ *STRUC (The reduplicant is exactly one light syllable)

input	/ $\sigma_{\mu[\text{RED}]}$ + kapo/	PARSE	*STRUC
a. ☞	<u>ka</u>-kapo		*σσσ
b.	<σ_μ>kapo	*!	*σσ
c.	<u>kapo</u>-kapo		*!σσσσ

The templatic analysis has a simpler grammar[5] than the nontemplatic one, by virtue of not requiring the morpheme-specific constraint that X is a light syllable; however, by the same token, it has a more complicated lexicon – the usual tradeoff.

In conclusion, we have seen that the same results can be achieved regardless of whether the prosodic content of the reduplicative morpheme is underlying metrical structure (a template which must be PARSEd), or is encoded in the grammar (as a constraint which must be satisfied). The equivalence of the two analyses shows that, at least in this simple type of example, templates are not logically necessary.[6]

For now, however, the goal is simply to set the stage for the analysis of Turkish stress. We have seen that there is good reason to doubt the need for underlying metrical structure in reduplication. Of course, this conclusion would be even more interesting if we could show that underlying metrical structure is unnecessary *generally* in phonological theory. From this perspective, we will examine a large body of data from Turkish stress, comparing an account which employs underlying metrical structure with one that does not. I will argue that the two types of analysis are not equivalent in explanatory power, and that the analysis using underlying metrical structure is superior. The conclusion will be, then, that the template-cum-object exists; it is not possible – yet – to eliminate it entirely from phonological theory.

2. Turkish

Turkish stress has been discussed in the literature for a long time. Prominent works analyzing different parts of the system are listed in (6); several have led to important theoretical claims.[7] However, none has attempted to analyze the full system. Thus one finds disparate and incompatible analyses of different aspects of Turkish stress. An aim of this chapter is to fit it all together.

(6) Literature analyzing Turkish stress: Lees (1961); Swift (1963); Lewis (1967); Foster (1970); Lightner (1978); Underhill (1976); Sezer (1981); Kardestuncer (1982); Poser (1984); Hameed (1985); Kaisse (1985); Dobrovolsky (1986); Hammond (1986); Kaisse (1986); Halle and Vergnaud (1987); Barker (1989); Kiparsky (1991); Idsardi (1992); Hayes (1995)

In (7) I list the stress-related phenomena of Turkish known to me. The phenomena in the right-hand column will not be treated here, either because they are too straightforward to be interesting (the case with compound stress and derived diminutive stress) or because the data are unclear.[8] We will thus be looking only at the five phenomena in the left-hand column.

(7)

Phenomena accounted for in this chapter	Phenomena not dealt with in this chapter
Final stress	Compound stress
Sezer stress	Stress of derived diminutive adjectives
Prestressing suffixes	Stress of adverbs in -en/an
Stressed suffixes	Vocative stress
Stressed roots	Secondary stress

3. Two productive patterns

Turkish exhibits two distinct and productive patterns of stress assignment. Each has its own morphological domain, and each is assigned by a different subgrammar, or cophonology, of Turkish. One pattern, imposed by the word-level cophonology, assigns final stress. The other, imposed by a stem-level cophonology, assigns a pattern of nonfinal stress termed here the "Sezer" pattern, after its discoverer, Engin Sezer (Sezer 1981). I will present each in turn.

(8) a. Sezer stress   assigned by Sezer stem cophonology
    b. Final stress   assigned by Word cophonology

(For recent discussion of cophonologies (subgrammars) in Optimality Theory see Itô and Mester 1995 and Inkelas, Orgun and Zoll 1997.)

3.1 Sezer (stems)

The Sezer pattern is imposed on place names and some borrowings. It is unfailingly nonfinal:

(9) Sezer stress pattern
    If the antepenultimate syllable is heavy (H) *and* the penultimate syllable is light (L), stress the antepenultimate syllable; otherwise, stress the penultimate syllable (Sezer 1981)

The pattern is illustrated in (10) on monomorphemic Sezer stems, grouped according to the weight of their antepenultimate and penultimate syllables. (The weight of the final syllable is irrelevant to the placement of stress.) Note that the Sezer pattern is imposed on names from other languages even when the stress in the source language is on a different syllable, as in *Ar.kán.sas* (from *Árkansas*) and *Santamoníka* (from *Santa Mónica*).

(10) Syllabic composition	Sezer stress pattern
...H H́ σ	İs.tán.bul, An.tál.ya, Hakʸ.kʸá:.ri,
	Ay.zɨn.hó:.ver, Kil.man.yá:.ro, Ar.kán.sas
...H́ L σ	Án.ka.ra, ša.mán.dɨra "buoy";
	Ka.li.fór.ni.ya, Mér.ji.mek, Ból.va.din,
	mán.di.ra "farm"
...L H́ σ	E.dír.ne, Va.šínk.ton, Ha.li.kár.nas,
	Ka.díl.lak
...L Ĺ σ	A.dá.na, İn.di.ya.na.pó.lis,
	Pa.pa.do.pú.los, Ke.né.di, O.ré.gon,
	Santamoníka

The productivity of the Sezer stress pattern is revealed by its applicability to derived stems. As shown in (11), derived words which do not normally exhibit Sezer stress do shift to the Sezer pattern when used as place names (Sezer 1981: 67; Inkelas, Orgun and Zoll 1997):[9]

(11)	Derived adjective (final stress)			Used as place name (Sezer stress)
...H H σ	kan.dil.-lí	"oil lamp-with"	>	Kan.díl.li
	ay.ran-ǰí	"yogurt drink-AGT (=yogurt drink seller)"	>	Ay.rán.ǰɨ
	kuz.gun-ǰúk	"raven-DIM"	>	Kuz.gún.ǰuk
...H L σ	sir.ke-ǰí	"vinegar-AGT (=vinegar seller)"	>	Sír.ke.ǰi
	tor.ba-lí	"bag-with"	>	Tór.ba.lɨ
...L H σ	ka.vak-lí	"poplar-with"	>	Ka.vák.lɨ
	ku.lak-síz	"ear-without"	>	Ku.lák.sɨz
...L L σ	o.va-ǰɨ́k	"valley-DIM"	>	O.vá.ǰɨk
	bo.ya-ǰí	"paint-AGT (=painter)"	>	Bo.yá.ǰi

3.2 Final (words)

The other productive pattern, final stress, exemplified in (12), is found in monomorphemic and suffixed words (not containing Sezer stems). Regardless of the number of suffixes, stress is unfailingly final. Because we will later see morpheme-specific perturbations in this pattern, let us refer to the morphemes in words showing final stress as neutral.

(12) Final stress: words containing only neutral morphemes

a. elmá   "apple"
   elma-lár   "apple-PL"
   elma-lar-dán   "apple-PL-ABL"
b. patlɨǰán   "eggplant"
   patlɨǰan-ím   "eggplant-1SG.POSS"
   patlɨǰan-ɨm-á   "eggplant-1SG.POSS-DAT"
c. gít   "go"
   gid-ér   "go-AOR"
   git-melí   "go-NEC"
d. yap   "do"
   yap-sín   "do-3SG.IMP"
   yap-tɨ-nɨ́z   "do-PAST-2PL"

e. gél   "come"
   gel-eǰék   "come-FUT"
   gel-eǰek-lér   "come-FUT-PL"
   gel-elím   "come-1PL.SUBJ"
f. tekmé   "kick (n.)"
   tekme-lé   "kick-VBL (v.)"
   tekme-le-dí   "kick-VBL-PAST"

3.3 Sezer stems in longer words: Sezer stress prevails

The word-level and Sezer stem cophonologies are not independent; in fact, Sezer stems can be included in longer words. When this occurs, the word as a whole inherits the stress of its Sezer stem. (13) shows Sezer stems combining with neutral suffixes which normally take stress when word-final. Here, however, the suffixes are unstressed; stress surfaces on the Sezer stem.

(13) a. Sezer stem + one neutral suffix: Sezer stress prevails
        [mándɨra]-da   "farm-LOC"   cf. araba-dá   "car-LOC"
        [Ánkara]-dan   "Ankara-ABL"   cf. araba-dán   "car-ABL"
        [Kandíl-li]-ye   "Kandilli-DAT"   cf. araba-yá   "car-DAT"
     b. Sezer stem + two neutral suffixes
        [mándɨra]-lar-da   "farm-PL-LOC"
     c. Sezer stem + four neutral suffixes
        [Ánkara]-lɨ-laš-tɨr-dɨ "Ankara-of-become-CAUS-PAST
                                 (=caused to become ones from A.)"

In sum, it appears that final stress is a default, imposed at the word level on strings not possessing stress from another source. The Sezer stem cophonology is one such source. Later, we will see other sources for nonfinal stress.

The diagram in (14) illustrates the interaction between the Sezer and word-level cophonologies (assuming the model of monotonic cyclicity, following Orgun 1994b). As shown in the left-hand example, the output of the Sezer-stem level is the input to the word level. In words not containing a Sezer stem, such as the example on the right, the entire string is input directly to the word-level cophonology for purposes of stress assignment.[10]

(14) Output of Sezer cophonology=input to word cophonology:

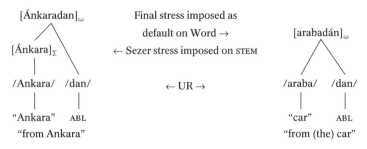

There is one important systematic exception to the generalization that Sezer stems block final stress in words containing them. As observed by Kaisse (1985: 204) and illustrated in (15), monosyllabic Sezer stems never retain stress when suffixed. Instead they permit a following neutral suffix to receive final stress at the word level.

(15) Bon-dán   "Bonn-ABL"   (cf. Adána-dan)
      Of-tá   "Of-LOC"   (cf. İstánbul-da)
      Kars-á   "Kars-DAT"   (cf. Kuláksɨz-a)

This is an important fact to keep in mind. We will return to it later.

4. Analyses of regular patterns

We turn now to optimality analyses of the two patterns we have just seen, starting with the Sezer stem cophonology.

4.1 Sezer stem cophonology

The Sezer stress pattern has the properties in (16): each stem has one stress, stress is normally penultimate, and stress is antepenultimate in case the penult is light and the antepenult, heavy.

(16) Properties of Sezer stress to be captured

One stress per stem

Nonfinality: stress is normally penultimate ⎤ Stress occurs in
                                             ⎬ final three-syllable
Quantity-sensitivity: stress shifts to   ⎰ window
antepenult in /… H L σ/ stems

The first property is easily captured using standard constraints in Optimality Theory (Prince and Smolensky 1993), shown in (17). HAVE-FT requires the domain to contain at least one foot; *STRUC, which militates against structure in general, ensures that the domain will contain at *most* one foot.[11]

(17) Constraints governing one-stress-per-domain:
HAVE-FT
The domain must contain a foot
*STRUC
Structure is prohibited
PARSE-SYL
Syllables must be parsed into feet

By ranking HAVE-FT above *STRUC and PARSE-SYL, as illustrated in (18), we ensure that exactly one foot occurs in each Sezer stem.

(18) Sezer stem cophonology: HAVE-FT ≫ *STRUC ≫ PARSE-SYL

	[Papadopulos]$_\Sigma$	HAVE-FT	*STRUC	PARSE-SYL
a. ☞	(x .) Pa.pa.do.pu.los		*	***
b.	(x .)(x .)(x) Pa.pa.do.pu.los		**!*	
c.	Pa.pa.do.pu.los	*!		******

There are numerous equally adequate ways to capture the nonfinality and quantity-sensitivity of Sezer stress. One approach would be, following Barker (1989) and Kiparsky (1991), to assume that the stress foot implicated in Sezer stress is iambic. This is consistent with its apparent quantity-sensitivity, a hallmark of iambic feet. On such an account, the final syllable would be "extrametrical" (perhaps by virtue of a NONFI NALITY constraint on stress feet, along the lines of Prince and Smolensky 1993) and an iambic foot would be built over the antepenultimate and penultimate syllables. Exactly when the antepenult is heavy and the penult light, however, the iambic foot would be disfavored by virtue of the complete mismatch between syllable weight and foot headedness. In this case, foot reversal is the preferred option; a trochaic foot is built instead. The resulting antepenultimate stress pattern is seen in words like *šamandira*:

(19) Iambic analysis

	(. x)	(. x)	(. x)
Iambic foot	İn.di.ya.na.po.lis	Ay.zɨn.ho:.ver	E.dir.ne

	(x .)
Trochaic foot	ša.man.dɨra

A closely related analysis would assign a ternary, left-headed foot to words like *šamandɨra*, rather than displacing the binary foot leftward; I see no way to choose between the two analyses.

The alternative analysis considered – and adopted here – is trochaic, fitting better with the trochaic foot used elsewhere in the system. As summarized in (20), a trochaic foot is assigned at the right edge of the stem (following Kaisse 1985, 1986; Hayes 1995: 262), capturing the fact that most Sezer stems have penultimate stress. Exactly when a final trochee would be headed by a light syllable and preceded by a heavy syllable, however, the foot occurs one syllable to the left – gaining a heavy syllable for its head:

(20) Trochaic analysis

	(x .)	(x .)	(x .)
Final trochee:	İn.di.ya.na.po.lis	Ay.zɨn.ho:.ver	E.dir.ne

	(x .)
Penultimate trochee:	ša.man.dɨra

Implementing the trochaic analysis requires three additional constraints. The first two are stated in (21). TROCHAIC requires stress feet to be trochaic. The second constraint, FINAL-FT, requires the stem to end in a foot.

(21) ◆TROCHAIC   ALIGN(ó, L, Foot, L)   Feet are trochaic
     FINAL-FT   Align(Domain, R,   The domain end
                  Foot, R)   coincides with a foot end

The diamond preceding the trochaic constraint in (21) signifies that the constraint is never violated in the cophonology under discussion, here the Sezer cophonology. I will use this convention throughout the chapter.

(22) Convention
     Diamonded constraints are unviolated in the cophonology under discussion.

Together, the constraints in (21) enforce penultimate stress in Sezer stems, as illustrated in (23).

(23) ◆Trochaic, Final-Ft together enforce penultimate stress

	[Adana]$_\Sigma$	◆Trochaic	Final-Ft
a. ☞	(x .) A.da.na		
b.	(x .) A.da.na		*!
c.	(. x) A.da.na	*!	

To capture the fact that stress appears on the antepenultimate syllable of a Sezer stem exactly when the penult is light and the antepenult is heavy, we introduce a new constraint, named "Contour," which baldly prohibits a sequence of heavy unstressed syllable followed by stressed light syllable. (Contour can be stated in terms of alignment (McCarthy and Prince 1993a) if, extrapolating from precedents in Prince and Smolensky 1993: 40, 43, 52, 57, we permit negative alignment constraints.)

(24) Constraint enforcing (local) quantity-sensitivity

Contour $*\sigma_{\mu\mu}\,\acute\sigma_\mu$ No heavy syllable may immediately
                                precede a stressed light syllable

[i.e., No-Align($\sigma_{\mu\mu}$, R, $\acute\sigma_\mu$, L)]

As illustrated in (25), Contour outranks Final-Ft, thus allowing a foot to be "displaced" leftwards whenever doing so prevents the violation of Contour. This is illustrated in the tableau with respect to *šamandıra*, a Sezer stem with a light penult and heavy antepenult. Candidate (b), with a final trochaic foot, violates Contour, and thus is rejected; candidate (a) violates only the lower-ranked Final-Ft, and therefore wins.

(25) Sezer cophonology: Contour ≫ Final-Ft

	[šamandıra]$_\Sigma$	[... H L σ]	Contour	Final-Ft
a. ☞	(x .) šamandıra	[... Ĥ L σ]		*
b.	(x .) šamandıra	[... H Ĺ σ]	*!H Ĺ	

The Contour constraint correctly predicts that stress can only depart by one syllable from its expected penultimate position. To see this, consider the word *Indiyanapólis*. Its initial syllable, five removed from the right edge, is heavy, while all other nonfinal syllables are light. The actual pronunciation of this Sezer stem has penultimate stress, not initial stress, even though an initial trochee would have a heavy syllable for its head. Feet cannot shift leftward indefinitely to gain a heavy head:

(26) a. final foot   (x .)

                   İn.di.ya.na.po.lis

     b. very left-shifted foot   (x   .)

                   *İn.di. ya.na.po.lis

As illustrated in the tableau in (27), our analysis correctly generates this result. Because the antepenultimate syllable (*na*) of *Indiyanapolis* is light, penultimate stress poses no threat to CONTOUR; hence there is no motivation for the stress-foot to dislocate.[12] Even though the left-shifted trochaic foot in candidate (b) has a heavy head, it does not fare any better than the final stress-foot in terms of CONTOUR; it simply gratuitously violates FINAL-FT, and is thus rejected.

(27) If antepenult is light, then a final foot cannot violate CONTOUR: no stress shift

	[İndiyanapolis]$_\Sigma$	CONTOUR	FINAL-FT
a. ☞	(x .) [... L Ĺ ...] İn.di.ya.na.po.lis		
b.	(x .) [ʜ́ ...] İn.di. ya.na.po.lis		*!

Stress shift is also correctly blocked when the penult is heavy, as in the Sezer stem *İstánbul* in (28). Here again, penultimate stress does not violate CONTOUR. Like the stem in (27), *İstánbul*, in (28), has penultimate stress.

(28) If penult is heavy, then a final foot cannot violate CONTOUR: no stress shift

	[İstanbul]$_\Sigma$	CONTOUR	FINAL-FT
a. ☞	(x .) [... H ʜ́ ...] İs.tan.bul		
b.	(x .) [ʜ́ ...] İs.tan.bul		*!

There is one fact not yet accounted for on this analysis, however, namely that a stress foot can displace only in the leftward direction. Consider the Sezer stem *Mérjimek*, in (29), which has a heavy-light-heavy syllable sequence and antepenultimate surface stress. If penultimate stress were assigned, as in candidate (d), CONTOUR would be fatally violated; hence, stress clearly must occur elsewhere. What we want is for it to shift one syllable to the left; *Mérjimek* has antepenultimate stress. However, our constraints incorrectly predict it to displace *rightward* to the final syllable. Candidate (b), with a final degenerate foot, is the only candidate to satisfy both CONTOUR and FINAL-FT in this tableau. The candidate that we *want* to win, namely (a), not only loses to (b), but also ties with (c), a catalectic candidate with unwanted final stress.

(29)   CONTOUR ≫ FINAL-FT incorrectly predicts final stress on …H-L-H Sezer stems:

	[Merjimek]$_\Sigma$	CONTOUR	FINAL-FT	
a.	(x .) Mer.ji.mek		*!	[This one *should* win: *Mérjimek*]
b. ☞	(x) Mer.ji.mek			
c.	(x .) Mer.ji.mek [σ]		*!	
d.	(x .) Mer.ji.mek	*!ʜ Ĺ		

To solve this problem, we must somehow reject candidates (29b) and (c). This means ruling out both degenerate feet, as in (b), and catalexis, as in (c), in the Sezer cophonology. To do so, we invoke the quite standard constraints (both from Prince and Smolensky 1993) in (30). ◆ FILL prohibits null syllables, effectively prohibiting catalexis, while ◆ FT-BIN requires feet to be binary, effectively prohibiting degenerate feet.[13] Both are unviolated in the Sezer cophonology.

(30) ◆ FILL   Syllables dominate segmental material
      ◆ FT-BIN   Feet are binary

(31), which is parallel to (29), illustrates the effects of making both constraints inviolable: no stress foot may be headed by the final syllable in the Sezer cophonology. This new constraint set correctly rejects candidates (b) and (c), leaving (a) as the clear winner.

(31)

	[Mer.ǰi.mek]$_\Sigma$	♦FILL	♦FT-BIN	CONTOUR	FINAL-FT
a. ☞	(x .) Mer.ǰi.mek				*
b.	(x) Mer.ǰi.mek	*!			
c.	(x .) Mer.ǰi.mek [σ]	*!			*
d.	(x .) Mer.ǰi.mek			*!H Ĺ	

A pleasing consequence of ranking ♦FT-BIN and ♦FILL so highly is that we can now explain the puzzling behavior of monosyllabic Sezer stems. Recall, as shown in the data in (32) (repeated from (15)), that monosyllabic Sezer stems do not retain stress when combined with neutral suffixes (Kaisse 1985, 1986). Instead, stress surfaces in word-final position.[14]

(32) Bon-dán   "Bonn-ABL"   (cf. İstánbul-dan)

This fact follows automatically from the inviolability of ♦FILL and ♦FT-BIN in the Sezer cophonology. Because these stems are monosyllabic, the only foot that could possibly be built on them would either be catalectic or degenerate; since neither option is available in the Sezer cophonology, these stems leave the Sezer cophonology without any stress at all (for a similar analysis, see Barker 1989). This is shown by the following tableau. The winning candidate, (a), is the one with no stress-foot.

(33) Sezer cophonology: ♦FILL, ♦FT-BIN ≫ HAVE-FT

	[Bon]$_\Sigma$	♦FILL	♦FT-BIN	HAVE-FT
a. ☞	Bon			*
b.	(x) Bon		*!	
c.	(x .) Bon [σ]	*!		

We will see shortly that as a consequence of acquiring no foot at the Sezer level, monosyllabic Sezer stems are stressed only at the word level, where the final pattern prevails.

(34) summarizes the constraints invoked in the analysis thus far.

(34) Unviolated   Violable (ranked where relevant)
♦TROCHAIC   HAVE-FT ≫ *STRUC ≫ PARSE-SYL
♦ FILL   CONTOUR ≫ FINAL-FT
♦ FT-BIN

We have now captured the pattern of stress within Sezer stems in a relatively simple fashion, using only trochaic feet. The next target is the word-level pattern, final stress.

4.2 Word cophonology

One thing the word and Sezer patterns have in common is that only one stress is permitted within each domain. The word cophonology thus requires the same constraint ranking seen earlier to achieve the one-stress-per-domain pattern.

(35) Word cophonology
♦ HAVE-FT (≫ FT-BIN, *STRUC)

In the word cophonology, however, ♦HAVE-FT is never violated: each word has a stress.

The word cophonology differs from the Sezer cophonology in imposing a pattern of fixed final stress. There are myriad ways to generate word-final stress, and virtually all of them have been proposed in the literature. A variety is listed in (36). Any of these would work reasonably well for Turkish.

(36) Some ways to generate final stress
    a. Right-headed unbounded iambic foot (Kaisse 1986; Halle and Vergnaud 1987)
    b. Final binary iambic foot
    c. Final grid mark (no foot) (Barker 1989; Hayes 1995: 61)
    d. Final binary trochee + catalexis (Kiparsky 1991; Kager 1993, 1995)

Of these analyses, (d) is optimal – and not merely because the trochaic foot it employs is useful elsewhere in the system. The iambic analyses (36a) and (36b) are highly disfavored in their own right because of the many final-stressed words in Turkish with a heavy penult. In the case of a word like *elma* "apple", for example, such an analysis would have to posit the undesirable "anti-iamb" (Prince 1990), with maximal mismatch between syllable weight and foot headedness.

As before, I choose to implement the trochaic analysis (36d), on the grounds that the trochee is the only foot which can capture the entire stress system of Turkish. A word with final catalexis and final stress is illustrated below:

(37)   (x   .)
        araba [σ]   [arabá]   "car"

The analysis of final stress is fairly simple, and I will not dwell on the details. The essential idea is that an alignment constraint, FINAL-STR, requires the word-final syllable to be stressed.

(38) FINAL-STR   Align(Domain, R, ó, R)

This constraint, when combined with the inviolable ♦TROCHAIC and ♦FT-BIN constraints seen earlier, requires catalexis, the existence of a phonetically null syllable (or grid beat) to the right of the word. Catalexis has been proposed, for Turkish and other languages, by Kiparsky (1991) and Kager (1992, 1993, 1995).[15] It permits a disyllabic trochee to be headed by the word-final syllable. In order to achieve catalexis, FILL, the constraint against null syllables, must be ranked low at the word level.[16]

(39) Word cophonology
     FINAL-STR ≫ FILL

The chart in (40) shows how this constraint ranking selects the proper outcome for a neutral root in combination with a neutral suffix. The winning candidate, (a), violates FILL once by possessing a single catalectic syllable, but it satisfies all the higher-ranked constraints: its foot is trochaic, binary, and is headed by the word-final syllable.

(40)

	[araba-da]$_\omega$ "car-LOC"	◆TROCHAIC	◆FT-BIN	FINAL-STR	FILL
a. ☞	(x .) a.ra.ba.da.[σ]				*
b.	(. x) a.ra.ba.da	*!			
c.	(x) a.ra.ba.da		*!		
d.	(x .) a.ra.ba.da			*!	

The FINAL-STR constraint should not be confused with the FINAL-FT constraint, which we saw was highly ranked in the Sezer cophonology. (41) compares the two and (42) gives their respective rankings in the two cophonologies:[17]

(41) FINAL-STR   Align(Domain, R, ó, R)
     FINAL-FT   Align(Domain, R, Ft, R)

(42)
(i) Word cophonology   FINAL-STR ≫ FINAL-FT
    (Stress is final, not penultimate)

	[araba]$_\omega$	FINAL-STR	FINAL-FT
a.	(x .) a.ra.ba	*!	
b. ☞	(x .) a.ra.ba [σ]		*

(ii) Sezer cophonology   FINAL-FT ≫ FINAL-STR
     (Stress is penultimate, not final)

	[Adana]$_\Sigma$	FINAL-FT	FINAL-STR
a. ☞	(x .) A.da.na		*
b.	(x .) A.da.na [σ]	*!	

4.3 Sezer stems in words: input wins

As stated earlier, and reschematized below, the output of the Sezer-stem cophonology serves as input to the word-level cophonology. Thus any interaction between Sezer stress and the final pattern is to be captured in the word-level cophonology.

(43) Output of Sezer cophonology=input to word-level cophonology

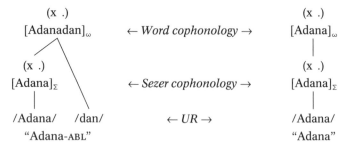

The generalization is that any Sezer stress existing in the input to the word level is preserved in the output. To capture this, we invoke the familiar constraint PARSE, here localized to the foot.[18]

(44) PARSE-FT

Preserve, in the output, any stress feet that are in the input

In the word cophonology, PARSE-FT outranks the FINAL-STR constraint, such that it is more important to parse an input foot than to build a new foot whose head is word-final. The option of doing both is, of course, ruled out by the constraints enforcing one stress per word.

(45) Word cophonology

PARSE-FT ≫ FINAL-STR

The chart in (46) illustrates the retention of stress on an unsuffixed Sezer stem, *Adána*, in the word cophonology: PARSE-FT forces the retention of the input foot, and the word-final syllable goes unstressed in the winning candidate.

(46)

	(x .) [[A.da.na]$_\Sigma$]$_\omega$	"Adana"	PARSE-FT	FINAL-STR
a. ☞	(x .) A.da.na [Adána]			*
b.	‹(x .)›(x .) A.da.na [σ] [Adaná]		*!	

The chart in (47) illustrates the same phenomenon, this time with a suffixed Sezer stem. Again, due to PARSE-FT, Sezer stress prevails over final stress under neutral suffixation (see (13)):

(47)

	(x .) [[A.da.na]$_\Sigma$ -dan]$_\omega$ "Adana-ABL"	PARSE-FT	FINAL-STR
a. ☞	(x .) A.da.na.dan [Adánadan]		*
b.	‹(x .)› (x .) A.da.na.dan [σ] [Adanadán]	*!	

In summary, input feet always prevail over "default" constraints on foot placement in the word cophonology. The constraint ranking guaranteeing this result is summarized below:

(48) Word cophonology: input wins
    ♦ HAVE-FT ≫ *STRUC   (The word must have one foot)
    PARSE-FT ≫ FINAL-STR   (Preserve an input [i.e. a Sezer] foot
                             rather than assign final stress)

This view of the Sezer–word level interface explains why monosyllabic Sezer stems, such as those in (49) and (50), permit the word-final stress pattern in words containing them. Recall from (15) and (33) that (due to FT-BIN and FILL) monosyllabic Sezer stems do not acquire a stress-foot in the Sezer cophonology. Because they are input to the word-level cophonology without metrical structure, PARSE-FT is inapplicable and thus does not hinder the imposition of final stress (by FINAL-STR).

(49)

	[[Of]$_\Sigma$]$_\omega$	♦ HAVE-FT	PARSE-FT	FINAL-STR
a. ☞	(x .) Of [σ]			
b.	Of	*!		*!

Both the unsuffixed monosyllabic Sezer stem in (49) and the suffixed one in (50) receive final stress.

(50)

	$[[Of]_\Sigma\text{-tan}]_\omega$	◆HAVE-FT	PARSE-FT	FINAL-STR
a. ☞	(x .) Of.tan [σ]			
b.	Of.tan	*!		*
c.	(x .) Of.tan			*!

In summary, Sezer stems disrupt the normal word-final stress pattern by virtue of possessing a stress foot in the input to the word cophonology. Only those Sezer stems not possessing such a foot allow the final-stress pattern to emerge.

Let us summarize the analysis arrived at so far. We have invoked ten constraints altogether, and they are ranked differently in the two cophonologies we have motivated. The constraints, and their respective rankings, are given below:

(51) List of all constraints invoked so far, and their rough definitions (diamonded constraints are violated in neither cophonology)

◆FT-BIN   Each foot is binary
◆TROCHAIC   Each foot has initial stress
CONTOUR $^*\sigma_{\mu\mu}\ \acute{\sigma}_\mu$
FILL   Syllables aren't null (i.e., no catalexis)
FINAL-FT   The right edge of the domain coincides with the right edge of a foot
FINAL-STR   The domain-final syllable is stressed
HAVE-FT   The domain has a foot
PARSE-FT   Each foot in the input is present in the output
PARSE-SYL   Each syllable belongs to a foot
*STRUC   No structure (evaluated here only with respect to feet)

(52) Summary of constraint ranking in Sezer cophonology

Unviolated	Crucially ranked		Irrelevant (so far)
FILL FT-BIN TROCHAIC	HAVE-FT — *STRUC — CONTOUR — FINAL-FT	⎧ PARSE-SYL ⎨ ⎩ FINAL-STR	PARSE-FT

(53) Summary of constraint ranking in word cophonology

Unviolated   Crucially ranked

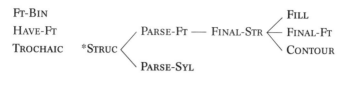

FT-BIN
HAVE-FT
TROCHAIC   *STRUC
                              PARSE-FT — FINAL-STR
                              PARSE-SYL

FILL
FINAL-FT
CONTOUR

5. Exceptions: morphemes which interrupt Sezer and/or final patterns

We now turn to exceptional, or nonneutral, morphemes. These disrupt the regular patterning we have seen thus far. As stated in (54), both suffixes and roots occur in this category. Prestressing suffixes, some of which are listed in (54a), place stress on the immediately preceding syllable. These can be monosyllabic, disyllabic, or trisyllabic.[19] Initially stressed suffixes, listed in (54b), are, by contrast, always disyllabic. There are no initially stressed monosyllabic suffixes. Finally, some examples of irregularly stressed roots are listed in (54c) and (54d).[20] Those in (54c) have fixed penultimate stress; those in (54d), fixed antepenultimate stress. All speakers have exceptional roots of this kind, though exactly which roots are exceptional varies across speakers.

(54) Nonneutral (stress-affecting) morphemes (uppercase letters indicate harmonic vowels):
a. Pre-stressing suffixes:

1 syllable	-mE	(NEG)
	-mI	(INTERR)
	-(y)lE	(INSTR/COM)
	-(y)In	(2.PL.IMP)
	-j̇E	(ADV)
	-j̇E	(MIT)
2 syllables	-leyin	(ADV)
3 syllables	-j̇EsInE	(ADV)

b. Initially stressed suffixes:

2 syllables	-Iyor	(PROG)
	-ErEk	("by")
	-Inj̇E	("when")

c. Sample penult-stressed roots (contents of this set vary across speakers)

ab.lú.ka	"blockade"	Pom.pé.i	"Pompeii"
Af.rí.ka	"Africa"	šev.ró.le	"Chevrolet"
Av.rú.pa	"Europe"	tar.há.na	"dried curd"
Mek.sí.ka	"Mexico"	Üs.kǘ.dar	(place name)
pen.ǰé.re	"window"		

d. Sample antepenult-stressed roots (contents of this set vary across speakers)

Ér.zin.ǰan	(place name)
Kas.tá.mo.nu	(place name)
pé.nal.tɨ	"penalty kick"
Zón.gul.dak	(place name)

The effect of these morphemes on the patterns we have seen is straightforward: the stress of nonneutral morphemes overrides both Sezer and final stress. To see this, we will examine all possible contexts in which nonneutral morphemes occur:

(55) a. Nonneutral morpheme within Sezer stem
b. Nonneutral morpheme within word (no Sezer stem)
c. More than one nonneutral morpheme within word (no Sezer stem)
d. Sezer stem + one nonneutral morpheme
e. Sezer stem + more than one nonneutral morpheme

The generalization is relatively simple:

(56) Generalization
Within a domain (word or Sezer stem), stress of leftmost nonneutral morpheme prevails; however, stress of Sezer stem prevails within word.

Let us now look at the data, case by case. We start with Sezer stems containing a nonneutral morpheme.

5.1 Nonneutral morphemes within Sezer stems: nonneutral wins

Sezer stems can be monomorphemic, composed of a single nonneutral root, as illustrated in (57). In such cases, the stress of the nonneutral root overrides the expected Sezer stress.

(57) Nonneutral roots as place names: Sezer stress is overridden

Af.rí.ka	"Africa"	*Áfrika
Av.rú.pa	"Europe"	*Ávrupa
Kas.tá.mo.nu	(place name)	*Kastamónu
Zón.gul.dak	(place name)	*Zongúldak

The same is true of derived place names containing nonneutral morph-emes. As shown in (58), adjectives formed by the prestressing suffix -ǰe/-ǰa can be used as place names, meaning they can form Sezer stems:

(58) Derived adjective   > used as place name (i.e. as Sezer stem)

süt-lǘ-ǰe	"milk-with-MIT (=sort of milky)"	Sütlǘǰe	(*Sútlüǰe)
kan-lɨ́-ǰa	"blood-with-MIT (=sort of bloody)"	Kanlɨ́ǰa	(*Kánlɨǰa)
čam-lɨ́-ǰa	"pine-with-MIT (=sort of piney)"	Čamlɨ́ǰa	(*Čámlɨǰa)

Each derived adjective in (58) has a heavy antepenultimate syllable and light penult, such that antepenultimate Sezer stress would be expected in the place name. However, these forms retain the penultimate stress dictated by the prestressing suffix they contain. Compare the adjectives-cum-Sezer stems in (58) to the derived adjective with all neutral morph-emes in (59) which, as we have already seen in (11), does shift to the Sezer pattern when used as a place name:

(59) Derived adjective with only neutral morphemes *does* shift to Sezer stress as place name

torba-lɨ́ "bag-with"   > Tórbalɨ (place name) (*Torbalɨ́)

From these data we can conclude that in the Sezer cophonology, the source for morpheme-specific stress outranks the constraints crucial to establishing the Sezer pattern (specifically CONTOUR, FINAL-FT).

(60) Sezer cophonology
Morpheme-specific stress prevails over Sezer stress

5.2 Nonneutral morpheme within word: nonneutral wins

When a word contains one nonneutral morpheme – and no Sezer stem – the stress associated with that morpheme overrides the expected final stress. This is illustrated in the data in (61a) and (61b). Compare the words in the left-hand data column, which contain a nonneutral suffix, to those in the right-hand column, which contain only neutral morphemes. The words in the right-hand column display the expected final stress pattern, but those in the left-hand column show the stress dictated by their nonneutral suffix.

(61)

a. Prestressing suffixes override final stress in word cophonology:

Suffix	Example	Gloss	Compare: same root with neutral suffix	
-mE	tekmelé-me	"kick-NEG"	tekmele-dí	"kick-PAST"
-mI	arabá-mɨ	"car-INTERR"	araba-lár	"car-PL"
-(y)lE	kedí-yle	"cat-INSTR/COM"	kedi-lér	"cat-PL"
	patlɨján-la	"eggplant-INSTR/COM"	patlɨjan-lár	"eggplant-PL"
-(y)In	yáp-ɨn	"do-2PL IMP"	yap-tí	"do-PAST"
	tekmelé-yin	"kick-2PL IMP"	tekmele-dí	"kick-PAST"
-ĵE	güzél-ĵe	"beautiful-ADV"	güzel-lík	"beautiful-NOM"
	insán-ĵa	"human-ADV"	insan-lɨk	"human-NOM"
-ĵE	tat-lí-ĵa	"taste-with-MIT"	tat-lɨ-lɨk	"taste-with-NOM"
-leyin	akšám-leyin	"evening-at"	akšam-lár	"evening-PL"
-ĵEsInE	hayván-ĵasɨna	"animal-like"	hayvan-lár	"animal-PL"

b. Stressed suffixes override final stress in word cophonology:

Suffix	Example	Gloss	Compare: same root with neutral suffix	
-íyor	yap-íyor	"do-PROG"	yap-malí	"do-NEC"
	gid-íyor	"go-PROG"	gid-eĵék	"go-FUT"
-ÉrEk	gid-érek	"go-by (=by going)"	git-melí	"go-NEC"
	yap-árak	"do-by (=by doing)"	yap-aĵák	"do-FUT"
-ínĵE	gel-ínĵe	"go-when"	gel-eĵék	"come-FUT"
	yap-ínĵa	"do-when"	yap-malí	"do-NEC"

The nonneutral suffix needn't be final to have an effect on stress; (62) and (63) show that the stress of a nonneutral suffix prevails even if neutral suffixes follow in the word. In each of these examples, the nonneutral morpheme is underlined:

(62) Prestressing suffix (underlined) + neutral suffix: prestressing suffix prevails

    a. okú-<u>ma</u>-aǰak   [okúmayaǰak]   "read-NEG-FUT"
      (cf. oku-aǰák   [okuyaǰák]   "read-FUT")
    b. gít-<u>me</u>-meli   "go-NEG-NEC"
      (cf. git-melí   "go-NEC")

(63) Stressed suffix (underlined) inside neutral suffix: stress of stressed suffix prevails

    a. gel-<u>íyor</u>-sa   "come-PROG-COND"
      (cf. gel-sé   "come-COND")
    b. gel-<u>íyor</u>-sa-nɨz   "come-PROG-COND-2PL"
      (cf. gel-se-níz   "come-COND-2PL")
    c. gel-<u>íyor</u>-du   "come-PROG-PAST"
      (cf. gel-dí   "come-PAST")
    d. gel-<u>íyor</u>-du-nuz   "come-PROG-PAST-2PL"
      (cf. gel-di-níz   "come-PAST-2PL")

As expected, nonneutral (i.e., stressed) roots work the same way that nonneutral suffixes do. In (64), several stressed roots are shown alone and in combination with a neutral suffix, the Ablative; in all cases, the expected word-final stress is overridden by root stress.

(64) Stressed roots (underlined) alone or inside neutral suffixes: root stress prevails

    a. <u>tarhána</u>   "dried curd"   (cf. arabá   "car")
       <u>tarhána</u>-da   "dried curd-LOC"   (cf. araba-dá "car-LOC")
    b. <u>Kastámonu</u>   "Kastamonu"
       <u>Kastámonu</u>-dan   "Kastamonu-ABL"
    c. <u>Üskúdar</u>   "Üsküdar"
       <u>Üskúdar</u>-a   "Üsküdar-DAT"
    d. <u>penǰére</u>   "window"
       <u>penǰére</u>-ler-i   "window-PL-3POSS"

The fact that prestressing suffixes, stressed suffixes, and stressed roots all manage to override the word-final stress pattern tells us that, at the word level, the compelling force behind these morpheme-specific stresses must overpower the constraint enforcing word-final stress.

(65) Word cophonology
    Morpheme-specific stress prevails over final stress

5.3 Sezer stem + nonneutral morpheme: input wins

We have looked at what happens when a nonneutral morpheme is contained within a Sezer stem or within a word. What happens when a
Sezer stem is suffixed with a nonneutral suffix? In (66) we see two Sezer
stems followed by nonneutral suffixes – in (66a), the prestressing negative suffix, and in (66b) the initially stressed progressive, three suffixes
away from the stem. In both cases, the Sezer stem stress prevails.

(66)
   a. Sezer stem + prestressing suffix
      Ánkara   "Ankara"
      Ánkara-mɨ "Ankara-INTERR" (cf. elmá-mɨ "apple-INTERR")
   b. Sezer root + neutral suffixes + initially stressed suffix
      Ánkara-li-   "Ankara-of-become-PROG (=becoming ones from
      laš-ɨyor   Ankara)"

These facts suggest a pattern of "input wins," illustrated graphically in
(67), a diagram of (66a). In the output of the Sezer level, the stem *Ánkara*
possesses a stress foot. This foot is input to the word-level cophonology,
which evaluates the Sezer stem together with the potentially prestressing interrogative suffix. The Sezer stress is preserved.

(67) Sezer + nonneutral suffix (*-mɨ*) in word cophonology:
      Sezer (=input) wins

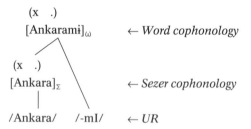

So far, we have examined stems and words containing at most one nonneutral morpheme. In such cases, the stress pattern of the nonneutral
morpheme (if any) prevails over final stress.

(68) Word-level cophonology
      Morpheme-specific stress prevails over final stress (though is itself
      prevailed over by Sezer stress)

But what happens when there is more than one nonneutral morpheme? We turn next to such cases, and uncover a scenario of "leftmost wins."

5.4 Nonneutral morphemes in combination: leftmost nonneutral wins

In (69) to (72) we see several examples of words containing more than one nonneutral morpheme (and no Sezer stem). In each case, the leftmost nonneutral morpheme, be it suffix, (69) to (71), or root, (72), determines the stress of the word as a whole. Nonneutral suffixes to the right have no effect on the stress pattern.

(69) Prestressing suffix < prestressing suffix: leftmost prestressing suffix prevails

    a. gél   "come"

       gél-me   "come-NEG"   (cf. gel-dí   "come-PAST")

       gél-me-sin   "come-NEG-   (cf. gel-eǰék-sin "come-FUT-

                  3.SG.IMP"   3.SG.IMP")

    b. arabá   "car"

       arabá-yla   "car-INSTR/COM"   (cf. araba-lár   "car-PL")

       arabá-yla-mɨ "car-INSTR/   (cf. araba-lár-mɨ "car-PL-INTERR")

                  COM-INTERR"

(70) Prestressing suffix < initially stressed suffix: prestressing suffix prevails

    a. bɨrák   "leave"

       bɨrák-ma   "leave-NEG"

       bɨrák-ma-ɨyor "leave-NEG-PROG"   (cf. bɨrak-íyor "leave-PROG")

       [bɨrákmɨyor]

    b. gél   "come"

       gél-me   "come-NEG"

       gél-me-inǰe   "come-NEG-ADV"   (cf. gel-ínǰe   "come-ADV")

       [gélmeyinǰe]

(71) Initially stressed suffix < prestressing suffix: initially stressed suffix prevails

    a. gel-íyor   "come-PROG"   (cf. gel-eǰék   "come-FUT")

       gel-íyor-mu   "come-PROG-   (cf. gel-eǰék-mi "come-FUT-

                INTERR"   INTERR")

    b. yap-árak   "do-ADV"   (cf. yap-malí   "come-NEC")

       yap-árak-mɨ "do-ADV-INTERR"   (cf. yap-malí-mɨ "come-NEC-INTERR")

(72) Stressed root < prestressing suffix (< prestressing suffix): root stress prevails

      penǰére   "window"   (cf. patlɨ́ján   "eggplant")

      penǰére-yle   "window-   (cf. patlɨ́ján-la "eggplant-

                INSTR/COM"   INSTR/COM")

      penǰére-mi   "window-INTERR"   (cf. patlɨ́ján-mɨ "eggplant-INT")

      penǰére-yle-mi "window-INSTR/   (cf. patlɨ́ján-la-mɨ "eggplant-INSTR/

                COM-INTERR")   COM-INTERR")

5.5 Sezer stem + more than one nonneutral morpheme: leftmost wins

The forms in (72), in which a stressed root surfaces with stress despite being combined with potentially prestressing suffixes, are of particular interest when compared to the data in (73). Here we find words composed of a Sezer stem plus two prestressing suffixes. In each case, the Sezer stem stress prevails – and neither suffix has an effect on the stress pattern of the word.

(73) In words with Sezer stem + two pre-stressing suffixes, stress on Sezer stem prevails

a. Adána-yla-mï   "Adana-INSTR/COM-INTERR"
b. mándïra-yla-mï   "farm-INSTR/COM-INTERR"

It is significant that roots, with idiosyncratic stress, as in (72), are behaving like Sezer stems, whose stress is predictable.

5.6 Summary

In summary, the interactions among nonneutral morphemes and productive stress patterns suggest the following: while an input foot prevails over any nonneutral morphemes within the same domain, if there is no input foot, then the leftmost nonneutral morpheme prevails.

(74) Generalization

Within a domain (word or Sezer stem), stress of leftmost nonneutral morpheme prevails over the pattern normally assigned to that domain; however, stress of Sezer stem prevails within word.

Notice that it is the stress of the leftmost nonneutral morpheme, rather than the leftmost potential stress, which prevails in the domain. To bring this point home, reconsider the examples in (75), also seen earlier. These are Sezer stems which contain nonneutral morphemes. The examples have been selected such that the nonneutral stress, which surfaces, is actually linearly to the right of where the Sezer stress would be if assigned. However, the data are consistent with the generalization in (74). The leftmost nonneutral morpheme in the Sezer stem is the one which dictates where stress goes.

(75) Actual stress (nonneutral morpheme   Outcome if Sezer stress
      underlined)   were assigned
      Kan-lï-ǰa (prestressing suffix)   *Kánlïǰa
      Üskúdar   (stressed root)   *Üsküdar

It should be noted here that "leftmost wins" is an attested pattern in Turkish even outside of irregularly stressed morphemes: in compounds, we also typically find that the first, or leftmost, word is stressed (see, e.g., Lewis 1967: 23, Swift 1963: 115–19). Thus, the generalization in (74) is not entirely unexpected.

We will now examine two approaches to the data we have seen so far. One approach utilizes underlying metrical structure to characterize the nonneutral morphemes. The other uses morpheme-specific grammatical constraints. We turn first to the grammatical approach.

6. A purely grammatical account: exceptionality by grammatical constraints

The exceptionality of the nonneutral morphemes of Turkish has to do with where stress is located in the word. Since stress is always located in the immediate vicinity of the relevant morpheme, the most suitable grammatical account within Optimality Theory is the theory of Generalized Alignment, developed by McCarthy and Prince (1993a).[21]

6.1 Alignment

Alignment constraints take the form shown below, in which one edge of some category (morphological or phonological) is aligned with some edge of another category. In the alignment constraints we will invoke for exceptional stress, a morphological "category" – actually, a specific morpheme – is aligned with a foot or stressed syllable.

(76) Generalized Alignment (McCarthy and Prince 1993a)
       Align(Cat$_1$, Edge$_1$, Cat$_2$, Edge$_2$)

       Variety of alignment constraint needed here: Align(morpheme$_i$, Edge$_i$, ó/Foot$_j$, Edge$_j$)

(77) illustrates how various nonneutral morphemes can easily be characterized in terms of alignment.[22] Prestressing suffixes are left-aligned with the right edge of a stressed syllable. Initially stressed suffixes are left-aligned with the *left* edge of a stressed syllable – or, alternatively, left-aligned with the left edge of a foot, assuming we can

somehow guarantee that the foot is a trochee. A guarantee of that sort is needed anyway for penult-stressed roots, as in (77c); these must be right-aligned with the right edge of a foot, and that foot is preferably a trochee.

(77) a. Prestressing suffix /-mE/   Align(mE, L, ó, R)
     b. Initially stressed suffix /-Iyor/   Align($Iyor$, L, ó, L)   *or*
                                     Align($Iyor$, L, Foot, L)
     c. Penult-stressed root /penǰere/   Align($penǰere$, R, Foot, R)

A problem arises with the fourth class of exceptional morpheme, namely the roots with irregular antepenultimate stress. There is no way to align a trochaic foot with the right edge of such a morpheme to achieve antepenultimate stress. In the case of three-syllable words, such as *Zónguldak*, of course the trochee could be aligned with the left edge of the root. However, this still leaves words like *Kastámonu* unaccounted for. I can imagine two possible solutions. Either *Kastámonu* requires an iamb to be aligned with its left edge, in which case alignment constraints must explicitly mention the type of foot involved; or, *Kastámonu* is subject to two alignment constraints, one of which requires its final syllable to be nonaligned with a foot.

(78) Problem: antepenult-stressed roots
     a. Zónguldak   Align($Zonguldak$, L, Foot, L)
     b. Kastámonu   Align($Kastamonu$, L, Iamb, L)   *or*
                            [No-Align($Kastamonu$, R, Foot, R) $\gg$
                            Align($Kastamonu$, R, Foot, R)]

Let us assume that at least one of these options is chosen; we thus have descriptively adequate constraints for all the known types of exceptional stress placement. Let us now see how the constraints must be ranked in the Sezer and word cophonologies in order to achieve the generalization in (74).

6.2 Ranking

We know that within the Sezer cophonology, morpheme-specific stress prevails over the Sezer stress pattern, and that within the word cophonology, morpheme-specific stress prevails over the final stress pattern. Therefore the following rankings must obtain:

(79) Sezer cophonology: alignment constraints ≫ Contour,
                                                  Final-Ft
      Word cophonology: alignment constraints ≫ Final-Str

These rankings are illustrated in (80) and (81). In (80) we see the pre-stressing adjectival /-ǰa/ embedded within a Sezer stem; its stress pattern, manifested in winning candidate (80a), prevails over that of the Sezer pattern, manifested in losing candidate (80b). Contour is the only relevant Sezer stress constraint in this example, and thus the only one shown in the tableau.

(80) Sezer cophonology: Align(ǰE, L, ó, R) ≫ Contour

	[Kan-lɨ-ǰa]ₛ "blood-with-MIT (place name)"		Align-ǰE	Contour
a. ☞	(x .) Kan.lɨǰa	[Kanlɨǰa]		*
b.	(x .) Kan.lɨǰa	[Kanlɨǰa]	*!	

(81) illustrates a word composed of the neutral root /bɨrak/ and the pre-stressing negative suffix /-ma/. Because the prosodic alignment needs of the negative suffix outrank Final-Str, the word surfaces with stress preceding the negative suffix, as in winning candidate (81a).

(81) Word cophonology: Align(mE, L, ó, R) ≫ Final-Str

	[bɨrak-ma]ω "leave-NEG"		Align-mE	Final-Str
a. ☞	(x .) bɨrak|ma	[bɨrákma]		*
b.	(x .) bɨrak|ma [σ]	[bɨrakmá]	*!	

To capture the fact that a Sezer stem keeps its stress when followed by a nonneutral morpheme, we must also ensure that the constraint responsible for Sezer stress, namely PARSE-FT, outranks each morphemic prosodic alignment constraint.

(82) Within the word, Sezer stress prevails over stress of a nonneutral suffix (or suffixes)

   word cophonology   PARSE-FT ≫ Alignment constraints
   (≫ FINAL-STR)

This is illustrated in the tableau in (83), where the Sezer stem /Adana/ combines with the prestressing interrogative suffix, which has an associated alignment constraint of the type in (77a). In (83), only the winning candidate in (83a) satisfies PARSE-FT, at the expense of violating the alignment constraint for the prestressing negative suffix.

(83)

	(x .) [Adana]$_\Sigma$-mɨ]$_\omega$	"Adana- INTERR"	PARSE- FT	ALIGN- mI	FINAL- STR
a. ☞	(x .) A.da.na.|mɨ	[Adánamɨ]		*	*
b.	‹(x .)›(x .) A.da.na.|mɨ	[Adanámɨ]	*!	*	*
c.	‹(x .)›(x .) A.da.na.|mɨ[σ]	[Adanamí]	*!		

The one case we have yet to look at is a word with two nonneutral morphemes. In such a situation, of course, only one of the morphemes successfully imposes its required stress pattern on the word. One means of implementing this competition would be to rank the morphemic alignment constraints, such that only one can be satisfied.[23] An illustration of this method is shown in (84). Here, a neutral root combines with the prestressing negative followed by the stressed progressive. If we suppose that the alignment constraint for the negative – which must follow a stressed syllable – outranks the alignment constraint for the progressive – which must initiate a foot – then we achieve the desired outcome: the candidate satisfying the alignment constraint for the negative suffix wins. (84b) shows the same root, this time with the progressive followed by a prestressing interrogative. Again, ranking the alignment constraint for the progressive above that for the interrogative achieves the desired result.

(84) i. Word cophonology: Align(mE, L, ó, R) ≫ Align($Iyor$, L, ó, L)

	[bɨrak-ma-ɨyor]_ω "leave-NEG-PROG"		ALIGN-mE	ALIGN-$Iyor$	FINAL-STR
a. ☞	(x .) bɨrak.|ma-|ɨyor	[bɨrákmɨyor]		*	*
b.	(x .) bɨrak.|ma-|ɨyor	[bɨrakmɨ́yor]	*!		*
c.	(x .) bɨrak.|ma-|ɨyor [σ]	[bɨrakmɨyór]	*!	*	

ii. Word cophonology: Align($Iyor$, L, ó, L) ≫ Align(mI, L, ó, R)

	[bɨrak-ɨyor-mu]_ω "leave-PROG-INTERR"		ALIGN-$Iyor$	ALIGN-mI	FINAL-STR
a. ☞	(x .) bɨrak.|ɨyor.|mu	[bɨrakɨ́yormu]		*	*
b.	(x .) bɨrak.|ɨyor.|mu	[bɨrakɨyórmu]	*!		*

Of course, this type of constraint ranking works only if the linear ordering properties of the morphemes happen to coincide with the ranking of their prosodic alignment constraints. Constraint ranking is only an indirect method for capturing "leftmostness"; it is an accident that the morpheme whose alignment constraint is ranked highest occurs to the left of the morpheme with the lower-ranked alignment constraint. This approach would fail if, for any pair of suffixes with competing stress requirements, order was shown to vary according, for example, to semantics.

One way of overcoming this problem would be to suppose that, in the word cophonology, *all* morphemic alignment constraints are satisfied, and that "leftmost wins" is a constraint on foot parsing imposed at a later (possibly phrasal) level.

(85) Leftmost wins in alignment account: add another cophonology
Word cophonology
 Morphemic alignment constraints ≫ *STRUC
Phrase cophonology
 ◆HAVE-FT ≫ *STRUC ≫ PARSE-FT ≫ STR-INITIAL

An illustration is provided in (86) and (87). Here we see a word composed entirely of nonneutral morphemes: a stressed root and two prestressing suffixes. (86) shows all three feet being imposed in the word cophonology; (87) shows how, at a later level (probably the phrase), all but the leftmost of these feet fail to be parsed.

(86)

	[penjere-yle-mi]$_\omega$ "window-INSTR/ COM-INTERR"	ALIGN- penjere	ALIGN- (y)lE	ALIGN- mI	*STRUC
a. ☞	(x) (x) (x .) pen.je.re|y.le.|mi [penjéréylémi]				***
b.	(x) pen.je.re|y.le.|mi [penjéreylemi]		*!	*	*

(87)

	(x) (x) (x .) [pen.je.re|y.le.|mi]$_\phi$	◆HAVE- FT	*STRUC	PARSE- FT	*STR-INIT
a. ☞	(x)‹(x)›‹(x .)› pen.je.rey.le.mi [penjéreylemi]		*	**	*
b.	(x)(x)(x .) pen.je.rey.le.mi [penjéréylémi]			**!*	*

Note that this analysis is also undesirable. The word level cophonology creates unwieldy, ill-formed representations, which must be cleaned up on a later, otherwise unmotivated level.[24]

7. A lexical account: exceptionality as prespecification

Having seen roughly how a grammatical account of the exception facts would work, let us develop a prespecification account with which to contrast it. On a prespecification account, an exceptional morpheme is affiliated in underlying representation with a stress-foot, which interacts with constraints in the grammar to determine the stress pattern of the word containing it. I will argue that all of the exceptional stress in Turkish can be handled by prespecifying a trochaic foot – a foot of the same type that the grammar normally assigns.

(88) shows the lexical entries that would be required. For inherently stressed morphemes, whether root or suffix, the trochee dominates material in the morpheme. For prestressing suffixes, the head of the trochee is unfilled, and must unify with material in the base for which the suffix selects. The difference between stressed and prestressing suffixes is merely a difference in the distribution of underlying structure; it is the presence of this underlying structure which distinguishes all nonneutral morphemes from neutral ones.

(88) Nonneutral stress=prespecified (disyllabic) trochee

	(x .)		
Stressed root	penǰere		
	(x .)		
Initially stressed suffix	-Iyor		
	(x .)	(x .)	(x .)
Prestressing suffix	-mI	-leyin	-ǰEsInE

As part of the underlying representation of a nonneutral morpheme, the trochaic template is subject to the PARSE-FT constraint of the word-level cophonology.

7.1 The grammar: leftmost input wins

On the prespecification account, the generalization about the interactions of various sources for stress in Turkish words, repeated below, is easy to capture:

(89) Generalization
      Within a domain (word or Sezer stem), stress of leftmost non-neutral morpheme prevails over the pattern normally assigned to that domain; in addition, stress of Sezer stem prevails within word.

The basic insight on the prespecification account is that the leftmost prespecified foot (in any given domain) wins. In the Sezer cophonology, the only sources for prespecified feet are the morphemes themselves; in the word cophonology, another potential source is the Sezer stem, which (unless monosyllabic) always has a stress foot. All that either cophonology has to do to generate the correct surface stress is identify the leftmost input foot – and parse it. This is illustrated in the following example, which shows the various sources for stress (Sezer stems, nonneutral morphemes) in their possible combinations. Within each bracketed domain, the leftmost input foot wins.

(90) Nonneutral morpheme
within Sezer stem

$$\begin{array}{ccc} (x\ .) & & (x\ .) \\ \text{Kan lɨ-jE} & \rightarrow & [\ \text{Kan lɨja}\ ]_\Sigma \end{array}$$

Sezer stem as word

$$\begin{array}{ccc} (x\ .) & & (x\ .) \\ [\ \text{Kan lɨja}\ ]_\Sigma & \rightarrow & [\ \text{Kanlɨja}\ ]_\omega \end{array}$$

Sezer stem + nonneutral
morpheme in word

$$\begin{array}{ccc} (x\ .)\ (x\ .) & & (x\ .) \\ [\ \text{Kanlɨja}\ ]_\Sigma\ \text{-mI} & \rightarrow & [\ \text{Kanlɨjamɨ}\ ]_\omega \end{array}$$

Two nonneutral morphemes
in word

$$\begin{array}{ccc} (x\ .)(x\ .) & & (x\ .) \\ \text{penjere -mI} & \rightarrow & [\ \text{penjeremi}\ ]_\omega \end{array}$$

$$\begin{array}{ccc} (x\ .)(x\ .) & & (x\ \ .) \\ \text{yap -mE -sIn} & \rightarrow & [\ \text{yapmasɨn}\ ]_\omega \end{array}$$

We already know how to guarantee that an input foot prevails over the "default" stress pattern in any given cophonology: PARSE-FT is highly ranked in both Sezer and word cophonologies. To fully implement the analysis we need only to formalize "leftmost wins." To this end, I invoke a new constraint, STR-INITIAL:

(91) STR-INITIAL: Align(ó, L, Domain, L)
     Each stressed syllable is initial in the domain

STR-INITIAL plays an observable role only when there are multiple stress-feet in the input. Consider the tableau in (92). Here we see a neutral root in combination with two nonneutral suffixes, each of which has an underlying stress-foot. We know independently that the output word must have exactly one stress-foot; PARSE-FT tells us that the output foot must be one of the input feet. The role of STR-INITIAL is to tell us which input foot surfaces. The winning candidate, (92a), is the one in which the leftmost input foot is parsed. Losing candidate (92b) preserves the rightmost of the two input feet, incurring a greater violation of STR-INITIAL; losing candidate (92c) satisfies STR-INITIAL but violates PARSE-FT. STR-INITIAL must, therefore, be ranked below PARSE-FT.

(92) Word-level cophonology: PARSE-FT ≫ STR-INITIAL

	(x .) (x .) [bɨrak-mE-Iyor]_ω	"leave-NEG- PROG"	PARSE-FT	STR- INITIAL
a. ☞	(x .)‹(x .)› bɨ.rak.mɨ.yor	[bɨrákmɨyor]	*	*
b.	‹(x .)›(x .) bɨ.rak.mɨ.yor	[bɨrakmɨyor]	*	**!
c.	(x .)‹(x .)›‹(x .)› bɨ.rak.mɨ.yor	[bɨrakmɨyor]	**!	

An advantage of the proposed account is that, in the word cophonology, Sezer feet, derived in the Sezer cophonology, look just like lexically prespecified feet. As a result, STR-INITIAL treats them alike, selecting
the leftmost to parse. This is illustrated in the following tableau, where
the word cophonology preserves the stress foot present in the input
Sezer stem *Adána*:

(93)

	(x .) (x .) [[Adana]_Σ-mI]_ω	"Adana-INTERR"	PARSE- FT	STR- INITIAL
a. ☞	(x .) ‹(x .)› A.da.na.mɨ	[Adánamɨ]	*	*
b.	(x .) ‹(x .)›‹(x .)› A.da.na.mɨ	[Ádanamɨ]	**!	

STR-INITIAL has no role to play when the input has fewer than two stress
feet. Because it is outranked by PARSE, in any form with just one input
foot, that foot prevails regardless of its location, as shown below:

(94) If there is only one input foot, PARSE-FT always prevails

i. a prespecified foot within the Sezer stem

	(x .) [Kan-lɨ-ǰa]_Σ	PARSE-FT	STR-INITIAL
a. ☞	(x .) Kan.lɨ.ǰa [kanlɨ́ǰa]		*
b.	(x .)‹(x .)› Kan.lɨ.ǰa [kánlɨǰa]	*!	

ii. a prespecified foot within the Word domain

	(x .) [penǰere]$_\omega$		PARSE-FT	STR-INITIAL
a. ☞	(x .) pen.ǰe.re	[penǰére]		*
b.	(x .)‹(x .)› pen.ǰe.re	[pénǰere]	*!	

Similarly, STR-INITIAL is ineffective in forms containing absolutely no prespecified stress feet. In both word and Sezer cophonologies, STR-INITIAL is dominated by the constraints governing where an inserted stress foot should be located. (95) shows that STR-INITIAL is ranked below FINAL-FT in the Sezer cophonology (95i) and below FINAL-STR in the word cophonology, (95ii):

(95) If there is no input stress foot, then the constraints on stress assignment prevail

    i. Sezer cophonology: FINAL-FT ≫ STR-INITIAL

	[Adana]$_\Sigma$		FINAL-FT	STR-INITIAL
a. ☞	(x .) A.da.na	[Adána]		*
b.	(x .) A.da.na	[Ádana]	*!	

    ii. Word cophonology: FINAL-STR ≫ STR-INITIAL

	[araba-lar-i]$_\omega$ "car-PL-ACC"		FINAL-STR	STR-INITIAL
a. ☞	(x .) a.ra.ba.la.ri[σ]	[arabalarí]		***
b.	(x .) a.ra.ba.la.ri	[árabalari]	*!	

A summary is provided, below, of the constraint ranking needed to implement the templatic, prespecification account of exceptionality. Note that all the constraints are highly general and independently needed.

(96) Constraint rankings needed to implement prespecification (templatic) account

Sezer   ◆HAVE-FT ≫ *STRUC ≫ PARSE-FT ≫
CONTOUR ≫ FINAL-FT ≫ STR-INITIAL

Word   ◆HAVE-FT ≫ *STRUC ≫ PARSE-FT ≫
FINAL-STR ≫ STR-INITIAL

8. Comparing the two accounts at the explanatory level

We have now seen two accounts, one purely grammatical and one using prespecification, of exceptional stress in Turkish. Both are descriptively adequate. In this section, I compare the two on explanatory grounds, giving three arguments for the superiority of the prespecification account on explanatory grounds:

(97) a. Under prespecification account, the generalization is simpler; Sezer stress, exceptional stress form natural class, explaining their identical behavior in words

b. Prespecification account treats exceptions as natural class

c. Prespecification account is more economical, using only one foot type

8.1 Generalization is simpler on prespecification account

Compare the generalizations reached about the word level on the two different analyses. On the grammatical account, the generalization is that in both cophonologies, the leftmost nonneutral morpheme prevails; however, in the word cophonology, Sezer stress takes precedence even over nonneutral morpheme stress.

(98) Grammatical account
Sezer wins (word cophonology), else top-ranked alignment constraint wins (both cophonologies)

Prespecification account
Leftmost input foot wins (both cophonologies)

Notice that it is only an accident on the grammatical account that the constraint enforcing preservation of Sezer stress and the alignment constraints all happen to be ranked in the same position relative to FINAL-STR. On this analysis, Sezer stress and morpheme-specific stress have nothing in common that would lead us to expect this similar behavior.

On the prespecification account, by contrast, Sezer stress and morpheme-specific stress are formally identical in the word cophonology. Thus there is no need to distinguish them. The generalization becomes simpler – leftmost wins – and holds for both cophonologies. In providing a neater generalization over the data, the prespecification account is at an advantage.

8.2 Exceptions form natural class

The second advantage of the prespecification account is that it provides a unitary representation for all exceptions, providing a further generalization. In particular, all exceptional morphemes have a prespecified disyllabic trochee. This generalization correctly predicts that certain exception types will be unattested. In particular, we expect no post-stressing morphemes, as shown in (99a), since to represent these an iambic foot would be required. Similarly, we predict the absence of underlying morpheme-final iambs or degenerate feet, with resulting fixed morpheme-final stress (b).[25]

(99) a.   (. x)   (.   x) No iambs
        *ara ba   *[[   ] mI]
      b.   (. x)   (.   x) No iambs
        *a raba   *[[   ] mI]
                 (x)   (x)   No degenerate feet
        *ara ba   *[[   ] mI]

By contrast, the grammatical account can make no such predictions. Each nonneutral morpheme is, to be sure, affiliated with an alignment constraint – but there are many more logically possible ways to align morphemes with stress and stress feet than are attested in the inventory of exceptional morphemes in Turkish, and there is no obvious way in which to narrow down the expected possibilities. To see why, examine the range of alignment constraints it was necessary to invoke to capture the types of exceptionality displayed.

(100) Attested alignment constraints (assuming independent guarantee
of trochaic foot shape)

Align(sfx, L, ó, R)	(=prestressing suffix)
Align(sfx, L, ó/Ft, L)	(=stressed suffix)
Align(root, R, Ft, R)	(=penult stressed root)
Align(root, L, ó/Ft, L)	(=*Zónguldak* etc.)
NoAlign(*Kastamonu*, R, Ft, R)	(=*Kastámonu* etc.)
∧ Align(*Kastamonu*, R, Ft, R)	

Leaving aside the troublesome *Kastámonu*, each alignment constraint
invoked in the analysis is of the same overall format shown in (101):
a morphological category is aligned with a prosodic category. In the
alignment account of Turkish developed above, the set of morphological categories referred to includes root and suffix. The set of prosodic categories referred to includes stress and foot. Both left and right
edges of morphological and prosodic categories are referred to. In short,
we have four binary choices, which leads us to expect sixteen possible
alignment constraints.

(101) Four binary choices available in the overall format of Align(MCat,
$Edge_1$, PCat, $Edge_2$):
MCat ∈ {sfx, root}
PCat ∈ {ó, Foot}
$Edge_1$ ∈ {L, R}
$Edge_2$ ∈ {L, R}

Yet certain of these are clearly unattested in the system, as illustrated in
(102). In particular, the alignment constraints that would generate post-
stressing behavior are not utilized in Turkish; nor are those which
would generate fixed morpheme-final stress.

(102) Why not the unattested:

Align(sfx, R, ó, R)	(=fixed suffix-final stress)
Align(sfx, R, ó, L)	(=poststressing suffix)
Align(sfx, R, Foot, L)	(=poststressing suffix)
Align(sfx, L, ó, L)	(=initially stressed monosyllabic suffix)
Align(sfx, L, Foot, L)	(=initially stressed monosyllabic suffix)
Align(root, R, ó, R)	(=fixed root-final stress)
Align(root, R, ó, L)	(=poststressing root)
Align(root, R, Foot, L)	(=poststressing root)

The basic problem is that the attested alignment constraints do not form a natural class to the exclusion of the unattested ones. No generalization about exceptionality is captured here; the analysis is not explanatory.[26]

8.3 Grammar constrains prespecification

A common criticism of prespecification accounts is that they predict too many types of underlying representations. For example, one could criticize the account proposed here by observing that in principle, any sort of weird metrical structure – such as a degenerate foot, or an iambic foot, or a ten-syllable foot – could be prespecified, and could have its own weird effects on the grammar. However, there is a simple response to this criticism, which is that prespecified structure *is* constrained by the grammar, in a way that other approaches to exceptionality are not.

For example, the proposed prespecification analysis of Turkish employs only disyllabic trochees. Exceptional words differ from regular words only in the location of the trochaic foot they all possess. It is easy to guarantee that no other type of foot can be used in the system. All we need is the statement in (103): ◆Ft-Bin and ◆Trochaic, both unviolated in Sezer and word cophonologies, dominate Parse-Ft. Note that this is a constraint ranking that we already arrived at, completely independently of exceptions: ◆Ft-Bin and ◆Trochaic were found to be unviolable (hence undominated by any of the other constraints we discussed), while Parse-Ft was found to be dominated by *Struc (see (17)).

(103) The guarantee that all, even prespecified (exceptional), feet are binary trochees

◆Ft-Bin, ◆Trochaic ≫ Parse-Ft

The location of the prespecified stress foot is another matter. As far as I know, there are no roots or suffixes prespecified for final stress.[27] The generalization about roots is easy to handle. According to Inkelas and Orgun (1995), Turkish requires a root level of phonology (on which syllabification takes place and a bimoraic minimality condition is imposed). In order to prohibit root stress on final syllables, we need only assume that in the root cophonology, Fill and ◆Ft-Bin are as highly ranked as they are in the Sezer cophonology. This will prohibit catalexis and degenerate feet – thus making it impossible for a final prespecified stress to survive.[28]

Consider, by comparison, how we would implement the generalization about foot form in exceptional words on the grammatical account. All along, I was assuming that the feet referred to in the alignment constraints would all somehow be guaranteed to be disyllabic trochees. But the relevant guarantee is, of course, simply the stipulation that each and every alignment constraint is outranked by a constraint to the effect that the foot in Turkish is trochaic.

(104) The guarantee that feet imposed by all alignment constraints are binary trochees

◆FT-BIN, ◆TROCHAIC ≫ ALIGNMENT CONSTRAINT 1

◆FT-BIN, ◆TROCHAIC ≫ alignment constraint 2

◆FT-BIN, ◆TROCHAIC ≫ alignment constraint 3

etc.

It is just an accident that the alignment constraints are all ranked in this fashion.

To summarize, prespecification is inherently constrained by the grammar, for which nonexceptional words provide independent motivation. But a grammatical analysis of exceptionality cannot be inherently constrained by the grammar in a similar way, because it *is* the grammar.

9. Conclusions

In conclusion, I have argued that the prespecification, template-based account of exceptional stress in Turkish is superior on explanatory grounds to the proposed alignment account. Note that both analyses have been formulated within Optimality Theory; the two approaches differ only on the theory-neutral issue of how much complexity should be allocated to the lexicon as opposed to the grammar. In fact, the prespecification analysis is perfectly suited to Optimality Theory, which avoids the rampant stress deletion processes that would be required on a rule-based, derivational account.

If it is generally agreed that the prespecification analysis of Turkish stress is superior to the one which does not use templates, then we must acknowledge some role for templates in phonological theory. This conclusion may be perfectly compatible with the claims about templates by McCarthy and Prince (1993, this volume), who are discussing only reduplication and infixation. Perhaps templates play a role in exceptional stress patterns but not in the more canonical types of prosodic morphology (though see Zoll 1993 for arguments that templates in Yawelmani Prosodic Morphology are referred to by the grammar and thus must be prespecified structure, and Itô and Mester 1994 for the proposal that a German suffix consists underlyingly of an empty mora). However, if true this can only be an accident, given the equivalence we saw earlier between the templatic and nontemplatic accounts of simple CV reduplication. There is no principled reason not to use templates, and in at least some cases they clearly improve analyses.

10. Implications: the role of exceptions in analysis

In closing, I would like to explore one further implication of the study of Turkish, namely the role that exceptions can play in phonological analysis. It has become increasingly clear to me that the common methodology of basing one's analysis on the "core" phenomena of a language and only gradually, if ever, extending the analysis to the more "marginal" phenomena can be misleading. It is not always the case that the study of regular patterns logically precedes and informs the study of exceptional patterns.

Working on Turkish stress has shown me that the direction of influence can, at least sometimes, be the reverse: in this case, the careful study of exceptions actually illuminates the analysis of the regular patterns by showing the predominance of the trochaic foot. Thus regardless of the details of the analysis, I hope that at least one implication of this study will be that exceptions should play a more central role in, rather than function as a footnote to, theoretical analysis.

Notes

1 I would like to thank Larry Hyman, René Kager, John McCarthy, Engin Sezer, Karl Zimmer, and an anonymous referee for helpful discussion during the preparation of this paper; Cheryl Zoll and Orhan Orgun provided pivotal help in the development of the analysis. The data analyzed in this paper are from Standard Istanbul Turkish. All examples have been checked with a single native speaker and represent a consistent idiolect. Speakers do vary somewhat with respect to the particular lexical items which exhibit exceptional stress; I have made no attempt to document this variation.

2 "Template" has become an ambiguous term, sometimes used to refer to any mechanism (whether lexical or grammatical) which characterizes the specific prosodic shape of a given morpheme. In this paper I use

"template" specifically to refer to the use of underlying metrical structure in specifying morpheme shape.

3 In deriving the phonological size of a reduplicant from its morphological category (STEM versus AFFI X), McCarthy and Prince make the strong prediction that the morphological behavior – not just the phonological shape – of the two reduplicant types will differ significantly. Any word formed through foot-sized reduplication will be a morphological compound (thus expected to display all the semantic, syntactic, and phonological properties accruing to compounds in the language in question); by contrast, all syllable-sized reduplication should be on a par morphologically with affixation. McCarthy and Prince do not go into detail about the morphology of the reduplication constructions they analyze, so it is not easy to confirm the morphological predictions. Should, however, the morphological predictions turn out not to be correct, then the phonological size of a reduplicant will not be derivable directly from its morphological structure; size will have to be governed instead by constraints stating directly that a given reduplicative morpheme is a prosodic word (X=PRWD) while another is no larger than one syllable (X ≤ σ). Note that there is no principled way (as far as I know) of excluding such constraints from the theory in any case.

4 If, following Orgun (1994a) and McCarthy and Prince (this volume), we assume that Containment (Prince and Smolensky 1993; McCarthy and Prince 1994, this volume) is no longer a principle of Optimality Theory, then PARSE can be understood simply as the command "structure present in input is present (and linked) in the output." This is how I use PARSE throughout the paper, although I follow the notational convention of past optimality work by showing deleted structure in angled brackets (simply to make deletions easier to observe in diagrams).

5 Though a similar number of constraints is invoked, the templatic analysis uses fewer morpheme-specific constraints (thus only universal ones), and in that sense is simpler.

6 McCarthy and Prince (1993b) also argue that at least in one case, from Axininca Campa (AC), templates are insufficient to characterize reduplicant shape. In AC, reduplicant size varies according to base size and is not capturable through a single, invariant template. The crucial data are shown below (roots are in boldface and reduplicants are underlined):

(i)	Size of input to reduplication	Output of reduplication	Size of reduplicant
a.	Polysyllabic root	**kawosi**-<u>kawosi</u>	3 syllables
b.	Disyllabic root	**kowa**-<u>kowa</u>	2 syllables
c.	Prefixed disyllabic root	noN-**koma**-<u>koma</u>	2 syllables
d.	Prefixed monosyllabic root	no-**naa**-<u>nonaa</u>	2 syllables
e.	Unprefixed monosyllabic root	**naa**-<u>naa</u>	1 syllable

The essential facts (see McCarthy and Prince (1993b), and references therein, for more detail) are that a root is reduplicated whole — unless it is monosyllabic, in which case a prefix, if any, is reduplicated as well. McCarthy and Prince's account of these data uses two constraints. R ≤ ROOT asserts that the reduplicant is no larger than the root. DISYLL states that "the left and right edges of the reduplicant must coincide, respectively, with the left and right edges of *different* syllables" (82), i.e., that the reduplicant is minimally disyllabic. By ranking DISYLL above R ≤ ROOT, McCarthy and Prince ensure that more than a root will be reduplicated only where needed to satisfy DISYLL.

McCarthy and Prince argue that DISYLL – the prosodic constraint in their analysis – cannot be identified with a standard template because it imposes only a lower bound on prosodic size. Templates, according to McCarthy and Prince, are by nature size-invariant and lack the flexibility needed to accommodate the AC facts.

However, all that is clear from this example is that a *single* template would not by itself be sufficient. What makes this case of reduplication special is that it has distinct upper and lower prosodic bounds. A single template would fail in just the same way that a single constraint would fail: note that McCarthy and Prince themselves rely on *two* morpheme-specific constraints, not the usual single constraint, on reduplicant size. A comparably enriched templatic account would work fine. Suppose, for example, McCarthy and Prince's account were altered minimally by eliminating the constraint DISYLL in favor of an underlying disyllabic foot in the lexical representation of the reduplicative affix. PARSE will ensure that this foot is preserved — guaranteeing a disyllabic lower bound — and the rest remains the same. In fact, since PARSE is independently needed while DISYLL is (so far) not motivated outside this example, the templatic analysis is arguably superior. (Note also that, by virtue of relating nonadjacent elements of the representation, DISYLL is nonlocal and requires an Alignment constraint outside of the bounds of Generalized Alignment theory (McCarthy and Prince 1993a), more reasons to try and eliminate it.)

7 For example, Poser (1984) proposed nonperipheral extrametricality; Barker (1989) proposed that prestressing suffixes are extrametrical and that stress is assigned cyclically; Kiparsky (1991) and Kager (1992) proposed catalexis; Hayes (1995) proposed foot extrametricality.

8 In most compounds, the first word of the compound retains its stress and the second does not (see e.g., Swift 1963: 115–19). Derived diminutive stress is strictly initial (e.g., *ĭne-ĭik* "very thin"), consistent with a fixed initial trochaic foot. Both phenomena are perfectly compatible with the analysis proposed in this chapter.

The stress of adverbs in *-en/an* is discussed in Sezer (1981), who describes stress as being penultimate if the penult is heavy (e.g., *ik.ti.sá:.d-en*

"economically") and antepenultimate otherwise (*te.kéf.fü.l-en* "by surety").
As Hayes (1995) observes, this pattern can be analyzed with a moraic
trochee (and final syllable extrametricality). However, the construction is
apparently not productive in Turkish, and the data are not consistent
across speakers. For these reasons I have chosen not to analyze the pattern here. Vocative stress is mentioned by Swift (1963: 180–81), Lewis
(1967: 22–23), and Foster (1970: 252); however, I have so far been unable
to confirm the pattern with a native speaker. Given that, as Swift observes
(181), vocatives have a distinctive intonation, one would also want to confirm instrumentally that their stress (not just pitch) is actually different
from that of nonvocatives.

Secondary stress in Standard Turkish is controversial; it exists according to some sources (Lees 1961; Foster 1970; Underhill 1976; Barker
1989) but not according to others (Swift 1963; Lewis 1967), and where it
is described, descriptions conflict. Those reporting secondary stress hear it
on closed syllables (Lees 1961: 49), or on final syllables in words with
nonfinal main stress (Underhill 1976: 19; Barker 1989), or on heavy syllables which precede potentially prestressing suffixes and occur near the
end of long verbs with main stress near the beginning (Lees 1961: 45). The
most liberal transcription of nonprimary stress is found in Foster (1970:
244–46), though Foster reports (248) that the stresses he transcribes "do
not always show up." To be on the safe side, I choose not to analyze secondary stress (which I myself do not hear) until better, preferably instrumental, evidence for it is found. Note, however, that none of the reported
secondary stress patterns poses any serious problem to the analysis to be
developed.

9 The following abbreviations are used in glosses: ABL (ablative), ADJ (adject-
ivalizer), ADV (adverbializer), AGT (agentive), AOR (aorist), CAUS (causative),
COM (comitative), COND (conditional), DAT (dative), DIM (diminutive), FUT
(future), IMP (imperative), INSTR (instrumental), INTERR (interrogative),
LOC (locative), MIT (mitigative), NEC (necessitative), NEG (negative), NOM
(nominalizer), PL (plural), POSS (possessive), PROG (progressive), SG (singular), SUBJ (subjunctive), VBL (verbalizer).

Following the standard tradition, uppercase letters are used to represent
underspecified segments in Turkish morphemes.

10 Actually, as argued in Inkelas and Orgun (1995), Turkish has four lexical
levels in addition to the Sezer level; these are omitted from the diagrams in
(14) in order to save space. As no unique stress patterns are associated
with any of these levels, they are irrelevant to the issues at hand. Note that
the interaction among cophonologies is determined by the morphological
constituent structure of the relevant word.

11 I am assuming that PARSE-SYL, together with FT-BIN, is what ensures that
feet are minimally disyllabic (instead of being minimally bimoraic). Note

that HAVE-FT is being used instead of the more standard LEX≈PRWD (Prince and Smolensky 1993); this is in order to allow the constraint to apply in different domains (namely the Sezer stem and the word, which are distinct), rather than holding only in the "prosodic word."

12 By contrast, if we had used WSP (the Weight-to-Stress Principle of Prince and Smolensky 1993), which is context-free, we would be unable to explain why the stress foot can shift only one syllable away from the right edge.

13 A final foot in *Mérjimek* might appear to be bimoraic, hence in satisfaction of FT-BIN; either we stipulate that FT-BIN refers to the syllable, which is presumably required anyway in languages with obligatorily disyllabic trochaic feet, or we rely on final consonant extrametricality (known anyway to be motivated in Turkish; see Rice 1990 and Inkelas and Orgun 1995) to ensure that the final syllable counts as monomoraic. (Of course, the latter solution works only for closed syllables.)

14 There are "exceptional" place names, such as *Anadolú*, which have final stress. However, it is easy to show that what is exceptional about these roots is simply that they are stressed as words, rather than as Sezer stems: when *Anadolu* is combined with neutral suffixes, stress appears at the end of the word, e.g., *Anadolu-dán* "Anadolu-ABL." As Sezer (1981) notes, the Sezer cophonology contains some members which are not place names; it seems that the converse is also true, and that not all place names are subject to the Sezer cophonology. See Inkelas and Orgun (1995) for some discussion of how morphemes exceptionally avoid or undergo given cophonologies.

15 Actually, Kager (1992, the first version) discusses Turkish, but Kager (1993, the second version) does not; however, both versions propose catalexis for monomoraic words in languages like Turkish. Kiparsky (1991) and Kager (1992, 1993, 1995) have argued that the existence of monomoraic words (e.g., Turkish *su* "water") provides further motivation for catalexis. However, see Inkelas and Orgun (1995) for an alternative account of such forms.

16 An alternative to FINAL-STR would be to propose, as suggested by René Kager (personal communication in June 1994), that catalexis results from a misalignment between grid and string: under catalexis, the grid extends one beat beyond the right edge of the string. Assuming that stress feet are constructed on the grid, then the same FINAL-FT constraint (Align(Domain, R, Foot, R)) would handle word-final stress as well as Sezer stress. There would be no need for FINAL-STR, which has the aesthetic disadvantage of referring directly to stressed syllables.

17 FINAL-STR must also outrank CONTOUR in the word cophonology, as shown by forms like *patlijan-dá* "eggplant-LOC."

18 This is the same conceptualization of PARSE employed earlier in the discussion of reduplication.

19 Barker (1989), based on a misstatement by Lewis (1967: 23), claims that all polysyllabic suffixes are exceptional (either prestressing or initially stressed). This claim is repeated in van der Hulst and van de Weijer (1991: 18). However, it is not true. See, for example, the neutral polysyllabic suffix -*EjEk* in (12) and those in *asker-va:rí* "soldier-like," *Mool-istan-í* "Mongolia-ACC," and *yešil-imtirak-lár* "green-ish-PL (greenish ones)."

20 Note: I am not considering any attempt to abstractly manipulate the syllable structure of these words so that Sezer stress would correctly be assigned to them. For example, it could be claimed that there is a catalectic mora in the second syllable of *Üskúdar*, leading to the assignment of penultimate stress; the same could be said for the stressed syllable of *Kastámonu*. In general, if underlying structure is to be used to capture exceptionality, then I would only use surface-true structure, since otherwise there are few constraints on what can be done.

21 An alternative, suggested by Kaisse (1985, 1986) and Hameed (1985), is level ordering: preaccenting suffixes are added at a level following that at which final stress is assigned. However, such an account has no explanation for initially stressed suffixes or idiosyncratically stressed roots and is at odds with affix ordering facts: as Kaisse (1985) notes, it is in fact possible for nonneutral suffixes to precede neutral ones.

22 (77) exemplifies only the *metrical* alignment constraints on stress-affecting morphemes; to each suffix X in Turkish (regardless of its effect – or lack thereof – on stress) there will also correspond a constraint of the form Align(X, L, base, R), which specifies the linear order of suffix and base.

23 McQuown and Koylan (1944: 864–65) provide a list of suffixes in order of "strength" from which to determine the stress of a word with multiple suffixes. While of course not conceptualized within Optimality Theory, the list serves the same purpose as ranking alignment constraints.

24 An anonymous reviewer suggests an alternative in which the morphemic alignment constraints are co-ranked, such that given *n* alignment constraints, all candidates in which only one alignment constraint is satisfied will tie with respect to their violations of the alignment constraint family. The candidate in which stress is leftmost will win. While potentially workable, the consequences of allowing a (possibly arbitrary) set of constraints to be co-ranked have been sufficiently unexplored (and hence the technique is sufficiently unconstrained) that I leave this type of analysis for future research.

25 Of course, the possibility of fixed morpheme-final stress still exists; it could be generated by means of an underlying trochaic foot headed by the morpheme-final syllable. This possibility is discussed later in the text.

26 Alan Prince pointed out at the workshop that if the theory of alignment were modified to exclude morpheme-specific alignment constraints of the type in (100) (not to mention those in (102)), the prespecification account might be the *only* descriptively adequate one.

It is hard to see how exactly to restrict the theory, however; as long as relations between metrical and morphological structure (e.g. the currently pivotal LEX≈PRWD (Prince and Smolensky 1993) and STEM=PRWD (McCarthy and Prince 1993b, 1994) exist, and as long as alignment constraints exist, there can be no principled reason *not* to align morphological entities with metrical ones. It is certainly worth pursuing ways in which the power of alignment could be pared down to just the needed level. However, I think there is a more general point to be made here, which is that the grammar is generally able to describe more types of exceptions than actually exist, and that, therefore, the theory must always locate exceptionality in the lexicon, which has fewer options. See Inkelas, Orgun, and Zoll (1997) for amplification of this point.

27 There also appear to be no roots prespecified for stress outside of the final 3-syllable window. However, since there are few roots this long in this first place, the generalization is not very striking. I have chosen not to account for it. However, it could be accounted for by the root cophonology; see Kager (1993, 1994) for discussion of the implementation of stress windows.

28 Note, however, that I have no way of enforcing a similar ban on final-stressed suffixes. Turkish levels are noncyclic (Inkelas and Orgun 1994), thus eliminating the possibility of banning degenerate feet/catalexis on each suffixation cycle. Orhan Orgun (personal communication) notes that there is one suffix, the NECESSITATIVE /-mElI/, whose final syllable is always stressed (e.g., *git-melí* "go-NECESS," *git-melí-ler* "go-NECESS-3PL"). It may just be a coincidence that this suffix never precedes a neutral suffix; its combinatory possibilities are rather limited. However, it might also be the case that /-mElI/ has fixed final stress.

References

Barker, Christopher. 1989. Extrametricality, the cycle, and Turkish word stress, in J. Itô and J. Runner (eds.), *Phonology at Santa Cruz* 1. University of California, Santa Cruz, CA: Syntax Research Center, 1–33.

Dobrovolsky, Michael. 1986. Stress and vowel harmony domains in Turkish, in V. Nikiforidou *et al.* (eds.), *Proceedings of the Twelfth Annual Meeting of the Berkeley Linguistics Society*. Berkeley, CA: Berkeley Linguistics Society, 61–71.

Foster, Joseph F. 1970. On some phonological rules of Turkish, Ph.D. dissertation, University of Illinois, Urbana-Champaign, IL.

Halle, Morris, and Jean-Roger Vergnaud. 1987. *An Essay on Stress*, Cambridge, MA: MIT Press.

Hameed, J. 1985. Lexical phonology and morphology of Modern Standard Turkish, *Cahiers Linguistiques d'Ottawa* 14: 71–95.

Hammond, Michael. 1986. The obligatory-branching parameter in metrical theory, *Natural Language and Linguistic Theory* 4: 185–228.

Hayes, Bruce. 1995. *Metrical Stress Theory: Principles and Case Studies*. University of Chicago Press.

Hulst, H. van der, and J. van de Weijer, 1991. Topics in Turkish phonology, in H. Boeschoten and L. Verhoeven (eds.), *Turkish Linguistics Today*, Leiden: E. J. Brill, 11–159.

Idsardi, William. 1992. The computation of prosody, Ph.D. dissertation, Massachusetts Institute of Technology, Cambridge, MA.

Inkelas, Sharon, and Cemil Orhan Orgun. 1995. Level ordering and economy in the lexical phonology of Turkish, *Language* 71: 763–93.

Inkelas, Sharon, Cemil Orhan Orgun, and Cheryl Zoll. 1997. Implications of lexical exceptions for the nature of grammar, in I. Roca (ed.), *Constraints and Derivations in Phonology*, Oxford: Clarendon Press, 393–418.

Itô, Junko and R. Armin Mester. 1994. Anaptyxis in Optimality Theory: the phonology and morphology of German *schwa*. Paper presented at Workshop on Prosodic Morphology, University of Utrecht, June 1994.

1995. Japanese phonology, in J. Goldsmith (ed.), *The Handbook of Phonological Theory*, Cambridge, MA: Blackwell, 817–38.

Kager, René. 1992. Stress in windows, ms. (first version) University of Utrecht.

1993. Stress in windows, ms. (second version) University of Utrecht.

1994. On eliminating directional foot-parsing, in H. P. Kolb (ed.), *Generative Linguistics in the Old World, Newsletter* 32, Spring 1994, Department of Language and Literature, Tilburg University, 30–31.

1995. Consequences of catalexis, in H. van der Hulst and J. van de Weijer (eds.), *Leiden in Last: HIL Phonology Papers I*. Den Haag: Holland Institute of Generative Linguistics, 269–98.

Kaisse, Ellen. 1985. Some theoretical consequences of stress rules in Turkish, in W. Eilfort, P. Kroeber, and K. Peterson (eds.), *Papers from the General Session of the Twenty-First Regional Meeting*. Chicago, IL: Chicago Linguistic Society, 199–209.

1986. Toward a lexical phonology of Turkish, in M. Brame, H. Contreras, and F. Newmeyer (eds.), *A Festschrift for Sol Saporta*, Seattle, WA: Noit Amrofer, 231–40.

Kardestuncer, A. 1982. A three-boundary system for Turkish, *Linguistic Analysis* 10: 75–117.

Kiparsky, Paul. 1991. Catalexis, ms. Stanford University, CA and Wissenschaftskolleg zu Berlin.

Lees, Robert. 1961. *The Phonology of Modern Standard Turkish*. Indiana University Publications Uralic and Altaic Series, vol. 6, Bloomington, IN: Indiana University Publications.

Lewis, Geoffrey. 1967. *Turkish Grammar*. Oxford University Press.

Lightner, Theodore. 1978. The main stress rule in Turkish, in M. A. Jazayery, E. Polomé, and W. Winter (eds.), *Linguistic and Literary Studies in Honor of Archibald A. Hill*. vol. 2: Descriptive Linguistics, The Hague: Mouton, 267–70.

McCarthy, John, and Alan S. Prince. 1986. Prosodic Morphology, ms. University of Massachusetts, Amherst, MA and Brandeis University, Waltham, MA.

1993a. Generalized alignment, in G. E. Booij and J. van Marle (eds.), *Yearbook of Morphology 1993*, Dordrecht: Kluwer, 79–153.

1993b. Prosodic Morphology I: constraint interaction and satisfaction, ms. University of Massachusetts, Amherst and Rutgers University, New Brunswick, NJ.

1994. The emergence of the unmarked: Optimality in Prosodic Morphology, in M. Gonzàlez (ed.), *Proceedings of the North East Linguistic Society* 24. Amherst, MA: Graduate Linguistic Student Association, University of Massachusetts, 333–79.

This volume. Faithfulness and identity in Prosodic Morphology.

McQuown, Norman A., and Sadi Koylan. 1944. *Spoken Turkish*. Henry Holt and Co.

Orgun, Cemil Orhan. 1994a. A short history of Containment, OT net posting, July 1994.

1994b. Monotonic cyclicity and Optimality Theory, in M. Gonzàlez (ed.), *Proceedings of the North East Linguistic Society* 24. Amherst, MA: Graduate Linguistic Student Association, University of Massachusetts, 461–74.

Poser, William J. 1984. The phonetics and phonology of tone and intonation in Japanese, Ph.D. dissertation, Massachusetts Institute of Technology, Cambridge, MA.

Prince, Alan, and Paul Smolensky. 1993. Optimality Theory: constraint interaction in generative grammar, ms. Rutgers University, New Brunswick, NJ and University of Colorado, Boulder, CO.

PTT. 1994. Türkiye Kod ve Telefon Numaraları Rehberi. [PTT guide to Turkish telephone numbers and area codes.]. Ankara: PTT.

Rice, Keren. 1990. Predicting rule domains in the phrasal phonology, in S. Inkelas and D. Zec (eds.), *The Phonology-Syntax Connection*. University of Chicago Press and CSLI Publications, 289–312.

Sezer, Engin. 1981. On non-final stress in Turkish, *Journal of Turkish Studies* 5: 61–69.

Swift, Lloyd B. 1963. *A Reference Grammar of Modern Turkish*. Indiana University Publications Uralic and Altaic Series, vol. 19, Bloomington, IN: Indiana University Publications.

Underhill, Robert. 1976. *Turkish Grammar*. Cambridge, MA: MIT Press.

Zoll, Cheryl. 1993. Directionless syllabification and ghosts in Yawelmani. Paper presented at Rutgers Optimality Workshop I, Rutgers University, New Brunswick, NJ.

6 Realignment

Junko Itô and R. Armin Mester

1. Introduction

The notion "alignment" entered Optimality Theory (OT) in the form of correspondence requirements that demand certain edges of grammatical constituents – say, the right edge of every stem – coincide with a corresponding edge of a prosodic constituent – say, with the right edge of some syllable. Alignment requirements control the prosodic shape of morphological and other grammatical constituents and in this way lay the foundation for Prosodic-Morphological analysis. The constraint just mentioned forces the end of a stem to coincide with the end of a syllable: it must be syllabified, and the syllable must not span a stem-suffix juncture. First proposed in Prince and Smolensky (1991, 1993) in the course of an analysis of the Australian language Lardil, this constraint was shown to be operative in Axininca Campa by McCarthy and Prince (1993a). In its concentration on the mapping relation between grammatical and prosodic categories, Alignment Theory has its roots in earlier work on the syntax–prosody interface (most notably the "end-based" theory of Selkirk 1986), extended to word-internal domains in Inkelas (1989) and Cohn (1989). The alignment concept has since been developed in several ways. Thus it has been shown that significant analytical advantages can be obtained by extending alignment to include an altogether different type of constraint linking two *prosodic* categories like prosodic words and feet: i.e., PCat-PCat constraints, in addition to the traditional GCat-PCat type. The internal prosody of words in Japanese is significantly shaped by the requirement that the left edge of every PrWd must correspond to the left edge of a foot (Itô and Mester 1992: 30). In different theoretical contexts, similar ideas have been explored in work by Burzio (1994) and Idsardi (1992). The most systematic and influential proposal in this direction is Generalized Alignment Theory (McCarthy and Prince 1993b), where alignment is systematically developed into a large family of constraints requiring coincidence of (left or right) edges for a wide variety of categories. This work has opened up a rich field of alignment-theoretic analysis including, for example, directionality effects in footing. In fact, this line of research has demonstrated that alignment constraints, even though logically independent of the central tenets of OT (ranking and violability of constraints, with optimality defined as "best-satisfaction"), can only unfold their full analytical and explanatory potential within the ranking network of an optimality-theoretic grammar. By further developing an alignment-theoretic approach to syllable structure and extending it to issues relating to structural complexity and the sonority profile of syllables, this chapter[1] brings empirical and formal considerations to bear on the proper definition of the notion "alignment," presenting old problems and exploring new ideas along the way.

2. Syllable theory and alignment

Syllable well-formedness conditions of various kinds have played a significant role in the optimality-theoretic analysis that grew out of Prince and Smolensky's (1993) inaugurating work. In particular, the ranking of the two most basic well-formedness conditions – ONSET (requiring/favoring the presence of onsets) and NO-CODA (requiring/favoring the absence of codas) – with respect to faithfulness constraints has been pivotal in numerous analyses.

(1) Basic syllable theory
     ONSET   Syllables without onsets are disallowed.
     NO-CODA   Syllables with codas are disallowed.

Exploring the limits of alignment-theoretic statements, McCarthy and Prince (1993b) suggest that ONSET and NOCODA can be formulated as requiring, respectively, that every syllable be left-aligned with a consonant (ONSET) and right-aligned with a vowel (NOCODA).[2]

(2) ONSET   Align-Left (σ, C)
     NO-CODA   Align-Right (σ, V)

As in all alignment constraints, the first argument is quantified universally ("every syllable"), the second existentially ("some consonant").
Generally speaking, one of the most fertile formal resources of Generalized Alignment Theory lies in the possibility of exchanging the two arguments, providing a rich network of related conditions with different
logical force. For example, McCarthy and Prince (1993b) show that
great mileage can be obtained from the interplay of mirror-image constraint pairs like those in (3).[3]

(3) ALIGN-LEFT   (PrWd, Ft)
    ALIGN-LEFT   (Ft, PrWd)

Regarding the alignment-theoretic versions of ONSET and NO-CODA
(2), however, McCarthy and Prince (1993b: 20) state that such combinatorial freedom of argument settings is unavailable, remarking that
"[h]ere G[eneralized] A[lignment] provides a way of formalizing the
substantively fixed constraints." Clarification and formalization are
certainly significant achievements in themselves; it appears, however,
to be premature to conclude that such combinatorial freedom of argument settings is unavailable for syllable theory.[4] As we will see, the
internal richness and symmetry of the emerging alignment-theoretic
syllable theory is considerably richer than a mere restatement of familiar
conditions.

2.1 Syllable alignment and segment alignment

The task before us, then, is to explore the formal and empirical content
of the mirror-image (reversed argument) versions of ONSET and NO-
CODA, given in (4).

(4) ALIGN-LEFT (σ, C)   ONSET
    ALIGN-LEFT (C, σ)   ALIGN-C (mirror-image of ONSET)
    ALIGN-RIGHT (σ, V)   NO-CODA
    ALIGN-RIGHT (V, σ)   ALIGN-V (mirror-image of NO-CODA)

Reversing the arguments for ONSET yields an alignment constraint
(ALIGN-C) which focuses on the consonant (formally, quantifies universally over consonantal segments), and requires it to be left-aligned with

some syllable. Similarly, reversing the arguments for No-Coda results in an alignment constraint (Align-V) which focuses on the vowel, and requires it to be right-aligned with some syllable. The following chart organizes the mirror-image constraint pairs in terms of their arguments: we will refer to Onset and No-Coda, with the syllable as the first argument, as "syllable(-to-segment) alignment" constraints, and the mirror-image versions, with consonant/vowel as first argument, as "segment(-to-syllable) alignment" constraints.

(5)

	Alignment	
	of syllables (σ,__)	of segments (seg,__)
Left edge	(σ, C) "Onset"	(C, σ) "Align-C"
Right edge	(σ, V) "No-Coda"	(V, σ) "Align-V"

The syllable-alignment constraints require every *syllable* to be left-aligned with a consonant (i.e., to have an onset) and to be right-aligned with a vowel (i.e., to be open). On the other hand, the mirror-image segment alignment constraints require every *segment* to be left/right-aligned with syllables: consonants must be syllable-initial, vowels must be syllable-final.

From a purely formal standpoint, it is obvious that the segment alignment constraints differ in logical force from the corresponding mirror-image syllable alignment constraints. More interesting, perhaps, is the fact, to be demonstrated below, that the new network of constraints yields a richer syllable typology, including systems with complex onsets, nuclei, and codas, bringing us one step closer to a serious approximation of the range of syllabification systems encountered in natural languages. For better or for worse, a characteristic feature of the new approach is its exclusively alignment-theoretic nature, without reliance on configuration-specific penalties like CodaCond, NoComplex, No-Long-Vowel, No-Diphthong found in the literature (see Prince and Smolensky 1993 and Rosenthall 1994, among others).

2.2 Align-C

Besides Onset and No-Coda, one of the most frequently discussed syllable structure conditions is the Coda Condition (Itô 1986, 1989), which restricts the *type* of consonant that can occupy the syllable-final position. As is well known, the Coda Condition (henceforth: "Coda-Cond," following the usage in Prince and Smolensky 1993) plays a pivotal role in accounting for the form and distribution of intervocalic clusters found in languages. In languages that allow codas at all, it restricts the type of consonants that can occupy this position. Typically, only unmarked elements (like coronal sonorants) and consonants homorganic (i.e., place-linked) to the following onset make licit codas. Itô and Mester (1994) argue that Coda-Cond is not a negative constraint disallowing certain syllable-final consonants, but is formally an Align-C constraint, requiring consonants to be left-aligned with syllables (6) – i.e., the mirror-image counterpart of Onset, in the sense of (4) and (5).

(6) Coda-Cond=Align-C   (Itô and Mester 1994)
     Align-Left (C, σ) $\forall C \, \exists \sigma$ [Coincide (Left-Edge-of (C),
                           Left-Edge-of (σ))]

   For every consonant C, there is a syllable σ such that the left edge
   of C coincides with the left edge of σ.

This is the general form of Coda-Cond, ruling out all consonantal elements syllable-finally. The fact that (6) is a positive statement is not an idiosyncrasy; rather, it shares this property with all alignment statements in the current framework.[5] In concrete cases, the consonantal element referred to by means of "C" in (6) is often more narrowly circumscribed by referring to CPlace, marked CPlace, or major segment types (resonants, obstruents). In this way, Coda-Cond, (6), is, properly speaking, an alignment scheme that in individual grammars is cashed in for some set of elementary alignment conditions.

   In order to see how the alignment constraint in (6) can do the work of earlier statements of Coda-Cond, consider the following simple example. McCarthy and Prince (1993b) note that like many other Semitic languages, Bedouin Arabic and biblical Hebrew have a constraint against pharyngeal codas, as a particular instantiation of Coda-Cond (McCarthy 1994). We reproduce their formulation below in (7), where "pharyngeal" refers exclusively to CPlace.

(7) Coda-Cond   *[pharyngeal])$_\sigma$ (McCarthy and Prince
     (Arabic, Hebrew)   1994: 44, (93))

In the theory advocated here, (7) is replaced by the alignment constraint (8).

(8) ALIGN-PHARYNGEAL   ALIGN-LEFT ([pharyngeal], σ)

Rather than disallowing pharyngeals in the coda, ALIGN-PHARYNGEAL (ALIGN-PHAR) assigns a mark to any pharyngeal consonant not left-aligned with a syllable.[6] Just as in the original analysis, this constraint dominates FILL, resulting in epenthesis (indicated by "□" in (9)). The constraint interaction resulting in outputs like those in (9) is depicted in tableau (10).

(9) ya.ʕ□.mōd   "he will stand"
    he.ħ□.zīq   "he strengthened"

(10)		ALIGN-PHAR	FILL
	.yaʕ.mōd.	*!	
☞	.ya.ʕ□.mōd.		*

The move towards stating CODA-COND as a constraint left-aligning consonants with syllables is conceptually attractive because it turns CODA-COND from an association condition loosely appended to the rest of syllable theory into a counterpart of alignment-theoretic ONSET (see (4) and (5)).

2.3 ALIGN-V

Having found a strong case for ALIGN-C in the form of traditional CODA-COND, it is a natural step to turn to ALIGN-V (repeated in (11)) and ask whether any known syllable well-formedness condition might fall under it.

(11) ALIGN-V   ALIGN-RIGHT (V, σ)

The answer is not difficult to find: if the right edge of every vowel must coincide with a right syllable edge, this does not only mean that vowels should stand in open syllables, but also that *vowels should not be part of complex nuclei.* Consider in this context the ban against diphthongs in Rosenthall (1994).

(12) NO-DIPHTHONG   *   (Rosenthall 1994: 27)

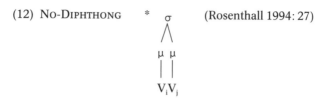

According to Rosenthall (1994), this is an undominated constraint in Yoruba, responsible for alternations as in (13).[7]

(13) /bu+ata/   [bata]   "pour ground pepper"
      /ra+ọgẹdẹ/   [rọgẹdẹ]   "buy bananas"

We propose that the formal expression of the ban against complex nuclei should be the alignment constraint ALIGN-V (11). The tableau in (14) (adapted from Rosenthall 1994: 67) illustrates how the correct empirical results are obtained.

(14)

Input: /bu+ata/	ALIGN-V ALIGN-RIGHT(V, σ)	ONSET ALIGN-LEFT (σ, C)	PARSE
a. .bua.ta.	*!		
b. .bu.a.ta.		*!	
c. ☞ .b<u>a.ta.			*

The segment alignment constraint ALIGN-V requires every vowel to be right-aligned with a syllable, hence in (14a) the vowel *u* violates this constraint, since it is not syllable-final. In (14b) all the vowels are indeed parsed syllable-finally, fulfilling ALIGN-V, but now the medial syllable *.a.* violates the syllable alignment constraint ONSET. Thus, (14c) is the winning candidate, violating the low-ranking PARSE, and fulfilling both ALIGN-V[8] and ONSET.

The constraint NO-DIPHTHONG (12) specifically targets a *sequence* of vowels within the syllable domain. The success of the corresponding nonsequential alignment constraint raises the prospect of further reducing the need for construction-specific sequential constraints in phonological theory.

2.4 Further segment-alignment effects

It would be a mistake to view this alignment-theoretic approach to syllable structure as merely a succinct restatement of familiar conditions

like ONSET, NO-CODA, CODA-COND, and NO-DIPHTHONG. There is a
deeper symmetry organizing the syllable structure constraints, quite comparable to the foot-related constraints; and we will see that the segment-
alignment constraints have more far-reaching effects than what is covered
by CODA-COND or NO-DIPHTHONG.

We start with the chart in (15) showing some correlations between
syllable and segment-alignment constraints in systems where $_\sigma$[CVC] is
the upper bound for syllable complexity. In (15a) and (15d), the four
constraints (ONSET, NO-CODA, ALIGN-C, ALIGN-V) are all satisfied in
.CV. and all violated in .VC. And in (15b) and (15c), ALIGN-C and
ALIGN-V have the same marks as the NO-CODA column.

(15)		Syllable alignment		Segment alignment	
		ONSET	NO-CODA	ALIGN-C	ALIGN-V
		ALIGN-LEFT (σ, C)	ALIGN-RIGHT (σ, V)	ALIGN-LEFT (C, σ)	ALIGN-RIGHT (V, σ)
a.	.CV.	✓	✓	✓	✓
b.	.V.	*	✓	✓	✓
c.	.CVC.	✓	*	*	*
d.	.VC.	*	*	*	*

This correlation between NO-CODA and the segment-alignment constraints might seduce unwary readers into concluding that only one
of the three constraints (NO-CODA, ALIGN-C or ALIGN-V) is necessary in the system.[9] This conclusion, however, would be erroneous: the
apparent marking correlation between NO-CODA and the segment-
alignment constraints exists only at the simplest level of syllabic organization, where many distinctions have collapsed due to the absence of
complex onsets, complex nuclei, and complex codas. The correlation
breaks down once we look beyond the $_\sigma$[CVC] barrier, as shown in
charts (16) and (17). The syllable types considered in (16) have various kinds of onsets and nuclei, but are all open. Those in (17) add
further complexities in their post-vocalic parts (codas, simple and
complex).

(16) (Complex) onset, (complex) nucleus, open

		Syllable alignment		Segment alignment	
		ONSET	NO-CODA	ALIGN-C	ALIGN-V
		ALIGN-LEFT (σ, C)	ALIGN-RIGHT (σ, V)	ALIGN-LEFT (C, σ)	ALIGN-RIGHT (V, σ)
a.	.CV.	✓	✓	✓	✓
b.	.CCV.	✓	✓	*	✓
c.	.CVV.	✓	✓	✓	*
d.	.CCVV.	✓	✓	*	*

(17) (Complex) onset, (complex) nucleus, (complex) coda

		Syllable alignment		Segment alignment	
		ONSET	NO-CODA	ALIGN-C	ALIGN-V
		ALIGN-LEFT (σ, C)	ALIGN-RIGHT (σ, V)	ALIGN-LEFT (C, σ)	ALIGN-RIGHT (V, σ)
a.	.CVC.	✓	*	*	*
b.	.CVCC.	✓	*	**	*
c.	.CCVCC.	✓	*	***	*
d.	.CCCVCC.	✓	*	****	*
e.	.CVVC.	✓	*	*	**
f.	.CVVCC.	✓	*	**	**
g.	.CCVVCC.	✓	*	***	**

With respect to ONSET and NO-CODA, these two groups of syllable types incur the same marks (✓ONSET, ✓NO-CODA in (16), ✓ONSET, *NO-CODA in (17)). But they differ widely with respect to the segment alignment constraints, which focus on every consonant and every vowel in the phonological string. Thus a syllable with a complex onset .CCV. (16b) fulfills ONSET, but the second C incurs one violation of ALIGN-C. Similarly, a syllable with a complex nucleus (diphthong or long vowel) of the form .CVV. (16c) fulfills NO-CODA, but the first V incurs one violation of ALIGN-V. Note that violations of ALIGN-C and ALIGN-V in (16) and (17) can simply be measured categorically (pass/fail), without having to rely on the gradient measures of disalignment suggested by

McCarthy and Prince (1993b) for foot-directionality effects. On the other hand, Mester and Padgett (1994) have found a potential use for gradient measures of violation (in terms of segmental or moraic distance) in syllable theory. We therefore leave the role of gradient violation in syllable alignment as an open question.

Multiple violation marks are incurred when several segments are independently evaluated by the constraint. For example, four consonants are evaluated by ALIGN-C in (17c). The first one passes, the other three fail the alignment test, incurring three marks.

As far as ALIGN-V is concerned, the requirement is not that every syllable should end in some vowel, but that every vowel[10] should end some syllable, and this requirement is violated by every diphthong and every long vowel. Similarly, ALIGN-C is violated by every complex onset (as well as by codas, whether simple or complex (17)).

In terms of the relations between the individual constraints under discussion here, we find the picture in (18), which reveals the extent to which the four constraints are orthogonal to each other (the cells are filled with examples illustrating the compatibility of the two constraint evaluations). Disregarding heterosyllabic geminate consonants and syllables without nuclear vowels, there are two implications (the corresponding cells are marked "*no*" in (18)): a violation of NO-CODA implies a violation of ALIGN-C (*[NO-CODA] ⊃ *[ALIGN-C]) and also a violation of ALIGN-V (*[NO-CODA] ⊃ *[ALIGN-V]).[11]

(18)

ONSET	✓							
	*							
NO-CODA	✓	.cv.	.v.					
	*	.cvc.	.vc.					
ALIGN-C	✓	.cv.	.v.	.cv.	*no*			
	*	.ccv.	.vc.	.ccv.	.cvc.			
ALIGN-V	✓	.cv.	.v.	.cv.	*no*	.cv.	.ccv.	
	*	.cvv.	.vv.	.cvv.	.cvc.	.cvv.	.vc.	
	✓	*	✓	*	✓	*	✓	*
	ONSET		NO-CODA		ALIGN-C		ALIGN-V	

The approach sketched above partially succeeds in deriving specific complexity facts from the interaction of general constraints and in this way achieves a deeper level of explanation than construction-specific constraints. As Scott Myers and an anonymous reviewer have reminded the authors, the alignment-theoretic approach is still programmatic and leaves open many questions in the area of syllable complexity, in particular the mutual independence of various factors: (i) onset complexity and coda complexity, (ii) long vowels and diphthongs, and (iii) nucleus complexity and the admission of closed syllables. Construction-specific constraints like NO-COMPLEX-NUCL, NO-LONG-VOWEL, NO-DIPHTHONG, NO-COMPLEX-ONS, NO-COMPLEX-CODA, etc., will obviously remain unsurpassed in terms of data coverage, but must by the same token remain purely descriptive and do not bring us closer to a theoretical understanding of such complexity issues and their interrelations, with or without Optimality Theory.

In order to illustrate what is involved, consider the third point mentioned above: some languages allow complex nuclei (long vowels and diphthongs), but no closed syllables; other languages allow closed syllables, but no complex nuclei; still other languages allow, or disallow, both. Consider now a language allowing codas but no complex nuclei: since closed syllables violate both ALIGN-C and ALIGN-V, ALIGN-V is clearly a violable constraint in such a language. But then, why would complex nuclei be excluded? One way of approaching this issue is to differentiate between PARSE-C and PARSE-V (as suggested in Prince and Smolensky 1993 and in many other studies). The reader can easily verify that the ranking (19a) derives a coda-language without complex nuclei, whereas (19b) derives a no-coda-language with complex nuclei.

(19) a. PARSE-C   b. PARSE-V

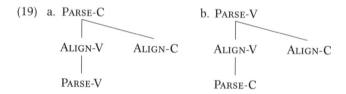

Whether or not such a faithfulness-based analysis is ultimately correct, it serves to illustrate the central strategy advocated here: instead of postulating construction-specific complexity constraints, the generalizations are derived by having segment-alignment constraints interact with members of other constraint families in crucial ways.

2.5 Segment alignment and segment sonority

A legitimate question to ask at this point concerns the role of segment-alignment constraints in phonology, including their interface with phonetics: why do segment-alignment constraints exist? (Note that this question is different from: what service can they perform in the analysis of complex syllable structures?)[12] We hypothesize that segment-alignment constraints are related to a more fundamental requirement: *segments should be prominent*. And being leftmost or rightmost in some domain counts as being prominent. The reason why consonants should be *left*-aligned with syllables, and vowels *right*-aligned, lies probably in their phonetic nature, involving both articulatory and acoustic factors; formal phonology records the asymmetry in terms of alignment constraints whose edge-orientation is substantively determined.

A syllable has only two edges, hence only two segments can be prominent in virtue of being adjacent to a syllable edge (*.CV.* violates no prominence constraints). This raises two intrinsically related questions: what does the prominence profile of larger syllables (like *.trend.*) look like? And what is the connection between the alignment-theoretic approach to syllable structure and classical (Sievers–Jespersen) sonority theory?[13]

Taking up an idea first brought up in Prince (1983) and to some extent developed in work by Borowsky (1984) and others, suppose we give formal expression to the sonority relations between segments by means of a sonority grid representation: the more sonorous a segment, the more grid-marks in its sonority grid column (as Sharon Inkelas reminds us, a different but related idea is the syllable-internal metrical constituency hypothesized by Kiparsky 1979 and Zec 1988). This is shown in (20a), which corresponds to the familiar depiction of syllable sonority in (20b) (by means of an upwards–downwards curving graph). Since there is good reason to believe that the notion of sonority itself, while phonetically grounded, does not represent a directly measurable phonetic quantity, discrete grid representations might in fact be more appropriate than the largely fictitious continuity of sonority "profiles" like (20b).

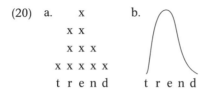

(20) a.   x   b.

      x x

      x x x

      x x x x x

      t r e n d   t r e n d

At first glance, it looks as if grid representations as in (20a) serve only an illustrative purpose and should not be part of the representational system admitted by formal phonology. But things begin to look different when we consider the familiar sonority profile in this grid from the point of view of alignment.[14] If being prominent means being foremost (leftmost, rightmost) in some domain, a segment can fulfill alignment with a syllable edge in two ways: (i) by literally occupying the edge position (*string alignment* – of the segment within the terminal string), and (ii) by occupying an edge position in terms of its highest sonority grid mark (*grid alignment* – of a segment's highest grid-mark, on its level of the sonority grid). The idea is that every segment in a syllable like *.trend.* fulfills grid alignment, as indicated in (21): the highest (circled) grid-mark in every segment column is adjacent to (aligned with) the syllable edge.

(21)
$$
\begin{array}{ccccc}
 & & ⓧ & & \\
 & ⓧ & x & & \\
 & x & x & ⓧ & \\
ⓧ & x & x & x & ⓧ \\
t & r & e & n & d
\end{array}
$$

The optimality of culminative sonority profiles lies in the fact that *any* permutation of two adjacent grid columns in (21) would cut off the segment with a shorter grid column from the edge (by an intervening segment with a higher grid column). In (22), we show various reorderings of the nonce string [klurd] and their representations on the sonority grid. For clarity, we denote the highest grid mark of the sonority grid column associated with some segment k as Ⓚ.[15]

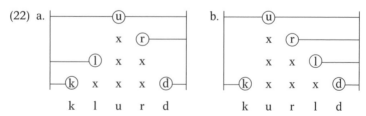

(22) a.   b.

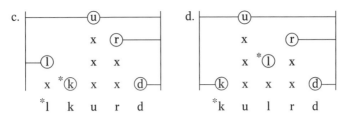

What is of interest for grid alignment, then, is the topmost entry in each segment column. For a segment s, we will refer to the highest sonority mark in its grid as Max(s) (written as Ⓢ). An alignment-theoretic version of the Sievers–Jespersen sonority sequencing principle then takes the form of a constraint requiring every segment s to be grid-aligned with a syllable edge.[16]

(23) ALIGN-EDGE (Max(s), σ)   (where Edge stands for "Left or Right")[17]

Finally, this alignment approach to syllable sonority may provide a new formal foundation for the notion "demisyllable" familiar from the work of Fujimura and Lovins (1978), Fujimura (1979), and Clements (1990): the initial demisyllable consists of the substring grid-aligned with the left edge of the syllable, while the final demisyllable consists of the substring grid-aligned with the right edge of the syllable. As seen in (22a) and (22b), the peak vowel is aligned with both edges, and hence is a member of both the initial and final demisyllable.

3. Crisp edges

What counts as aligned/misaligned becomes less straightforward when we consider junctures with multiple linking. In order to illustrate the problem, let us consider the four different situations in (24) with respect to ALIGN-R constraints (both ALIGN-R (A, C) and ALIGN-R (C, A)). There is little doubt that (24a) should count as aligned and (24b) and (24c) as misaligned. But how about (24d)? Here the rightmost element of C, α, is indeed linked to an element at the right edge of A – but not exclusively: α is also linked to an element at the left edge of B. It is such situations of nonexclusive linkage (in the terminology of Merchant 1996) that we turn to next.

(24) a.

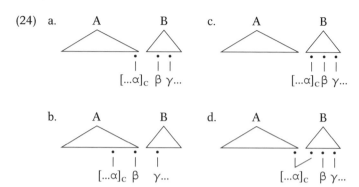

We will first take a closer look at some past OT analyses that deal with such cases, and then consider the consequences for syllable-theoretic alignment constraints. As we will show, the double-linking scenario provides access to details of alignment structure, and helps us settle an open question regarding the formal definition of alignment.

3.1 Nonexclusive linking and the Lardil–Axininca alignment dilemma

The two most influential syllable-based analyses in Optimality Theory, that of Lardil (Prince and Smolensky 1993) and that of Axininca Campa (McCarthy and Prince 1993a), both employ the GCat-PCat alignment constraint ALIGN-RIGHT (25), requiring right stem edges to coincide with right syllable edges.

(25) ALIGN-RIGHT (stem, σ)   (See Prince and Smolensky 1993: 103 [Lardil]; McCarthy and Prince 1993a: 35–36 [Axininca Campa].)

An unresolved problem arises in situations where the crucial stem-suffix juncture is multiply linked: the interpretation of this alignment constraint diverges for Lardil and Axininca Campa. In order to capture the facts in the two languages, "ALIGN-RIGHT (stem, σ)" must be interpreted as *fulfilled* for the multiply linked structure in Lardil (Prince and Smolensky 1993: 103), but as *violated* in the parallel Axininca Campa situation (McCarthy and Prince 1993a: 39–40).

(26) a. Lardil /kaŋ+a/ "speech"   b. Axininca Campa /kim+aancʰi/
                                         "to hear"
   [.kaŋ.ka.], *[.ka.ŋa.]   *[.kim.paan.cʰi.], [.ki.maan.cʰi.]

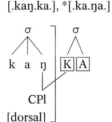

   CPl
   [dorsal]

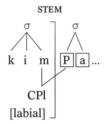

                                         CPl
                                         [labial]

   [.kaŋ.⊥Ka.] (aligned?)   *[.kim.⊥Paan.cʰi.] (misaligned?)

In Lardil (26a), [.kaŋ.⊥Ka.] (where [K] denotes an epenthetic onset
filler homorganic (⊥) with the stem-final [ŋ]) is taken to satisfy align-
ment, and is for this reason preferred to the misaligned *[.ka.ŋ|a.]. In
Axininca Campa (26b), on the other hand, both the multiply linked
*[.kim.⊥ Paan.cʰi.] (where [P] denotes an epenthetic onset filler homor-
ganic with the stem-final [m]) and the nonepenthetic [.ki.m|aan.cʰi.] are
taken as misaligned ("ALIGN requires sharply defined morpheme edges,
but linking…undoes the desired relation between the morphological
and prosodic constituency of a form" (McCarthy and Prince 1993a: 39–
40)). Since the two competing candidates [.ki.m|aan.cʰi.] and [.kim.⊥
Paan.cʰi.] tie on ALIGN-RIGHT (violations are crucially reckoned categorically, not gradiently), FILL decides in favor of the first candidate (which
gets by with less epenthesis).

The inconsistency in the interpretation of alignment is illustrated in
ranking tableau format in (27).[18] The correct results are obtained only if
double-linking at the crucial juncture fulfills ALIGN-RIGHT for Lardil,
but violates ALIGN-RIGHT for Axininca Campa.[19]

(27) a. Lardil:

/kaŋ + a/	ONSET	ALIGN-R	FILL
☞Lardil .kaŋ.⊥Ka.			*
.ka.ŋ|a.		*!	
.kaŋ.|a.	*!		

b. Axininca

/kim + a .../	Onset	Align-R	Fill
.kim.⊥Pa.		*	*!
☞ Axininca .ki.m|a.		*	
.kim.|a.	*!		

3.2 Alignment as crisp alignment

The formal definition of Alignment offered in McCarthy and Prince (1993b: 10, reproduced below in (28)) leads to the interpretation that is necessary for the Axininca analysis, where multiple linking at the relevant juncture entails misalignment.[20] Formally, the sharp edge requirement is built into the definition of alignment reproduced in (28). The definition is cast in string-theoretic terms and makes use of the notion "is-a," familiar from the formal theory of syntactic constituency (see section 3.3 below for further discussion of this notion).

(28) Definition
      Align (Cat$_1$, Edge$_1$, Cat$_2$, Edge$_2$) (McCarthy and Prince 1993b: 10)
      Let Edge$_1$, Edge$_2$ be either L or R. Let S be any string. Then, for any substring A of S that is-a Cat$_1$, there is [a] substring B of S that is-a Cat$_2$, such that there is a decomposition D(A) of A and a decomposition D(B) of B, both sub-decompositions of a decomposition D(S) of S, such that Edge$_1$ (D(A)) = Edge$_2$ (D(B)).

The definition in (28) is one possible way of making the alignment concept precise, among several alternatives; in particular, there is no *a priori* reason to make the definition so crucially dependent on the strict *is-a* relation. Before scrambling to find some reanalysis for Lardil that is compatible with (28), it would therefore be advisable to look at other alignment constraints and consider the consequences of the various ways of understanding alignment. It turns out that the view of alignment which interprets cross-linkage as misaligning is particularly problematic for the syllable-theoretic alignment constraints discussed above in section 3.1. Consider a situation where Align-C (Coda-Cond) refers specifically to CPlace (29), as in Japanese, Ponapean, Diola Fogny, Axininca Campa, and many other languages.

(29) a. ALIGN-C (Japanese, etc.)   ALIGN-LEFT (CPlace, σ)
     b. ONSET   ALIGN-LEFT (σ, C)

As is well known, the central property of such cases is that multiply linked CPlace (linked to both coda and onset) does not count as a violation of CODA-COND; earlier theories (starting with Itô 1986, 1989) take account of this by exempting geminate consonants and place-linked clusters in some way or other (by means of underlying placelessness persisting into the derivation, by linkage count, by licensing through ONSET, or by other theoretical devices bestowing special privileges on geminates and partial geminates: see Goldsmith 1990, Lombardi 1991, Scobbie 1991, and Itô and Mester 1993 for discussion; see Itô, Mester, and Padgett 1995 for an approach to some aspects of feature linkage, feature (under)specification, and assimilation within OT). In a situation where CODA-COND is a highly-ranked constraint, then, as in Japanese, geminates and place-linked clusters should not count as violating alignment. For example, just as the CPlace in (30a) fulfills alignment with the left edge of the second syllable, the CPlace in the linked cases (30b) and (30c) must also fulfill alignment with the left edge of the second syllable, in spite of the additional link to the preceding syllable.

(30) a. kama "kettle"   b. kampai "cheers"   c. kappa "water
                                                         imp"

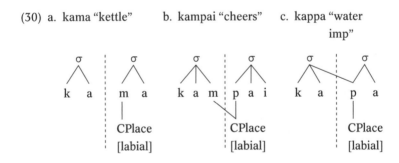

This alignment scenario is not restricted to CODA-COND: all syllables in (30) clearly also fulfill ONSET, irrespective of whether the targeted consonant is exclusively linked as a leftmost syllable daughter (30a) or whether it is *also* linked as the rightmost daughter of another syllable (30c). Fulfilling ONSET by linking to an adjacent segment is quite common (e.g., leading to ambisyllabicity, see McCarthy 1993). These results cannot be obtained with the definition of alignment in (28). In (30b) and (30c), the two syllables share segmental material; therefore, in the technical sense of the relation "*is-a*," neither (30b) nor (30c) contains a string that *is-a* syllable. It is hence impossible for ALIGN-C (CODA-COND) (29a), as a condition seeking to align a consonant *to a syllable*, ever to be fulfilled in these forms. On the other hand, since there is no string that *is-a* syllable, ONSET (29b) is vacuously fulfilled (in the absence of a string that *is-a* syllable, there can never be a string that *is-a* syllable and fails to be left-aligned with a consonant), irrespective of the absence or presence of onsets.

The foregoing discussion makes it clear that under the definition of alignment in (28), our attempt to state basic syllable laws in terms of alignment constraints cannot succeed – we end up with absurd results (see Itô and Mester 1994 for further discussion). Note, however, that the culprit is not the notion "alignment" by itself, but rather the idea that alignment is built on the notion "*is-a*," which is responsible for the crisp alignment requirement.

Like ALIGN-R in Lardil, ONSET and ALIGN-C are constraints whose alignment requirements are fulfilled even when double linking has blurred the crucial edge. From this perspective, the "odd man out" is not the Lardil case, but rather the Axininca case (and the conception of alignment on which it is built). Before throwing out the baby with the bathwater, however, we should also note the kernel of truth that remains in the thesis of crisp alignment: there is a penalty against cross-junctural linkages, as shown by the facts of the Axininca case.

Our conclusion is that the crisp-edge requirement and the general notion "alignment" are independent elements of the theory that must be decoupled. In other words, we propose that alignment constraints are indeed fulfilled in noncrisp linkage situations.[21] Furthermore, there is a family of constraints favoring crisp edges of prosodic categories that we will refer to as "CRISP-EDGE." We develop the formal details in the next section, and show that CRISP-EDGE is independent of the various alignment constraints in terms of its function and its ranking with respect to other constraints.

3.3 Alignment and crisp edges: definitions and further issues

Allowing noncrisp linkage to fulfill alignment constraints requires only a small formal change in the definition of alignment. The idea is to employ a relation which traces downwards from a category to the terminal string and finds the category's content. This relation will take the place of the *is-a* relation which traces upwards from a terminal substring towards a category and requires uniqueness of the higher category, in the sense explained above (see (28) and the related discussion). We will make use of the relation *is-the-content-of* (identical with Pierrehumbert and Beckman's (1988: 156) notion "substantive fringe of a node"); for our purposes here, it will be sufficient to note that within a phonological representation a terminal substring A *is-the-content-of* a category $\mathfrak{C}$ if and only if A is the maximal terminal substring dominated by $\mathfrak{C}$. Note that a string A can *be-the-content-of* a category, $\mathfrak{C}$, even if some element of A is also linked to some node outside of $\mathfrak{C}$.

In (31), we first introduce some notation designed to facilitate formal development.

(31) Notation

$\|...\|$	the content of…	$\|\mathfrak{C}\|=/\beta/$	the content of $\mathfrak{C}$ is the string β
$\equiv$	*is-a*	$/\beta/ \equiv \mathfrak{C}$	the string β *is-a* $\mathfrak{C}$
$\subseteq$	is a substring of	$/xy/ \subseteq /wxyz/$	the string xy is a substring of the string $wxyz$

Consider next the example in (32).

(32) a.

```
      σ₁          σ₂
      |  \      / |
      a    t   a        atta
```

b. $|\sigma_2|=/ta/$

c. $/ta/ \not\equiv \sigma$

In (32a), /ta/ *is-the-content-of* σ_2 (32b): a trace downwards from σ_2 converges on /ta/ as the maximal terminal substring dominated by σ_2. On the other hand, /ta/ *is-not-a* σ (32c): a trace upwards from the terminal elements of /ta/ does not converge on a single node labelled "σ." We note without proof that /x/ $\equiv \mathfrak{C}$ implies $|\mathfrak{C}_i| = /x/$ (for some i), whereas the converse does not always hold. Equipped with this understanding of *is-the-content-of* ("$|...|$"), we can proceed to the revised definition of *alignment* in (33) (built on (28), with the changes noted earlier).

(33) Revised definition of alignment: ALIGN ($\mathfrak{C}_1$,E_1,$\mathfrak{C}_2$,E_2)
Let E_1, E_2 be either Left or Right. Let S be any string. Then, for any
A⊆S with A=|$\mathfrak{C}_1$|, there is a B⊆S with B=|$\mathfrak{C}_2$|, such that there is a
decomposition D(A) of A and a decomposition D(B) of B, both
sub-decompositions of a decomposition D(S) of S, such that
E_1(D(A))=E_2(D(B)).

Turning then to the CRISP-EDGE constraint, its intuitive aim is to rule
out any linking across the edges of prosodic categories, as depicted in
(34).

(34) Multiple linking between prosodic categories is prohibited

(35) is a formal version of the CRISP-EDGE constraint (or rather, constraint scheme); every prosodic category has an associated constraint of
this kind, and the different CRISP-EDGE constraints can be separately
ranked.

(35) CRISP-EDGE[PCat]
Definition
Let /A/ be a terminal substring in a phonological representation,
$\mathfrak{C}$ a category of type PCat, and /A/= |$\mathfrak{C}$| (*the-content-of* $\mathfrak{C}$). Then
$\mathfrak{C}$ is *crisp* (has *crisp edges*) if and only if A *is-a* $\mathfrak{C}$: ∀ A (/A/ = |$\mathfrak{C}$| ⊃
/A/≡ $\mathfrak{C}$)

CRISP-EDGE[PCat]: A PCat has crisp edges.

CRISP-EDGE remains to be further developed in terms of categories and
L–R edges. Of central importance is CRISP-EDGE[PrWd], which figures for
example in the analysis of the prosodic morphology of Sino-Japanese by
Itô and Mester (1996); if in most dialects of English (word-internal)
ambisyllabicity is only possible in non-foot-initial position (see Kiparsky
1979, among others), this can be viewed as a consequence of CRISP-
EDGE[Ft]. CRISP-EDGE[σ] rules out gemination and similar cases of
double-linking. In the version of the CRISP-EDGE constraint in (35), there
is no attempt to distinguish between left and right edges. If this turns out
to be necessary, relativization to particular edges can be introduced

(general notions like "edge," "left," and "right" are not the exclusive property of alignment theory). An apparatus more complex than the one in (35) is certainly imaginable, for example, with crispness requirements coupled with particular alignment configurations, but would have to be supported by empirical evidence. Until such evidence emerges, the plain form in (35) seems adequate.

The independence of ALIGNMENT and CRISP-EDGE is brought home in chart (36). We are here considering CRISP-EDGE[σ] and ALIGN-C (both binary constraints, i.e., evaluated categorically: pass/fail). (36a) to (36d) are examples for all four marking combinations: (✓ ✓), (✓ *), (* ✓), and (* *).

(36)		CRISP-EDGE[σ]	ALIGN-LEFT (C, σ)
a. σ σ ∧ ∧ C V C V		✓	✓
b. σ σ ∧ ∣ C V C V		✓	*
c. σ σ ∧∧ C V C V		*	✓
d. σ σ ∧∧ C V C C V		*	*

3.4 Resolving the dilemma

Once alignment constraints and CRISP-EDGE constraints are distinguished, the resolution of the Lardil–Axininca dilemma is straightforward: from the current perspective, the dilemma arose out of a notion of "alignment" which was in reality a conflation of two separate notions. In the present theory, we can distinguish the two systems simply by ranking the relevant constraints differently for Axininca (CRISP-EDGE ≫ ALIGN-R), and Lardil (ALIGN-R ≫ CRISP-EDGE). The tableaux in (38) and (37) illustrate that the correct candidate is chosen as the winner (compare (26) and (27) above).

(37) Lardil:[22]

/kaŋ + a/	Onset	Align-R	Crisp-Edge(σ)	Fill
a. ☞ .kaŋ.⊥Ka.			*	*
b. .ka. ŋ|a.		*!		
c. .kaŋ|.a.	*!			

(38) Axininca:[23]

/kim + a .../	Onset	Crisp-Edge(σ)	Align-R	Fill
a. .kim.⊥Pa.		*!		*
b. ☞ .ki.m|a.			*	
c. .kim|.a.	*!			

Candidates with noncrisp linkages, (38a) and (37a), do not violate Align-R but violate Crisp-Edge. Axininca ranks Crisp-Edge above Align-R (38), hence the winning candidate has crisp-edged but misaligned syllables. On the other hand, the ranking of the two constraints is the reverse in Lardil (37), hence the winner has aligned but noncrispedged syllables.

4. Summary

This chapter has pursued two independent but interrelated lines of inquiry into Alignment Theory. First, it shows that a small extension of the theory results in the subsumption of a significant part of traditional syllable theory, including various conditions on syllable structural complexity (conditions on codas, complex onsets, complex nuclei, and complex codas), and it offers some speculations regarding an alignment-theoretic approach to classical sonority theory in terms of grid alignment. Second, the chapter takes up a problem arising for the alignment concept (as defined in McCarthy and Prince 1993b) in connection with the multiply linked structures that are the hallmark of modern nonlinear phonological representations. The central idea is that, different from the standard view, alignment per se must be decoupled from the requirement that prosodic categories need sharp edges, not blurred by double linking. This requires the formal notion "Crisp Edge" for prosodic categories and concomitantly a revised definition of alignment.

Notes

1 For stimulating questions and suggestions, we would like to thank the participants at the 1994 Utrecht Workshop on Prosodic Morphology, an anonymous reviewer, and the editors. For helpful comments on an earlier version of this paper, we are grateful to Diana Archangeli, Sharon Inkelas, René Kager, Dan Karvonen, John McCarthy, Jason Merchant, Scott Myers, Orhan Orgun, Jaye Padgett, Janet Pierrehumbert, Alan Prince, Doug Pulleyblank, Curt Rice, Philip Spaelti, Rachel Walker, Moira Yip, and Cheryl Zoll.

2 The formulation in McCarthy and Prince (1993b) has four arguments: ONSET "ALIGN (σ, L, C, L)" and NO-CODA "ALIGN (σ, R, V, R)." We have extracted the same-edge argument here to simplify the discussion. The condensed notation also brings out the fact that alignment conditions (apart from the separate category of opposite-edge alignment conditions like "Suffix-to-PrWd" (McCarthy and Prince 1993a)) have two, and not four, arguments (see also Pierrehumbert 1993 for discussion).

3 The first requires every prosodic word to have a foot flush with its beginning but is silent about other feet contained within a prosodic word. The second requires the left edge of every foot to coincide with the left edge of some prosodic word but does not require anything of prosodic words in general. The latter constraint incurs multiple violations in foot parsing; violations are reckoned in a gradient manner; selection proceeds under the criterion of minimum violation, as usual, and picks the foot parse most clustering towards the edge-to-be-aligned-to: every other parse incurs more alignment violations. (The idea that directionality effects can in this way be viewed as minimal violation effects is attributed to R. Kirchner in McCarthy and Prince 1993b.)

4 This is not to say that substantively fixed argument settings do not exist. As we will see in section 2.5, the edge orientation (Left/Right) appears to be phonetically determined.

5 Negative alignment statements are in principle not impossible: NonFinality (Prince and Smolensky 1993), for example, could be viewed as a negative constraint of this kind, i.e., as an antialignment constraint ruling out the right-alignment of any head of PrWd with PrWd: ~Align-Right (H(PrWd), PrWd). This constraint (which calls for categorical and not gradient evaluation) makes use of H(PrWd), a generalized notion of "head" denoting *any* head of PrWd, i.e., its immediate head (foot), the most prominent foot of the word, and in addition the head of the head foot, i.e., the most prominent syllable of the word, an idea first explored in Prince and Smolensky (1993): H(X) = Head(X), Head(Head(X)), etc. Many questions regarding the proper treatment of nonfinality effects remain open, as demonstrated by Hung (1994); in a related vein, Spaelti

(1993) proposes a WEAKEDGE constraint that favors sparseness of structure at right edges of prosodic trees, and obtains some interesting results
that are not directly replicable with standard versions of NONFINALITY. In
the present context, questions regarding the existence of antialignment
constraints must remain unexplored, and we will confine our discussion
to positive alignment statements.

6 In this case, double-linking issues do not arise in connection with ALIGN-
PHAR because of a high-ranking constraint against geminate pharyngeals
(see McCarthy 1986, 1994). We will return to the important question of
multiple linking in connection with our discussion of crisp and noncrisp
alignment in section 3.

7 Doug Pulleyblank (electronic communication, 16 February 1995) has
pointed out to us that the Yoruba facts are more complex than what is
portrayed in (13), with grammatical conditioning, optionality, and other
conditions entering as independent factors.

8 Note that unparsed segments must count as vacuously fulfilling the segment-alignment constraint.

9 Thus it has been suggested to us in comments on our previous work on
AlIGN-C (Itô and Mester 1994) that ALIGN-C takes the place of No-CODA,
making the latter superfluous.

10 Or "vowel mora." For simplicity of presentation, our segmental representations here abstract away from the more sophisticated representational
apparatus in the current literature.

11 Heterosyllabic geminate consonants violate No-CODA, but do not violate
ALIGN-C, under our conception of (noncrisp) alignment; see section 3.
And a syllable without any vowel cannot violate ALIGN-V, even if it viol-
ates No-CODA.

12 See Itô and Mester (1994: 32–33) and in particular Smolensky (1995) for
potential extensions in the area of onset maximization, syllable contact,
and minimal sonority distance.

13 See Sievers (1881) and Jespersen (1904); see also Saussure (1916) for a
closely related aperture-based approach; among the numerous developments in contemporary phonology, see Zec (1988) and Clements (1990)
and references therein. The latter work also contains a clear statement
of the assumption that sonority in the sense relevant for syllable theory is
not a single phonetic parameter which could be directly measured, but
rather a composite phonological notion based on several different phonetic
parameters, an assumption explicitly or implicitly made by most modern
work on the topic; see Ladefoged (1990) for a concurrent view from a
phonetic perspective.

14 This idea was suggested to us by A. Prince (electronic communication,
21 April 1994).

15 Not all permutations that fulfill grid alignment (and thus conform to
   universal sonority sequencing) are well-formed (e.g. *[klrud]). Clearly,
   further constraints are at work (e.g., demisyllabic constraints) whose
   nature and role remain to be investigated within the current framework.
16 Grid Column Continuity (Liberman and Prince 1977, Prince 1983, Hayes
   1995) would make it possible to state the constraint in a looser way,
   such that, for every segment, *some* grid-mark in its grid column must be
   aligned with the syllable, without requiring the grid-mark to be the topmost one in its column. Given grid-column continuity, edge-adjacency of
   some nonmaximal grid-mark *g* entails edge-adjacency of all grid-marks
   above *g*.
17 In each case, Max(*s*) will occupy some level *L* of the grid. We assume here,
   postponing formal development for another occasion, that evaluating the
   alignment of Max(*s*) with a syllable σ means evaluating its alignment with
   the string of grid marks associated with σ at level *L*.
18 In order to focus on the point under discussion, we treat the epenthetic
   final /a/ in Lardil (forced by prosodic word minimality, see Prince and
   Smolensky 1993: ch. 7 and reference cited there) as a suffix. (We note that
   another possible attack on the Lardil/Axininca dilemma, different from
   the one pursued in the text, could focus on precisely this difference
   between the two cases: in Lardil, the input contains no suffixal material,
   and the free play of Gen results in the epenthesis of a whole syllable in
   many cases. In Axininca, on the other hand, the input already comes
   with a (vowel-initial) suffix. This raises the possibility that the emergence
   of an epenthetic onset filler in Lardil could be viewed as an instance of
   the emergence of the unmarked (here: syllable with an onset), in the sense
   of McCarthy and Prince (1994). It is not entirely clear, however, how
   this idea could be formally executed; furthermore, a full analysis of Lardil
   would have to take into account a number of allomorphy facts relevant
   for stem alignment, such as Hale's (1973: 423) observation that the future
   suffix /-uŋ/ appears as /-kuŋ/ after all nasal-final stems (perhaps a case
   of prosodically controlled allomorph selection, in the sense of Mester
   1994).
19 It is not possible to resolve the paradox by reranking FILL over ALIGN-R
   in Axininca: as shown by McCarthy and Prince (1993a: 36) ALIGN-R
   must dominate FILL: /iN + koma + i/ → .iŋ.koma|.Ti., *.iŋ.koma|i. "he
   will paddle."
20 This "thesis of crisp alignment" is further articulated in McCarthy and
   Prince (1993b: note 44), which reinforces the impression – with some
   reservations – that unique graph-theoretic mothering is indeed a precondition for successful alignment. See also McCarthy (1993) for an English example.

21 Independent arguments in support of this can be found in other recent studies. Merchant (1996) shows that ambisyllabic consonants in German fulfill a constraint requiring stem-syllable alignment at right edges. Cohn and McCarthy (1994: 46) make a similar point, *viz.*, that Indonesian vocoids linked simultaneously to nucleus and onset position do not count as violating root-to-foot alignment.

22 Further aspects of the analysis of Lardil stem alignment (in particular, the emergence of unmarked homorganicity over coronality) are discussed in Itô and Mester (1994: 39–43).

23 Another possibility is to make ALIGN-R and CRISP-EDGE(σ) crucially unranked in Axininca (which would require weakening the standard theory of constraint ranking, as noted at various points in Prince and Smolensky 1993). Then the two constraints would tie, and lower-ranked FILL would cast the decisive vote in favor of *kima*...(thus replicating an aspect of the analysis of McCarthy and Prince 1993a).

References

Borowsky, Toni. 1984. On a grid-based theory of the syllable, ms. University of Massachusetts, Amherst, MA.

Burzio, Luigi. 1994. *Principles of English Stress*, Cambridge University Press.

Clements, G. N. 1990. The role of the sonority cycle in core syllabification, in J. Kingston and M. Beckman (eds.), *Papers in Laboratory Phonology* 1: *Between the Grammar and Physics of Speech*, New York, NY: Cambridge University Press, 283–333.

Cohn, Abigail C. 1989. Stress in Indonesian and bracketing paradoxes, *Natural Language and Linguistic Theory* 7: 167–216.

Cohn, Abigail C., and John J. McCarthy. 1994. Alignment and parallelism in Indonesian phonology, ms. Cornell University, Ithaca, NY and University of Massachusetts, Amherst, MA.

Fujimura, Osamu. 1979. An analysis of English syllables as cores and affixes, *Zeitschrift für Phonetik, Sprachwissenschaft und Kommunikationsforschung* 32: 471–76.

Fujimura, Osamu, and Juliette B. Lovins. 1978. Syllables as concatenative phonetic units, in A. Bell and J. B. Hooper (eds.), *Syllables and Segments*, Amsterdam: North-Holland, 107–20.

Goldsmith, John. 1990. *Autosegmental and Metrical Phonology*, Oxford: Blackwell.

Hale, Kenneth. 1973. Deep-surface canonical disparities in relation to analysis and change: an Australian example, in T. A. Sebeok (ed.), *Cur-*

rent *Trends in Linguistics* vol. 11, Mouton: The Hague and Paris, 401–58.

Hayes, Bruce. 1995. *Metrical Stress Theory: Principles and Case Studies*. University of Chicago Press.

Hung, Henrietta. 1994. The rhythmic and prosodic organization of edge constituents, Ph.D. dissertation, Brandeis University, Waltham, MA.

Idsardi, William. 1992. The computation of prosody, Ph.D. dissertation, Massachusetts Institute of Technology, Cambridge, MA.

Inkelas, Sharon. 1989. Prosodic constituency in the lexicon, Ph.D. dissertation, Stanford University, Stanford, CA.

Itô, Junko. 1986. Syllable theory in prosodic phonology, Ph.D. dissertation, University of Massachusetts, Amherst, MA.

1989. A prosodic theory of epenthesis, *Natural Language and Linguistic Theory* 7: 217–60.

Itô, Junko, and R. Armin Mester. 1992. Weak layering and word binarity, Report no. LRC-92-4, Linguistics Research Center, University of California, Santa Cruz, CA.

1993. Licensed segments and safe paths, *Canadian Journal of Linguistics* 38: 197–213.

1994. Reflections on CodaCond and alignment, in J. Merchant, J. Padgett, and R. Walker (eds.), *Phonology at Santa Cruz III*, University of California, Santa Cruz, CA, 27–46.

1996. Stem and word in Sino-Japanese, in T. Otake and A. Cutler (eds.), *Phonological Structure and Language Processing*, Speech Research 12, Berlin: Mouton de Gruyter, 13–44.

Itô, Junko, R. Armin Mester, and Jaye Padgett. 1995. Licensing and underspecification in Optimality Theory, *Linguistic Inquiry* 26: 571–614.

Jespersen, Otto. 1904. *Lehrbuch der Phonetik*, Authorized translation by Hermann Davidsen, Leipzig and Berlin: B. G. Teubner.

Kiparsky, Paul. 1979. Metrical structure assignment is cyclic, *Linguistic Inquiry* 10: 421–41.

Ladefoged, Peter. 1990. On dividing phonetics and phonology, in J. Kingston and M. Beckman (eds.), *Papers in Laboratory Phonology* 1: *Between the Grammar and Physics of Speech*, Cambridge University Press, 398–405.

Liberman, Mark, and Alan S. Prince. 1977. On stress and linguistic rhythm, *Linguistic Inquiry* 8: 249–336.

Lombardi, Linda. 1991. Laryngeal Features and Laryngeal Neutralization, Ph.D. dissertation, University of Massachusetts, Amherst, MA.

McCarthy, John J. 1986. OCP effects: gemination and antigemination, *Linguistic Inquiry* 17: 207–63.

1993. A case of surface constraint violation, *Canadian Journal of Linguistics* 38: 169–95.

1994. The phonetics and phonology of Semitic pharyngeals, in P. Keating (ed.), *Papers in Laboratory Phonology* 3, Cambridge University Press, 191–233.

McCarthy, John J., and Alan S. Prince. 1993a. Prosodic Morphology I: constraint interaction and satisfaction, ms. University of Massachusetts, Amherst, MA, and Rutgers University, New Brunswick, NJ.

1993b. Generalized Alignment, in G. E. Booij and J. van Marle (eds.), *Yearbook of Morphology 1993*, Dordrecht: Kluwer, 79–153.

1994. The emergence of the unmarked, *Proceedings of the North East Linguistic Society* 24, GLSA, University of Massachusetts, Amherst, MA: Graduate Linguistic Student Association, 333–79.

Merchant, Jason. 1996. Alignment and fricative assimilation in German, *Linguistic Inquiry* 27: 709–19.

Mester, R. Armin. 1994. The quantitative trochee in Latin, *Natural Language and Linguistic Theory* 12: 1–61.

Mester, R. Armin, and Jaye Padgett. 1994. Directional syllabification in Generalized Alignment, in J. Merchant, J. Padgett, and R. Walker (eds.), *PASC III*, University of California, Santa Cruz, CA, 79–85.

Pierrehumbert, Janet. 1993. Alignment and prosodic heads. Paper presented at *Eastern States Conference on Linguistics*.

Pierrehumbert, Janet, and Mary Beckman. 1988. *Japanese Tone Structure*, Cambridge, MA: MIT Press.

Prince, Alan S. 1983. Relating to the grid, *Linguistic Inquiry* 14: 19–100.

Prince, Alan S., and Paul Smolensky. 1991. Notes on Connectionism and Harmony Theory in linguistics, TR CU-CS-533–91, Department of Computer Science, University of Colorado, Boulder, CO.

1993. Optimality Theory: constraint interaction in generative grammar, ms. Rutgers University, New Brunswick, NJ, and University of Colorado, Boulder, CO.

Rosenthall, Samuel. 1994. Vowel/glide alternation in a theory of constraint interaction, Ph.D. dissertation, University of Massachusetts, Amherst, MA.

Saussure, Ferdinand de. 1916. *Cours de linguistique générale*, Publié par Charles Bally et Albert Sechehaye; avec la collaboration de Albert Reidlinger, Paris: Payot.

Scobbie, James M. 1991. Attribute value phonology, Ph.D. dissertation, University of Edinburgh.

Selkirk, Elisabeth. 1986. On derived domains in sentence phonology, *Phonology Yearbook* 3: 371–405.

Sievers, Eduard. 1881. *Grundzüge der Phonetik, zur Einführung in das Studium der Lautlehre der indogermanischen Sprachen*. [5th improved edition, Leipzig: Breitkopf and Härtel, 1901, Hildesheim, New York, NY: G. Olms, 1976.]

Smolensky, Paul. 1995. On the internal structure of the constraint component of UG, colloquium handout, University of California, Los Angeles, April 1995.

Spaelti, Philip. 1993. Final geminates in Swiss German, in *Proceedings of the North East Linguistic Society* 24, Amherst, MA: Graduate Linguistic Student Association, University of Massachusetts.

Zec, Draga. 1988. Sonority constraints on prosodic structure, Ph.D. dissertation, Stanford University, Stanford, CA.

7 Faithfulness and identity in Prosodic Morphology

John J. McCarthy and Alan S. Prince

1. Introduction

The theory of Prosodic Morphology (PM)[1] addresses a range of empirical problems lying at the phonology-morphology interface: reduplication, infixation, root-and-pattern morphology, and canonical shape requirements (such as word minimality). Its goal is to explain the properties of these phenomena in terms of general, independently motivated principles of morphology, of phonology, and of their interface. If the enterprise is fully successful, then these principles alone will suffice, and there will be no PM-specific principles or apparatus lurking anywhere in linguistic theory. Put in this way, the goal of PM is the same as the rest of linguistic theory: to achieve greater empirical coverage and deeper explanation with fewer resources – in the happiest case, with no resources at all that are specific to the domain under investigation.

This program was initiated by identifying templates with prosodic categories, eliminating the freedom to stipulate the form of templates independent of the theory of prosodic forms. This is the Prosodic Morphology Hypothesis of McCarthy and Prince (1986). The successor to the Prosodic Morphology Hypothesis is Generalized Template Theory (McCarthy and Prince 1994a, b), which carries the explanatory goals of PM up to the next level: the elimination of templates *per se* in favor of widely applicable constraints on prosody, morphology, and their interface. In this view, typical templatic categories like the "Minimal Word" are given no independent status, but rather emerge in reduplicative contexts through appropriate ranking of constraints on foot parsing and grammar → prosody mapping (see section 4.3 below for discussion and illustration).

218

Another line of development in PM has been the study of infixation and related phenomena. The first effort at greater generality and explanation in this domain was the introduction of prosodic circumscription (McCarthy and Prince 1990) to connect the locus of infixation with extrametricality, which plays an independent role in the characterization of prosodic-structural domains. The theory of infixation and extrametricality has been much transformed by the perspective of Optimality Theory, and now infixation can be understood as the result of the domination of morphological affixal-placement constraints by prosodic-structural ones, all independently motivated (Prince and Smolensky 1991, 1993; McCarthy and Prince 1993a, b; McCarthy 1997a).

In these two areas, templates and infixation, the explanatory goals of PM have been advanced by first connecting PM-specific principles to external domains (prosodic structure, extrametricality), and then by eliminating the PM-specific principles and stipulations in favor of constraints of complete generality, ranked under Optimality Theory. This chapter follows the same course in relation to a third area of PM investigation: template satisfaction. Initially, template satisfaction under Optimality Theory was *sui generis*, based on a special relation of correspondence between a base and its reduplicative copy (called the "reduplicant").[2] Here we argue that correspondence should be generalized to include other kinds of linguistic relations, such as input-output faithfulness in particular (section 2). In this way, the apparatus of copying constraints is combined with faithfulness into a broadly applicable Correspondence Theory. The key notion underlying this generalization is "identity."

Reduplication is a matter of identity: the reduplicant copies the base. Perfect identity cannot always be attained, though; templatic requirements commonly obscure it. Base-copy parallelism is most striking when carried to an extreme – when otherwise well-behaved phonological processes are disrupted by the demands of reduplicative identity. It may happen that parallel phonological developments occur in both the base and the copy, even though the regular triggering conditions are found only in one or the other. This is "overapplication."[3] Similarly, regular phonological effects may fail to appear in the base or in the copy, when the relevant environment is found in just one of them. This is "underapplication." Either way, a phonologically expected asymmetry between the base and the copy is avoided, and identity between the base and the copy is maintained. Phonological processes of all types, at all levels, have been observed to show such behavior.

Identity figures much more widely in phonology proper, though perhaps less obviously. According to Optimality Theory, *faithfulness* constraints demand that the output be as close as possible to the input, along all the dimensions upon which structures may vary (Prince and Smolensky 1993). Derivation is determined to a large degree by the interaction between faithfulness constraints, demanding identity, and constraints on output structural configurations, which may favor modification of the input, contravening faithfulness. Input-output faithfulness and base-reduplicant identity, we argue, are effectively the same thing, controlled by exactly the same set of formal considerations, played out over different pairs of compared structures. The interplay between them leads to a number of significant results concerning the direction of reduplicative copying (sections 4.2 and 4.3), the connection between Generalized Template Theory and Correspondence Theory (section 4.3), the typology of reduplication/phonology interactions (section 5), and underapplication (section 6). The conclusion (section 7) summarizes the results and offers some prospects for future work.

2. Correspondence Theory

2.1 The role and character of correspondence

To comprehend phonological processes within Optimality Theory, we require a model of constraints on faithfulness of the output to the input (expanding on Prince and Smolensky 1991, 1993). To provide a basis for the study of over- and underapplication, we need to develop a model of constraints on identity between the base and the reduplicant (expanding on McCarthy and Prince 1993a). These twin goals turn out to be closely related, since they are united in Correspondence Theory, thereby eliminating the need for special, distinct theories of input-output faithfulness and base-reduplicant identity.

The motivation for a unified theory of faithfulness and identity is particularly clear when we consider the range of parallels between them:

Completeness of mapping

In the domain of base-reduplicant identity, completeness is total reduplication and incompleteness is partial reduplication, normally satisfying some templatic requirement on the canonical shape of the reduplicant.

In the domain of input-output faithfulness, incompleteness is phonological deletion.

Dependence on input/base

In the domain of base-reduplicant identity, the phonological material of the reduplicant normally is just that of the base. This dependence on the base is violated in systems with fixed default segments in the reduplicant: e.g., Yoruba, with fixed default *i*, as in /mu/ → *mí–mu* (Akinlabi 1984, McCarthy and Prince 1986, Pulleyblank 1988).

The parallel in the input-output domain is epenthesis, with default segments inserted under syllabic or other conditions.

Contiguity of mapping

In the domain of base-reduplicant identity, the copy is usually a *contiguous* substring of the base. For instance, in Balangao prefixing reduplication (Shetler 1976, McCarthy and Prince 1994a), contiguity protects reduplicant-medial coda consonants, though not reduplicant-final ones: ...*tagta–tagtag*, *...*tata–tagtag*. Violation of the contiguity property is met with conspicuously in Sanskrit reduplication: *du–druv*.

Contiguity effects are also known in the input-output domain, though they are less well studied than other constraints on epenthesis or deletion. In Axininca Campa and Lardil, epenthetic augmentation is external to the root (McCarthy and Prince 1993a and references cited there): /tʰo/ → *tʰota*, *tʰato; /ɽil/ → *ɽilta*, *ɽatil, *ɽital. Likewise, in Chukchee (Kenstowicz 1994, Spencer 1993), morpheme-edge epenthesis is preferred to morpheme-internal epenthesis: /miml-qaca-n/ → *mimləqacan*, *miməlqacan. And in Diyari (Austin 1981, McCarthy and Prince 1994a), a prohibition on all syllable codas leads to deletion of word-final consonants, but not of word-medial ones, with the effect that all words are vowel-final; this provides an exact parallel to the Balangao reduplicant.

Linearity of mapping

Reduplication normally preserves the linear order of elements. But in Rotuman (Churchward 1940 [1978]), there is metathetic reduplication of disyllabic roots: /RED–pure/ → *puer-pure*. Similarly, the I-O map typically respects linear order, but metathesis is a possibility. In the phonology of Rotuman, for example, a metathesis similar to the reduplicative phenomenon is observed in a morphological category called the incomplete phase (McCarthy 1995): *pure* → *puer*.

Anchoring of edges

The reduplicant normally contains an element from at least one edge of the base, typically the left edge in prefixed reduplicants and the right edge in suffixed reduplicants.
Edge-anchoring has been observed and studied even more extensively in the input-output domain, where it has been identified with the class of constraints on the *alignment* of edges of morphological and prosodic constituents (Prince and Smolensky 1991, 1993; McCarthy and Prince 1993a, b).

Featural identity

Copied segments in the base and the reduplicant are normally identical to one another, but may differ featurally for phonological reasons. For instance, nasal place-assimilation in Tübatulabal leads to imperfect featural identity of copied segments, as in *zam̱–ba̱ṉin* (Voegelin 1935, Alderete *et al.* 1996). The same sort of identity, or phonologically motivated non-identity, of segments in input and output is the very crux of phonological alternation.

This range of parallels is remarkable, and demands explanation. Linguistic theory must relate the constraints on the matching of reduplicant and base (the copying constraints) to the constraints on the matching of phonological output and input (the faithfulness constraints). We propose to accomplish this by generalizing the notion of *correspondence*. Correspondence was introduced into OT as a base-reduplicant relation (McCarthy and Prince 1993a); here, we extend it to the input-output domain, and other linguistic relationships besides. The parallels observed above are accounted for if Universal Grammar (UG) defines *types* of constraints on correspondence, with distinct realizations of the constraint types for each domain in which correspondence plays a role.

Correspondence itself is a relation between two structures, such as base and reduplicant (B-R) or input and output (I-O). To simplify the discussion, we focus on correspondence between strings.[4]

(1) Correspondence

Given two strings S_1 and S_2, *correspondence* is a relation $\Re$ from the elements of S_1 to those of S_2. Elements $\alpha \in S_1$ and $\beta \in S_2$ are referred to as *correspondents* of one another when $\alpha \Re \beta$.

Here we will assume that the structural elements α and β are just (tokens of) segments, but it is a straightforward matter to generalize the approach to other units of phonological representation. For instance, correspondence of moras, syllables, feet, heads of feet, as well as tones, and even distinctive features or feature-class nodes, may be appropriate to support the analysis of quantitative transfer, compensatory lengthening, and floating features.[5]

Correspondence need not be limited to the B-R and I-O relations. For example, the same notions extend directly to relations between two stems, as in root-and-pattern, circumscriptional, or truncating morphology (Benua 1995, McCarthy and Prince 1994b, McCarthy 1995), and they can be connected with the types of cyclic or transderivational relationships within paradigms explored by Benua (1995, 1997) and Burzio (1994a, b).

In a correspondence-sensitive grammar, candidate reduplicants or outputs are subject to evaluation together with the correspondent base or input. Each candidate pair (S_1, S_2) comes from Gen equipped with a correspondence relation between S_1 and S_2. There is a correspondence relation for each (B, R) candidate-pair. There is also a correspondence relation for each (I, O) candidate-pair. Indeed, one can simply think of

Gen as supplying correspondence relations between S_1 and all possible structures over some alphabet.[6] Eval then considers each candidate pair with its associated correspondence relations, assessing the completeness of correspondence in S_1 or S_2, the featural identity of correspondent elements in S_1 and S_2, and so on.

A hypothetical illustration will make these ideas more concrete. In (2a), we provide some (B, R) correspondences, and in (2b) we do the same for (I, O) correspondence. The comments on the right describe any interesting imperfections of correspondence. Correspondent segments are indicated here by subscripted indices, a nicety that we will usually eschew in the discussion later.

(2) Hypothetical illustrations

    a. Some B-R Correspondents   Input = /RED–badupi/

    $b_1\,a_2\,d_3\,u_4\,p_5\,i_6 - b_1\,a_2\,d_3\,u_4\,p_5\,i_6$ Total reduplication – perfect B-R correspondence.

    $b_1\,a_2\,d_3 - b_1\,a_2\,d_3\,u_4\,p_5\,i_6$ Partial reduplication – *upi* in B has no correspondents in R.

    $b_1\,a_2\,t_3 - b_1\,a_2\,d_3\,u_4\,p_5\,i_6$ The *t* in R has a non-identical correspondent in B, for phonological reasons (final devoicing).

    $?\,a_2\,d_3 - b\,a_2\,d_3\,u_4\,p_5\,i_6$ The *?* is *not* in correspondence with the base-initial *b*. This is a type of fixed-segment reduplication (cf. Tübatulabal in Alderete *et al.* 1996).

    $?_1\,a_2\,d_3 - b_1\,a_2\,d_3\,u_4\,p_5\,i_6$ The *?* in R has a non-identical correspondent in B. This and the preceding candidate are formally distinct, since Eval considers candidates with their correspondence relations.

    b. Some I-O Correspondents   Input = /$p_1\,a_2\,u_3\,k_4\,t_5\,a_6$/

    $p_1\,a_2\,u_3\,k_4\,t_5\,a_6$ A fully faithful analysis – perfect I-O correspondence.

    $p_1\,a_2\,?\,u_3\,k_4\,t_5\,a_6$ Hiatus prohibited by high-ranking ONSET, so epenthetic *?* in O has no correspondent in I.

$p_1 u_3 k_4 t_5 a_6$ Hiatus prohibited, leading to
   Λ V-deletion. The segment a_2 in I
                                         has no correspondent in O.
$p_1 a_2 u_3 t_4 t_5 a_6$ The k_4 in I has a non-identical
   Λ correspondent in O, for
                                         phonological reasons
                                         (assimilation).
b l u r k   No element of O stands in
$\Lambda \Lambda \Lambda \Lambda \Lambda$ correspondence with any
                                         element in I. Typically fatal.

The variety of candidates shown emphasizes some of the richness of the Gen-supplied set. It falls to Eval, and the language-particular constraint hierarchy, to determine what is optimal, what is not, and what can never be optimal under any ranking of the constraints in UG.

2.2 Some constraints on correspondent elements

Constraints must assess correspondence and identity of correspondent elements. There are separate (and therefore separately rankable) constraints for each correspondence relation (input/output, base/reduplicant, etc.). The following are three of the constraint families that will play a leading role in our discussion; all relate the string S_1 (base, input, etc.) to the string S_2 (reduplicant, output, etc.).

(3) The MAX constraint Family
    General Schema
        Every segment of S_1 has a correspondent in S_2.
    Domain-specific instantiations
        MAX-BR
            Every segment of the base has a correspondent in the reduplicant.
            (Reduplication is total.)
        MAX-IO
            Every segment of the input has a correspondent in the output.
            (No phonological deletion.)

(4) The DEP constraint family
    General schema
        Every segment of S_2 has a correspondent in S_1.
        (S_2 is "dependent on" S_1.)

Domain-specific instantiations

DEP-BR

Every segment of the reduplicant has a correspondent in the base.

(Prohibits fixed default segmentism in the reduplicant.)

DEP-IO

Every segment of the output has a correspondent in the input.

(Prohibits phonological epenthesis.)

(5) The IDENT(F) constraint family

General schema

IDENT(F)

Let α be a segment in S_1 and β be any correspondent of α in S_2.

If α is [γF] , then β is [γF].

(Correspondent segments are identical in feature F.)

Domain-specific instantiations

IDENT-BR(F)

Reduplicant correspondents of a base [γF] segment are also [γF].

IDENT-IO(F)

Output correspondents of an input [γF] segment are also [γF].

Some constraints on other aspects of the correspondence relation are listed in the appendix. Note further that each reduplicative affix has its own correspondence relation, so that in a language with several reduplicative affixes there can be several distinct, separately rankable constraints of the MAX-BR type, etc. This means that different reduplicative morphemes within a language can fare differently with respect to constraints on correspondence – for example, one can be total reduplication, obeying MAX-BR, and one can be partial, violating MAX-BR. It also means that reduplicative morphemes can differ in how they interact with the phonology, in one and the same language, as Urbanczyk (1996a, this volume) argues. It must be, then, that correspondence constraints are tied not only to specific dimensions (B-R, I-O), but also, in some cases at least, to specific morphemes or morpheme classes. Thus, the full schema for a faithfulness constraint may include such specifics as these: the element preserved, the dimension of derivation along which the two structures are related, the *direction* of inclusion along that dimension (as in the contrast between MAX and DEP), and the morphological domain (stem, affix, or even specific morpheme) to which the constraint is relevant.

Now some comments on the specific constraints. MAX-IO is a reformulation of the constraint PARSE in Prince and Smolensky (1991, 1993) and other OT work, which liberates it from its connection with syllabification and phonetic interpretation. In addition, the MAX family subsumes the reduplication-specific MAX in McCarthy and Prince (1993a). Depending on which correspondence relation they regulate, the various MAX constraints will (*inter alia*) prohibit phonological deletion, demand completeness of reduplicative copying, or require complete mapping in root-and-pattern morphology.

The DEP constraints approximate the function of FILL in Prince and Smolensky (1991, 1993) and other OT work. They encompass the anti-epenthesis effects of FILL without demanding that epenthetic segments be literally unfilled nodes, whose contents are to be specified by an auxiliary, partly language-specific component of phonetic interpretation. They also extend to reduplication and other relations.

The IDENT constraints require that correspondent segments be featurally identical to one another. Unless dominated, the full array of these constraints will require complete featural identity between correspondent segments. Crucial domination of one or more IDENT constraints leads to featural disparity and phonological alternation.

Various extensions of IDENT have emerged from continuing research. One, proposed by Pater (this volume), differentiates IDENT(+F) and IDENT(–F) versions for the same feature; the typological consequences of this move for the present theory are taken up in section 5.4 below. Another, adopted by Urbanczyk (1996a), posits identity of moraic analysis of correspondent segments. Extensions of IDENT to other aspects of prosodic structure are treated in Benua (1995) and McCarthy (1995). Another important development, pursued by Alderete (1996), Beckman (1997), and Selkirk (1995), is differentiation of IDENT and other correspondence constraints by position: onset versus coda, stressed versus unstressed, root versus affix.[7] The first-named, more prominent position typically receives more faithful treatment, as evidenced by phenomena of position-sensitive neutralization. Finally, in the light of work in feature geometry (Clements 1985b, Padgett 1995a, etc.), it is plausible that constraints of the IDENT family will quantify over classes of features.

The IDENT constraint family is constructed here on the assumption that segments alone stand in correspondence, so identity of features is always demanded indirectly, through the segments bearing those features. As we noted above, it is a reasonably straightforward matter, though, to extend the correspondence relation to features as well as segments. Then the constraint IDENT(F) would be replaced by the MAX(F)/ DEP(F) pair, plus an apparatus of additional constraints to ensure faithfulness of features to their original segmental associations. Featural correspondence is arguably necessary to deal with some floating feature phenomena (Zoll 1996) and with entailments between segmental and featural deletion (Lombardi 1995).

In section 2.1 we listed many parallels between B-R Identity and I-O Faithfulness. These parallels now have an explanation: they follow from the fact that both B-R and I-O are related by correspondence and that identical constraint types apply to each (and to other domains of correspondence as well).

There is an important further parallel to be drawn, which the generality of correspondence affords us. The correspondence constraints proposed above and in the appendix are strongly reminiscent of some principles and rules of autosegmental association. For example, MAX, DEP, and LINEARITY recall the clauses of Goldsmith's (1976) Well-Formedness Condition: every tone-bearing element is associated with some tone; every tone is associated with some tone-bearing element; association lines do not cross. Likewise, CONTIGUITY and ANCHORING can be analogized to the requirement of directional one-to-one linking and the Initial Tone Association Rule in Clements and Ford (1979). These parallels are explained if we generalize correspondence still further, to include not only identity relations (like I-O and B-R) but also the relation of autosegmental association. The phenomena comprehended by the theory of autosegmental association are therefore a special case of correspondence.[8]

These parallels, and the consequent reduction of autosegmental association to correspondence, recapture one of the original ideas of Prosodic Morphology, one which was lost in the solely reduplicative correspondence theory of McCarthy and Prince (1993a): that template satisfaction is a special case of autosegmental association, involving associating floating melodemes to a templatic skeleton (McCarthy 1979, Marantz 1982, Clements 1985a, Mester 1986, McCarthy and Prince

1986, etc.). We now see that exactly the same relation – correspondence – and the same constraints – MAX, DEP, etc. – are at work in both domains, just as they are in faithfulness.

2.3 Correspondence theory and the PARSE/FILL Model

Most work within OT since Prince and Smolensky (1991, 1993) assumes that the phonological output is governed by a requirement that no input element may be literally removed. To-be-deleted elements are present in the output, but marked in some way. (This property is dubbed "Containment" in McCarthy and Prince 1993a;[9] ideas like it have played a role throughout much of modern syntactic theory, e.g., Postal 1970, Perlmutter (ed.) 1983, and Chomsky 1975.) Under this assumption, phonologically deleted segments are present in the output, but unparsed syllabically, making use of the notion of *Stray Erasure* in Steriade (1982). The I-O Faithfulness constraint PARSE regulates this mode of deletion, by prohibiting unsyllabified segments.

Because they reduce the prohibition on deletion to an easily stated structural constraint, these moves provide a direct and convenient way to handle a variety of basic cases. But this is by no means the only possible approach to faithfulness in OT (cf. Prince and Smolensky 1993: 25, note 12; Yip 1993; Myers 1993; and Kirchner 1993 for some other alternatives). Indeed, there are very significant differences in formal architecture between the serial operational theory from which Stray Erasure originated and OT's parallel, evaluative-comparative approach to well-formedness. The shared goal of both theories is to derive the properties of deletion patterns from independent principles of syllabification. Under standard deterministic Markovian serialism, there is no clear way to combine rules of literal deletion with operational rules of syllabification so as to get this result. So the burden must be placed entirely on the rules of syllabification, with deletion postponed to sweep up afterwards. OT's architecture admits this as a possible line of attack on the problem, but since all manners of alteration of the input are considered in parallel, there is no intrinsic need to limit Gen to an output representation without deletions, so long as the relation between input and output is kept track of – for example, by correspondence relations. An immediate (and desirable)[10] consequence of the correspondence/full-deletion approach is that deleted elements simply cannot play a role in determining the performance of output structures on constraints defined strictly on output representations. There is then no need to restrict these constraints to seeing only *parsed elements*, as for example Myers (1993) demonstrates to be true of the OCP; the point applies with equal force to a class of alignment constraints, as shown by J. Beckman (1995). Along the same lines, B-R correspondence sees only what is manifest in B, a fact that leads directly to strong predictions about over-application in the reduplicative theory.

Much OT work since Prince and Smolensky (1991) assumes as well that no segment can be literally *added* to the output. Phonological epenthesis is seen as the result of providing prosodic structure with no segment to fill it, the phonetic identity of the epenthetic segment being determined by extra-systemic rules of (phonetic) interpretation, exactly as in Selkirk (1981), Lowenstamm and Kaye (1985), and Itô (1986, 1989). The constraint FILL militates against these unfilled prosodic nodes. Here again, a faithfulness issue is given a simple structural interpretation that allows for easy formulation and direct assault on the basic generalizations about the relation between epenthesis and syllabifiability. But, just as with deletion, the architectural shift opens new perspectives. Under OT, it is no longer formally necessary to segregate the cause of epenthesis (principles of syllabification) from the fact itself. Under correspondence, the presence of epenthetic elements is regulated by the DEP constraint family, and they appear in optimal forms with whatever kind and degree of featural specification the phonological constraints demand of them. An immediate, desirable consequence is that the choice of epenthetic material comes under *grammatical* control: independently required constraints on featural markedness select the least offensive material to satisfy (or better satisfy) the driving syllabic constraints. (See Prince and Smolensky 1993, ch. 9, Smolensky 1993, McCarthy 1993, and McCarthy and Prince 1994a for relevant discussion of featural markedness in epenthetic segments.) In addition, the actual featural value of epenthetic segments can figure in phonological generalizations (Spring 1994, Davis 1995), as is known to be the case in many situations (for example, Yawelmani Yokuts harmony, discussed in Kuroda 1967 and Archangeli 1985). This contrasts sharply with the FILL theory, in which the feature composition of epenthetic segments is determined post-phonologically, by a further process of phonetic implementation. This "phonetics" nevertheless deals in the very same materials as phonology, and is subject to interlinguistic variation of a sort that is more than reminiscent of standard constraint-permutation effects. Correspondence makes immediate sense of these observations, which appear to be in principle beyond the reach of FILL-based theories.

This discussion has brought forth a significant depth of empirical motivation behind the proposal to implement faithfulness via correspondence of representations. A primary motive is to capture the parallels between B-R Identity and I-O Faithfulness. This is reinforced by the observation that mapping between autosegmental tiers is regulated by the same formal principles of proper correspondence, allowing us to recapture the formal generality of earlier, autosegmental-associative theories of template satisfaction. By contrast, a Containment or PARSE/ FILL approach to inter-tier association is hardly conceivable.[11] Correspondence also allows us to explain why certain constraints, such as Myers's tonal OCP, are totally insensitive to the presence of deletion sites, and why epenthetic elements show an unmarked feature composition, which can nevertheless play a role in phonological patterns such as vowel harmony. To these, we can add the ability to handle phenomena such as diphthongization and coalescence through the use of one-to-many and many-to-one relations. It is certainly possible, bemused by appearances, to exaggerate the differences between the PARSE/FILL approach and correspondence – both being implementations of the far more fundamental faithfulness idea, without which there is no OT – but it seems quite clear at this point that correspondence is the more promising line to pursue.

Correspondence Theory also raises broader issues about the character of phonology and phonological constraints generally, as several of the other contributions to this volume make clear. Readers interested in further exploring these matters might begin with the following (non-exhaustive) list: Agbayani and Harada (1996); Bat-El (1996); Beckman (1997); Beckman *et al.* (1995); Benua (1997); Burzio (1997); Bye *et al.* (1996); Chen (1996); Fulmer (1997); Gerfen (1996); Gnanadesikan (1997); Green (1997); Hermans and van Oostendorp (to appear); Itô, Kitagawa, and Mester (1996); Itô and Mester (1997); Kim (1997); Letterman (1997); Myers and Carleton (1996); Orgun (1996a, b); Spaelti (1997); Zoll (1996). All are relatively accessible, contain significant discussion of topics in Correspondence Theory, and provide further pointers to the literature.

3. Approaches to reduplication/phonology interaction

3.1 Reduplication/phonology interaction in Correspondence Theory

The full theory of reduplication involves correspondence between underlying stem and surface base, between surface base and surface reduplicant, and between underlying stem and surface reduplicant. The following
diagram portrays this system of relations:

(6) Full Model

$$\text{Input} \qquad /\text{Af}_{\text{RED}} + \text{Stem}/$$

I-R Faithfulness   *I-B Faithfulness*

$$\text{Output} \qquad R \rightleftarrows B$$

B-R Identity

In keeping with our practice so far, we will continue to employ a purely
terminological distinction between identity and faithfulness, but we do
this solely to emphasize the distinct dimensions along which these perfectly homologous notions are realized.

The relation between stem and reduplicant – *I-R Faithfulness* in the
diagram – turns out to play a subsidiary role in the theory, essentially because of a universal metacondition on ranking, discussed in McCarthy
and Prince (1995: section 6), which ensures that faithfulness constraints
on the stem domain always dominate those on the affixal domains.
From this, it follows that I-R Faithfulness appears in a subordinate
position in every ranking, dominated by I-B Faithfulness, significantly
limiting its effects. In many rankings, its presence will be completely or
almost completely hidden; it therefore becomes convenient to study a
simplified model, a proper sub-theory, in which I-R Faithfulness is not
considered. Let us call this the "Basic Model," which directly follows
McCarthy and Prince (1993a).

(7) Basic Model

$$\text{Input} \qquad /\text{Af}_{\text{RED}} + \text{Stem}/$$

I-O Faithfulness

$$\text{Output} \qquad R \rightleftarrows B$$

B-R Identity

The Basic Model will be the major focus below; for extension to the Full
Model, see McCarthy and Prince (1995: section 6).

The identity-preserving interactions between phonology and reduplication were named overapplication and underapplication in the pion-
eering work of Wilbur (1973a, b, c). Although these terms emerge from
a particular conception of rules and rule application which is no longer
viable, they can be given a more neutral characterization, in terms of
relations rather than processes, and we will use them throughout in a
strictly descriptive sense. A phonological mapping will be said to overapply when it introduces, in reduplicative circumstances, a disparity
between the output and the lexical stem[12] that is not expected on purely
phonological grounds. To put it even more neutrally, we can say that,
in a situation where there is a two-way opposition between a marked
element of limited distribution and an unmarked default element, overapplication is the appearance of the marked element outside of its
normal distributional domain. A typical example is given in (8).

(8) Overapplication in Madurese nasal harmony (Stevens 1968, 1985;
    Mester 1986: 197–200)

Stem	Simple	Reduplicated	Expected	Gloss
/neat/	nẽỹãt	ỹãt-nẽỹãt	*yat-nẽỹãt	"intentions"

A nasal span runs rightward from nasal consonants (column two). In
the reduplicated form (column three), nasal spreading in the base is replicated in the reduplicant, even though the triggering nasal consonant is
not copied. If reduplication were thought of as copying the underlying
form of the base, the expected result would be the one in column four; it
is from this perspective that nasal harmony is thought to overapply to
force nasalized ỹ and ã in the reduplicant. Regardless of the mechanism
involved, the effect is to introduce an unexpected disparity between the
presumed lexical stem and the output – the presence of the nasalized ã.
In terms of the surface repertory, we can say that the marked member of
the ã/a opposition is found outside its canonical, post-nasal position.

Similarly, a phonological process will be said to underapply when
there is a *lack* of expected disparity between the input stem and the output. In the most straightforward case, this amounts to the unmarked
member of an opposition putting in an appearance where the marked
member is expected. Akan reduplication provides a typical example:
palatalization fails to apply in the reduplicant when it is not phonologically motivated in the base:

(9) Underapplication in Akan (Christaller 1875, Schachter and Fromkin
     1968, Welmers 1946)

	Stem	Reduplicated	Expected	Gloss
a.	ka?	kɪ-ka?	*tɕɪ-ka?	"bite"
b.	haw?	hɪ-haw?	*ɕɪ-haw?	"trouble"

Though Akan typically disallows velars and other back consonants
before front vowels, the offending sequence is found in reduplicated
forms like kɪ-ka?. In Wilbur's terms, the velar palatalization process
underapplies in the reduplicant. More neutrally, we can observe that
the general phonological pattern of the language leads us to expect a
disparity between the underlying stem (with k) and the reduplicant
(where we ought to see tɕ), and we do not find it. Put in markedness
terms, the unmarked member of k/tɕ appears here not in its default
environment, but in a position where, it seems, the marked member
is required. The effect is to make the actual reduplicant more closely
resemble the stem.

The third relevant descriptive category is that of *normal application*,
whereby both base and reduplicant are entirely well-behaved phonologically, being treated as completely independent entities. Tagalog
flapping provides an instance: there is an allophonic alternation between
d and *r* in Tagalog, with the flap found intervocalically, much as in English. Reduplication makes no inroads on this generalization:

(10) Normal application in Tagalog (Carrier 1979: 149f.)

	Stem	Reduplicated	Over	Under	Gloss
a.	datiŋ	d-um-ā-ɾatiŋ	*ɾ-um-ā-ɾatiŋ	*d-um-ā-datiŋ	"arrive"
b.	diŋat	ka-ka-ɾiŋat-diŋat	*ka-ɾiŋat-ɾiŋat	*ka-diŋat-diŋat	"suddenly"

As with underapplication and overapplication, it must be emphasized
that the expression "normal application" is a term of art, describing a
certain state of affairs, and there is no implication that normal application is particularly usual or more commonly encountered than its rivals,
or even universally available. Indeed, the typology we develop below
(section 5) includes circumstances where the theory does not always
admit normal application as an option (see also McCarthy and Prince
1995: section 3.2).

Since the earliest work on this subject (e.g., Wilbur 1973a), it has been
recognized that over- and underapplication support reduplicant-base

identity. Suppose the cited phonological processes in Madurese and Akan had applied *normally*, yielding the results in the columns labeled "Expected": they would then increase disparity between base and reduplicant. If reduplication, by its very nature, involves identity between base and reduplicant, then any special interaction with phonology that serves to support reduplicant-base identity is functioning in aid of the reduplicative pattern itself. This is the insight we will explore, by examining the range of interactions between the competing and often irreconcilable demands of faithful correspondence between different representations.

Working within the Basic Model, (7), we will sketch the overall lie of the land. The constraints demanding B-R Identity are evaluated in parallel with the constraints on phonological sequences and on I-O Faithfulness that are responsible for relations like Madurese $V \sim \tilde{V}$ and Akan $k \sim t\varsigma$. With B-R Identity constraints dominant, we need only take seriously those candidates in which base and reduplicant actually match. With the relevant phonological constraints dominant as well, overapplication can result. Consider the Madurese case, which offers the following comparison of potential outputs:

(11) Overapplication of nasal harmony in Madurese (from /neat/)

	Candidate	Chief Flaw	Remarks	Type
a. ☞	ỹãt-nẽỹãt	*I-O Faithfulness: nasal V in stem	Forced violation	Over
b. *	yat-nẽyat	*Phonological constraint against NV$_{Oral}$	Fatal	Under
c. *	yat-nẽỹãt	*B-R Identity	Fatal	Normal

The sequence NV$_{Oral}$ is disallowed in the language, where N = any nasal segment, including nasalized vowels and glides. The doubly nasalized form, (11a), is optimal, because it achieves perfect identity of base and reduplicant while still avoiding the forbidden sequence. The cost is the introduction of extra marked segments – nasal vocoids – into the representation; indeed, into an environment where they are not tolerated elsewhere in the language. Such considerations lead to a ranking requirement on this kind of overapplication. which characterizes the interplay among constraints on B-R Identity and markedness relative to some structural condition, "Phono-Constraint" (Phono-Con).

(12) An overapplication ranking pattern
       B-R Identity, Phono-Constraint ≫ Markedness

This ranking asserts that reduplicative identity and some phonological requirement (like the prohibition on NV_{Oral}) both take precedence over another phonological requirement, here the markedness constraint against nasality in vocoids. (This accords with the observation that in case of a simple marked versus unmarked contrast, classic overapplication involves the otherwise unexpected appearance of a marked element.) The primacy of base-reduplicant identity leads here to overapplication, examined in section 4. The responsible rankings, including (12) and others that involve conflict between B-R Identity and I-O Faithfulness, are examined and refined in the factorial typology of section 5.

Strikingly, classic underapplication does not emerge in this theory as a separate descriptive category that can be freely imposed *via* B-R Identity constraints. The reason is not far to seek. B-R Identity is equally respected in both underapplication and overapplication; by itself, therefore, B-R Identity cannot decide between them. Compare forms (11a) and (11b): *ỹãt-nẽỹãt*, versus **yat-nẽỹat*. Base and reduplicant are entirely identical in both candidates. Any decision between them must be made on other grounds.

To get phonology happening at all, the relation Phono-Constraint ≫ I-O Faithfulness must be maintained. In Madurese, this is what yields nasal spread in the language at large. With Phono-Constraint as the final arbiter, overapplication must result, because the underapplicational candidate fails to satisfy it. There is simply no way that the force of Phono-Constraint can be blunted by B-R Identity.

Normal application or reversion of the reduplicant to a less marked repertory, however, remains an option, when B-R Identity is crucially subordinated. In this case, reduplicative identity cannot compel the extension of phonology from base to reduplicant, or vice versa. Base and reduplicant therefore enjoy an independence measured by the number and kind of B-R Identity constraints that are crucially subordinated.

The theory, then, basically distinguishes two conditions: one in which B-R Identity is respected (to some degree, along certain dimensions), yielding overapplication; and one in which B-R Identity is set aside, yielding normal application or reversion to the unmarked in the reduplicant. The choice between under- and overapplicational candidates must be made on grounds other than B-R Identity. In the Madurese case just reviewed, the overapplicational candidate is chosen because it alone satisfies the phonological constraint banning NV_{Oral} while maintaining the required level of identity. How, then, does classic underapplication come about? It can only be that another independent constraint excludes the naively expected result, and that we are really looking at overapplication involving that other constraint.

The underapplication of palatalization in Akan provides an example. The independent constraint here is the OCP, which can be independently observed in the language to prevent palatalization when a coronal-coronal sequence would result (see McCarthy and Prince 1995: section 5 for the details). Indeed, one might expect the OCP to figure commonly in such interactions, since reduplication often produces nearby replications of features; and this is exactly what the OCP can rule out, through high rank. In such cases, the reduplicative situation will reflect a more general restriction on the language – though it may be one that is not particularly salient to the casual observer. Here and in McCarthy and Prince (1995: section 5) we argue that all proposed cases of underapplication are of this type, leading to a schema along these lines (where C stands for, for example, the relevant subcase of the OCP that is visibly active in Akan).

(13) A skeletal ranking for underapplication as overapplication
      B-R Identity, C ≫ Phono-Constraint ≫ I-O Faithfulness

This ranking results in underapplication, because the mapping due to the subhierarchy Phono-Constraint ≫ I-O Faithfulness is blocked in certain circumstances by C, and reduplication happens to provide one of those circumstances. B-R Identity demands that base and reduplicant mirror each other quite closely, and the only way to attain this while satisfying C is to avoid the mapping triggered by Phono-Constraint. Thus, the full phonology – the mapping involving C – is *overapplied*. This line of argument is pursued in section 6.

A further significant property of Correspondence Theory emerges from the parallelism of constraint evaluation. The base and the reduplicant are evaluated symmetrically and simultaneously with respect to the language's constraint hierarchy. The base does not have serial priority over the reduplicant, and reduplication is not, in fact, the copying or replication of a previously fixed base. Instead, both base and reduplicant can give way, as it were, to achieve the best possible satisfaction of the entire constraint set. The result is that, under certain circumstances, when B-R Identity crucially dominates I-O Faithfulness, the base will be predicted to copy the reduplicant. An overapplicational case of this type (Malay) is examined in section 4.2; others can be found in McCarthy and Prince (1995: section 3.6 to section 3.8, section 5.3). (Lushootseed may be yet another overapplicational case; see Urbanczyk 1996a, this volume.) Such analyses offer very strong evidence for Correspondence Theory as articulated here, and with it, for the claims of parallelist OT, particularly as contrasted with serialist theories of grammatical derivation.

For the theory of reduplicative phonology, the principal interest of the architecture proposed here is this: the phenomena called overapplication and underapplication follow in Correspondence Theory from the very constraints on reduplicant-base identity that permit reduplication to happen in the first place. The constraints responsible for the ordinary copying of a base also govern the copying of phonologically derived properties. Effectively, there is no difference between copying and over- or underapplication, and therefore such phonological interactions, along with normal application, turn out to be a fully expected concomitant of reduplicative structure, obtainable through the permutation of ranked universal constraints, as expected in OT.

3.2 Correspondence Theory in relation to earlier work

Previous theories of reduplication have been framed within a serialist conception of grammar as a sequence of operations. On this view, identity is asserted by a rule of exact copying and has no special, durable status: like other rule effects, it is guaranteed to hold only at the derivational instant when the copying rule applies, and it is as subject to the same vagaries of earlier and later derivation as any other rule product. Here is the first discussion of a serial model, due to Bloomfield (1933: 222), writing about nasal substitution in Tagalog:

the form [pa-mu-muːtul] "a cutting in quantity" implies, by the actual sequence of the parts, that the reduplication is made "before" the prefix is added, but at the same time implies, by the presence of [m-] for [p-] in both reduplication and main form, that the prefix is added "before" the reduplication is made.

Bloomfield's ordering paradox can be untwisted into the following succession of stages (the interesting steps are highlighted by ➢).

(14) Root   /puːtul/
      Prefixation   paN-puːtul
      ➢Nasal Substitution   pa-muːtul
      ➢Reduplication   pa-mu-muːtul

The reduplicative copying operation targets the transformed root *muːtul*, rather than the underlying root /puːtul/. The defining characteristic of the Ordering Theory is that some phonological process precedes reduplication, so that its effects are felt – or not felt – prior to copying, and thus are observed – or not observed – in both base and copy. If a rule is ordered before reduplicative copying, then its effects or non-effects will be seen in both base and copy. If the relevant phonological rule applies to the base, its output is copied; this is overapplication, ordering-wise. If the rule fails to apply to the base (because its context is only met through later affixation, including reduplication itself), then by the principle of strict serialism, it has forever lost its chance to apply; underapplication results. Normal application is obtained when the phonological process applies after reduplicative copying.

Ordering Theory first emerges in generative phonology with analyses of Akan by Schachter and Fromkin (1968: 162) and of Luiseño by Munro and Benson (1973). The theory is worked out in detail by Wilbur (1973a, b), and since then has been accepted almost universally. It has engendered a very substantial secondary literature, including detailed treatments by Aronoff (1976: 72–78); Carrier-[Duncan] (1979; 1984); Kiparsky (1986); Marantz (1982); and Shaw (1976 [1980]); as well as less comprehensive discussions by Anderson (1974, 1975); Hollenbach (1974); Odden and Odden (1985); Schlindwein (1991); Sietsema (1988); Steriade (1988: 107–108). This body of work has been extremely important in defining the character of the problem and engendering insights into its properties. It has achieved substantial analytic and descriptive success.

The basic Ordering Theory gives an appealing account of reduplicative phonology: either phonology precedes reduplication, or reduplication precedes phonology. In section 4 and McCarthy and Prince (1995), we show that the theory is deeply flawed in empirical predictions, and that it cannot, in fact, comprehend the range of phonology/reduplication interactions, even when subject to further refinements. Its fundamental defect, we suggest, is that it cannot reckon appropriately with the notion of *identity*. The identity-preserving character of the interaction between reduplication and phonology follows in Ordering Theory from the fact that reduplication gets the last crack at the representation, after the phonological rules have applied. We instead find effects that depend crucially on parallel development of the base and reduplicant, in Malay, Tagalog, and Southern Paiute below, and in Axininca Campa, Chumash, Kihehe, and Klamath in McCarthy and Prince (1995).

Some versions of Ordering Theory also encounter conceptual difficulties. To the extent that late ordering of a morphological process is unique to reduplication, there are then *two* special ways in which reduplication works in favor of base-reduplicant identity: reduplicative copying itself demands identity, but late ordering of reduplication serves to support it, in the face of phonological alterations. In contrast, Correspondence Theory sees identity as intrinsic to reduplication, with no separation between these two ways of achieving and maintaining it. (This issue in Ordering Theory has been recognized previously; Lexical Phonology responds to it by adverting to the possibility of late ordering of *any* morphological process, as in Kiparsky 1986. This mitigates, but does not eliminate, the conceptual objection, since reduplicative identity is still achieved by means extrinsic to the notion of identity itself.)

Though she develops it fully, Wilbur herself ultimately rejects Ordering Theory and adopts a very different approach, Global Theory, that connects somewhat more closely with the fundamental insight that over- and underapplication support reduplicative identity. The proposal is that phonology can detect the results of copying, through global rule interaction. Wilbur writes:

As I see it, the solution centers around the necessity for a rule to make use of the information that two segments...are in a copy relationship to each other (one is the copy of the other) as a result of a morphological rule (Reduplication, Vowel Copy, etc.)...If the relationship of the original segment (in [the base]) and its copy (in [the reduplicant]) can be captured by the term "mate" and represented by a notation such as X and X', then a global condition on a phonological rule which *overapplies* (regardless of whether it overapplies to [the base] or [the reduplicant]) can be written as:

X (and X') → Y if AXB

When a rule *fails to apply*, it can be formulated as:

X (and X') → Y if X (and X') / A___B   (1973a: 115–17)

In other words, a rule of reduplication establishes the "mate" relation between each original segment and its copy. Subsequent phonological rules have access to the mate relation, with identity-preserving effects. Rules can affect both mates, though only one meets the structural description, yielding overapplication. Or rules can demand that both mates meet the structural description, leading to underapplication when only one mate satisfies it. This second possibility arises from a key difference between Wilbur's proposal and the theory pursued here: by fundamental architectural construction, only *faithfulness* constraints work off correspondence. There is no way of stipulating that a structural constraint is violated only if its preconditions are met simultaneously in base and reduplicant; were this statable, it would parallel Wilbur's mate condition on satisfaction of the Structural Description of a rule. It follows that there can be no analogue of classic underapplication in the present theory. Finally, normal application is permitted in Wilbur's approach, because rules can also ignore the mate relation, applying freely in ways that disrupt identity of reduplicative mates. The choice among over-, under-, or normal application is made in the statement of each rule, through stipulation (or not) of the "(and X′)" codicils.

This is an important conceptual alternative to the Ordering Theory, because it tries to connect the phonological unity of reduplicated segments with the fact that one is a copy of the other. But Global Theory sits uneasily on the edifice of most phonological theory of the 1970s and 1980s. Early generative phonology relies on a step-wise serial derivation, in which each rule has access only to the output of the immediately preceding rule. The only global relation among rules is the stipulated ordering itself. The mate relation represents a major relaxation of this requirement with no compensating simplification or restriction elsewhere in the phonology. Indeed, rule ordering itself is still required within the phonology proper, even though the mate relation has been added to the theory. In contrast, the Ordering Theory of phonology/reduplication interaction requires nothing except what early generative phonology had in abundance: serial ordering of rules.

For this reason, it is not surprising that the Global Theory received relatively little attention in later work[13] and that there has been a decided preference for solutions based on Ordering Theory. A significant exception to this trend is the structural approach to base-reduplicant relations, studied in depth by Mester (1986: ch. 3), as well as variations in work

John J. McCarthy and Alan S. Prince

by Clements (1985a), Hirschbühler (1978: 118–21), McCarthy (1979: 373–87, 1983, 1985), McCarthy and Prince (1986: 102–108), Pulley-blank (1988: 265–67), Tateishi (1987), and Uhrbach (1987). Mester's work is particularly relevant in the present context, since it achieves considerable descriptive and explanatory success with many of the empirical issues that will be dealt with here.

The structural model works from an enriched phonological representation in which Wilbur's "mate" relation can be inspected directly, in terms of across-the-board form, autosegmental spreading, or some other aspect of the representation. Rules confronted with this complex representation will over- or underapply, depending on context.[14] This reification of the copying relation marks a significant advance over Ordering Theory, with connections to Wilbur's (1973a) ideas on the one hand and Correspondence Theory on the other. Yet even the structural approach must also call on rule ordering to deal with normal application. After some phonology applies to the structure in which the mate relation is represented directly, the whole structure is regularized ("linearized" is the usual term), obliterating all traces of the copying relation. Later rules apply to it normally, without reference to the base-reduplicant connection, since no evidence of reduplication remains present. Thus, the linearization step in the derivation has much the same effect as the copying step in Ordering Theory proper, in that it severs the base-reduplicant tie.[15]

Though the Global Theory cannot be reconciled with the serial derivation that is typical of earlier work in phonological theory, more recent developments have greatly altered the field in which this matter is played out. Since the mid-1970s, with the advent of metrical and auto-segmental phonology, the serial Markovian derivation, which lies at the heart of Ordering Theory, has been progressively marginalized, with the greater explanatory weight (and the bulk of actual research) falling on structural conditions and global principles of well-formedness (see Padgett 1995b for a recent review). In particular, most versions of Optimality Theory assume that constraints on all aspects of phonological structure are applied in parallel (Prince and Smolensky 1993). Inputs are mapped directly to outputs, in an essentially flat derivation whose outcome is determined by a parochial constraint hierarchy.

From an *a priori* perspective, it is not too surprising that Ordering Theory should be replaced by parallelism within OT. The principal function of rule ordering in standard phonology is to state general-izations that are not surface true (cf. Bromberger and Halle 1989); this has significance in the context of a restrictive Universal Grammar that severely delimits the set of possible generalizations. Rule ordering oper-ates with that limited set by asking that every rule be a true generaliza-tion, but only at the stage of the derivation when it applies; subsequent rules may very well obscure its result or the conditions that led to its application. Adherence to the doctrine of truth-in-generalization leads immediately to the need for multiple (sub-)levels of representation. At each (sub-)level, rules are literally, if momentarily, true.

In contrast, the constraints of OT are evaluated at the output (with faithfulness determined by reference to the input), but they are not guar-anteed to be true of the output, because the language-particular ranking establishes precedence relations among them. Rather, they are guaran-teed only to be *minimally violated* in optimal forms, in the technical sense explicated in Prince and Smolensky (1993). With the recognition that universal linguistic constraints can have significant force in deter-mining representational form, even when they are not *true*, it becomes possible to reckon in parallel, while preserving, and indeed strengthen-ing considerably, the universality of Universal Grammar. Reduplicative identity is just a special case of this general property of OT.

4. Correspondence Theory and overapplication

In this section, we analyze overapplication under Correspondence Theory. We begin (section 4.1) with a relatively straightforward case, Madurese nasal harmony, where a phonological process active in the base is paralleled in the reduplicant. We then turn (section 4.2) to phe-nomena that prove the descriptive superiority of Correspndence Theory to Ordering Theory. These include *back-copying*, in which phonology that is derived in the reduplicant is replicated in the base, and copying of phonology that occurs at reduplicant-base juncture. The possibility of back-copying raises a signficant issue in connection with reduplicative templates, and this is addressed in section 4.3. Finally, section 4.4 sums up the results.

4.1 Simple overapplication: Madurese nasal harmony

In Madurese, nasality extends rightward from a primary nasal segment until it encounters an oral obstruent. It spreads to vowels, *y*, and *w*, and passes unimpeded through *ʔ* and *h*. Such nasal spans are the only environment in which nasalized vowels and glides appear – except for reduplication. The reduplicant will have nasalized vocoids to echo those in the base, even when the triggering nasal consonant is present only in the base (Stevens 1968, 1985; Mester 1986: 197; McCarthy and Prince 1995):

(15) Nasalization and reduplication in Madurese

/neat/	ỹãt-nẽỹãt	"intentions"
/moa/	w̃ã-mõw̃ã	"faces"
/maen-an/	ẽn-mãẽn-ãn	"toys"
/ŋ-soon/	ɔ̃n-nɔ̃ʔɔ̃n	"request (verb)"
cf. /soon/	ɔn-sɔʔɔn	"request (noun)"

The final example confirms that nasality does not spread leftward. Indeed, the nasalized portion of the reduplicant in *ỹãt-nẽỹãt* isn't even adjacent to a nasal consonant. Thus, there is no explanation, other than copying, for the nasality in the prefixed reduplicant. (These examples exhibit glide formation and other interesting phonology as well, which we will abstract away from in this discussion.)

Correspondence Theory asserts that such effects derive from the impact of reduplicative identity constraints on the independently established phonology of the language. We therefore begin with a characterization of the relevant phonological infrastructure.

The language lacks nasal vocoids except in specific circumstances. We take the lack of nasal vocoids to reflect the force of a universal markedness relation:

(16) $*V_{Nas} \gg *V_{Oral}$

According to Prince and Smolensky (1993: ch. 9), pretheoretic ideas of featural markedness reflect universally fixed rankings, as in (16), of constraints against featural combinations, rather than underspecification or privativity. The universal ranking (16) entails the elementary implicational markedness observation that any language that has nasal vocoids will also have the corresponding oral vocoids.

But constraints like those in (16) are ineffectual unless they dominate a relevant faithfulness constraint. In the case at hand, we have:

(17) $*V_{Nas} \gg$ IDENT-IO(nas)

The constraint IDENT-IO(nas) requires that segments in I-O correspondence show exactly the same value of nasality (see section 2.2, (5) for the family of IDENT constraints).

The effect of the hierarchy in (17), taken by itself, is to eliminate all nasal vocoids from the output of the phonology. To see this, consider what happens to any hypothesized input containing a nasal vowel, for example *bã*:

(18) $*V_{Nas} \gg$ IDENT-IO(nas)

/bã/	$*V_{Nas}$	IDENT-IO(nas)
a. ☞ ba		*
b. bã	*!	

Denasalization occurs, due to compelled violation of IDENT-IO(nas). Any nasal vowel or glide will be mapped to its nonnasal counterpart. Under natural assumptions about lexicon optimization (Prince and Smolensky 1993: ch. 9; Stampe 1972 [1980], Dell 1980), no learner would bother to posit an underlying feature when its fate is merely to disappear without a trace. Consequently, given such a constraint system, it follows that the lexicon will be free of nasal vocoids, so long as there is no morphological advantage to positing them.

Thus far we have a language without nasal vowels. Madurese admits them in one general circumstance – postnasally – in violation of the segmental markedness constraint $*V_{Nas}$. We assume that nasal vocoids are compelled by a constraint $*NV_{Oral}$, which militates against the sequence [+nas]⁀[–nas, vocalic]:[16]

(19) $*NV_{Oral}$
      $*$[+nas]⁀[–nas, vocalic].

This constraint must dominate $*V_{Nas}$, because it forces the presence of nasal vowels in the output. It also dominates IDENT-IO(nas), because it must also be able to force a change in nasality: any input oral vowel must gain nasality in a postnasal context. In addition, the complete hierarchy must dispose of all other faithfulness constraints whose violation would aid in the satisfaction of $*NV_{Oral}$ – for example, MAX-IO, which would allow segment deletion, and IDENT-IO(son), which, taken with IDENT-IO(nas), would force nasal consonants to suffer denasalization, turning into obstruents. Writing F'(nas) to indicate this class of constraints, we have the following as the full hierarchy:

(20) $*NV_{Oral}, F'(nas) \gg *V_{Nas} \gg$ IDENT-IO(nas), $*V_{Oral}$

The constraints in the faithfulness set F' (nas) must dominate $*V_{Nas}$, because they speak to ways of satisfying $*NV_{Oral}$ other than by introducing nasal vowels.

The effects of the hierarchy in (20) are illustrated in the following tableau, which examines the fate of various candidates from underlying /na/.

(21) /na/ → nã

/na/	$*NV_{Oral}$ ⋮ F' (nas)	$*V_{Nas}$	IDENT-IO(nas)
a. ☞ nã	⋮	*	*
b. na	*! ⋮		
c. da	⋮ *!		*

In this grammar, oral and nasal vocoids are placed in complementary distribution – it is, then, a canonical case of allophonic alternation through constraint interaction. (See Baković 1994 and Kirchner 1995 for parallel developments.) The alternation is allophonic because no hypothetical lexical contrast between V_{Nas} and V_{Oral} can survive to the surface. A potential input /bã/, just like an input /ba/, will surface as *ba*; underlying /na/, just like /nã/, as *nã*. As a structuralist analysis would assert, no phonemic contrast between /ã/ and /a/ is possible.

The hierarchy in (20) characterizes, *via* constraint ranking, a typical situation of allophonic distribution: nasalized vowels occur in nasal contexts and oral vowels occur elsewhere. The default or "elsewhere" status of oral vowels follows from the universal markedness relation (16) which asserts, by fixing a ranking in Universal Grammar, that nasalized vowels are more marked than oral ones. Generalizing from the allophonicity schema (20) and the markedness relation (16), we can see that universal markedness relations will have consequences for the analysis of allophonic alternation. If $*\alpha \gg *\beta$ universally, then β must have the elsewhere status in any $\alpha \sim \beta$ alternation. In this way, Optimality

Theory relates observations about the markedness of phonological systems to alternations within those systems. Furthermore, the mere fact of such an alternation means that UG must provide a constraint with the effect of banning β or requiring α in some context (like the constraint *NV$_{Oral}$ in (20)), since otherwise the more marked α member of the alternation would never emerge. On the other hand, when there is no universal markedness relation between α and β, either one is free to assume default status in any allophonic alternation between them.

A final representational question arises: are nasal vowels in the lexicon? Is *nã* underlyingly /na/ or /nã/? In either case, the surface output is the same, and the answer turns on assumptions about lexicon optimization which are independent of OT *per se*, and perhaps lose some of their interest in this context. Is it better to have optimal forms derived with less violation – delivered by /nã/; or is it better to have a more sparsely or uniformly specified lexicon – delivered by /na/? Under earlier structuralist and generative views, complementary distribution between segment types α and β devolves from two types of conditions: a crucially lexical constraint *β that bars one segment type, say β, from all underlying representations; and a rule α→β/E__F that introduces lexically banned β in another component (the phonology).[17] OT shifts the burden of explanation to output constraints, thereby removing the lexical situation from the explanatory focus. Under OT, *β is recognized as an output constraint – a structural markedness constraint – as is *EαF, and their relation to each other and to relevant faithfulness constraints through ranking determines the outcome. When, as in Madurese, both dominate a relevant faithfulness constraint such as IDENT-IO(nas), lexical specification is irrelevant to the outcome, and lexical representation will be decided, if at all, on less tangible grounds (such as Lexicon Optimization in Prince and Smolensky 1993: chs. 4, 9) than in previous conceptions. For further discussion, see also Stampe (1972), Dell (1980), and Itô, Mester, and Padgett (1995).

Reduplication complicates the distributional situation: it introduces nasal vowels in nonnasal contexts. We repeat some of the typical data here:

(22) Nasalization and reduplication in Madurese
    /neat/   ỹãt-nẽỹãt   "intentions"
    /moa/   w̃ã-mõw̃ã   "faces"

No independent word could have the form $\tilde{y}\tilde{a}t$, as is predicted by the constraint hierarchy just developed. The independent appearance of $\tilde{y}\tilde{a}t$, $\tilde{w}\tilde{a}$ and the like can only be an effect of a reduplication-specific constraint, demanding featural identity between base and copy. Several possibilities exist for the exact formulation of the crucial constraint: does the constraint demand identity in all features, in some subset of features, or just in the feature [nasal]? Here we conservatively characterize the constraint as demanding identity only in the feature [nasal]:[18] IDENT-BR(nas). IDENT-BR(nas) must dominate $*V_{Nas}$, thereby compelling nasalized vocoids to appear in places where they are not otherwise allowed. This is the only addition that need be made to the basic grammar of nasalization in Madurese to encompass reduplication. The resulting hierarchy looks like this:

(23) Full ranking for nasality in Madurese

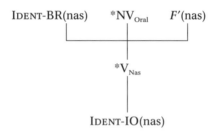

The following tableau illustrates the reduplication of /neat/, comparing a few of the most plausible candidates. (For clarity, we suppress mention of the residual faithfulness constraints as well as of $*V_{Oral}$.)

(24) /RED + neat/ → $\tilde{y}\tilde{a}t$-$n\tilde{e}\tilde{y}\tilde{a}t$

/RED + neat/	IDENT-BR(nas)	$*NV_{Oral}$	$*V_{Nas}$[19]	IDENT-IO(nas)
a. ☞ $\tilde{y}\underline{\tilde{a}t}$-$n\tilde{e}\underline{\tilde{y}\tilde{a}t}$			*****	**
b. $y\underline{at}$-$n\tilde{e}\underline{yat}$		*!	*	*
c. $y\underline{at}$-$n\tilde{e}\underline{\tilde{y}\tilde{a}t}$	**!		***	**

The imposition of B-R Identity eliminates the phonologically transparent form (c), in which nasal vocoids only occur postnasally. Forms (a) and (b) both satisfy B-R featural identity in different ways. The choice between them is therefore governed by the background phonology of the language. Form (b), a kind of underapplication, fatally violates the constraint responsible for nasal harmony, since it has oral vocoids in a postnasal context (*nẽyat). (Recall that *NV$_{\text{Oral}}$ is violated whenever a nasal segment is immediately followed by an oral vowel or glide.) Only form (a) succeeds in achieving the requisite identity of base and reduplicant, while also satisfying the dominant phonological constraint *NV$_{\text{Oral}}$ that drives the nasal harmony alternation. The downside of (a) is extra violation of *V$_{\text{Nas}}$, but the necessary subordination of *V$_{\text{Nas}}$ renders this inevitable.

The existence of forms like ỹãt-nẽỹãt means that the distribution of nasality in Madurese vowels does not accord perfectly with the structuralist requirements for allophonicity – nasal and oral vowels are fully predictable except in the reduplicant. But this follows, very simply, from the high rank of B-R Identity. Because it dominates the antinasal constraint *V$_{\text{Nas}}$, identity of base and reduplicant infringes on the perfection of complementary distribution; the system is allophonic except in this special circumstance. Identity-driven interactions of this type are common in reduplicative morphology (see appendix B of McCarthy and Prince 1995 for a list of cases) and in truncating and "cyclic" morphology as well (Benua 1995, 1997).

The Madurese outcome is of the sort termed overapplication, and in the Global Theory of Wilbur (1973a), the very *rule* of Nasal Spread literally applies to the vocoids in the reduplicant, as "mates" of the vocoids in the base. Nasal Spread then truly *over*applies, since it operates outside its canonical domain. Correspondence Theory works quite differently. The enforcement of B-R Identity – exactness of the copying relation – suppresses the *denasalization* ordinarily evoked by the subhierarchy *V$_{\text{Nas}}$ ≫ IDENT-IO(nas). Thus, the analysis here could be better described, in terms internal to the present theory, as involving underapplication, or blocking, of denasalization (see section 5.4 below for further discussion of this point).

Because OT is inherently typological in nature, it is important to scrutinize the analysis for predicted interlinguistic variation through permuted ranking (see section 5 for a more fine-grained version of the typology). Holding the basic phonology constant, the B-R Identity constraint can be intercalated at various positions in the ranking. A glance at tableau (24) indicates that the crucial pivot point is the constraint *V$_{\text{Nas}}$. When dominated by the relevant B-R Identity constraint, the outcome is overapplication, as we have seen. When this ranking is inverted, so that $*V_{Nas} \gg$ IDENT-BR(nas), the phonologically unmotivated nasal vocoids are no longer admitted, and the base and the reduplicant each show no more than their locally expected phonology: this is a kind of *normal application*, in which the reduplicant correspondents revert to their unmarked state along the nasal dimension, as exemplified in candidate (24c) *ỹat-nẽỹãt*.

There is yet a third type of candidate, *ỹat-nẽỹat*, (24b), in which the general phonological process of nasal spread is inhibited, yielding another form of identity between base and reduplicant. This is underapplication in the classic sense, where a phonological rule is said to be blocked by considerations of identity; or, in our somewhat more neutral formulation, an expected stem-output disparity is not found; or more neutrally yet, an unmarked element appears in a context where a marked element is generally demanded. As we have emphasized, it is impossible to produce this effect by reranking of B-R Identity constraints. The constraint $*NV_{Oral}$ must be crucially dominated to elevate the classically underapplicational candidate (24b), *yat-nẽyat*; yet no matter where it sits in the hierarchy, IDENT-BR(nas) simply cannot interfere with the effectiveness of $*NV_{Oral}$. The choice between the two candidates respecting B-R Identity – here, *ỹãt-nẽỹãt* and *yat-nẽyat* – has to be made on grounds other than B-R Identity. Phonology will always favor the one that does best on the higher-ranking phonological constraint. If the language is to have nasal spread at all, it must have $*NV_{Oral} \gg *V_{Nas}$ and this dooms all output representations containing oral vocoids in a postnasal environment. Thus, the correspondence theory of faithfulness entails an important general limitation: classical underapplication can never be achieved by reranking of B-R Identity; *some other constraint must be involved.* We believe this to be a correct result, and we return in section 6 to the interpretation of underapplication phenomena.

From these examples, one main line of analysis is now clear. When a phonological process is observed to affect both base and reduplicant, though the conditions for its application are met only in the base or only in the reduplicant, B-R Identity requirements are responsible.

Under Ordering Theory (section 3.2), any phonological process that overapplies must occur prior to reduplication, as in the following schematic derivation for Madurese nasal harmony:[20]

(25) Madurese nasal harmony, serially

Underlying Form	/neat/	
Glide Epenthesis	neẏat	
Nasal Harmony	nẽỹãt	
Reduplicative Copy	ỹãt-nẽỹãt	
Surface Form	ỹãt-nẽỹãt	Matched nasality

In this model, overapplication is a consequence of a particular rule-ordering configuration, in which reduplication happens to apply after some phonological rules. Similarly, normal application – independence of phonology and reduplication – is attributed to the opposite ordering, in which reduplication precedes phonological rules. All effects of identity must follow from the one identity-imposing event of reduplicative copy. Once made, the copy is no more related to the base than any other morpheme is, and it is freely subject to the vagaries of further derivation.

We argue, on the contrary, that reduplicative identity is a relation defined on the output; and that constraints on reduplicative identity are evaluated in parallel with other constraints on output structure and on input-output correspondence (faithfulness). Reduplicative identity is a part of the output: it is never lost. Reduplicative Correspondence Theory is not commensurable with the Ordering Theory; the effects and noneffects of re-ranking in parallel OT are not the same as those of reordering under operational serialism. Indeed, there are circumstances where only overapplication is possible (see the discussion of Madurese glide copy in McCarthy and Prince 1995: section 3.2). In such cases, Correspondence Theory predicts a more limited range of possibilities than Ordering Theory.

4.2 Parallelism in reduplicative correspondence

There are circumstances where Correspondence Theory predicts a wider range of interactions than can be accommodated in serial theories. These involve effects deriving from parallel evaluation of output forms for phonology and goodness of B-R Identity. Two types can be observed, back-copying and copying of phonology that is derived at the reduplicant-base juncture.

In Tagalog *pa-mu-mu:tul*, the phonology of the reduplicant is transmitted back to the base by correspondence, an outright impossibility in operational theories, where the reduplicant copies the base and not vice versa. This is back-copying, and the analysis of it relies on parallel evaluation of the phonology of the reduplicant and the B-R match. Here, schematically, is the Tagalog situation (see also section 5.3):

(26) Overapplication in Tagalog nasal substitution

/paN–RED–puːtul/	Phono- Constraint	B-R Identity	I-O Faithfulness
a. pam̲-p̲u-puːtul	*!		
b. ☞ pa-m̲u-m̲uːtul			*
c. pa-m̲u-p̲uːtul		*!	

Form (26a) simply fails to show the effects of Phono-Con, which is responsible for the nasal substitution process (on which see Pater this volume). Form (26c) is an instance of so-called normal application, with B-R mismatch. The actual output form (26b) satisfies B-R Identity but pays the price of violating low-ranking I-O Faithfulness, because the surface form of the base is different from its underlying form. This alternation in the base produces a good base-reduplicant match, back-copying the effect of a phonological process from the reduplicant to the base.

In general, back-copying will occur whenever the reduplicant undergoes a phonological process and, by virtue of the ranking B-R Identity ≫ I-O Faithfulness, the effects of that process are transmitted from reduplicant to base. No version of Ordering Theory can make sense of such interactions, except sometimes by the expedient of dodging them entirely (as in the Bloomfieldian derivation (14), with postphonological infixation of the reduplicative morpheme). Yet back-copying interactions are by no means uncommon; see the discussion of Southern Paiute below (section 6) and of Axininca Campa, Chumash, Kihehe, and Klamath in McCarthy and Prince (1995).

Perhaps even more striking are cases where the transmitted phonology occurs at the reduplicant-base juncture itself (a phenomenon whose significance was first noted by Wilbur 1973a, c). Under parallelism, the reduplicant can provide an environment that determines properties of the base, which must then, by correspondence, also appear in the reduplicant itself. Similarly, the base can impose phonology on the reduplicant, which is back-copied to the base. But Ordering Theory excludes back-copying entirely and allows no interaction between the reduplicant and the base until after the reduplicant has been brought into existence by the copying operation, after which it is too late to do anything about base-reduplicant identity. Thus, these effects raise severe difficulties for Ordering Theory, and, if well-substantiated, provide definitive evidence in favor of reduplicative Correspondence Theory.

Cases of this type will not be thick on the ground, because they require the coincidence of several independent factors, some rare. Quite aside from overapplication, phonological interaction between reduplicant and base is relatively uncommon: most reduplication is total or near-total, with base and reduplicant in a compound structure, so that the usual processes of intra-word phonology will typically not apply between them. Wilbur (1973a, c) tentatively cites two possible examples, from Chukchee and Serrano. Both have turned out to have empirical problems, and we will not consider them here, though further examination may be merited. In later work, Onn (1976: 114) and Kenstowicz (1981) provide the example of nasal harmony in Malay, and we will examine it closely here.

The basic distribution of nasality in Malay is identical to Madurese (see section 4.1): nasal and oral vocoids are in complementary distribution, with nasals appearing only in a postnasal environment. As in Madurese, base and reduplicant are featurally identical, and thus the very same constraint hierarchy (23) must be at work. In Malay, however, nasal spreading also applies across the reduplicant-base juncture. This establishes the precondition for the kind of interactions we're interested in. The consequences for reduplication are shown below:

(27) Malay reduplication²¹
    hamɔ̃   h̲a̲mɔ̃-hãmɔ̃   "germ/germs"
    waŋĭ   w̃ãŋĭ-w̃ãŋĭ   "fragrant/(intensified)"
    aŋãn   ãŋãn-ãŋãn   "reverie/ambition"
    aŋẽn   ãŋẽn-ãŋẽn   "wind/unconfirmed news"

Remarkably, nasality whose source is a nasal consonant in the *first* conjunct reappears in that very morpheme, outside the context where Malay phonology admits nasals. Thus, nasality spreads from the ŋ of /waŋɪ/ rightward to yield *waŋĭ*. But in *w̃ãŋĭ-w̃ãŋĭ*, the nasal span anchored in the first ŋ runs across the R-B juncture, incorporating the following *wa* in the base; and the nasalization of the second instance of *w̃ã* compels the first *w̃ã* to nasalize, extraphonologically, as well.

Observe that nasality spreads only to the right: witness examples like *tahan/mənāhān* "withstand," in which prefixation of /məN/ and nasal substitution lead to an alternation in the nasality of the root vowels, even though the root itself ends in *n*. Since there is no leftward spreading, the only possible source of nasality in the first syllable of *w̃ãŋĩ-w̃ãŋĩ* is reduplicative identity – its nasality matches the phonologically motivated nasality of its correspondent in the second conjunct.

Because reduplication is total, it is unclear from available information which conjunct is the reduplicant and which is the base. We will explore both alternatives, showing that the difference has essentially no significance for the analysis under Correspondence Theory.

Let us first assume that reduplication is pre-positive, with the order R+B. The copying of nasality follows directly from the hierarchy in (23) above. The important candidates are contrasted here:

(28) Malay reduplicative identity, assuming pre-positive reduplication

/RED–waŋi/	IDENT-BR(nas)	*NV_{Oral}	*V_{Nas}	IDENT-IO(nas)
a. ☞ w̃ãŋĩ_R-w̃ãŋĩ_B			*****	***
b. waŋĩ_R-waŋĩ_B		*!	**	*
c. waŋĩ_R-w̃ãŋĩ_B	**!		****	***

In forms (28a) and (28b), reduplicant and base match in nasality. Form (28b) is out for very general reasons, discussed above, in reference to tableau (24): B-R Identity can never block a dominant phonological constraint in its native environment. Candidate (28c) exemplifies normal application, which can be achieved *via* subordination of B-R Identity. In fact, B-R Identity is undominated, so candidate (28a) wins easily, and the reduplicant must take on the nasality of the base, even though the reduplicant is itself a crucial source of that nasality.

No familiar version of Ordering Theory can account for examples like this one. Neither way of ordering the rules of nasal harmony and reduplication yields the right result, as the following derivations show:

(29) Serial Theory: reduplication precedes phonology (assuming R+B)

Underlying Form	/RED–waŋi/	
Copy	waŋi–waŋi	
Spread Nasal	waŋĩ–w̃ãŋĩ	
Outcome	*waŋĩ–w̃ãŋɪ	Mismatched nasality

(30) Serial Theory: phonology precedes reduplication (assuming R+B)

Underlying Form	/RED-waɲi/	
Spread Nasal	RED-waɲĩ	
Copy	waɲĩ-waɲĩ	
Outcome	*waɲĩ-waɲĩ	Matched orality

When reduplication precedes, as in derivation (29), normal application is the result, echoing the outcome when B-R Identity is crucially subordinated. When phonology precedes, as in derivation (30), the result is underapplication of nasal spreading, a pattern not obtainable by any ranking in Correspondence Theory. This shows once again that the standard Ordering Theory is incommensurable with the parallel Correspondence Theory advocated here – and it is wrong too, if Malay truly has R+B reduplication.

The correct output can be obtained serially if Reduplicative Copy is allowed to reapply. The most general reformulation of the theory would treat Copy as a persistent or everywhere rule, which applies whenever its structural description is met (Chafe 1968, Myers 1991). The process would then proceed as follows, incorporating derivation (29), on the (random) assumption that Copy gets the first crack:

(31) Persistent Serial Theory: derivation I (assuming R+B)

Underlying Form	/RED-waɲi/	
Copy	waɲi-waɲi	
Spread Nasal	waɲĩ-w̃ãɲĩ	
Copy	w̃ãɲĩ-w̃ãɲĩ	
Outcome	w̃ãɲĩ-w̃ãɲĩ	Matched nasality

If, on the other hand, Spread Nasal applies first, we must extend derivation (30), and assume as well that Spread is also persistent:[22]

(32) Persistent Serial Theory: derivation II (assuming R+B)

Underlying Form	/RED-waɲi/	
Spread Nasal	/RED-waɲĩ/	
Copy	waɲĩ-waɲĩ	
Spread Nasal	waɲĩ-w̃ãɲĩ	
Copy	w̃ãɲĩ-w̃ãɲĩ	
Outcome	w̃ãɲĩ-w̃ãɲĩ	Matched nasality

The Persistent Serial Theory may seem like no more than an extension of familiar (if controversial) proposals, but there is a significant twist when free iteration of rules is set loose in the reduplicative realm. A persistent rule applies whenever its structural description is met: but what is the structural description of Reduplicative Copy? To work in the present context, the answer must be this: persistent Copy applies whenever R and B are *not* identical; equivalently, unless they *are* identical. One may also think of it as an output condition: apply Copy until R=B; this frames the requirement like a convergence condition on an iterative process. In either case, direct reference must be made to reduplicative identity, above and beyond copying itself. The B-R Identity requirements of Correspondence Theory must therefore be recapitulated in the Persistent Serial Theory, no doubt in excruciating detail once a finer level of analysis is undertaken. (This embodies an odd conceptual quirk as well: the very operation of copying exists to produce identity; persistence superadds another identity requirement to ensure its success.) Thus, Persistent Serialism really *abandons* the serialist goal of reducing identity to the existence of a copying operation, and fails to solve the identity problem in a satisfactorily unitary way.

Let us now explore the consequences of the assumption that Malay reduplication is post-positive, yielding the order B+R. This has no effect whatever on the prediction of the theory developed here, as the following tableau makes clear:

(33) Malay reduplicative identity, assuming post-positive reduplication

/waŋi-RED/	IDENT-BR(nas)	*NV$_{Oral}$	*V$_{Nas}$	IDENT-IO(nas)
a. ☞ w̃ãŋĩ$_B$-w̃ãŋĩ$_R$			*****	***
b. waŋĩ$_B$-waŋĩ$_R$		*!	**	*
c. waŋĩ$_B$-w̃ãŋĩ$_R$	**!		****	*

The only difference is that candidate (33c) now accumulates but one violation of IDENT-IO(nas), a fact that plays no role in the outcome.

With this B+R structure, it is the base that accommodates itself to the reduplicant. Nasalization of the initial vocalic sequence of the reduplicant springs from the base, and to the base it returns, under compulsion of B-R Identity. This result is clearly unobtainable in copying theories, for the simple reason that the reduplicant copies the base and never vice-versa. Even more striking, perhaps, is the pathological interaction between the B+R structure and the theory of Persistent Serialism. Examine the following partial derivation:

(34) Persistent Serial Theory (assuming B+R)
      Underlying Form   /waŋi-RED/
      Spread Nasal   waŋĩ-RED
      Copy   waŋĩ-waŋĩ
      Spread Nasal   waŋĩ-w̃ãŋĩ
      Copy   waŋĩ-*waŋĩ*
      Spread Nasal   waŋĩ-w̃ãŋĩ
      Copy   waŋĩ-*waŋĩ*
      etc...   ... ...

Each application of Spread Nasal from the base introduces a difference between base and reduplicant: the initial round of Copy yields the result *waŋĩ*$_B$-*waŋĩ*$_R$, which then undergoes nasal spreading to become *waŋĩ*$_B$-*w̃ãŋĩ*$_R$, thereby triggering yet another round of Copy, which triggers another hit from Spread Nasal, triggering yet another round of reduplicative copying, *ad infinitum*. The derivation, in short, does not converge;[23] it has no single output. This appears to be a disastrous result, with consequences extending far beyond the success or failure of one analysis of one pattern of Malay reduplication. It shows that constraints of identity cannot be casually invoked to trigger rule application in Persistent Serialism, because the very notion of "output of a derivation" then ceases to be well defined, in the general case. In sharp contrast, identity constraints are perfectly well behaved in nonserial OT.

The interaction of nasal spread and reduplicative identity in Malay provides a compelling argument in favor of the parallel-evaluation Correspondence Theory. If the B+R construal of the pattern is correct, then no serial base-copying theory can even generate the facts. If the R+B construal is correct, then a revised serial theory can be made to work, one that incorporates the option of free iterative application of rules. The revision is drastic, however, in its formal consequences. It requires the direct inclusion of special identity criteria to determine convergence of the iterative process – that is, when to reapply a rule and extend the derivation; these criteria mirror those in Correspondence Theory. The burden of proof falls on the speculative iterativist to demonstrate that reduplicative Correspondence Theory need not be recreated entire within Persistent Serialism. Even more seriously, the notion "output of a derivation" falls prey to endless iterative looping in one plausible range of cases; this indicates that Persistent Serialism, driven by identity conditions, may well not even be minimally workable as a linguistic theory.

To sum up, the material from Malay shows that phonological processes can be both triggered by the reduplicant and copied by it. Serial theories, even when assisted by various auxiliary assumptions, are unable to account for this type of behavior. The best serial theory is the persistent one, but it requires a theory of reduplicative correspondence to get off the ground, and is even then beset by fundamental problems that come immediately from invoking identity within an iterative regime. If base-reduplicant identity is regarded as a relation, rather than the effect of a copying process (or as a condition on serial processing), and if phonological alternations are seen as consequences of constraint satisfaction, the Malay pattern (and back-copying, as in Tagalog) emerges directly from parallel evaluation of fully formed outputs.

4.3 Back-copying and Prosodic Morphology

Correspondence Theory entails, as one of its central claims in the reduplicative realm, that there is symmetry of base-reduplicant identity. In overapplication situations, the base may be altered to match the reduplicant, just as the reduplicant is altered to match the base. This assumption follows from the conceptual structure of the theory. It is also essential to the analysis of back-copying cases like Tagalog /paN+ RED+putul/ → *pa-mu-mu:tul*, where the process of nasal substitution affects the reduplicant and, through high-ranking B-R Identity, the base is altered to match the nasal in the reduplicant. As we have emphasized, although back-copying cannot be reconciled with the demands of serial derivation, it is an expected consequence of an approach like OT that evaluates fully formed output candidates in parallel.

An important observation about back-copying has been brought to our attention independently by René Kager and Philip Hamilton, and the goal of this section is to explain it in terms of general properties of the theory of Prosodic Morphology. The issue is this: though phonological processes like Tagalog nasal substitution are observed to backcopy, the reduplicative template itself never does. Consider, for example, reduplication in the Australian language Diyari.

(35) Reduplication in Diyari (Austin 1981; Poser 1982, 1989; McCarthy and Prince 1986, 1991a, b)

Root	RED+Root	
wiḷa	wiḷa-wiḷa	"woman"
kanku	kanku-kanku	"boy"
kuḻkuŋa	kuḻku-kuḻkuŋa	"to jump"
tʲilparku	tʲilpa-tʲilparku	"bird species"
ŋankaṇṭi	ŋanka-ŋankaṇṭi	"catfish"

Descriptively, the reduplicant is identical to the first syllable of the base plus the initial CV of the second syllable. This is just exactly the shape of the minimal word of the language, and so it has in the past been standard Prosodic-Morphology practice to say that the reduplicative template for Diyari is the constituent MinWd (McCarthy and Prince 1986, 1991a, b).

No known language shows back-copying of this MinWd template, though. Such a language, referred to here as Diyari', would be expected to show alternations like the following:

(36) Reduplication in (hypothetical) Diyari'

Root	RED+Root	
wiḷa	wiḷa-wiḷa	"woman"
kanku	kanku-kanku	"boy"
kuḻkuŋa	kuḻku-kuḻku !	"to jump"
tʲilparku	tʲilpa-tʲilpa !	"bird species"
ŋankaṇṭi	ŋanka-ŋanka !	"catfish"

The interesting point about Diyari' is that it achieves a perfect match between base and reduplicant – perfect B-R Identity – and perfect satisfaction of the MinWd template. It does so at the expense of (many) I-O Faithfulness violations, since unmatched segments of the underlying root are lost when the root is reduplicated.

From this example we can develop a somewhat more formal statement of the Kager–Hamilton problem. Assume that there is an undominated templatic constraint RED=MinWd, unviolated in any reduplicant of Diyari' (or real Diyari). Likewise, there is perfect B-R matching in Diyari' (unlike real Diyari), indicating that Max-BR is also undominated. The following tableau shows that Max-IO suffers in the encounter with these two top-ranked constraints:

(37) Red=MinWd, Max-BR ≫ Max-IO in hypothetical Diyari′

/red+tʲilparku/	Red=MinWd ⦙ Max-BR	Max-IO
a. ☞ tʲilpa-tʲilpa	⦙	*
b. tʲilpa-tʲilparku	⦙ *!	
c. tʲilparku-tʲilparku	*! ⦙	

Unreduplicated forms receive a fully faithful analysis in Diyari′, though, because neither of the top-ranked reduplicant-specific constraints has anything to say, and so Max-IO emerges as decisive:

(38) Derivation of unreduplicated forms in hypothetical Diyari′

/tʲilparku/	Red=MinWd ⦙ Max-BR	Max-IO
a. ☞ tʲilparku	⦙	
b. tʲilpa	⦙	*!

The rankings in the two contrasting systems are therefore these:

(39) Ranking properties of the Kager–Hamilton problem
    a. Ranking in real Diyari – normal application of templatic constraint
       Red=MinWd, Max-IO ≫ Max-BR

    b. Ranking in hypothetical Diyari′ – back-copying overapplication of templatic constraint
       Red=MinWd, Max-BR ≫ Max-IO   (cf. (61) below)

The constraint hierarchy for real Diyari in (39a) is typical of normal application (see (62) below). With Max-BR low ranking, neither templatic conformity nor I-O Faithfulness is sacrificed to achieve better B-R Identity. Diyari′, on the other hand elevates templatic conformity and B-R Identity above the dictates of I-O Faithfulness (cf. the ranking for Tagalog back-copying in (26)). Ranking permutations like these predict possible interlinguistic differences: the Kager–Hamilton problem, quite simply, is that languages like Diyari′ do not exist, contrary to prediction.

Of course, this prediction depends on the assumption that all the constraints in (39) are indeed part of UG; if they are not, then permutations of their ranking are irrelevant. The status of MAX-BR and MAX-IO is not in doubt. Rather, the flaw in (39b) lies in the assumption that UG contains templatic constraints like RED=MINWD. There are no such constraints, and without them the Kager–Hamilton problem evaporates.

To deny that there are prosodic-morphological templates may seem nihilistic – after all, aren't templates the very essence of Prosodic Morphology? But recall the goal of Prosodic Morphology, as set out in section 1: to derive the characteristics of reduplication and like phenomena from general properties of morphology, general properties of phonology, and general properties of the interface between morphology and phonology. To the extent that PM-specific devices like templates are posited, this goal remains distant.

The program of deriving the descriptive effects of templates from independently required constraints on phonology, morphology, and their interface is called Generalized Template Theory (GTT – McCarthy and Prince 1994a, b; Carlson 1996; Colina 1996; Downing 1994, 1996a, b, this volume; Futagi to appear; Gafos 1995, 1996; Itô, Kitagawa, and Mester 1996; Moore 1995; Spaelti 1997; Urbanczyk 1996a, b; cf. Shaw 1987, Steriade 1988, Itô and Mester 1992 for precursors). The main thesis is that templates are obtained by entirely general constraints *via* the emergence-of-the-unmarked ranking pattern (McCarthy and Prince 1994a; section 5.2 below). A structural constraint rendered inactive in the language as a whole because of domination by I-O Faithfulness may nonetheless emerge as visibly active in situations where I-O Faithfulness is not relevant. In particular, it may determine the form of the reduplicant, which is subject to constraints on B-R Identity rather than I-O Faithfulness. The ranking schema that leads to this situation is the following.

(40) Skeletal ranking for emergence of the unmarked
      I-O Faithfulness ≫ Phono-Constraint ≫ B-R Identity

Because I-O Faithfulness dominates Phono-Constraint, its effects are typically not visible in the language as a whole. Phono-Constraint cannot compel inexact correspondence between the underlying stem and the surface base. It can, however, affect the perfection of correspondence in the horizontal, B-R dimension. This means that the reduplicant will obey Phono-Constraint even when obedience means inexactness of copying. The reduplicant then obeys a constraint that is otherwise violated freely in the language as a whole – one that may even be violated in the base of reduplication.

Let us apply these ideas to the Diyari MinWd template, based on McCarthy and Prince (1994b), which should be consulted for further discussion. As the irreducible starting point of the analysis, we observe that every morpheme must surely be categorized for its position in the morphological hierarchy: affix, root, stem, and so on. The core idea is that once this morphology has been fixed, constraints on the morphology-prosody relationship will define the prosodic correlates of morpheme-category membership. With the prosodic correlates thus broadly fixed, constraints on the canonical realization of prosodic categories will fully determine the lower-level details. In the case of Diyari, the key morphological observation is that the reduplicative morpheme is lexically categorized as a *stem*, so that reduplication is structurally a form of stem-stem compounding. The canonical realization of *stem*, accomplished via Generalized Alignment (McCarthy and Prince 1993b), is as prosodic word (PrWd). This much we take to be uncontroversial; the challenge is to make the transition from the coarse-grained characterization of *stem* as a prosodic word to the exact details of the bisyllabic, vowel-final reduplicant structure that is observed in the language. This, we claim, is emergent as the most harmonic possible prosodic word (PrWd), as defined by independently motivated constraints of metrical theory. The relevant constraints are these:

(41)

Constraint Name	Definition	Discussion	References
HEADEDNESS (PRWD)	Every PrWd must contain a foot.	A standard assumption about the Prosodic Hierarchy. Unviolated in Diyari (and perhaps universally).	Selkirk (1980a, b, 1995); McCarthy and Prince (1986, 1991a, b); Itô and Mester (1992).
FT-BIN	Feet are binary under syllabic or moraic analysis.	Unviolated in Diyari, which lacks monosyllabic feet.	Prince (1980); McCarthy and Prince (1986); Hayes (1995).

PARSE-SYLL	Every syllable belongs to some foot.	Instantiates as a violable constraint the maximal parsing assumption of metrical theory.	Prince and Smolensky (1993); McCarthy and Prince (1993a, b).
ALL-FT-LEFT	Align(Ft,L,PrWd, L)≈Every foot stands in initial position in the PrWd.	Responsible for directional footing – see immediately below.	Kirchner (1993); McCarthy and Prince (1993b).

The stress pattern of Diyari (morphological complications aside – see McCarthy and Prince 1994b) locates main stress on the initial syllable and secondary stress on every odd-numbered syllable thereafter, except that lone final syllables are not stressed: $(\acute{\sigma}\sigma)(\grave{\sigma}\sigma)(\grave{\sigma}\sigma)\sigma$. This pattern of directional footing is obtained under the ranking PARSE-SYLL ≫ ALL-FT-LEFT. According to ALL-FT-LEFT, all feet should be at the left edge. But dominance of PARSE-SYLL requires that the form be fully footed (subject only to FT-BIN). Under minimal violation of ALL-FT-LEFT, a multi-foot form must have its feet as close to the left edge as possible. (See McCarthy and Prince 1993b, elaborating on the proposal of Kirchner 1993, for additional discussion.)

In a form with the stress pattern $(\acute{\sigma}\sigma)(\grave{\sigma}\sigma)(\grave{\sigma}\sigma)\sigma$, both PARSE-SYLL and ALL-FT-LEFT are violated. PARSE-SYLL is violated because there is always an unparsed syllable in odd-parity words, to preserve FT-BIN, which is undominated in this language. ALL-FT-LEFT is violated because the non-initial feet are misaligned. Both constraints, however, *can* be obeyed fully. In that case,

every syllable is footed (PARSE-SYLL is obeyed), and
every foot is initial (ALL-FT-LEFT is obeyed).

Only one configuration meets both of these requirements, the minimal word, since it has a single foot that parses all syllables and is itself properly left-aligned.

(42) $[\text{ Ft }]_{\text{PrWd}}$ *i.e.*, disyllabic $[(\sigma\ \sigma)_{\text{Ft}}]_{\text{PrWd}}$ or bimoraic $[(\mu\ \mu)_{\text{Ft}}]_{\text{PrWd}}$

Thus, the minimal word is the most harmonic PrWd possible, with respect to PARSE-SYLL and ALL-FT-LEFT – indeed, with respect to every form of Ft/PrWd alignment. Of course, the single foot contained within the minimal word is optimally binary, because of FT-BIN. Hence, the most harmonic PrWd with respect to these metrical constraints is a disyllable in any language that does not make quantitative (moraic) distinctions.

Returning to reduplication, we can apply this insight using the emergence of the unmarked ranking in (40). The reduplicant is a free-standing prosodic word (PrWd), as evidenced by its stress behavior and vowel-final status (Austin 1981). With PARSE-SYLL and ALL-FT-LEFT ranked so that their effects are emergent, the reduplicant is the most harmonic PrWd possible, even at the cost of imperfect copying. Thus, these constraints compel violation of MAX-BR, as shown in the following tableaux.

(43) PARSE-SYLL ≫ MAX-BR, from /RED+tⁱilparku/

	PARSE-SYLL	MAX-BR
a. ☞ [(tⁱilpa)$_{Ft}$]$_{PrWd}$ -[(tⁱilpar)$_{Ft}$ ku]$_{PrWd}$	*	***
b. [(tⁱilpar)$_{Ft}$ ku]$_{PrWd}$ -[(tⁱilpar)$_{Ft}$ ku]$_{PrWd}$	**!	

This tableau shows incomplete copying of odd-parity roots. Form (43b) is a perfect copy, but it also involves an extra PARSE-SYLL violation. Incomplete copying avoids this unparsed syllable, and, as (43a) shows, this is more harmonic prosodically.[24] The next tableau shows the same thing, but with ALL-FT-LEFT as the decisive constraint.

(44) ALL-FT-LEFT ≫ MAX-BR, from (hypothetical) /RED+ŋandawalka/

	ALL-FT-LEFT	MAX-BR
a. ☞ [(ŋanda)$_{Ft}$]$_{PrWd}$– [(ŋanda)$_{Ft}$ (walka)$_{Ft}$]$_{PrWd}$	*	*****
b. [(ŋanda)$_{Ft}$ (walka)$_{Ft}$]$_{PrWd}$– [(ŋanda)$_{Ft}$ (walka)$_{Ft}$]$_{PrWd}$	**!	

In (44b), the reduplicant fatally violates ALL-FT-LEFT, since it contains an unaligned foot, while form (44a) spares that violation by incomplete copying. The "minimalization" of the reduplicant follows from these rankings. But ordinary roots of the language can be nonminimal, indicating that MAX-IO dominates both PARSE-SYLL and ALL-FT-LEFT.

(45) MAX-IO ≫ PARSE-SYLL, from /tʲilparku/

	MAX-IO	PARSE-SYLL
a. ☞ [(tʲilpar)_Ft ku]_PrWd		*
b. [(tʲilpar)_Ft]_PrWd	**!	

(46) MAX-IO ≫ ALL-FT-LEFT, from /RED+ŋandawalka/

	MAX-IO	ALL-FT-LEFT
a. ☞ [(ŋanda)_Ft (walka)_Ft]_PrWd		*
b. [(ŋanda)_Ft]_PrWd	*****!	

The full ranking for Diyari, then, is this (cf. (40)):

(47) Diyari ranking using emergence of the unmarked
     MAX-IO ≫ PARSE-SYLL, ALL-FT-LEFT ≫ MAX-BR

Minimality – here interpreted as prosodic optimality with respect to syllabic parsing (PARSE-SYLL) and foot alignment (ALL-FT-LEFT) – is an emergent property of the reduplicant. MAX-BR is subordinated to these requirements of prosodic harmony, but MAX-IO dominates them. No template or templatic constraint like RED=MINWD is necessary or desirable – the independently necessary constraints of the prosodic-morphology interface, of prosodic theory itself and of correspondence are enough. Indeed, it is not even possible, we assert, to declare that the Diyari reduplicant is a PrWd. It suffices to identify the lexical status of the reduplicative morpheme, surely an ineliminable property of its mor-phology. Once it is understood that *stem* is most harmonically aligned with a PrWd (McCarthy and Prince 1994b), there is a cascade of phono-logical consequences, controlled by emergence of the unmarked. Fur-ther direct evidence for the role in reduplication of morphology and its canonical expression is found in Downing (this volume), Itô, Kitagawa, and Mester (1996), and Urbanczyk (1996a, b).

This account of the shape of the Diyari reduplicant is superior, on explanatory grounds, to an analysis that posits templatic constraints like RED=MINWD, RED=PRWD, or the like. Significantly, it also provides an immediate explanation for the nonexistence of Diyari′. To get back-copying, the constraints defining the shape of the reduplicant must dominate MAX-IO (compare (39b)). But now every word of the language

– not just reduplicated words – will obey these constraints! That is not what Diyari' is supposed to look like.

To put the matter more generally, back-copying an emergent template is impossible because it demands mutually incompatible rankings. Let C denote the constraints that define the shape of the reduplicant. For C to be emergent, it must fit the following ranking schema:

(48) Ranking for emergence of C (cf. (40))
      I-O Faithfulness ≫ C ≫ B-R Identity

For a constraint C to be back-copied, a different ranking is necessary:

(49) Ranking for back-copying of C (cf. (26))
      B-R Identity, C ≫ I-O Faithfulness

These rankings are inconsistent. In (48), C is obeyed only in the reduplicant, where BR-Identity suffers. But in (49), C is obeyed in the whole language. There is an obvious ranking contradiction, and by virtue of it we have a solution to the Kager–Hamilton problem – Diyari' cannot exist because no constraint C can emerge and be back-copied in the same language, since emergence and back-copying require mutually incompatible constraint rankings.

Projecting from the Diyari situation, we can say that no template of any type can be back-copied. To secure this general result, two additional assumptions need to be made explicit. One is the Generalized Template Hypothesis, according to which UG countenances no templates or any other affix-specific constraints. As we have just seen, templatic constraints like RED=MINWD are the source of the Kager–Hamilton conundrum, and elimination of them through reanalysis under emergence of the unmarked is the main goal of Generalized Template Theory. A related assumption, brought to our attention by Ed Keer, is that the emergence of the unmarked must work by combining general markedness constraints (like PARSE-SYLL) with grammatically restricted faithfulness constraints (like MAX-IO versus MAX-BR), and not the other way around. Grammatically restricted markedness constraints are just another type of templatic constraint, and so their existence would subvert this result.

Templates are never back-copied, something of a surprise given the ubiquity of templates in reduplication. This gap is a principled one, and it is explained by uniting two hitherto distinct themes of Prosodic

Morphology: Correspondence Theory and Generalized Template Theory. Templates are not back-copied because there are no templates; there are only rankings of universal constraints with templatic effect, and these rankings contradict those that lead to back-copying. This convergence of results from very different domains is encouraging and suggests that both aspects of the approach may very well be on the right track.

4.4 Summary

We have argued in this section for an account of reduplicative overapplication, set within parallelist Optimality Theory under the Correspondence Theory of faithfulness and identity. Phonological alternations or distributional restrictions require a ranking in which some phonological constraint dominates I-O Faithfulness; this defines the background phonology of the language at hand. When B-R Identity constraints are also active, then phonological effects on the base are carried over to the reduplicant. But effects may be carried as well from reduplicant to base, since the form of both is determined in parallel. Indeed, even phonological alternations arising from the interaction of base and reduplicant may be duplicated, because of parallel evaluation. All three types of overapplication – base to reduplicant, reduplicant to base, and interactional – have been exemplified in this section. Moreover, all types of alternations may be observed to behave in this way – segmental and featural, morphophonemic and allophonic.

Serial approaches are strikingly less successful in dealing with the diversity of overapplication effects. Indeed, the best serial theory departs markedly from standard assumptions, requiring the option of persistent reapplication of rules, in order to assure output B-R Identity in the face of B-R interaction effects. But it evidently presupposes a characterization of "identity" which, in all likelihood, merely recapitulates the very Correspondence Theory it is meant to replace. With this, because of its serialism, it suffers from grave problems of ill definition arising from the existence of nonconvergent (oscillatory) derivations. Further, cases in which the base itself is shaped so as to match the reduplicant are absolute impediments to any serial theory which sees the copying operation as the basis of reduplicative identity. In Correspondence Theory, though, the same constraints responsible for copying are also responsible for overapplication. Therefore, with full symmetry, given parallelism, the base can copy the reduplicant and phonological effects conditioned jointly by reduplicant and base can be observed in both.

The book is not closed, of course. In the many-celled multidimensional matrix of predicted empirical possibilities, many cells are as yet empty or incomplete. A meticulous and final argument would match every case of full reduplication with one or more of partial reduplication that has exactly the same properties; every case of overapplication with a case of normal application that assumes the same background phonology and templatic form. Many contrasts between the effects of different types of phonology need to be examined, as well. In particular, broader cross-linguistic study is needed to establish more securely some of the typological results that emerge under permutation of the identity constraints with the variety of phonological constraints that drive alternations.[25] Consider, for example, the constraint responsible for nasal place assimilation. Is it possible to have R-to-B overapplication yielding a hypothetical relation like /RED+panit/ → *pam-pamit*? Cases of this specific type have not been observed, yet it is not clear how (or whether) they are to be distinguished from true R-to-B interaction in Malay (section 4.2) and other cases analyzed in McCarthy and Prince (1995). Indeed, one might ask whether there can be B-to-R overapplication of the same process, exemplified by /RED+an+bit/ → *am-ambit*. Again, we have located no such cases, which are nonetheless predicted to exist under all theories of overapplication, serial and parallel alike. It could be that structural factors, here having to do with the formal properties of assimilated nasal stop clusters, offer a principled explanation for this sort of gap in R-to-B overapplication. It could be that there is no real gap, merely ignorance. It could be that there are indeed real gaps like this, as yet unpredicted by Correspondence Theory, due to principles of R/B asymmetry that have not yet been uncovered. Similarly, free emergence of the unmarked allows for fine distinctions among different prosodic types, depending on which of the various relevant constraints are ranked above B-R Identity; yet the observed set of templatic forms shows a substantial clumping together of prosodic constraints. Given the success of the approach in providing a very general account of the character of canonical forms, including "templates," it will likely be useful to pursue the further explanatory and descriptive issues that it discloses.

5. Factorial typology

Permutation of ranking exposes the content of a proposed sub-theory of constraints. What mappings and relationships are admitted by the various rankings? Do all the rankings yield possible grammars? The full set of permuted rankings constitutes a *factorial typology* of a linguistic domain (Prince and Smolensky 1991, 1993: ch. 6).

The Basic Model posits faithfulness constraints on two distinct dimensions of correspondence, as represented here:

(50) Basic Model

Input   /Af$_{\text{RED}}$ + Stem/
                           $\updownarrow$ *I-O Faithfulness*
Output   R $\rightleftharpoons$ B
                   B-R Identity

In this section, we will examine the ways that phonology and reduplication interact in the Basic Model's factorial typology, which counterposes B-R Identity, I-O Faithfulness, and structural markedness constraints. Extension to the Full Model (6), which imposes I-R Faithfulness as well, is taken up in McCarthy and Prince (1995: section 6).

The project falls into two halves. First, we consider those systems where there is no relevant language-wide phonology at work; among these is a pattern in which the reduplicant shows phonology that the base does not ("emergence of the unmarked"). Second, we examine the cases where significant language-wide phonology exists and can interact nontrivially with reduplication. The most important results, adumbrated at various points, include the availability of reduplicant-to-base back-copying and the nonavailability of underapplication and even of certain kinds of "normal application." The model enforces a distinction between overapplication patterns that extend base phonology to the reduplicant and those that extend reduplicant phonology back to the base; this arises because only the back-copying pattern requires otherwise unmotivated violations of I-O Faithfulness.

5.1 Nonapplication

For a feature-changing map to be present in the phonology, a Phono-Constraint C must dominate *some* relevant constraint on I-O

Faithfulness[26] as well as every other phonological constraint *M that militates against the desired output M. For instance, in Madurese nasal harmony (section 4.1), the phonological constraints $*V_{Nas}$ and $*NV_{Oral}$ are active because they dominate the faithfulness constraint IDENT-IO(nas); this allows nasality values to switch between input and output forms. It is also necessary that $*NV_{Oral}$, *qua* "Phono-Constraint," dominate $*V_{Nas}$, so that the otherwise-banned nasal vocoids V_{Nas} are allowed into output representations.

(51) Necessary conditions for Phono-Constraint to be enforced in I-O mapping

   Phono-Constraint ≫ I-O Faithfulness, {*M}

In this schema, the term "I-O Faithfulness" is used here to refer to *some* relevant constraint of that type, while "{*M}" means *every* relevant structural constraint. Though we will not be dwelling on formal details in this overview, the distinction between *some* and *every* seems worthy of note, and we will draw attention to it *via* an *ad hoc* notation: {X} will mean "every relevant constraint of type X," while unbraced X means simply "some relevant constraint of type X."

The force of Phono-Constraint is blunted when the negation of condition (51) holds. If all relevant I-O Faithfulness constraints crucially dominate the Phono-Constraint C, it will not be active in defining the input-output mapping. If some structural constraint *M dominates it, then typically nothing can be done to enforce C by introducing M: for example, if $*V_{Nas} ≫ *NV_{Oral}$, then the constraint $*NV_{Oral}$ simply cannot be satisfied by the introduction of nasal vocoids.

(52) Phono-Constraint rendered ineffectual

   {I-O Faithfulness} ≫ Phono-Constraint

   OR   *M ≫ Phono-Constraint

Things are similar on the reduplicative front. Subordination of some B-R Identity constraint to a sufficiently high-ranked Phono-Constraint C can force inexactness of copying; the reduplicant will respect C whether or not the base does.[27] But if all relevant B-R Identity constraints dominate C, then C cannot compel a base-reduplicant disparity. Thus, when Phono-Constraint C is subordinated to all relevant B-R

Identity constraints *and* all relevant I-O Faithfulness constraints, it is completely out of action. This gives us the ranking in (53):

(53) A skeletal ranking for total nonapplication
      {B-R Identity}, {I-O Faithfulness} ≫ Phono-Constraint

In its dominated position, Phono-Constraint can compel neither unfaithfulness nor inexact identity; it is inert.[28] Pursuing the second disjunct of (52), we note that nonapplication can also be obtained by ranking relevant *markedness* constraints above Phono-Constraint, regardless of the disposition of I-O Faithfulness and B-R Identity. Should $*V_{Nas}$ dominate $*NV_{Oral}$, nasal vocoids will be admitted in neither base nor reduplicant to assuage $*NV_{Oral}$.

Examples of non-application ranking patterns are legion, although they do not always attract attention. For example, the constraint $*NV_{Oral}$ is thoroughly dominated in many languages, so that it has no effects on either base or reduplicant. Such rankings allow constraints to be universally *available* without being universally *active*. Nonapplicational ranking is one of the ways in which the activity of any constraint of Universal Grammar is controlled by its systematic relation to other constraints; in the limiting case, its activity can be entirely suppressed.

5.2 Emergence of the unmarked

The universal availability of Phono-Constraint assumes particular importance in rankings where it dominates B-R Identity, though ranked below I-O Faithfulness.

(54) Skeletal ranking for emergence of the unmarked
      {I-O Faithfulness} ≫ Phono-Constraint ≫ B-R Identity, {*M}

Because every relevant I-O Faithfulness constraint dominates Phono-Constraint, the effects of Phono-Constraint are not visible in the language generally. Phono-Constraint cannot compel disparity between input stem and output base, whose correspondence relation is indicated by the vertical arrows in the portrait of the Basic Model in (50). This amounts to "no application" in general. Phono-Constraint can, however, affect the perfection of correspondence in the horizontal, B-R dimension of (50). This means that the reduplicant will obey

Phono-Constraint even when obedience means inexactness of copying.[29] The reduplicant *obeys* a constraint that is otherwise violated freely in the language at large – one that may even be violated in the reduplicative base itself.

This state of affairs is a type of *emergence of the unmarked*. The idea is that the phonologically unmarked structure – unmarked because it obeys Phono-Constraint – emerges in reduplicated forms, though it is not required in the language as a whole. Initially developed in McCarthy and Prince (1994a), where the ranking schema (54) is presented,[30] emergence of the unmarked supports the OT conception of constraints as ranked, rather than parameterized (Prince and Smolensky 1991, 1993): parameterization of Phono-Constraint would be an all-or-nothing matter and could never produce emergence of the unmarked. Emergence of the unmarked is invoked in section 4.3 above as the basis of Generalized Template Theory; the emergent unmarked structures include the kind of prosodic configurations realizing morpheme-types that have been previously understood as templates.

An illuminating example comes from the Philippine Austronesian language Balangao (Shetler 1976). The Balangao reduplicant copies the first two syllables of the base, minus the final coda: /RED–tagtag/ → *tagta-tagtag*. This means that the constraint No-CODA crucially dominates the reduplicant-maximizing constraint MAX-BR.

(55) No-CODA ≫ MAX-BR in Balangao

/RED–tagtag/	No-CODA	MAX-BR
a. ☞ tag.ta.–tag.tag.	***	*
b. tag.tag.–tag.tag.	****!	

Form (55a) violates MAX-BR, because the final *g* of the base has no correspondent in the reduplicant. It does so, as the tableau makes apparent, to spare a No-CODA violation. Undominated CONTIG-BR (see the appendix) protects the reduplicant-medial coda, ruling out the further codaic economy obtained by a reduplicant like *ta.ta.–*.[31]

Though No-CODA dominates MAX-BR in Balangao, it has the opposite ranking with respect to MAX-IO. The language obviously has codas, both medially and finally, so it must value faithfulness to the input higher than coda avoidance:

(56) MAX-IO ≫ NO-CODA in Balangao

/tagtag/	MAX-IO	NO-CODA
a. ☞ tag.tag.		**
b. tag.ta.	*!	*

Here, form (56b) violates MAX-IO, since input-final *g* has no correspondent in the output. Violation is fatal, because NO-CODA ranks
below the input-output faithfulness constraint. (To flesh out the analysis, we must have DEP-IO and all other relevant I-O Faithfulness
constraints dominating NO-CODA, to ensure that every avenue of escape
from faithful parsing is blocked off.)

Combining the two results, we have MAX-IO, ...≫ NO-CODA ≫ MAX-
BR – a special case of the emergence of the unmarked schema (54).

(57)
Schema   {I-O Faithfulness} ≫ Phono-Constraint ≫ B-R Identity
Instantiation   MAX-IO, ...   ≫ NO-CODA   ≫ MAX-BR

The following tableau shows the force of these constraints:

(58) Emergence of the unmarked in Balangao

/RED–tagtag/	MAX-IO	NO-CODA	MAX-BR
a. tag.ta.-tag.ta.	*!	**	
b. tag.tag.-tag.tag.		****!	
c. ☞ tag.ta.-tag.tag.		***	*

The coda-sparing but inexact reduplicant (58c) is optimal, even though
the language as a whole allows codas. Indeed, the *base* in the very same
form has a coda (two, even), as does the medial syllable of the reduplicant (where it is protected by CONTIG-BR). The situation can be
diagrammed as in (59) below:

(59) Input   /Af$_{\text{RED}}$ + tagtag/
                              ↑↓ *exact faithfulness*
      Output   tagta ⇆ tagtag
                     inexact identity

Here we see exactness of correspondence in the vertical dimension, because the input form of the base is identical to its output form, but inexactness in the horizontal dimension, because the base and reduplicant are distinct.

In comparison, B-R Identity is respected in forms (58a) and (58b). But form (58a) *tagta-tagta* fatally sacrifices input material (*MAX-IO) to gain codaic advantage, while form (58b) *tagtag-tagtag* has a final coda in the reduplicant (*NO-CODA) that can be avoided at the mere price of incomplete copying. This, then, is emergence of the unmarked: the constraint NO-CODA is better respected in the reduplicant than it is in the language as a whole.

Reduplicative emergence of the unmarked, derived from rankings like (57), enforces template-like conditions. A segmental theorist from the dawn of Prosodic Morphology would have been tempted to declare a template like "CVCCV" for the reduplicative morpheme. On this view, the lack of a reduplicant-final coda in Balangao is the result of a chance arrangement of Cs and Vs. But of course this CV-template echoes a familiar type of canonical restriction on general word-form (holding in Italian, for example, where there are closed syllables internally, e.g., *pasta*, but not word-finally). Emergence of the unmarked allows us to recruit the structural principles that delimit word- and morpheme-form for use in defining templatic restrictions on reduplicative affixes and other objects of Prosodic Morphology. Generalizing from this kind of initial success, the natural proposal (section 4.3) is that all conditions formerly attributed to templates follow from morphology-prosody interface constraints (such as "Stem aligns with PrWd") taken together with the various constraints on the shape of prosodic categories (such as NO-CODA) under the ranking regime of emergence of the unmarked. This provides a maximally general theory of "templates," building them from the interaction of constraints independently recognized as part of Universal Grammar. In addition to its generality, this approach immediately provides a principled limitation on reduplicative back-copying, resolving the Kager–Hamilton problem.

5.3 Modes of overapplication and normal application

In the grammatical patterns reviewed so far, there is either no relevant phonology (nonapplication) or it is restricted to the reduplicant (emergence of the unmarked). When language-wide phonology exists and when its conditioning environment is found in one member but not the other of the base-reduplicant pair, reduplicative identity is threatened and the potential for extending the phonology outside its normal venue arises. That is overapplication.

Since by assumption there is language-wide phonology at play, we will presuppose the following rankings throughout the discussion:

(60) Phonology with Phono-Constraint

Phono-Constraint ≫ I-O Faithfulness, {*M}

Phono-Constraint will therefore be factored out of the ranking schemata adduced below in order to highlight the interactions of B-R Identity.

With an architectural distinction between I-O Faithfulness and B-R Identity, conflict can arise between analogous constraints on the two dimensions, and when it arises, it must be settled in favor of one or the other. This leads to a fundamental morphological distinction in the typology: overapplication from R to B (back-copying), where R is the target of the basic phonology, requires otherwise unnecessary violations of I-O Faithfulness to obtain optimal B; but overapplication from B to R, where B is already the primary target of phonological unfaithfulness, requires only that the extra markedness violations in R be forced. Consequently, back-copying requires not only Phono-Constraint ≫ I-O Faithfulness, but also B-R Identity ≫ I-O Faithfulness, since it is exactly the demand for B-R Identity that compels otherwise unmotivated faithfulness violations. The extra markedness violations must also be compelled, leading to the following schema:

(61) Back-copying overapplication in B, when R is the target of *Phono-Constraint*

{B-R Identity} ≫ I-O Faithfulness, {*M}

This schema shows that B-R Identity formally parallels Phono-Constraint in schema (60) as a provider of impetus for I-O phonology.

The base is protected from incursions in all rankings that do not have this character. Holding constant the relation between Phono-Constraint and the I-O Faithfulness constraint that yields the relevant phonology, the ranking {I-O Faithfulness} ≫ B-R Identity will preserve the base from back-copying. Similarly, domination of B-R Identity by any member of the set {*M} will be sufficient to prevent the effects of

Phono-Constraint from being carried back to the base. These two conditions for normal application are collected in the following schema:

(62) Normal Application in B, When R is the Target of *Phono-Constraint*

{I-O Faithfulness} ≫ B-R Identity
OR   *M   ≫ B-R Identity

Under the first disjunct in (62), the base cannot be unfaithful to the input merely to take on Phono-Constraint-motivated phonology from the reduplicant – the excess cost in I-O Faithfulness violations is too high. The same base-protective effect also results when a relevant markedness constraint dominates B-R Identity, regardless of I-O Faithfulness, as in the second disjunct. Either of these disruptions of the back-copying ranking yields a type of normal application: base and reduplicant go their separate ways phonologically, without regard to the B-R linkage between them.

Concrete examples of both ranking schemata come from Austronesian nasal substitution (on which see Pater this volume). In (63a), we have data from Balangao (Shetler 1976), in which nasal substitution applies normally, with indifference to reduplicative structure. In (63b), Bloomfield's Tagalog example is recalled from section 1. Nasal substitution overapplies, with its effects transmitted from reduplicant to base:

(63) Contrast in application of Austronesian nasal substitution
   a. Normal application in Balangao
      /maN+tagtag/   ma-n̲agtag   "running"
      /maN+RED+tagtag/ ma-n̲agta-t̲agtag[32] "running everywhere"
   b. Overapplication in Tagalog
      /paN+putul/   pa-m̲uːtul
      /paN+RED+putul/   pa-m̲u-m̲uːtul

In both cases, the reduplicant has the N+voiceless stop configuration that is the target of the responsible Phono-Constraint. The difference between the two lies in whether or not B-R Identity is supported by duplicating the derived nasal in the base. In Balangao, with the ranking (62), faithfulness takes precedence over identity, so the base is not affected by changes in the reduplicant.

(64) Normal application in Balangao nasal substitution

/maN–RED–tagtag/	Phono-Constraint	I-O Faithfulness	B-R Identity
a. man-tagta-tagtag	*!		
b. ma-nagta-nagtag		*!	
c. ☞ ma-nagta-tagtag			*

The comparison between (64b) and (64c) is the interesting one. In (64b), the base has n for underlying /t/, violating the faithfulness constraint IDENT-IO(-nas), as in Pater (this volume), which forbids the relation /t/$_I$ ~ [n]$_O$. In (64c), though, only the reduplicant has the n, and this is optimal because all the B-R Identity constraints forbidding t_B ~ n_R are decisively dominated.[33] This is one type of normal application, in which a phonological process, visibly active in the language as a whole, also applies to the reduplicant, leading to a B-R mismatch.

Tagalog, by contrast, instantiates the ranking schema (61), where dominant B-R Identity can compel I-O unfaithfulness, transmitting changes in the reduplicant back to the base, as in section 4.2. The results are illustrated schematically in the following tableau.

(65) Overapplication in Tagalog nasal substitution

/paN–RED–puːtul/	Phono-Constraint	B-R Identity	I-O Faithfulness
a. pam-pu-puːtul	*!		
b. ☞ pa-mu-muːtul			*
c. pa-mu-puːtul		*!	

The interesting comparison is between forms (65b) and (65c). The base in form (65b) pays the price of unfaithfulness to the input – /p/$_I$ ~ [m]$_O$ here, with nasal mismatch – in order to achieve a good base-reduplicant match.

The Balangao-Tagalog contrast shows how the ranking of B-R Identity relative to I-O Faithfulness effectively distinguishes between normal application and overapplication, when the primary target of Phono-Constraint is the *reduplicant*. But when Phono-Constraint targets the *base*, the relative ranking of I-O Faithfulness is of no consequence, as we have noted, because modifications of the reduplicant are not reck-oned as I-O violations. Control of overapplication must therefore fall to the relationship between B-R Identity and the relevant structural con-straints (*M) other than the Phono-Constraint that is directly involved in the basic phonology: for example, segmental markedness constraints. Thus in a Madurese/Malay-type nasal harmony system (section 4), the crucial pivot is *V$_{Nas}$ – if the relevant B-R Identity constraint dominates it, then the additional identity-preserving nasal vocoids will be forced in the reduplicant, as in *ỹãt-nẽỹãt*. This is B-to-R overapplication descript-ively, and here again the relevant B-R Identity constraint plays a role much like that of *NV$_{Oral}$ in forcing violations of *V$_{Nas}$.

(66) Overapplication in R when B is target
      B-R Identity ≫ {*M}

This kind of overapplication ensures that the reduplicant accurately imitates the base, even when the phonological circumstances in B are different from those in R. Thus, in the Madurese/Malay case, given underlying input /ỹãt/, the grammar will produce denasalized output [yat]; but given base [...ỹãt...], we get reduplicant [ỹãt].

If the ranking runs the other way, with *V$_{Nas}$ ≫ B-R Identity, then any reduplicant vocoids corresponding to base vocoids will be nonnasal. The cost of faithfully echoing nasal vocoids as nasal is too high; the reduplicated form in this modified language would be *yat-nẽỹãt*. Observe that the nonnasality of such reduplicant vocoids does not come from exact copying of the input stem, which is not visible to the reduplic-ant (and which need not contain oral vocoids anyway – see section 4.1). Rather, the mapping of [ỹãt]$_B$ to [yat]$_R$ is a kind of emergence of, or reversion to, the unmarked: the correspondents of [ỹãt]$_B$ are chosen the same way that the grammar would deal with input /ỹãt/ in the absence of faithfulness restraints on nasality. In systems where there is no nasal-oral contrast in vowels, the unmarkedness that would emerge in the reduplicant is just that seen everywhere else in the language. In a lan-guage where free-standing nasal vowels are allowed, the situation would be classic emergence of the unmarked, with the reduplicant alone show-ing the less marked repertory. Thus, although this is "normal applica-tion," it should be clear that it is not at all guaranteed to be "normal" in any sense referring to the expected phonological development of a chunk of underlying stem to which the reduplicant owes its existence.

Thus, reversion to the unmarked is as close as the Basic Model comes to normal application in the reduplicant when the base is the target of phonology.

(67) Reversion to the unmarked in R
      *M ≫ B-R Identity

The Full Model, or something like it, is required for those cases where access to the underlying stem is absolutely necessary in the construction of the reduplicant. See McCarthy and Prince (1995: section 6) for discussion.

The Basic Model, then, exhibits exactly four distinct modes of handling potential phonological asymmetries between base and reduplicant. (71) illustrates that when a reduplicant R is targeted by phonology, we have either (Ia) back-copying overapplication from R to B, securing B/R identity, (61), or (Ib) completely normal development of B, yielding B/R disparity, (62). Again in (71), when a base B is targeted, we have either (IIa) overapplication from B to R, (66), or (IIb) reversion to the unmarked in R, often a normal-looking pattern, (67). In the general case, the grammar can freely choose one from each of these two targeting categories, generating four predicted systems. For example, in one language the very same process can affect the reduplicant with no carryover to the base, (Ib), but it can affect the base with overapplication in the reduplicant, (IIa). An instance of this behavior in Indonesian is examined in McCarthy and Prince (1995: section 4.3).

5.4 Illustration of the typology

In order to pursue the detailed force of the general points just surveyed, it is useful to run through a system that concretely embodies the entire typology of section 5.3.

Let us imagine a language with exactly the nasal harmony situation of Madurese or Malay, and a reduplication pattern similar to that of Madurese. Adopting a proposal by Pater (this volume), let us further divide the featural constraint IDENT(F) into IDENT(+F) and IDENT(−F). IDENT-IO(+F) means that +F-elements in the input should correspond to +F-elements in the output; it forbids a "denasalizing" I-O relationship, but it says nothing about -F-elements. More formally, one can write:

(68) IDENT-IO(+F)   For α ∈ I, β ∈ O, with α, β in correspondence,
if α is [+F], then β is [+F].

(69) IDENT-BR(+F)   For α ∈ B, β ∈ R, with α, β in correspondence,
if α if [+F], then β is [+F].

Parallel definitions apply to the [−F] case. Observe that the constraint
IDENT(F) conflates the +F and the −F constraints; splitting IDENT into
two independently rankable parts is necessary, as we will see, for developing the full fourfold typology.

The background phonology of the language is then given by the following ranking diagram.

(70) Vocoid is nasal in nasal span, otherwise oral.

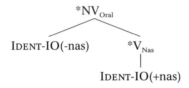

Observe that *V_Nas does not crucially dominate IDENT-IO(-nas), because
this faithfulness constraint pertains only to the nasalizing map /-nas/_I →
[+nas]_O. However, the constraint *V_Nas must dominate IDENT-IO(+nas),
in order to rid the output of free-standing nasals via a *de*nasalizing map,
as /bã/_I → [ba]_O.

The typology will emerge from interpolation of IDENT-BR(+nas) and
IDENT-BR(−nas) into the purely phonological system, (70), in accord
with the schemata of the previous section. Let us imagine two stems and
some relevant morphology to provide the crucial test cases. Let one be
/peyak/, suitable for receiving (or rejecting) overapplicative influence
from a reduplicant lying in a nasal span; let the other be /meyad/, suitable for transmitting nasality to a nasal-free reduplicant. Let us also
imagine a prefix /paŋ/, capable of initiating a nasal span. The range of
attainable outputs, and their status in the typology, is outlined here, with
the potential focus of overapplication underlined:

(71) Application types
    I. Reduplicant targeted by phonology
       /peyak/
       Ia. R →B Overapplication   paŋ-ỹãk-peỹãk
       Ib. Normal   paŋ-ỹãk-peyak

II. Base targeted by phonology
/meyad/

IIa. B →R Overapplication   ỹãd-mẽỹãd
IIb. Reversion in R   yad-mẽỹãd

Underlying forms such as /pẽỹãk/ and /mẽỹãd/ would give exactly the same outputs, since we are in a complementary distribution situation. There can be no candidates where postnasal vocoids are left oral in the output; these, which fatally violate *NV$_{Oral}$ and cannot be redeemed by any ranking of BR-Identity, will be left out of the discussion.

The behavior of the viable candidates with respect to the constraint hierarchy can be tabulated as follows:

(72) The viable candidates considered

R as Target: /peyak/	*NV$_{or}$	IO(–nas)	*V$_{Nas}$	IO(+nas)	BR(+nas)	BR(–nas)
Ia. paŋ-ỹãk- peỹãk		**	****			
Ib. paŋ-ỹãk- peyak			**			**
B as Target: /meyad/						
IIa. ỹãd-mẽỹãd		***	*****			
IIb. yad-mẽỹãd		***	***		***	

Since the comparison in each case is strictly pair-wise, a more perspicuous tabularization is possible, which notes the winner of the comparison rather than the low-level enumeration of constraint violations:

(73) Comparative representation of the viable candidates

R as Target: /peyak/	*NV$_{or}$	IO(–nas)	*V$_{Nas}$	IO(+nas)	BR(+nas)	BR(–nas)
Ia. paŋ-ỹãk- peỹãk						☞ a
Ib. paŋ-ỹãk- peyak		☞ b	☞ b			
B as Target: /meyad/						
IIa. ỹãd-mẽỹãd					☞ a	
IIb. yad-mẽỹãd			☞ b			

In this table, the four phonological constraints are ranked according to (70). We can now proceed to consider how the B-R Identity constraints are to be ranked among them:

(74) Normal application in B
   a. Winning candidate is Ib, so
         IDENT-IO(-nas) ≫ IDENT-BR(-nas)
      OR   *V$_{\text{Nas}}$ ≫ IDENT-BR(-nas)
   b. Accords with schema (62):
         {I-O Faithfulness} ≫ B-R Identity
      OR   *M ≫ B-R Identity

(75) Reversion to the unmarked in R
   a. Winning candidate is IIb, so
         *V$_{\text{Nas}}$ ≫ IDENT-BR(+nas)
   b. Accords with schema (67)
         *M ≫ B-R Identity

(76) R-to-B overapplication
   a. Winning candidate is Ia, so
         IDENT-BR(-nas) ≫ IDENT-IO(-nas), *V$_{\text{Nas}}$
   b. Accords with schema (61)
         {B-R Identity} ≫ I-O Faithfulness, {*M}

(77) B-to-R overapplication
   a. Winning candidate is IIa, so
         IDENT-BR(+nas) ≫ *V$_{\text{Nas}}$
   b. Accords with schema (66)
         B-R Identity ≫ {*M}

Comparing (77) to (76) shows that the B-to-R regime turns on a sense of B-R Identity different from the one relevant to R-to-B back-copying. For B-to-R overapplication, the pivotal constraint is IDENT-BR(+nas), which militates against a *denasalizing* map from B to R, like $\tilde{a}_{\text{B}} \sim a_{\text{R}}$ in *ỵad-mẽỹãd*. By contrast, back-copying from R to B, as in *paŋ-ỹãk-peỹãk*, avoids the nasalizing relationship $a_{\text{B}} \sim \tilde{a}_{\text{R}}$, and the relevant identity constraint that must prevail is IDENT-BR(-nas), which forbids *paŋ-ỹãk-peỵak*.

We conclude with some comments on key aspects of the theory brought to light in this constructed example.

Overapplication. The account developed here involves not one but two distinct featural maps: *oral → nasal* and *nasal → oral*. Each is controlled by different faithfulness/identity constraints and each can play a role – either as active or as blocked – in every condition we have enumerated. Consider standard B-to-R overapplication (IIa), as in *ỹãd-mẽỹãd*. It earns the name "overapplication" because of the featural disparity between a hypothesized lexical stem /meyad/ and the reduplicant *ỹãd*. But what's really happening in the Basic Model is that the general default map *nasal → oral* is being blocked along the B-R dimension by the identity constraint IDENT-BR(+nas). Thus, from the internal point of view this has more the character of underapplication. B-to-R back-copying involves unexpected activity/inactivity by both maps. As before, there is inhibition of the default denasalizing map along the B-R dimension; furthermore, there is unexpected activity along the I-O dimension of *oral → nasal*, to deal with inputs like /peyak/, and therefore unexpected suppression of *nasal → oral* to handle possible inputs like /pẽỹãk/. (Under complementary distribution, free-standing input nasals must be eliminated from output representations; but in just this one non-postnasal case, when R falls in the nasal span, they are allowed to remain.) Thinking of overapplication as the appearance of a marked element in unexpected circumstances, it is clear that this can only be achieved by limiting the activity of the map that removes the marked element (*nasal → oral*), and by extending the map that introduces the marked element along the I-O dimension.

Faithfulness. The theory has significant sensitivity to the character of faithfulness constraints. Substantive assumptions about what kind of faithfulness constraints exist will determine predictions about the range of possible systems of overapplication. For example, if IDENT(F) is *not* split into two constraints, then there can be only two systems: Ia/IIa (symmetrical overapplication) and Ib/IIb (no overapplication).

Even more striking, perhaps, if there is no IDENT(–nas) or equivalent – no faithfulness constraint militating against the transition from unmarked to marked – then there can be no back-copying at all of [+nas], because the crucial driving constraint is IDENT-BR(–nas), as shown above in the discussion of type Ia overapplication.

Finally, observe that in the set of systems examined here, it is predicted that the occurrence of R-to-B back-copying and standard B-to-R overapplication are entirely independent of each other, since each submits to the control of independent faithfulness constraints – IDENT(+F) and IDENT(–F). However, if we assume a dependency between the two, recognizing IDENT(–F) and IDENT(±F), where failure on the first implies failure on the second – a "stringency" relationship of the type discussed in Prince (1997) – then we find that back-copying Ia implies B-to-R overapplication IIa, but not vice versa; a kind of implicational markedness prediction over possible systems.

Underapplication. As noted throughout, and as is evident from the factorial-typological survey, classical underapplication is not a category recognized by the present theory. Broadly speaking, underapplication requires the appearance of an unmarked or default element in circumstances where the marked, nondefault element is required by the phonology of the language. B-R Identity simply cannot force this to happen: there is always a choice between identity-satisfying overapplication (like Madurese *ỹãt-nẽỹãt*) and identity-satisfying but phonology-defying underapplication (as in impossible **yat-nẽ*<u>*yat*</u>). Since the phonology is driven by an undominated structural constraint (*NV_{Oral} here) that is not sensitive to correspondence, the choice between the two candidates is irresistibly in favor of the phonologically superior one, which is overapplicational.

The appearance of underapplication can be achieved, however, when the actual opposition in the phonology is not a simple two-way "marked/here" ~ "unmarked/there" type of pattern. If the phonology contains a further context in which the unmarked element appears, due to a constraint ranked *above* what we have called "Phono-Constraint," then something that looks quite like underapplication can result. For example, suppose (as René Kager has suggested to us) that there were a hypothetical constraint forbidding nasal vocoids in word-initial positions. With this constraint and IDENT-BR(+nas) ranked above *NV_{Oral} in a Malay/Madurese type of system, the grammar would pick *yat-nẽyat* as the phonologically superior candidate. But this is really overapplication – the extension of word-initial denasalization to word-medial position *via* reduplicative correspondence. It is nothing more than an instance of the back-copying schema (61), with the Phono-Constraint implicit there reidentified as Kager's putative **#V_{Nas}$. In the absence of such a constraint – and we believe it to be absent in this case – the apparently underapplicational form can never be obtained. Classical underapplication, then, is admitted only as the overapplication of some aspect of the language's phonology, in accord with the overapplication schemata. We turn now to a particularly striking case.

6. Underapplication

In Southern Paiute, the segments w and η^W stand generally in complementary distribution: w is found word-initially, and η^W postvocalically, as illustrated in the following examples (Sapir 1930: 49; Mester 1986: 214).

(78) Southern Paiute w/η^W distribution

	Initial	Postvocalic	Gloss
a.	wa?aŋi-	tïˑ'-ŋʷa?aŋi	"to shout/to give a good shout"
b.	waixa-	nıaˑ'vı-ŋʷaixap·ı	"to have a council/council (of chiefs)"
c.	wʌ'tcï'-	cu(w)a'-ŋʷʌ'tcïp·ïya'	"to catch up with/nearly caught up with"
d.	w(')itsï'-	tï'raŋ'ʷıntsï'ıts·	"bird/horned lark (literally, desert bird)"

Of postvocalic w like the one parenthesized in example (78c), column two, Sapir remarks

After a primary u (o) a w, indicated as ^{W} if weak, often slips in before an immediately following vowel. (1930: 57)

We therefore take the variable and evanescent w to be a phonetic matter. Morphophonemic lenition of /m/ to a labial glide (Sapir 1930: 62) results in intervocalic η^W (not w), just as would be expected, given the way the allophones are distributed.

The interaction with reduplication is remarkable: it is the base that copies the reduplicant, defying the distributional pattern, when there is an asymmetry of environments:

(79) Differing contexts in B and R

	Simple	Reduplicated	Gloss
a.	wïn·ai-	wï-wï'-n'nai-	"to throw/several throw down"
b.	wayi-	wa-wa'x·ıpïya'	"several enter/all entered"
c.	wïyï-	wï-wï'xïʌ	"vulva/vulvas (obj.)"
d.	wïnı-	wï-wïn'nï-q·u-	"to stand/to stand (iterative)"

Here the reduplicant's word-initial w is transmitted back to the base; no other explanation is viable. It cannot be that the base-reduplicant boundary is word-like and impervious to lenition: observe that lenition runs across all other prefix boundaries, and even compound boundaries, as in (78b). Furthermore, the stress pattern (famously iambic and left-aligned) shows that the reduplicant is very much a part of the phonological word. Finally, when both base and reduplicant provide the same context, the lenited variant appears in both.

(80) Same context in B and R
    Simple   Reduplicated   Gloss
    w̱ịnɩ-   ya-ṉʷ ɩ́-ṉʷ ịnɩx̱a'   "to stand/while standing and holding"

With equivalent conditions in B and R, there is no possible threat to reduplicative identity and normal application is found. This same-context case also shows that Southern Paiute is not easily analyzed as a freak of lexical-phonological level ordering or the like, with a $w \rightarrow \eta^w$ process stuck in a stratum prior to reduplication. Were this the case, other post-reduplicative affixation like that of ya- in (80) should be unable to lenite postvocalic w. The only way out – as in the structurally similar Tagalog case discussed above in section 5.3 (65) – would be to portray reduplication as a late "head rule" applying after all other morphology has been accomplished (cf. Aronoff 1988). Aside from resting on a theoretical move that severely compromises the affix-ordering generalization upon which so much of lexical phonology rests, this analysis seems particularly ill-founded because lenition is applicable to the results of all word-constructing morphology, including compounding.

Do forms like w̱ï-w̱ï'-n'nai- evidence under- or overapplication? If w is taken to be the default or unmarked element of the w/η^w alternation, then it must be underapplication in the descriptive sense we have used throughout, with the unmarked variant appearing in a context that ordinarily demands the marked one. As we have just seen, simple underapplication is not recognized by the general typology. To see how this works out in particular, let us analyze the complementary distribution relationship.

First, we must construct the neutralizing map $w, \eta^w \rightarrow w$, which will eliminate η^w from all surface representations unless inhibited. This makes w the default.

(81) $^*\eta^w \gg {}^*w$, IDENT-IO(nas)

Observe that this follows the form of the ranking schema (51), which gives necessary conditions for having a nontrivial map in the phonology. We simplify the discussion by mentioning only the change in nasality, and by collapsing together the separate faithfulness constraints having to do with + and − values of the feature.

The map defined by (81) fails to take place in the intervocalic (or perhaps merely postvocalic) environment. This indicates the force of a higher-ranked constraint against w in that context, which partly suppresses the activity of $*\eta^W$. We can assume that the constraint militates against VwV; it must sit in a dominant position in the hierarchy:

(82) $*\text{VwV} \gg *\eta^W \gg *\text{w}, \text{IDENT-IO(nas)}$

Now, with the tacit understanding that the other relevant constraints are properly disposed of, it will happen that underlying ...*awa*... comes out as ...*aŋ^Wa*..., just like potential underlying...*aŋ^Wa*.... But underlying #*w* will be preserved, since if there is a less-marked state (say, *p*), unmentioned faithfulness constraints which dominate $*w$ will prevent it from slipping down the slope of unmarkedness. Furthermore, any potential input #*ŋ^W* will still be mapped to #*w*, in violation of the lowest rung of dominated constraints in (82). Thus, complementary distribution is established.

B-R Identity can demand that reduplicant and base match closely, but it cannot distinguish between matching η^Ws and matching ws. With $*\text{VwV}$ undominated, as in (82), choice of the η^W-matched form is inevitable. Yet it is w that prevails when there is contextual asymmetry between base and reduplicant:

(83) Differing context in R and B

Simple Form	Reduplicative Candidates	Remarks
w̱ïn·nai-	w̱ï-w̱ï′-n'nai-	☞ B back-copies phonology of R
	*ṉ^Wï-ṉ^Wï′-n'nai-	*R copies phonology of B
	*w̱ï-ṉ^Wï′-n'nai-	*normal phonology; bad B-R Identity

Consequently, as observed in our earlier discussions of underapplication (sections 3.1, 4.1, 5.4), there must be another constraint in action, ranked above $*\text{VwV}$. We propose that this constraint, which we will write as $*[\eta$, bans the velar nasal, labialized or not, from initial position. In support of framing the constraint at this level of generality, observe that of the nasals only m and n, and not η, may begin a word (Sapir 1930: 62). By itself, this observation does not determine that there is a *constraint* embodying the fact; it could also emerge from interaction, just as the ban on initial η^W does in the system (82). If so, the [__ environment would merely be the complement of the real assimilatory context(s) in which η is admitted (or from which other nasals are banned). McCarthy and Prince (1995: section 5.4) offer a specific argument to the contrary, showing that the $g \sim \eta$ alternation in Tokyo Japanese (Itô and Mester 1990, 1997) turns on the existence of exactly such a constraint. They further suggest, as Stampe has, that typological considerations show the need for the *[ŋ constraint independent of conditions on the appearance of assimilated and word-final elements. There is good evidence, then, that the constraint *[ŋ is part of the universal repertory, even though some of its effects are sometimes deducible from other constraints. According to this analysis, word-initial w in Southern Paiute is not merely a complementary default, as it first seems, but is rather the specific response to a specific constraint *[ŋ, just as η^W is a response to the specific constraint *VwV.

The grammar must therefore run as follows:

(84) *[ŋ, IDENT-BR(nas) $\gg$ *VwV $\gg$ *η^W $\gg$ *w, IDENT-IO(nas)

This hierarchy ensures that no velar nasals can appear in initial position under any circumstances, including reduplicative, and guarantees as well that the base and reduplicant must match w to w and η^W to η^W. Under analysis, the apparent underapplication system of Southern Paiute has turned out to be a kind of back-copying overapplication: word-initial rejection of η^W in favor of w is transmitted back to the base.

Thus far we have assumed that w is the less-marked member of the opposition: formally, that *$\eta^W \gg$ *w, perhaps universally. This is certainly plausible on intrinsic structural grounds, since η^W has everything that w has, and more; and it is typologically plausible as well, since the presence of η^W may well entail the presence of w, and the converse implication is certainly invalid. It is worth noting, however, that if *w $\gg$ *η^W were allowed, the system could be portrayed as simple overapplication, with the *marked element* w being backcopied. In such a case, the constraint *[ŋ would still be present and active, driving the default η^W out of initial position in favor of "marked" w. The constraint *VwV would be descriptively superfluous; but there is no theoretical gain in this result, since constraints militating against intervocalic glides are clearly motivated. (In Southern Paiute itself, for example, many such sequences coalesced historically into long vowels, creating the surface effect that long vowels can be stressed on either mora (K. Hale, personal communication.) Thus, the fundamental disagreement between the two analyses is not over which constraints are available in UG, but only over the relative markedness status of the allophones. If it is right to recognize w as universally the less marked member of w/η^W, then the analysis of Southern Paiute is fixed once and for all.

Southern Paiute reduplication provides, then, a canonical example of how apparent underapplication must be resolved within the present theory. (Additional examples – from Chumash, Akan, Klamath, Dakota, Japanese, Luiseño, Javanese, and Malay – are discussed in McCarthy and Prince 1995: section 5.) Furthermore, since there is no ambiguity as to which member of the (B, R) pair is the affix and which the base, the pattern also serves as a striking instance of back-copying, supporting the results of section 4, no matter how the relevant alternation is construed. The Southern Paiute pattern, which eludes a principled serialist account, thus yields strong evidence for the most basic predictions of the parallel-evaluation theory of B-R Identity.

7. Conclusion

Correspondence Theory originates as a revision of the PARSE/FILL implementation of the key notion of *faithfulness*. The following remarks hint at the richness of the issues (yet to be) explored.

Correspondence generalizes over different types of linguistic relatedness: underlying-surface, base-reduplicant, simple-derived. It sees these in terms of a relation $\mathfrak{R}$ between forms, and it offers a family of rankable, violable constraints on the integrity of $\mathfrak{R}$. These constraints demand completeness of the $\mathfrak{R}$ map, in either direction, identity of individual elements standing in an $\mathfrak{R}$ relation, and other aspects of categorial or string-based identity.

Correspondence Theory treats identity between reduplicant and base just like faithfulness of output to input. Faithfulness and identity follow from the same kind of formal constraints on the correspondence relation between representations. Because B-R Identity is a *relation* between B and R, rather than an *operation* creating R from B, the phonology of one conjunct may be matched in the other, and vice-versa, with full symmetry. When imposition of B-R Identity leads to effects not expected in extra-reduplicative circumstances, the results earn the name of over-application or of underapplication, depending on the character of the rest of the constraint system. High-ranking B-R Identity narrows the candidate set down to (B, R) pairs that are sufficiently closely matched; other considerations select the optimal candidate.

The evidence analyzed here and in McCarthy and Prince (1995) demonstrates that Correspondence Theory is superior, empirically and conceptually, to serial derivational approaches. All serial theories are incapable of dealing with cases in which B copies (or, more neutrally, *reflects*) R. Other interactions make finer distinctions among the various serialist alternatives. The most familiar theories – those with fixed rule ordering – are incapable of expressing patterns in which R imposes phonology on B that then reappears in R. A fundamental revision of ordering theory to include *persistent rules*, which reapply freely, brings the R $\rightarrow$ B $\rightarrow$ R cases under control, but brings in its wake major problems connected with nonconvergent (oscillating) derivations; and, of course, it does not solve the problem of comprehending R-to-B influence. Conceptually, serial theories are also prey to charges of non-unified explanation: the basic copying procedure enforces identity, and then other devices are called on exactly to *re*inforce it.

Correspondence Theory, as developed here, is accompanied by a well-instantiated factorial typology, which admits identity defying *normal application* and *emergence of the unmarked* as well as aggressive imposition of reduplicative identity. Underapplication, a prominent feature of serial theories, cannot be freely obtained by some special ranking of B-R Identity constraints. Rather, it is always the result of the intervention of some high-ranking constraint, of general import in the language, that happens to bar alternative ways of achieving identity between base and reduplicant; thus, in many situations, it will be predicted to be impossible.

Apart from their intrinsic interest, these results relate to several broad issues: parallelism versus serialism in Optimality Theory; explanation in Prosodic Morphology; the nature of faithfulness relations; the character of phonological constraints; and the formal properties of prosodic circumscription, the cycle, "paradigm uniformity," and other transderivational relationships. Here we briefly suggest how present work is relevant to these issues and what direction future investigations might take.

Although Optimality Theory in any form relies on parallel evaluation of a candidate set with respect to a hierarchy of ranked constraints, it is still entirely possible, as Prince and Smolensky (1993: ch. 2) emphasize, to distinguish various serialist and parallelistic architectures within this basic commitment. For example, transition from step to step in a derivation based on application of simple constructional principles could be governed by an OT system evaluating possible outputs at each step. (See Prince and Smolensky 1993: 79–80 for a worked example.) By far the bulk of research in the theory has, of course, been conducted under the contrary assumption that candidate outputs are evaluated nonserially, all at once, in complete parallel. Crucial evidence distinguishing serialist from parallelist conceptions is not easy to come by; it is therefore of great interest that reduplication-phonology interactions supply a rich body of evidence in favor of parallelism. Malay (section 4.2), Southern Paiute (section 6), and other examples cited in McCarthy and Prince (1995) (Axininca Campa epenthesis and augmentation; Chumash, Kihehe, and Tagalog coalescence; and Klamath syncope/reduction) either cannot be analyzed serially or can be analyzed only in formally-problematic and conceptually-flawed recastings of conventional serialism. Yet the same phenomena are readily captured by a system where reduplicative identity and phonological constraints are assessed in parallel. A crucial aspect of this success is that reduplicative identity is seen as a relation, formalized within Correspondence Theory and subject to evaluation by ranked constraints.

The goal of Prosodic Morphology is to derive the properties of reduplication and kindred phenomena from general principles of phonology and morphology, reducing and ultimately eliminating the principles that are specific just to reduplication. Correspondence Theory recognizes B-R Identity and I-O Faithfulness as identical relations governed by identical constraints; there is no special reduplication-specific copying relation that is unconnected with faithfulness. Furthermore, the constraints on string-to-string correspondence are mirrored in the theory of autosegmental association of tone and other elements, allowing Correspondence Theory to recapture, and greatly extend, the original insight behind modern work on nonconcatenative morphology. Similar results have been achieved in eliminating the Prosodic-Morphological template in favor of independently required constraints on prosody and the prosody-morphology relation (McCarthy and Prince 1994a, b) and in eliminating circumscriptional infixation in favor of independently required alignment constraints (Prince and Smolensky 1991, 1993; McCarthy and Prince 1993a, b; McCarthy 1997a). We are therefore closer to realizing the Prosodic Morphology program of, effectively, generalizing itself out of existence.

The Correspondence Theory of faithfulness has phonological extensions well beyond the issues considered here; the interested reader might wish to consult some of the literature cited at the end of section 2. It is also possible to imagine using the correspondence relation to support constraints demanding *non*identity – antifaithfulness constraints, as it were. The result would be constraints with the same basic character as the "two-level" rules introduced by Koskenniemi (1983) (also see Karttunen 1993, Lakoff 1993, and Goldsmith 1993); an example is found in Baković (1996). This move would not only greatly loosen the theory, but also profoundly change its formal character (see Moreton 1996), and should accordingly be viewed with considerable scepticism. A major descriptive advantage of admitting antifaithfulness constraints lies in the area of treating certain opaque interactions; on this see McCarthy (1997b) for an approach that extends Correspondence Theory but maintains the limitation to faithfulness.

Within the faithfulness/identity system, Correspondence Theory presupposes a different view of the output from the familiar PARSE/FILL nexus of most previous OT work (Prince and Smolensky 1991, 1993; and others), with a variety of interesting consequences for the characterization of prosodic and segmental phonology. Furthermore, the idea that autosegmental association instantiates the correspondence relation may be expected to impact on many aspects of phonology.

Finally, Correspondence Theory opens up a new way to look at the sorts of transderivational relationships among linguistic forms that have previously been understood in terms of a serial derivation (Benua 1995, 1997; McCarthy 1995). The most familiar serial mechanism recruited to account for transderivational relationships is the phonological cycle (Chomsky and Halle 1968); less familiar ones include prosodic circumscription (McCarthy and Prince 1990) and late ordering of morphological truncation rules (Anderson 1975). In each case, serial approaches see phonological identity in derivational terms: one representation must be created directly from another if they are to be similar. In contrast, Correspondence Theory provides a model of how to approach these transderivational relationships nonserially. With B-R correspondence, base and reduplicant are related to one another as parallel representations, and identity between them is demanded by rankable constraints. There is no need for a serial derivational relationship, in which the reduplicant is operationally copied from the base; in fact, the evidence of section 4.2 establishes the empirical inadequacy of serial relatedness.

In transderivational relationships, a correspondence relation holds between forms sharing the same root. The clearest case of this is afforded by interactions between phonology and morphological truncation, in a near-exact parallel to reduplicative over- and underapplication, as proposed by Benua (1995). But correspondence also engages with broader issues of supposed cyclic or level-based effects (Benua 1997), connecting with proposals in Burzio (1994a, b).

Prosodic circumscription is another serial mechanism that can be reexamined in this light (McCarthy 1995, 1997a). Under prosodic circumscription, a form is first provided with prosodic constituency (syllable and foot structure); then a prosodic constituent is identified and subjected to morphological derivation, up to and including provision of new prosodic structure *via* template mapping. Many proposed cases of prosodic circumscription have been reanalyzed in other terms, as a result of developments in Optimality Theory (Prince and Smolensky 1991, 1993; McCarthy and Prince 1993a, b). But a significant residue remains. This residue, it turns out, can be understood in terms of constraints demanding that certain segments have identical prosodic analyses in paradigmatically related forms; appropriate constraints demand that correspondent segments within the paradigm share foot-initiality, main stress, or similar prosodic characteristics. Moreover, the same constraints are responsible for faithfulness to lexical prosody, thereby contributing to the Prosodic Morphology goal of relying only on mechanisms that are independently available.

Appendix

A set of constraints on the correspondence relation

This appendix provides a tentative list of constraints on correspondent elements. Affinities with other constraint types are noted when appropriate. All constraints refer to pairs of representations (S_1, S_2), standing to each other as (I, O), (B, R), etc. The constraints also refer to a relation $\Re$, the correspondence relation defined for the representations being compared. Thus, each constraint is actually a constraint family, with instantiations for I-O, B-R, I-R, Tone to Tone-Bearer, and so on.

The formalization is far from complete, and aims principally to clarify. As in section 2, we imagine that a structure S_i is encoded as a set of elements, so that we can talk about $\Re$ on (S_1, S_2) in the usual way as a subset, any subset, of $S_1 \times S_2$. We use the following standard jargon: for a relation $\Re \subset A \times B$, $x \in \text{Domain}(\Re)$ iff $x \in A$ and $\exists y \in B$ such that $x\Re y$; and $y \in \text{Range}(\Re)$ iff $y \in B$ and $\exists x \in A$ such that $x\Re y$.

(A.1) MAX
　　　Every element of S_1 has a correspondent in S_2.
　　　Domain$(\Re) = S_1$

(A.2) DEP
　　　Every element of S_2 has a correspondent in S_1.
　　　Range$(\Re) = S_2$.

MAX (= (3)) and DEP are analogous respectively to PARSE-segment and FILL in Prince and Smolensky (1991, 1993). Both MAX and DEP should be further differentiated by the type of segment involved, vowel versus consonant. The argument for differentiation of FILL can be found in Prince & Smolensky (1993), and it carries over to FILL's analogue DEP. In the case of MAX, the argument can be constructed on the basis of languages like Arabic or Rotuman (McCarthy 1995), with extensive vocalic syncope and no consonant deletion.

(A.3) IDENT(F)
　　　Correspondent segments have identical values for the feature F.
　　　If $x\Re y$ and x is $[\gamma F]$, then y is $[\gamma F]$.

IDENT (= (5)) replaces the PARSE-feature and FILL-feature-node apparatus of Containment-type OT. See Pater (this volume) and section 5.4 above for further developments. As stated, IDENT presupposes that only segments stand in correspondence, so all aspects of featural identity must be communicated through correspondent segments. Ultimately, the correspondence relation will be extended to features, to accommodate "floating" feature analyses, like those in Archangeli and Pulleyblank (1994) or Akinlabi (1996). (Also see Lombardi 1995, Zoll 1996.)

(A.4) Contiguity

    a. I-CONTIG ("No Skipping")

        The portion of S_1 standing in correspondence forms a contiguous string.

        Domain($\Re$) is a single contiguous string in S_1.

    b. O-CONTIG ("No Intrusion")

        The portion of S_2 standing in correspondence forms a contiguous string.

        Range($\Re$) is a single contiguous string in S_2.

These constraints characterize two types of contiguity (see also Kenstowicz 1994). The constraint I-CONTIG rules out deletion of elements *internal* to the input string. Thus, the map $xyz \rightarrow xz$ violates I-CONTIG, because the Range of $\Re$ is $\{x, z\}$, and xz is not a contiguous string in the input. But the map $xyz \rightarrow xy$ does not violate I-CONTIG, because xy is a contiguous string in the input. The constraint O-CONTIG rules out internal epenthesis: the map $xz \rightarrow xyz$ violates O-CONTIG, but $xz \rightarrow xzy$ does not. The definition assumes that we are dealing with strings. When the structure S_k is more complex than a string, we need to define a way of plucking out a designated substructure that is a string, in order to apply the definitions to the structure.

(A.5) {RIGHT, LEFT}-ANCHOR(S_1, S_2)

    Any element at the designated periphery of S_1 has a correspondent at the designated periphery of S_2.

    Let *Edge*(X, {L, R}) = the element standing at the *Edge* = L, R of X.

    RIGHT-ANCHOR. If x = Edge(S_1, R) and y = Edge(S_2, R) then x$\Re$y.

    LEFT-ANCHOR. Likewise, *mutatis mutandis*.

In prefixing reduplication, L-ANCHOR ≫ R-ANCHOR, and vice versa for suffixing reduplication. It is clear that ANCHORing should subsume Generalized Alignment; as formulated, it captures the effects of Align(MCat, E_1, PCat, E_2) for $E_1 = E_2$ in McCarthy and Prince (1993b). It can be straightforwardly extended to (PCat, PCat) alignment if correspondence is assumed to be a reflexive relation. For example, in *bí.ta*, the left edge of the foot and the head syllable align because *b* and its correspondent (which is, reflexively, *b*) are initial in both.

(A.6) LINEARITY ("No Metathesis")

S_1 is consistent with the precedence structure of S_2, and vice versa.

Let $x, y \in S_1$ and $x', y' \in S_2$.

If $x\Re x'$ and $y\Re y'$, then

$x < y$ iff $\neg (y' < x')$.

(A.7) UNIFORMITY ("No Coalescence")

No element of S_2 has multiple correspondents in S_1.

For $x, y \in S_1$ and $z \in S_2$, if $x\Re z$ and $y\Re z$, then $x = y$.

(A.8) INTEGRITY ("No Breaking")

No element of S_1 has multiple correspondents in S_2.

For $x \in S_1$ and $w, z \in S_2$, if $x\Re w$ and $x\Re z$, then $w = z$.

LINEARITY excludes metathesis. UNIFORMITY and INTEGRITY rule out two types of multiple correspondence – coalescence, where two elements of S_1 are fused in S_2, and diphthongization or phonological copying, where one element of S_1 is split or cloned in S_2. On the prohibition against metathesis, see Hume (1995, 1996) and McCarthy (1995). On coalescence, see Gnanadesikan (1995), Lamontagne and Rice (1995), McCarthy (1995), and Pater (this volume).

Notes

1 This chapter is excerpted from a longer work, which appeared as McCarthy and Prince (1995). We are grateful to René Kager for his extensive comments on a previous version, and to him, Harry van der Hulst, and Wim Zonneveld for arranging the workshop at which this material was first presented. For comments on this material, we are also grateful to several other workshop participants: Sharon Inkelas, Junko Itô, Armin Mester, Orhan Orgun, Joe Pater, David Perlmutter, Sam Rosenthall, Pat Shaw, and Suzanne Urbanczyk. Additionally, audiences at Harvard University, the University of Maryland, the University of Arizona, University of California, Irvine, University of California, Los Angeles, and the University of Texas at Austin have provided valuable feedback; and the comments, questions, and suggestions from the participants in the (eventually joint) University of Massachusetts and Rutgers Correspondence Theory seminars were particularly important for the development of this work. For useful discussion of numerous points, we would like to thank Akin Akinlabi, John Alderete, Diana Archangeli, Eric Baković, Jill Beckman, Laura Benua, Nicola Bessell, Luigi Burzio, Andrea Calabrese, Katy Carlson, Abby Cohn, Laura Walsh Dickey, Vicki Fromkin, Amalia

Gnanadesikan, Mike Hammond, Bruce Hayes, Caroline Jones, Ed Keer, Michael Kenstowicz, Takeo Kurafuji, Claartje Levelt, Mark Liberman, Linda Lombardi, Ania Lubowicz, Scott Myers, Sharon Peperkamp, Paul Portner, Sharon Rose, Lisa Selkirk, Jen Smith, Donca Steriade, Bert Vaux, Rachel Walker, and Moira Yip; additional thanks are due to Alderete, Beckman, Benua, Carlson, Gnanadesikan, Jones, Lubowicz, Smith, and Urbanczyk for their contributions as grant research assistants. Special thanks to Paul Smolensky for discussion of key foundational issues. This work was supported in part by grant SBR-9420424 from the National Science Foundation and by research funds from Rutgers, the State University of New Jersey, at New Brunswick.

2 The term "reduplicant" is due to Spring (1990).

3 The terms "overapplication" and "underapplication" are due to Wilbur (1973a, b, c). See section 3.1 below.

4 We will simplify the discussion in a further respect: we will speak of ℜ relating string to string, though relations are properly defined on "sets." A string can always be regarded as a set of ordered pairs of its members with positional indices, and similar constructions can be put together for structures more complex than strings. Ultimately, ℜ can be defined over such sets.

Correspondence is treated as a relation rather than a function to allow for one-to-many relationships, as in diphthongization, for example, or coalescence. On these phenomena, see among others Cairns (1976), de Haas (1988), Hayes (1990), and, using correspondence, Gnanadesikan (1995), Lamontagne and Rice (1995), McCarthy (1995), and Pater (this volume).

5 For formal development relevant to the full complexity of phonological structures, see Pierrehumbert and Beckman (1988), Kornai (1991), and van Oostendorp (1993). On quantitative transfer, see Levin (1983), Clements (1985a), Mester (1986: 239 note), McCarthy and Prince (1988), and Steriade (1988). On floating features, see among others Archangeli and Pulleyblank (1994), Akinlabi (1996), and Zoll (1996).

6 This way of characterizing Gen under correspondence was suggested to us at the Utrecht workshop by Sharon Inkelas and Orhan Orgun.

7 On differentiation of root versus affix faithfulness, see McCarthy and Prince (1995: section 6.2).

8 Stated as correspondence relations, the components of the Well-Formedness Condition and other autosegmental principles form a set of rankable, hence violable, constraints, leading to significant empirical differences from standard conceptions of autosegmental phonology. See Myers (1993) for an incisive discussion of tonal association under (pre-Correspondence) OT.

9 "Containment" is offered here as a term of art; hence, free association from the ordinary language homophone is unlikely to provide a reliable guide to its meaning.

10 Usually desirable. There are cases, going under the rubric of "opacity" (Kiparsky 1973), where deleted elements do influence the outcome, on which see McCarthy (1997b).

11 A Containment or PARSE/FILL approach to B-R Identity is conceivable, but flawed empirically. See the discussion in McCarthy and Prince (1995: section 2.3).

12 In this discussion, we assume that underlying forms are represented in the familiar fashion with predictable allophonic information absent, so that "disparity" is disparity from this structure. Whether such predictable information appears in underlying forms is independent of the assumptions of OT, as noted below (section 4.1, discussion of (48)). The formulation of over- and underapplication in terms of marked/unmarked elements and defaults circumvents this ambiguity.

13 Exceptions are Dudas (1976: 218–26) and Shaw (1976 [1980]: 319–91), who entertain this possibility along with others, Onn (1976), and the brief discussion in Kenstowicz (1981).

14 For further discussion, see McCarthy and Prince (1995: section 3.8). Compare the role of geminate structures in determining the (non)application of phonological processes (Hayes 1986, Schein and Steriade 1986, McCarthy 1986).

15 Another type of representational theory is given by Cowper and Rice (1985). They propose that the base and copy melodies are on different autosegmental tiers, with locality of phonological operations observed over both tiers.

16 This constraint is understood to prohibit linear concatenation of a nasal segment and an oral vocoid (glide or vowel). Obviously, a fuller treatment of the typology and theory of nasal harmony is required, but would be far removed from our concerns here. For relevant discussion, see Cohn (1990, 1993) and Cole and Kisseberth (1995).

17 It is worth emphasizing that the use of underspecification does not change the basic point of the argument. With underspecification, the lexicon is barred from containing both β and α (*α at least in the environments where β shows up). In their place is some underspecified entity Γ. The phonology proper provides both the fill-in rule $\Gamma \rightarrow \beta/E\_\_F$ and the default rule $\Gamma \rightarrow \alpha$ to spell out Γ. (See Archangeli 1988, and the references cited therein.) The default rule resembles the lexical implication $[\Gamma] \Rightarrow [\alpha]$ that disallows β in full-specification theories; default status of α is derived in this case not by specification at the lexical level, but through later specification via the default rule. Nevertheless, lexical form is crucial to the

descriptive mechanism, and some sort of constraint must still guarantee that β cannot appear lexically alongside Γ.

18 Since the reduplicant is featurally identical to its correspondent substructure in the base, it is clear that all such featural identity constraints are undominated in Madurese. We could regard them as being just one constraint, IDENT-BR(F), quantifying universally over all features. This would not allow individual feature identity constraints to be ranked separately. See Alderete *et al.* (1996) for some discussion of featural disparity in B-R correspondence.

19 The marks in the tableau follow the assumption that $*V_{Nas}$ pertains to all vocoids, including glides. The *y*, because epenthetic, suffers no defects in IDENT-IO(nas), since it has no underlying commitments to remain faithful to.

20 One particular version of Ordering Theory cannot account for Madurese, though. According to Marantz (1982: 460–61), only allomorph-selection rules can overapply. Madurese nasal harmony is obviously not an allomorph-selection process; on the contrary, it is allophonic. See Stevens (1985) for further discussion.

21 Onn (1976) does not transcribe nasality in glides; we have altered his transcriptions in this respect.

22 See Mester (1986: 190), where Sanskrit *ruki* is posited to be an everywhere rule to obtain combined overapplication and normal application effects.

23 "Converge" as opposed to "diverge" rather than "crash." Thanks to Bruce Tesar for the contrast.

24 Failed candidates like $*[(t^jil\text{-}t^jil)(parku)]$ or $*[(t^jilpar)(ku\text{-}t^jil)(parku)]$ incorporate the reduplicant into the same PrWd as the base. This option is ruled out by designating the reduplicative morpheme of Diyari as a root, from which PrWd status follows (McCarthy and Prince 1994b).

25 We are indebted to Donca Steriade for challenges on this point.

26 We are assuming that each feature- or structure-changing map is banned by at least one faithfulness constraint. This need not be the case logically – for example, epenthesis could in principle be controlled by markedness constraints alone – but it accords with most current practice.

27 The qualification "sufficiently high-ranked" is meant to exclude the possibility that another phonological constraint dominating Phono-Constraint blocks it. For example, in the nasalization phenomena discussed in section 4, $*V_{Nas} \gg$ IDENT-IO(nas), but this does not mean that $*V_{Nas}$ always gets its way; $*NV_{Oral}$ has the final say.

28 As noted, we assume that feature-changing mappings are at issue. Some constraints can be active without faithfulness violation, so long as Gen supplies equally faithful alternatives: ONSET, for example, distinguishes V.CV from VC.V, no matter where it is ranked (Prince and Smolensky 1993: 86).

29 Any relevant markedness constraints that militate against the desired output must also be subordinated to Phono-Constraint, as shown by the subordinate position of {*M} in (54).

30 See also McCarthy and Prince (1994b), Urbanczyk (1996a, b), Shaw (1994), and Alderete et al. (1996) for further discussion.

31 The more deviously constructed candidate $tag_{3,6}ta$–tag_3tag_6 spares MAX-BR violation via an odd correspondence relation, but at the expense of violating two other constraints defined in the appendix, LINEARITY-BR and UNIFORMITY-BR. It is an interesting further issue to explain why such fusion is, in all likelihood, impossible (as are many other LINEARITY-violating maps, here and elsewhere). Notice too that the banning of reduplicant-internal codas, in violation of CONTIG-BR, may be impossible as well, requiring further elaboration of the account.

32 The actual example in Shetler (1976) is *ma-nagta-tagta-tagtag*, with double reduplication. This form presents a further question: why not *ma-nagta-nagta-tagtag*? The matter is resolved by I-R correspondence, discussed in McCarthy and Prince (1995: section 6).

33 A formal alternative, following the second disjunct of the anti-back-copying schema (62) above, would be to rank the markedness constraint *NASAL-C above B-R Identity. Then considerations of B-R Identity would never be able to force the appearance of an additional *n* into the base, regardless of the ranking position of I-O Faithfulness.

References

Agbayani, Brian, and Naomi Harada (eds.). 1996. *UC Irvine Working Papers in Linguistics, vol. 2: Proceedings of the South-Western Optimality Theory Workshop (SWOT 2)*, Irvine, CA: Irvine Linguistics Students Association.

Akinlabi, Akinbiyi. 1984. Tonal underspecification and Yoruba tone, Ph.D. dissertation, University of Ibadan, Nigeria.

1996. Featural affixation, *Journal of Linguistics* 32: 239–90.

Alderete, John. 1996. Faithfulness to prosodic heads, to appear in B. Hermans and M. van Oostendorp (eds.) [ROA-94, http://ruccs.rutgers.edu/roa.html]

Alderete, John, Jill Beckman, Laura Benua, Amalia Gnanadesikan, John McCarthy, and Suzanne Urbanczyk. 1996. Reduplication and segmental markedness, ms. University of Massachusetts, Amherst, MA. [ROA-134, http://ruccs.rutgers.edu/roa.html]

Anderson, Stephen R. 1974. On the typology of phonological rules, in A. Bruck, R. Fox, and M. LaGaly (eds.), *Papers from the Parasession on Natural Phonology*, Chicago Linguistic Society, 1–12.

1975. On the interaction of phonological rules of various types, *Journal of Linguistics* 11: 39–62.

Archangeli, Diana. 1985. Yokuts harmony: evidence for coplanar representation in nonlinear phonology, *Linguistic Inquiry* 16: 335–72.

1988. Aspects of underspecification theory, *Phonology* 5: 183–208.

Archangeli, Diana, and Douglas Pulleyblank. 1994. *Grounded Phonology*, Cambridge, MA: MIT Press.

Aronoff, Mark. 1976. *Word Formation in Generative Grammar*, Cambridge, MA: MIT Press.

1988. Head operations and strata in reduplication: a linear treatment, *Yearbook of Morphology* 1: 1–15.

Austin, Peter. 1981. *A Grammar of Diyari, South Australia*, Cambridge University Press.

Baković, Eric. 1994. Strong onsets and Spanish fortition, in C. Giordano and D. Adron (eds.), *MIT Working Papers in Linguistics* 23, Cambridge, MA: Department of Linguistics and Philosophy, Massachusetts Institute of Technology.

1996. Foot harmony and quantitative adjustment, ms. Rutgers University. [ROA-168, http://ruccs.rutgers.edu/roa.html]

Bat-El, Outi. 1996. Selecting the best of the worst: the grammar of Hebrew blends, *Phonology* 13: 283–328.

Beckman, Jill. 1995. Shona height harmony: markedness and positional identity, in Beckman *et al.* (eds.), 1995, 53–75.

1997. Positional faithfulness, Ph.D. dissertation, University of Massachusetts, Amherst, MA.

Beckman, Jill, Laura Walsh Dickey, and Suzanne Urbanczyk (eds.). 1995. *University of Massachusetts Occasional Papers in Linguistics* 18: *Papers in Optimality Theory*, Amherst, MA: Graduate Linguistic Student Association.

Benua, Laura. 1995. Identity effects in morphological truncation, in Beckman *et al.* (eds.), 1995, 77–136. [ROA-74, http://ruccs.rutgers.edu/roa.html]

1997. Transderivational identity: phonological relations between words, Ph.D. dissertation, University of Massachusetts, Amherst, MA.

Bloomfield, Leonard. 1933. *Language*, New York, NY: Holt.

Bromberger, Sylvain, and Morris Halle. 1989. Why phonology is different, *Linguistic Inquiry* 20: 51–70.

Burzio, Luigi. 1994a. *Principles of English Stress*, Cambridge University Press.

1994b. Anti-allomorphy, handout of talk presented at "Going Romance 1994," Utrecht.

1997. Strength in numbers, *University of Maryland Working Papers in Linguistics* 5.

Bye, Patrik, Ove Lorentz, and Curt Rice (eds.). 1996. *Papers from the 2nd Workshop on Comparative Germanic Phonology = Nordlyd* 24. Tromsø University Working Papers on Language and Linguistics.

Cairns, Charles E. 1976. Universal properties of umlaut and vowel coalescence rules: implications for Rotuman phonology, in A. Juilland (ed.), *Linguistic Studies Offered to Joseph Greenberg*, 3 vols. (Phonology), Saratoga, CA: Anma Libri, II, 271–83.

Carlson, Kathryn. 1996. Reduplication in Nakanai: an OT account, ms. University of Massachusetts, Amherst, MA.

Carrier, Jill. 1979. The interaction of phonological and morphological rules in Tagalog: a study in the relationship between rule components in grammar, Ph.D. dissertation, Massachusetts Institute of Technology, Cambridge, MA.

Carrier-Duncan, Jill. 1984. Some problems with prosodic accounts of reduplication, in M. Aronoff and R. T. Oehrle (eds.), *Language Sound Structure*, Cambridge, MA: MIT Press, 260–86.

Chafe, Wallace. 1968. The ordering of phonological rules, *International Journal of American Linguistics* 24: 115–36.

Chen, Su-I. 1996. A theory of palatalization and segment implementation, Ph.D. dissertation, State University of New York, Stony Brook, NY.

Chomsky, Noam. 1975. *Knowledge of Language*, New York, NY: Pantheon.

Chomsky, Noam, and Morris Halle. 1968. *The Sound Pattern of English*, New York, NY: Harper and Row.

Christaller, Rev. J. G. 1875 [1964]. *A Grammar of the Asante and Fante Language, called Tshi [Chee, Twi]: based on the Akuapem Dialect with Reference to the other (Akan and Fante) Dialects*, Basel: Basel Evangelical Missionary Society. [Reproduced Farnborough, Hants., England: Gregg Press.]

Churchward, C. Maxwell. 1940. *Rotuman Grammar and Dictionary*, Sydney: Australasian Medical Publishing Co. [Reprinted 1978. New York, NY: AMS Press.]

Clements, G. N. 1985a. The problem of transfer in nonlinear morphology, *Cornell Working Papers in Linguistics* 7: 38–73.

1985b. The geometry of phonological features, *Phonology* 2: 225–52.

Clements, G. N. and K. Ford. 1979. Kikuyu tone shift and its synchronic consequences, *Linguistic Inquiry* 10: 179–210.

Cohn, Abigail. 1990. Phonetic and phonological rules of nasalization, Ph.D. dissertation, University of California, Los Angeles, CA. [Later published in *UCLA Working Papers in Phonetics* 76.]

1993. A survey of the phonology of the feature [±nasal], *Working Papers of the Cornell Phonetics Laboratory* 8: 141–203. [Originally circulated as UCLA ms. 1987.]

Cole, Jennifer, and Charles Kisseberth. 1995. Nasal harmony in Optimal Domains Theory, Cognitive Science Technical Report UIUC-BI-CS-95-02 (Language Series), Beckman Institute, Urbana-Champaign, IL.

Colina, Sonia. 1996. Spanish truncation processes: the emergence of the unmarked. *Linguistics* 34, 1199–1218.

Cowper, Elizabeth, and Keren Rice. 1985. Phonology and reduplication, ms. University of Toronto. Presented at the Canadian Linguistic Association meeting, June 1985.

Davis, Stuart. 1995. Emphasis spread in Arabic and grounded phonology. *Linguistic Inquiry* 26: 465–98.

Dell, François. 1980. *Generative phonology and French phonology* (trans. Catherine Cullen), Cambridge University Press.

Downing, Laura J. 1994. SiSwati verbal reduplication and the theory of Generalized Alignment, in M. Gonzàlez (ed.), *Proceedings of the North East Linguistic Society* 24: 81–95.

1996a. On the prosodic misalignment of onsetless syllables, ms. University of British Columbia.

1996b. Prosodic misalignment and reduplication, paper presented at the Linguistic Society of America annual meeting, San Diego, CA, 4–7 January 1996.

This volume. Verbal reduplication in three Bantu languages.

Dudas, Karen. 1976. The phonology and morphology of modern Javanese, Ph.D. dissertation, University of Illinois, Urbana-Champaign, IL.

Fulmer, Sandara Lee. 1997. Parallelism and planes in Optimality Theory: evidence from afar, Ph.D. dissertation, University of Arizona, Tucson, AZ.

Futagi, Yoko. To appear. Root-Reduplicant faithfulness, Proceedings of the Sixteenth West Coast Conference on Formal Linguistics, Stanford, CA: CSLI.

Gafos, Adamantios. 1995. On the proper characterization of "nonconcatenative" languages, ms. Johns Hopkins University, Baltimore, MD. [ROA-106, http://ruccs.rutgers.edu/roa.html]

1996. The Articulatory Basis of Locality in Phonology, Ph.D. dissertation, Johns Hopkins University, Baltimore, MD.

Gerfen, Henry. 1996. Topics in the phonology and phonetics of Coatzospan Mixtec, Ph.D. dissertation, University of Arizona, Tucson, AZ.

Gnanadesikan, Amalia. 1995. Markedness and faithfulness constraints in child phonology, ms. University of Massachusetts, Amherst. [ROA-67, http://ruccs.rutgers.edu/roa.html]

1997. Phonology with ternary scales, Ph.D. dissertation, University of Massachusetts, Amherst. [ROA-195, http://ruccs.rutgers.edu/roa.html]

Goldsmith, John. 1976. Autosegmental phonology, Ph.D. dissertation, Massachusetts Institute of Technology, Cambridge, MA.

1993. Harmonic phonology, in Goldsmith (ed.), 21–60.

Goldsmith, John (ed.). 1993. *The Last Phonological Rule: Reflections on Constraints and Derivations*, University of Chicago Press.

Green, Antony Dubach. 1997. The prosodic structure of Irish, Scots Gaelic, and Manx, Ph.D. dissertation, Cornell University, NY. [ROA-196, http://ruccs.rutgers.edu/roa.html]

Haas, Willem G. de. 1988. A formal theory of vowel coalescence, Ph.D. dissertation, Catholic University of Nijmegen.

Hayes, Bruce. 1986. Inalterability in CV phonology, *Language* 62: 321–51.

1990. Diphthongization and coindexing, *Phonology* 7: 31–71.

1995. *Metrical Stress Theory: Principles and Case Studies*, University of Chicago Press.

Hermans, Ben, and Mark van Oostendorp (eds.). To appear. *The Derivational Residue in Phonology*, Amsterdam: John Benjamins.

Hirschbühler, Paul. 1978. Reduplication in Javanese, *University of Massachusetts Occasional Papers in Linguistics* 3: 102–25.

Hollenbach, Barbara. 1974. Reduplication and anomalous rule ordering in Copala Trique, *International Journal of American Linguistics* 40: 176–83.

Hume, Elizabeth. 1995. Metathesis effects. Paper presented at the Montréal-Ottawa-Toronto Phonology Workshop, February 1995.

1996. A non-linearity based account of metathesis in Leti, ms. Ohio State University, Columbus, OH.

Itô, Junko. 1986. Syllable Theory in Prosodic Phonology, Ph.D. dissertation, University of Massachusetts, Amherst, MA.

1989. A prosodic theory of epenthesis, *Natural Language and Linguistic Theory* 7: 217–60.

Itô, Junko, and R. Armin, Mester. 1990. Proper containment and phonological domains, handout of talk presented at KATL, Osaka University, December 22, 1990.

1992. Weak layering and word binarity, ms. University of California, Santa Cruz, CA.

1997. Correspondence and compositionality: the *Ga-gyo* variation in Japanese phonology, in I. Roca (ed.), *Constraints and Derivations in Phonology*, Oxford University Press, 419–62.

Itô, Junko, Yoshihisa Kitagawa, and R. Armin, Mester. 1996. Prosodic faithfulness and correspondence: evidence from a Japanese argot, *Journal of East Asian Linguistics* 5: 217–94.

Itô, Junko, R. Armin Mester, and Jaye Padgett. 1995. Licensing and underspecification in Optimality Theory, *Linguistic Inquiry* 26: 571–614.

Karttunen, Lauri. 1993. Finite-state constraints, in Goldsmith (ed.), 173–94.

Kenstowicz, Michael. 1981. Functional explanations in generative phonology, in D. L. Goyvaerts (ed.), *Phonology in the 1980s*, Ghent: E. Story-Scientia, 431–44.

1994. Syllabification in Chukchee: a constraints-based analysis, in A. Davison, N. Maier, G. Silva, and W. S. Yan (eds.), *Proceedings of the Formal Linguistics Society of Mid-America* 4, Iowa City, IA: Department of Linguistics, University of Iowa, 160–81.

Kim, No-Ju. 1997. Tone, Segments, and Their Interaction in North Kyungsang Korean, Ph.D. dissertation, Ohio State University, Columbus, OH. [ROA-186, http://ruccs.rutgers.edu/roa.html]

Kiparsky, Paul. 1973. Phonological representations, in O. Fujimura (ed.), *Three Dimensions of Linguistic Theory*. Tokyo: Taikusha, 1–136.

1986. The phonology of reduplication, ms. Stanford University, CA.

Kirchner, Robert. 1993. Turkish vowel disharmony in Optimality Theory. Talk presented at Rutgers Optimality Workshop I, Rutgers University, New Brunswick, NJ.

1995. Contrastiveness is an epiphenomenon of constraint ranking, *Berkeley Linguistics Society Proceedings* 21, 198–208.

Kornai, András. 1991. Formal phonology, Ph.D. dissertation, Stanford University, CA.

Koskenniemi, Kimmo. 1983. *Two-level Morphology: a General Computational Model for Word-form Recognition and Production*, Publication no. 11, Helsinki: Department of General Linguistics, University of Helsinki.

Kuroda, S.-Y. 1967. *Yawelmani Phonology*, Cambridge, MA: MIT Press.

Lakoff, George. 1993. Cognitive phonology, in Goldsmith (ed.), 117–45.

Lamontagne, Greg, and Keren Rice. 1995. A correspondence account of coalescence, in Beckman *et al.* (eds.), 211–24.

Letterman, Rebecca. 1997. The effects of word-internal prosody in Sinhala: a constraint-based analysis, Ph.D. dissertation, Cornell University, Ithaca, NY.

Levin, Juliette. 1983. Reduplication and prosodic structure, ms. Massachusetts Institute of Technology, Cambridge, MA.

Lombardi, Linda. 1995. Why Place and Voice are different: constraint interactions and feature faithfulness in Optimality Theory, ms. University of Maryland, College Park. [ROA-105, http://ruccs.rutgers.edu/roa.html]

Lowenstamm, Jean, and Jonathan Kaye. 1985. Compensatory lengthening in Tiberian Hebrew, in L. Wetzels and E. Sezer (eds.), *Studies in Compensatory Lengthening*, Dordrecht: Foris.

Marantz, Alec. 1982. Re reduplication, *Linguistic Inquiry* 13: 435–82.

McCarthy, John J. 1979. Formal problems in Semitic phonology and morphology, Ph.D. dissertation, Massachusetts Institute of Technology, Cambridge, MA.

1983. Consonantal morphology in the Chaha verb, in M. Barlow, D. Flickinger, and M. Wescoat (eds.), *Proceedings of the West Coast Conference on Formal Linguistics* 2, Stanford Linguistics Association, 176–88.

1985. Some notes on ATB (Ross 1967, Williams 1981) phonology: data, analyses, theory, ms. AT&T Bell Laboratories.

1986. Lexical phonology and nonconcatenative morphology in the history of Chaha, *Revue québécoise de linguistique* 16: 209–28.

1993. The parallel advantage: containment, consistency, and alignment. Talk presented at Rutgers Optimality Workshop I, Rutgers University, New Brunswick, NJ.

1995. Extensions of faithfulness: Rotuman revisited, ms. University of Massachusetts, Amherst, MA. To appear in *Natural Language and Linguistic Theory*. [ROA-110, http://ruccs.rutgers.edu/roa.html]

1997a. Faithfulness and prosodic circumscription. (To appear in J. Dekkers, F. van der Leeuw, and J. van de Weijer (eds.), *Optimality Theory: Phonology, Syntax, and Acquisition*, Oxford University Press.)

1997b. Sympathy and phonological opacity, ms. University of Massachusetts, Amherst, MA.

McCarthy, John J., and Alan S. Prince. 1986. Prosodic Morphology, ms. University of Massachusetts, Amherst, MA and Brandeis University, Waltham, MA.

1988. Quantitative transfer in reduplicative and templatic morphology, in Linguistic Society of Korea (ed.), *Linguistics in the Morning Calm* vol. 2, Seoul: Hanshin Publishing Company, 3–35.

1990. Foot and word in Prosodic Morphology: the Arabic broken plural, *Natural Language and Linguistic Theory* 8: 209–83.

1991a. Prosodic minimality. Paper presented at University of Illinois Conference *The Organization of Phonology*.

1991b. Linguistics 240: Prosodic Morphology, lectures and handouts from 1991 Linguistic Society of America Linguistic Institute Course, University of California, Santa Cruz, CA.

1993a. Prosodic Morphology I: constraint interaction and satisfaction, ms. University of Massachusetts, Amherst, MA and Rutgers University, New Brunswick, NJ, RuCCS-TR-3.

1993b. Generalized alignment, in G. E. Booij and J. van Marle (eds.), *Yearbook of Morphology 1993*, Dordrecht: Kluwer, 79–153.

1994a. The emergence of the unmarked: Optimality in Prosodic Morphology, in M. Gonzàlez (ed.), *Proceedings of the North East Linguistic Society* 24, Amherst, MA: Graduate Linguistic Student Association, University of Massachusetts, 333–79.

1994b. Prosodic Morphology: an overview, papers presented at the Workshop on Prosodic Morphology, University of Utrecht, June 1994.

1995. Faithfulness and reduplicative identity, in Beckman *et al.* (eds.), 249–384. [ROA-60, http://ruccs.rutgers.edu/roa.html]

Mester, R. Armin. 1986. Studies in tier structure, Ph.D. dissertation, University of Massachusetts, Amherst, MA.

Moore, Deanna. 1995. Reduplication and optimization of prosodic structure, ms. University of Massachusetts, Amherst, MA.

Moreton, Elliott. 1996. Non-computable functions in Optimality Theory, ms. University of Massachusetts, Amherst, MA.

Munro, Pamela, and Peter Benson. 1973. Reduplication and rule ordering in Luiseño, *International Journal of American Linguistics* 39: 15–21.

Myers, Scott. 1991. Persistent rules, *Linguistic Inquiry* 22: 315–44.

1993. OCP effects in Optimality Theory, ms. University of Texas, Austin.

Myers, Scott, and Troi Carleton. 1996. Tonal transfer in Chichewa, *Phonology* 13: 39–72.

Odden, David, and Mary Odden. 1985. Ordered reduplication in Kíhehe, *Linguistic Inquiry* 16: 497–503.

Onn, Farid M. 1976. Aspects of Malay phonology and morphology: a generative approach, Ph.D. dissertation, University of Illinois, Urbana-Champaign, IL. [Published later in 1980. Universiti Kebangsaan Malaysia, Bangi.]

Oostendorp, Marc van. 1993. Phonological lines in bracketed grids and autosegmental representations, ms. University of Tilburg.

Orgun, Cemil Orhan. 1996a. Correspondence and identity constraints in two-level OT, in *Proceedings of the West Coast Conference on Formal Linguistics* 15. [ROA-62, http://ruccs.rutgers.edu/roa.html]

1996b. Sign-based morphology and phonology with special attention to Optimality Theory, Ph.D. dissertation, University of California, Berkeley, CA. [ROA-171, http://ruccs.rutgers.edu/roa.html]

Padgett, Jaye. 1995a. Feature classes, in Beckman *et al.* (eds.), 1995, 385–420.

1995b. Review of John Goldsmith (ed.), (1993) in *Phonology* 12: 147–155.

Pater, Joe. This volume. Austronesian nasal substitution and other *NÇ effects.

Perlmutter, David (ed.). 1983. *Studies in Relational Grammar*, vol. 1, University of Chicago Press.

Pierrehumbert, Janet, and Mary Beckman. 1988. *Japanese Tone Structure*, Cambridge, MA: MIT Press.

Poser, William. 1982. Why cases of syllable reduplication are so hard to find, ms. Massachusetts Institute of Technology, Cambridge, MA.

1989. The metrical foot in Diyari, *Phonology* 6: 117–48.

Postal, Paul. 1970. On coreferential complement subject deletion, *Linguistic Inquiry* 1: 439–500.

Prince, Alan. S. 1980. A metrical theory for Estonian quantity, *Linguistic Inquiry* 11: 511–62.

1997. Stringency and anti-Paninian hierarchies. Lecture notes from Topics in Optimality Theory, Linguistic Society of America Summer Institute, Cornell University, Ithaca, NY.

Prince, Alan S., and Paul Smolensky. 1991. Notes on Connectionism and Harmony Theory in linguistics, Technical report CU-CS-533-91, Department of Computer Science, University of Colorado, Boulder, CO.

1993. Optimality Theory: constraint interaction in generative grammar, ms. Rutgers University, New Brunswick, NJ, and University of Colorado, Boulder, CO.

Pulleyblank, Douglas. 1988. Vocalic underspecification in Yoruba, *Linguistic Inquiry* 19: 233–70.

Sapir, Edward. 1930. Southern Paiute, a Shoshonean language, *Proceedings of the American Academy of Arts and Sciences* 65, nos. 1–3.

Schachter, Paul, and Victoria Fromkin. 1968. *A Phonology of Akan: Akuapem, Asante, and Fante, UCLA Working Papers in Phonetics* 9.

Schein, Barry, and Donca Steriade. 1986. On geminates, *Linguistic Inquiry* 17: 691–744.

Schlindwein, Deborah. 1991. Reduplication in lexical phonology: Javanese plural reduplication, *The Linguistic Review* 8: 97–106.

Selkirk, Elisabeth. 1980a. Prosodic domains in phonology: Sanskrit revisited, in M. Aronoff and M.-L. Kean (eds.), *Juncture*, Saratoga, CA: Anma Libri, 107–29.

    1980b. The role of prosodic categories in English word stress, *Linguistic Inquiry* 11: 563–605.

    1981. Epenthesis and degenerate syllables in Cairene Arabic, in H. Borer and J. Aoun (eds.), *Theoretical Issues in the Grammar of the Semitic Languages*, Cambridge, MA: Department of Linguistics and Philosophy, Massachusetts Institute of Technology.

    1995. Surface restrictions in the distribution of lexical contrasts: the role for root faithfulness. Handout for *Linguistics 751*, University of Massachusetts, Amherst.

Shaw, Patricia. 1976. Dakota phonology and morphology, Ph.D. dissertation, University of Toronto.

    1987. Non-conservation of melodic structure in reduplication, in Anna Bosch *et al.* (eds.), *Papers from the 23rd Annual Regional Meeting of the Chicago Linguistic Society, Part Two: Parasession on Autosegmental and Metrical Phonology*, 291–306.

    1994. Minimality and markedness. Paper presented at the Workshop on Prosodic Morphology, Utrecht University, June 1994.

Shetler, Joanne. 1976. *Notes on Balangao Grammar*, Huntington Beach, CA: Summer Institute of Linguistics.

Sietsema, Brian. 1988. Reduplications in Dakota, in L. MacLeod, G. Larson, and D. Brentari (eds.), *Papers from the 24th Annual Regional Meeting of the Chicago Linguistic Society*, 337–52.

Smolensky, Paul. 1993. Harmony, markedness, and phonological activity. Paper presented at Rutgers Optimality Workshop I, Rutgers University, New Brunswick, NJ.

Spaelti, Philip. 1997. Dimensions of variation in multi-pattern reduplication, Ph.D. dissertation, University of California, Santa Cruz, CA.

Spencer, Andrew. 1993. The optimal way to syllabify Chukchee. Paper presented at Rutgers Optimality Workshop I, Rutgers University, New Brunswick, NJ.

Spring, Cari. 1990. Implications of Axininca Campa for Prosodic Morphology and reduplication, Ph.D. dissertation, University of Arizona, Tucson, AZ.

1994. The Axininca future reflexive, ms. California State University, San Marcos, CA. [Presented at 23rd Western Conference on Linguistics, 1993.]

Stampe, David. 1972. How I Spent my summer vacation [A dissertation on natural phonology], Ph.D. dissertation, University of Chicago, Chicago, IL.

Steriade, Donca. 1982. Greek prosodies and the nature of syllabification, Ph.D. dissertation, Massachusetts Institute of Technology, Cambridge, MA.

1988. Reduplication and syllable transfer in Sanskrit and elsewhere, *Phonology* 5: 73–155.

Stevens, Alan M. 1968. *Madurese phonology and morphology*, American Oriental Series 52, New Haven, CT: American Oriental Society.

1985. Reduplication in Madurese, in *Proceedings of the Second Eastern States Conference on Linguistics*, Columbus, OH: Linguistics Department, Ohio State University, 232–42.

Tateishi, Koichi. 1987. Consonant mutation in Mende, Loma, and Bandi and its implications, ms. University of Massachusetts, Amherst, MA.

Uhrbach, Amy. 1987. A formal analysis of reduplication and its interaction with phonological and morphological processes, Ph.D. dissertation, University of Texas, Austin, TX.

Urbanczyk, Suzanne. 1996a. Patterns of reduplication in Lushootseed, Ph.D. dissertation, University of Massachusetts, Amherst, MA.

1996b. Morphological templates in reduplication, in *Proceedings of the North East Linguistic Society 26*, Amherst, MA: Graduate Linguistic Student Association, 425–40.

This volume. Double reduplications in parallel.

Voegelin, C. F. 1935. Tübatulabal grammar, *University of California Publications in American Archaeology and Ethnology* 34: 55–190.

Welmers, William. 1946. *A Descriptive Grammar of Fanti, Language* dissertation 39, *Language* vol. 22, no. 3 Supplement.

Wilbur, Ronnie. 1973a. The phonology of reduplication, Ph.D. dissertation, University of Illinois, Urbana-Champaign, IL.

1973b. Reduplication and rule ordering, in *Papers from the Ninth Regional Meeting of the Chicago Linguistic Society*, Chicago, IL: Chicago Linguistic Society, 679–87.

1973c. The Identity Constraint: an explanation of the irregular behavior of some exceptional reduplicated forms, *Studies in the Linguistic Sciences* 3: 143–54.

Yip, Moira. 1993. Cantonese loanword phonology and Optimality Theory, *Journal of East Asian Linguistics* 2: 261–91.

Zoll, Cheryl. 1996. Parsing below the segment in a constraint-based framework, Ph.D. dissertation, University of California, Berkeley, CA. [ROA-143, http://ruccs.rutgers.edu/roa.html]

8 Austronesian nasal substitution and other NÇ̥ effects

Joe Pater

1. Introduction

Nasal substitution[1] occurs in Austronesian languages as far flung as Chamorro (Topping 1969, 1973), and Malagasy (Dziwirek 1989), as well as in several African languages (Rosenthall 1989: 50). However, it is most famous for its appearance in the Indonesian *məN-* prefixation paradigm (see, for example, Halle and Clements 1983: 125).[2] Nasal substitution refers to the replacement of a root-initial voiceless obstruent by a homorganic nasal (1a). If the obstruent is voiced, a homorganic cluster results instead (1b). As illustrated by the data in (1c), NÇ̥ (nasal/voiceless obstruent) clusters are permitted root-internally:

(1) a. /məN+pilih/   məmilih   "to choose, to vote"
       /məN+tulis/   mənulis   "to write"
       /məN+kasih/   məɲasih   "to give"
    b. /məN+bəli/   məmbəli   "to buy"
       /məN+dapat/   məndapat   "to get, to receive"
       /məN+ganti/   məŋganti   "to change"
    c. əmpat "four"   untuk "for"   muŋkin "possible"

Though familiar to most students of phonology, Austronesian nasal substitution has not engendered much theoretical discussion. The standard analysis invokes two ordered rules to generate the single nasal from the underlying pair of segments: nasal assimilation, followed by a rule of root-initial, postnasal, voiceless consonant deletion (e.g., Topping 1973: 49; Onn 1980: 15; Herbert 1986: 252; Teoh 1988: 156; though cf. Lapoliwa 1981: 111, Uhrbach 1987: 72).

In this chapter, I reanalyze nasal substitution as fusion of the nasal and voiceless obstruent, driven by a phonetically motivated constraint that disallows nasal/voiceless obstruent clusters (*NÇ). This analysis is cast in the framework of Optimality Theory, as developed in Prince and Smolensky (1993), and McCarthy and Prince (1993a, b, 1994a, b, 1995, this volume). In particular, aspects of Correspondence Theory, and the theory of morphology-phonology interaction expounded in McCarthy and Prince (1994b, 1995, this volume), play a central role.

Nasal substitution is just one of a range of processes that languages make use of to rid themselves of NÇ clusters, which also include post-nasal voicing, nasal deletion, and denasalization. Permutation of the constraint rankings posited for nasal substitution is all that is needed to provide a unified account of these NÇ effects. Nasal substitution occurs when the antifusion constraint Linearity is dominated by *NÇ and the other faithfulness constraints. Each of the other NÇ effects is similarly generated when the faithfulness constraint that it violates falls to the bottom of the hierarchy. Especially strong motivation for a unified treatment of the NÇ effects comes from the existence of languages in which two of the processes act in a "conspiracy" (Kisseberth 1970) to eliminate NÇ clusters. In this chapter I introduce conspiracies between nasal substitution and each of nasal deletion and postnasal voicing (see Pater 1996 for others). Since neither the standard rule-based analyses of nasal substitution or postnasal voicing, nor Itô, Mester, and Padgett's (1995) recent analysis of postnasal voicing extend to the full range of these processes, they fail to yield an account of the conspiracies between them.

The analysis of nasal substitution, and the other NÇ effects, appears in section 2 through section 4. Section 2.1 introduces the *NÇ constraint. In section 2.2, I discuss the segmental violations of Input-Output Faith-fulness that satisfy *NÇ (e.g., fusion and deletion), and provide an account of the morphological restrictions on Indonesian nasal substitu-tion. Section 4 is concerned with the Input-Output mismatches in the featural makeup of NÇ sequences (e.g., denasalization and postnasal voicing), and contains a modification to the formulation of McCarthy and Prince's (1995) Featural Identity, which is necessitated by the Iden-tity violations incurred by fusion. Section 5 focuses on the OshiKwanyama conspiracy between nasal substitution and postnasal voicing, and on Itô, Mester, and Padgett's (1995) redundant-feature licensing approach to postnasal voicing. The results are summarized in the final section, with directions for further research.

2. *NÇ̊

In a wide variety of languages, NÇ̊ clusters seem to be disfavored. That is, Input NÇ (nasal/voiced obstruent) sequences are represented faithfully in the Output, while NÇ̊ sequences are somehow altered. The usual result is for the obstruent to be voiced, though there are other possibilities, as enumerated in the introduction, and below.

The fact that these NÇ̊ effects, in particular postnasal voicing, occur with such frequency has long been assumed to stem from the ease of articulation of NÇ clusters relative to NÇ̊ (see Kenstowicz and Kisseberth 1979: 37; Herbert 1986), but without a specific hypothesis about the articulatory difficulty inherent in NÇ̊ being proposed. However, Huffman's (1993: 310) observation that the raising of the velum occurs very gradually during a voiced stop following a nasal segment, with nasal airflow only returning to a value typical of plain obstruents during the release phase, suggests an articulatory basis for a *NÇ̊ constraint, since a NÇ cluster allows a more leisurely raising of the velum than a NÇ̊. Put another way, a NÇ̊ cluster requires an unnaturally quick velar closure. The fact that this constraint is asymmetrical (i.e., *NÇ̊, and not *Ç̊N – see the discussion in section 6), can then be understood in the light of Zuckerman's (1972) finding that "the velum can be lowered more quickly and with greater precision than it can be raised" (Herbert 1986: 195).[3] Ohala and Ohala (1991: 213 – cited in Ohala and Ohala 1993: 239) provide the following complementary perceptually oriented explanation for nasal deletion in the NÇ̊ configuration.

(2) Among the auditory cues for a voiced stop there must be a spectral and amplitude discontinuity with respect to neighbouring sonorants (if any), low amplitude voicing during its closure, and termination in a burst; these requirements are still met even with velic leakage during the first part of the stop as long as the velic valve is closed just before the release and pressure is allowed to build up behind the closure. However, voiceless stops have less tolerance for such leakage because any nasal sound – voiced or voiceless – would undercut either their stop or their voiceless character.

Additional evidence for the markedness of NÇ̊ clusters comes from Smith's (1973: 53) observation that they emerged considerably later than NÇs in his son's speech, with the nasal consonant of an adult NÇ̊ being deleted in the child's production. This pattern has also been observed in the speech of learners of Greek (Drachman and Malikouti-Drachman 1973) and Spanish (Vogel 1976). Thus, data from typology, phonetics, and acquisition all converge on the existence of a universal, but violable, *NÇ̊ constraint:

(3) *NÇ̊
     No nasal/voiceless obstruent sequences

One of the primary strengths of a constraint-based theory like Optimality Theory is that phonetically grounded contextual markedness statements like *NÇ̊ can be directly incorporated into the phonology (Mohanan 1993: 98; Prince and Smolensky 1993: section 5; Archangeli and Pulleyblank 1995; see Flemming 1995, Hayes 1995, Jun 1995, Kirchner 1995, and Steriade 1995b for extensive development of this sort of approach within Optimality Theory). In what follows, I demonstrate how the interaction between *NÇ̊ and constraints on input-output correspondence creates grammars that generate nasal substitution, as well as the other NÇ̊ effects.[4]

3. *NÇ̊ and segmental correspondence

3.1 Segmental fusion

Rather than positing discrete steps of nasal assimilation and voiceless consonant deletion, or of complete assimilation of the voiceless consonant to the nasal and degemination (Uhrbach 1987: 72; cf. Herbert 1986: 252), I assume that the relationship between input *məN+pilih* and output *məmilih* is mediated by fusion, or coalescence of segments (Lapoliwa 1981: 111). Part of the motivation for this assumption is specific to the model of phonology being assumed here – a fusional analysis allows nasal substitution to be treated as a one step Input-Output mapping, without the intermediate derivational stage that assimilation + deletion requires. There are, however, two relatively theory-neutral arguments for fusion: one is from typology, the other is internal to the phonology of Indonesian.

In arguing for fusion-based analyses of other processes, Stahlke (1976) makes the point that an ordered-rule account predicts that each of the rules should be independently observed. While place assimilation of nasals is of course extremely common, postnasal voiceless consonant deletion seems never to apply without the prior assimilation of the nasal. As we will see below, there are examples of other NÇ effects applying without place assimilation, such as Zoque postnasal voicing (Wonderly 1951, Kenstowicz and Kisseberth 1979: 36, Padgett 1994), and denasalization in both Toba Batak (Hayes 1986) and Kaingang (Henry 1948, Piggott 1995). By using fusion rather than ordered rules, we avoid the "false step" of voiceless consonant deletion.

There is also evidence from within the phonology of Indonesian for the fusional analysis. Lapoliwa (1981: 110) notes that reduplication copies a substituted nasal (4a), while prefixal nasals preceding a voiced obstruent (4b), or a vowel (4c), fail to be copied:

(4) a. /məN+kata+RED+i/   məɲataɲatai   "to speak ill about someone"

   b. /məN+gerak+RED/   məgerakgerak   "to move something repeatedly"

   c. /məN+əlu+RED+kan/   məɲəluəlukan   "to praise"

Lapoliwa formulates the rule of nasal substitution as one of phonological and morphological coalescence, so that the substituted nasal in (4a) becomes part of the morphological stem, unlike the unassimilated nasal in (4c). Building on work by Uhrbach (1987), Cohn and McCarthy (1994) propose an entirely prosodic approach to these facts, in which the prefix-final nasal in (4a) becomes initial to the prosodic word, while the one in (4c) ends up in coda position outside of the prosodic word. The differing prosodic position of these consonants is due to an ALIGN WORD constraint, which forces coincidence of the edges of the root and prosodic word. If the root-initial consonant simply deleted, this analysis would be difficult, if not impossible, to maintain.

To formalize the fusional input-output mapping, I draw on McCarthy and Prince's (1994b, 1995, this volume) proposal that the relationship between input and output is directly assessed by constraints on correspondence. This approach contrasts with the indirect method of using purely output-based constraints, and stipulating that the phonological and morphological properties of the input must be contained in the

output, by the principles of containment and consistency of exponence
(Prince and Smolensky 1993, McCarthy and Prince 1993a, b). In the
containment approach to Input-Output Faithfulness, the constraint
PARSE-SEGMENT forces the realization of underlying segments (unpro-
nounced input segments are present in the output, but unparsed). The
equivalent in correspondence terms is a MAX constraint that demands
that every segment in the input map to a segment in the output, in other
words, that every input segment have an output correspondent. The
replacement of PARSE-SEGMENT with MAX allows an interpretation of
fusion as a two-to-one mapping from input to output: two input segments stand in correspondence with a single output segment (McCarthy
and Prince 1995; see also Gnanadesikan 1995 and Lamontagne and
Rice 1995). This results in the satisfaction of MAX, though under a strict
interpretation of containment, PARSE SEGMENT would be violated in this
situation (McCarthy and Prince 1993a: 163, Myers 1994, Russell 1995).
I illustrate the difference between input and output in (5), where sub-
scripting is used to indicate the crucial correspondence relationship:

(5) Input   Output
    $məN_1+p_2ilih$ $məm_{1,2}ilih$

Even though fusion does not involve deletion, and so satisfies MAX, it
does incur violations of other constraints. At the featural level, fusion
between non-identical segments violates constraints demanding Identity between input and output segments (see section 4 below for elaboration of Identity constraints, and for an example in which NC̥ fusion
is overruled by a Featural Identity constraint). Because fusion incurs
violations of Featural Identity, it tends to occur between segments that
are identical, or nearly so (cf. McCarthy and Prince 1993a: 163, where
fusion is restricted to identical elements). However, even fusion between identical segments is not automatic or universal, so it must violate
at least one constraint other than Featural Identity. One such constraint
is LINEARITY, which is independently needed in Correspondence Theory
to militate against metathesis.[5] McCarthy and Prince's (1995) formulation of LINEARITY is as in (6), where S_1 and S_2 refer to input and output
strings (or any other string of correspondent segments, such as base and
reduplicant):

(6) LINEARITY
    S_1 reflects the precedence structure of S_2, and vice versa.

In the fusional I-O relationship depicted in (5), /N/ precedes /p/ in the input, but not in the output, so LINEARITY is violated.[6] To command a violation of LINEARITY, *NÇ must be ranked above the faithfulness constraint, as illustrated in the tableau in (7). A pointing index indicates a grammatical form, and exclamation marks show where other candidates fail. Solid lines between constraints are used when the constraints are ranked, and dashed lines when there is no evidence for their ranking. Unless noted otherwise, all of the following tableaux apply to Indonesian.

(7) Nasal substitution: *NÇ ≫ LIN

Input: məN₁+p₂ilih	*NÇ	LIN
a. ☞ məm₁,₂ilih		*
b. məm₁p₂ilih	*!	

With the ranking reversed, the candidate without substitution (7b) would be optimal. Such a ranking characterizes languages that tolerate NÇ clusters.

3.2 Morphological conditions on fusion

The fact that fusion violates LINEARITY leads to a straightforward account of the lack of root-internal nasal substitution in Indonesian. McCarthy and Prince (1994b) and Urbanczyk (1996) show that a large number of disparate phonological phenomena, reduplicative and otherwise, result from stricter faithfulness requirements within the root than elsewhere in the word, that is, from the relative markedness of roots. The greater markedness of roots is no doubt driven by the need to maintain more contrasts between roots than between affixes. McCarthy and Prince formalize this difference in markedness by proposing a general ranking schema in which root-specific versions of faithfulness constraints are intrinsically ranked higher than the general, or affix-specific, version of the constraints. If nasal substitution were to apply within the root, massive neutralization would result. A root-specific ranking of LINEARITY (RootLIN) above *NÇ stops this from happening. A tableau illustrating the blocking of substitution within the root appears in (8):

(8) Root-internal NC̥ tolerance: RootLin ≫ *NC̥

Input: əm₁p₂at	RootLin	*NC̥	Lin
a. əm₁,₂at	*!		*
b. ☞ əm₁p₂at		*	

RootLin rules out fusion within the root because fusion destroys the precedence relationship between input root segments /m/ and /p/ (8a). Since the nasal in /meN+pilih/ is not part of the root, nasal substitution across the morpheme boundary does not disturb the precedence structure of root elements, and RootLin is obeyed.[7]

RootLin is effective in blocking substitution within the root because it is a constraint on the relationship between input and output strings, rather than between individual input and output segments, or features. If we attempted to rule out root-internal fusion with a root-specific constraint on Identity between input and output correspondents, substitution in the middle of the root, and at the beginning of it would be assessed equally, since both would turn a voiceless obstruent belonging to the root into an output nasal. As Donca Steriade (personal communication) has pointed out, it is not at all clear how a theory with faithfulness constraints demanding only faithful segmental and featural parsing would handle these and other segmental "derived environment" effects (see Kiparsky 1993 for recent discussion). The main difference between Indonesian nasal substitution, and more commonly discussed cases such as the Sanskrit Ruki rule and Finnish assibilation, is that the latter involve segmental change, rather than segmental fusion. However, if linearity is generalized to sub-segmental elements, such that it forces their underlying precedence relationship to be maintained, and if these cases can all be analyzed as involving partial segmental overlap, then root-specific rankings of sub-segmental linearity would generate non-derived environment blocking effects.[8] Clearly, a great deal of work needs to be done to determine the empirical coverage of root-specific Linearity constraints, but it seems plausible that the ranking of morpheme-specific faithfulness constraints above phonotactic constraints is the source of this sort of phenomenon.

3.3 Segmental deletion and insertion

So far we have only considered candidates with and without NÇ fusion. Deletion and epenthesis could also satisfy *NÇ, without incurring violations of LINEARITY. This means that in Indonesian, the constraints MAX and DEP, which are violated by deletion and epenthesis respectively (McCarthy and Prince 1995), must be ranked above LINEARITY. In fact, these constraints must be placed even higher in the hierarchy, above *NÇ, since neither deletion nor epenthesis is used to resolve *NÇ violations root-internally, where fusion is ruled out by ROOTLIN:

(9) Deletion and epenthesis blocked by MAX, DEP ≫ *NÇ

Input: əmpat	MAX	DEP	*NÇ
a. ☞ əmpat			*
b. əpat	*!		
c. əməpat		*!	

If MAX or DEP were ranked beneath *NÇ, deletion (9b) or epenthesis (9c) would be wrongly preferred over the optimal candidate (9a).

Though neither deletion nor epenthesis is resorted to in Indonesian to avoid *NÇ violations, permutation of the rankings of these constraints (Prince and Smolensky 1993: section 6) predicts the existence of other languages in which MAX and DEP are dominated by *NÇ and the other faithfulness constraints, producing NÇ deletion and NÇ epenthesis.

Examples of segmental deletion in the NÇ configuration include the aforementioned cases of child English (Smith 1973: 53), child Greek (Drachman and Malikouti-Drachman 1973), and child Spanish (Vogel 1976). Amongst the adult languages with NÇ deletion is the Kelantan dialect of Malay, which differs from standard Johore Malay in that it lacks nasals before voiceless obstruents, though it permits homorganic NÇ clusters (Teoh 1988). This pattern is replicated in African languages such as Venda (Ziervogel, Wetzel, and Makuya 1972 – cited in Rosenthall 1989: 47), Swahili[9] and Maore (Nurse and Hinnebusch 1993: 168), as well as several others cited by Ohala and Ohala (1993: 239).[10]

What unites all of these examples is that the nasal, rather than the obstruent, is deleted. This parallels the nasal/fricative cluster effects detailed, in Padgett (1994), which sometimes involve nasal, but never fricative, deletion. The constraints posited thus far assess obstruent and nasal deletion equally, as violations of MAX. How to formalize nasal-obstruent asymmetries in deletion, as well as in assimilation, remains unaddressed in Optimality Theory (and more generally, in phonology: see Mohanan 1993). One possibility is to introduce intrinsic rankings of the faithfulness constraints. For example, the fact that nasals tend to assimilate in place to obstruents, rather than the other way around, could be captured by a fixed ranking of OBSPLACEIDENT ≫ NASPLACE-IDENT (i.e., the identity requirement between an obstruent and its underlying correspondent is intrinsically higher ranked than that between a nasal and its correspondent; see Jun 1995 for development of this type of approach). For deletion, a ranking of an obstruent specific MAX constraint (OBSMAX) above the nasal specific (NASMAX) achieves the desired result. Establishing the phonetic basis, and typological correctness of this presumed fixed ranking is beyond the purview of this study, but it can be noted that its universality is supported by the observation that a few languages lack nasals, but none are without oral segments (Maddieson 1984 – cited in McCarthy and Prince 1994a, who provide a different explanation for this generalization).

The tableau in (10) demonstrates how an /NT/ cluster would be treated in a language such as Kelantan Malay, in which *NÇ̥ dominates MAX (note that all other faithfulness constraints, including LINEARITY, are also ranked above MAX).

(10) Tableau for Kelantan-like languages

Input: N_1T_2	*NÇ̥	OBSMAX	NASMAX
N_1T_2	*!		
N_1		*!	
☞ T_2			*

In future tableaux, I will merge the two MAX constraints, and show only the candidate with the deleted nasal.

For some reason, languages seem not to make use of epenthesis to resolve *NÇ̥ violations. One might stipulate that DEP universally dominates *NÇ̥, but without any independent motivation for this fixed ranking, such a formalization would remain in the realm of description, rather than explanation.[11] With this potential gap in the typology of NÇ̥ effects duly noted, I will now turn to the featural changes that can be used to satisfy *NÇ, and propose constraints to rule them out in Indonesian. In these instances, we will see the predicted factorial typology is indeed fulfilled.

4. *NÇ and featural faithfulness

4.1 Denasalization

Instead of completely deleting the nasal, another way to meet the *NÇ requirement is to change the underlying nasal into an obstruent. There are at least three languages that take this route: Toba Batak[12] (Hayes 1986), Kaingang (Henry 1948; cf. Piggott 1995), and Mandar (Mills 1975). Mandar, a language spoken in South Sulawesi, is particularly interesting because it has a prefixation paradigm that differs minimally from that of Indonesian. A homorganic nasal appears before voiced obstruents (11a), but instead of nasal substitution with the voiceless ones, there is gemination (11b) (in Toba Batak and Kaingang, the resulting obstruent retains its place specification, and can be heterorganic with the following consonant).

(11) Mandar *maN*- prefixation
    a. /maN+dundu/   mandundu   "to drink"
    b. /maN+tunu/   mattunu   "to burn"

In Mandar, unlike Indonesian, the prohibition against NÇ extends throughout the language:

(12) Nowhere in my material nor in Pelenkahu's extensive lists of minimal pairs is there a single instance of nasal plus voiceless stop.[13] Where such a cluster would be expected, because of cognate items or at certain morpheme boundaries, there is invariably a geminate voiceless stop. In this respect, [Mandar] is far more consistent than [Buginese]; perhaps it reflects greater freedom from outside influence. (Mills 1975: 82)

There are a number of potential constraints, or sets of constraints, that could rule out denasalization in Indonesian, as well as in languages like Kelantan Malay that have nasal deletion. Before turning to them, a short discussion of featural faithfulness within Correspondence Theory is in order.

To replace the containment-based PARSE-FEATURE (see, for example, Itô, Mester, and Padgett 1995) in Correspondence Theory, McCarthy and Prince (1994a, 1995) outline two approaches. One is to extend correspondence into the featural domain, and require mappings between instances of features such as [voice] in the input and output. A less elaborate theory, and the one that McCarthy and Prince adopt, invokes a set of identity requirements between segmental correspondents. A general formulation for such constraints is given in (13):

(13) Featural Identity: IDENT-(F)
      Correspondents are identical in their specification for F

Formulated in this way, featural faithfulness is not violated if a segment is deleted, since if an input segment has no output correspondent, identity constraints do not come into force. On the other hand, if there were a whole set of correspondence constraints that examined features, then every time an underlying segment failed to be realized in the output, all of the applicable featural correspondence constraints would be violated. This would force all of the featural correspondence constraints to be dominated by whatever constraint favored deletion. Whether this is a fatal flaw, or a happy result,[14] can only be assessed through careful study of the relationship between segmental deletion and feature changing processes, but it is evident that Featural Identity has the advantage of analytic convenience, especially when considering reduplication, which often involves long strings of correspondence violations.[15]

In cases of fusion, however, the simple statement of Featural Identity given in (13) does lead to some complications. Consider the input-output mappings in (14):[16]

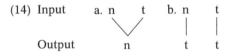

(14) Input   a. n   t   b. n   t

      Output   n   t   t

Nasal substitution is represented in (14a), and denasalization in (14b). One consequence of the symmetrical nature of identity is that IDENT[NAS] is violated to the same degree in (14a) and (14b), since in both instances a nasal and a voiceless obstruent stand in correspondence with one another. Nasal substitution also violates LINEARITY, so in terms of the constraints considered thus far, it is impossible for a language to prefer (14a) over (14b), since the faithfulness violations incurred by (14b) are a subset of those for (14a).

One might consider ruling out (14b) with constraints against coda obstruents, and/or gemination. By using a syllable-structure constraint to rule out denasalization, however, the resulting prediction should be that languages that display nasal substitution have tight restrictions on possible codas. To some extent, this is borne out. However, Chamorro, which has nasal substitution in *man-* and *fan-* prefixation, also has geminates and coda obstruents (Topping 1973: 36–49), even in prefixes, such as *hat-*, *chat-*, and *tak-* (Topping 1973: 66). Thus, nasal substitution does not appear to be driven by a desire to avoid coda obstruents, or gemination.

Another response to this problem is to elaborate identity somewhat, so that we have a way of stating that in nasal substitution an input nasal maps to an output one, while in denasalization an input nasal maps to an obstruent. With this shift away from symmetry the theory of featural faithfulness begins to look more like segmental correspondence, which has separate MAX and DEP constraints. However, I will preserve the analytic advantage of identity noted above by stating the constraint in such a way that featural faithfulness is not violated in cases of deletion:

(15) IDENTI → O[F]
     Any correspondent of an input segment specified as F must be F

Nasal substitution does not violate IDENTI → O[NAS], while denasalization does. [NAS] here would refer to the feature [nasal] in monovalent feature theory, or [+nasal] if bivalent features were assumed. The choice is not crucial, but since the feature [–nasal] seems not to be active in any phonological process, I will assume there is but a single monovalent feature [nasal] (Piggott 1993, Rice 1993, Steriade 1993, Trigo 1993; cf. Cohn 1993). Note that if bivalent features were used, and Featural Identity were stated without any reference to the value of the feature (i.e., "any correspondent of input segment X must be identical to X in its specification for F"), then the effects of this constraint would remain symmetrical, and the problem of differentiating I → O and O → I Identity would remain.

For a language like Mandar, IDENTI → O[NAS] is ranked beneath *NÇ̊ and the rest of the faithfulness constraints. In Indonesian, IDENTI → O[NAS] is ranked above LINEARITY, so that fusion is preferred over denasalization. A tableau for Mandar is given in (16).

(16) Mandar denasalization: *NÇ̥ ≫ IDENTI→O[NAS]

Input: maN₁+t₂unu	DEP	MAX	LINEARITY	*NÇ̥	IDENTI→O[NAS]
a. man₁,₂unu			*!		
b. man₁t₂unu				*!	
c. ☞ mat₁t₂unu					*
d. mat₂unu		*!			
e. maŋ₁at₂unu	*!				

Some further motivation for the recognition of separate IDENTI →
O[NAS] and IDENTO → I[NAS] constraints comes from the fact that
there is at least one language in which a geminate nasal is created to
avoid a *NÇ̥ violation (the South Sulawesi language Konjo; see Friberg
and Friberg 1991: 88). To distinguish Konjo from its near neighbour
Mandar, IDENTO → I[NAS] can be ranked beneath IDENTI → O[NAS], so
that having an output nasal in correspondence with an input obstruent
(i.e., NT → NN) is a better resolution of *NÇ̥ than having an input nasal
in correspondence with an output obstruent (i.e., NT → TT). In Mandar,
of course, the ranking between these constraints would be reversed.[17]

4.2 Postnasal voicing

The most common and most widely discussed NÇ̥ effect is postnasal
voicing. A particularly relevant and perhaps less familiar example is that
of the Puyo Pungo dialect of Quechua (Orr 1962, Rice 1993). As shown
in (17), postnasal voicing only affects affix consonants. Root-internally,
postnasal consonants can remain voiceless.

(17) Puyo Pungo Quechua
       a. Root-internal N
          šiŋki "soot" untina "to stir the fire" pampalʸina "skirt"
       b. Suffixal alternations
          sinik-pa "porcupine's"   kam-ba   "yours"
          sača-pi   "in the jungle" hatum-bi "the big one"
          wasi-ta   "the house"   wakin-da "the others"

Obviously, postnasal voicing satisfies *NÇ. Again, the question of what it violates is not as straightforward as it might at first seem. Compare the I-O correspondences for nasal substitution and postnasal voicing:

(18) Input   a. n   t   b. n   t

Output   n   n   d

If we assume full specification of the traditional set of features (i.e., those of Chomsky and Halle 1968), IDENT[VOICE] is the only constraint violated in (18b), yet it is also violated in (18a) since input /t/ corresponds to output /n/. Nasal substitution violates LINEARITY, while postnasal voicing does not, so again, there is some difficulty in establishing how Indonesian could prefer (18a) over (18b).

In this case, it is pointless to consider constraints that would rule out the NÇ configuration itself, since this does occur in Indonesian as the output of an underlying NÇ sequence. Nor does the problem lie in the symmetry of identity, since in both cases a voiceless input segment stands in correspondence with a voiced output segment. Rather, it is due to the mistaken assumption that [voice] on a sonorant and on an obstruent are equivalent (see Chomsky and Halle 1968: 300; Lombardi 1991; Rice and Avery 1989; Piggott 1992; Rice 1993; Steriade 1995a for discussion from a variety of perspectives). Because the exact method adopted for capturing the nonequivalency of sonorant and obstruent [voice] is of no particular consequence in the present context, I will simply invoke an identity constraint that specifically targets obstruent [voice]. There is no need to specify the constraint as applying from I-to-O or O-to-I:

(19) Obstruent voice identity: IDENT[OBsVCE]
     Correspondent obstruents are identical in their specification for [voice]

As it applies only to obstruents in correspondence, this constraint is not violated by nasal substitution, in which an obstruent is in correspondence with a nasal. For Indonesian, we can thus block postnasal voicing by ranking IDENT[OBsVCE] above *NÇ. In Puyo Pungo Quechua, a root-specific version of IDENT[OBsVCE] ranks above *NÇ, and the general IDENT[OBsVCE] ranks below it, thus producing affixal postnasal voicing only.

As this completes the analysis of nasal substitution, it is appropriate to provide an illustrative tableau.

(20) Final tableau for nasal substitution

Input: /məN₁+p₂ilih/	DEP	IDENTI → O[NAS]	MAX	ROOT LIN	IDENT [OBSVCE]	*NÇ	LIN
a. ☞ məm$_{1,2}$ilih							*
b. məm₁p₂ilih						*!	
c. məp₁p₂ilih		*!					
d. məm₁b₂ilih					*!		
e. məp₂ilih			*!				
f. məŋ₁əp₂ilih	*!						

Noteworthy in this tableau is the fact that all of the nonoptimal candidates, with the exception of the epenthetic (20f), do turn up as optimal in other languages, and that each of these cases can be generated simply by having one of the constraints fall beneath all the others. Candidate (20b) is generated if *NÇ ranks beneath the faithfulness constraints, as in languages that permit NÇ clusters. With IDENTI → O[NAS] at the bottom of this hierarchy, candidate (20c) is made optimal, as we have seen in Mandar. Candidate (20d) is preferred when IDENT[OBSVCE] is lowest ranked, as in Puyo Pungo Quechua. Finally, candidate (20e) wins with MAX dominated by the others, as in Kelantan Malay.

With the introduction of constraints such as ROOTLIN that disallow one of the NÇ effects in a particular environment, we would also expect to see cases where an alternate process takes place in the environment in which the usual one is ruled out. Such conspiracies between NÇ effects can be modeled simply by having both of the relevant faithfulness constraints ranked beneath *NÇ. It is a powerful argument for this approach that this expectation is indeed fulfilled.

4.3 NÇ fusion overruled by Featural Identity

In this section, I show how a high ranking Featural Identity constraint can disallow fusion between particular segments. This discussion also serves to introduce evidence of a conspiracy between nasal substitution and nasal deletion. The data to be accounted for involve a parametric difference between Austronesian and African nasal substitution. In all the Austronesian examples of which I am aware, the fricative /s/ undergoes substitution:[18]

(21) /məN+sapu/   [məɲapu]   "to sweep"   (Indonesian)
     /man+saga/   [maɲaga]   "stay"   (Chamorro; Topping
                                            1973: 50)
     /N+sambuŋ/   [ɲambuŋ]   "to connect" (Javanese;
                                            Poedjosoedarmo
                                            1982: 51)

African languages with nasal substitution demonstrate a split in behavior between stops and fricatives, as in the following examples cited by Rosenthall (1989: 49) (see also Odden and Odden 1985 on Kíhehe):

(22) a. /N+tuma/   [numa]   "I send"
        /N+seva/   [seva]   "I cook"   (Umbundu: Schadeberg 1982)
     b. /N+tabi/   [nabi]   "prince"
        /N+supa/   [supa]   "soup"   (Si-Luyana: Givón 1970)

To stem any suspicion that deletion before the fricatives is motivated solely by the markedness of nasal/fricative clusters (see Padgett 1994), note that voiced fricatives undergo postnasal hardening in Kíhehe (Odden and Odden 1985: 598). This shows that *NC̥ is needed for deletion in a nasal/voiceless fricative sequence, since one would otherwise predict that /ns/ should surface as [nt].

As in Indonesian, fusion with the voiceless stops can be attributed to the ranking of LINEARITY beneath *NC̥ and the rest of the faithfulness constraints, including MAX. However, unlike Indonesian, deletion occurs with root-initial voiceless fricatives instead of fusion. This indicates that preservation of input continuancy is more highly valued than preservation of the input nasal segment in these languages; in other words, that IDENTI → O[CONT] dominates MAX. The fact that deletion does occur rather than a *NC̥ violation places *NC̥ above MAX. Combining these rankings, we get *NC̥, IDENTI → O[CONT] ≫ MAX ≫ LINEARITY. The following tableaux show how this hierarchy generates the different responses to *NC̥ violations in fricative-initial and stop-initial roots.

(23) Fusion with stops

Input: N_1+t_2abi	*NC̥	IDENTI → O[CONT]	MAX	LIN
a. n_1t_2abi	*!			
b. ☞ $n_{1,2}abi$				*
c. t_2abi			*!	

With a stop-initial root, IDENT[CONT] is satisfied in fusion, so MAX is free to choose fusion (23b) over deletion (23c) as the best alternative to a *NC̥ violation (23a).

When the root begins with a fricative, as in (24), fusion creates a violation of IDENTI → O[CONT], since an input fricative has a stop as an output correspondent (assuming an undominated constraint against nasal fricatives in all these languages – see Cohn 1993, Padgett 1994). With IDENTI → O[CONT] ≫ MAX, the candidate with deletion, (24c), becomes optimal in this instance.

(24) Deletion with fricatives

Input: N_1+s_2upa	*NC̥	IDENTI → O[CONT]	MAX	LIN
a. n_1s_2upa	*!			
b. $n_{1,2}upa$		*!		*
c. ☞ s_2upa			*	

Austronesian nasal substitution evinces the opposite ranking MAX ≫ IDENT[CONT], since loss of input continuancy, as in (24b), is preferred to deletion.

As Kisseberth (1970) originally pointed out, cases like this in which two processes conspire to avoid a single configuration provide strong motivation for the formal recognition of output constraints. Under a purely rule-based analysis of nasal substitution, such as the standard one of nasal assimilation followed by voiceless consonant deletion, the functional connection between nasal substitution and nasal deletion would have to be stated independently of the rules themselves; their shared property of eliminating NC̥ clusters is only obliquely retrievable from the rule formulation. This contrasts with the present Optimality Theoretic analysis of African nasal substitution and nasal deletion, in which the functional motivation for these processes is directly incorporated into the formal explanation, thus allowing for a perspicuous account of the conspiracy between them.

5. *NC̥ versus redundant-feature licensing

It is of course not the case that simply being framed within Optimality Theory automatically endows an analysis of one of the NC̥ effects with the power to extend to the whole set. A case in point is Itô, Mester, and Padgett's (1995) account of postnasal voicing, which ingeniously reduces the phenomenon to what appear to be more basic and general constraints, but fails to cope with nasal substitution, and also straightforwardly generates an unattested pattern of nasal-obstruent voicing. The existence of a conspiracy between postnasal voicing and nasal substitution in the Bantu language OshiKwanyama, as well as the nonexistence of prenasal voicing, argue for the use of a relatively parochial, locally motivated constraint like *NC̥, which, by hugging the phonetic ground, stays closer to the attested facts.

5.1 Postnasal voicing

The basic premise of Itô, Mester, and Padgett's analysis is that because [voice] is redundant in sonorants, it cannot be licensed by sonorants. With this restriction, a nasal specified for [voice] violates the constraint License[Voice], as in the first candidate in the tableau in (25):

(25) Postnasal voicing as redundant-feature licensing

Input: NT	License[Voice]	SonVoi	Faith
a. NT [VOICE]	*!		
b. NT		*!	
c. ND \/ ☞ [VOICE]			*

As can be seen in (25b), the alternative of leaving the nasal unspecified for [voice] runs foul of the implicational constraint SonVoi, which

demands that sonorants must be specified for [voice]. The final candidate manages to satisfy both LICENSE[VOICE] and SONVOI by having
a single [voice] feature linked to both the nasal and the obstruent, the
latter of which is able to license it. This candidate is optimal when the
faithfulness constraint that is violated by non-identity between the voicing specification on input and output obstruents is ranked beneath
LICENSE[VOICE] and SONVOI. I have labeled this faithfulness constraint
"FAITH" so as to abstract from irrelevant differences in formulation
between Itô, Mester, and Padgett (1995) and the present analysis.

5.2 Nasal substitution?

To understand why redundant-feature licensing cannot deal with nasal
substitution, consider the table in (26):

(26) Nasal substitution and redundant-feature licensing

Input: NT	LICENSE[VOICE]	SONVOI	LINEARITY
a. N ⎮ [VOICE]	*		*
b. N		*	*
c. NT ⎮ [VOICE]	*		
d. NT		*	

In a language with nasal substitution, either (26a) or (26b) must be
optimal. However, the violations incurred by each of those candidates
are a superset of those of one of the faithful ones, (26c) and (26d) respectively. Therefore, fusion could not be the result of any ranking of this set
of constraints.

   Intuitively, one might think that nasal substitution and postnasal
voicing are in some way related, since both act to get rid of NÇ sequences.
This intuition is borne out by the facts of OshiKwanyama, a western
Bantu language discussed by Steinbergs (1985), which demonstrates a
conspiracy between nasal substitution and postnasal voicing. While there

are no alternations, root-internal postnasal voicing is evidenced by the complementary distribution of [k] and [g] – [k] appears word-initially and intervocalically, while [g] occurs after nasals. Furthermore, loan-words are modified by voicing the postnasal obstruent. The following are borrowings from English.

(27) Postnasal voicing in OshiKwanyama loanwords
    [sitamba]   "stamp"
    [pelenda]   "print"
    [oinga]   "ink"

Root-initially, nasal substitution, rather than postnasal voicing, occurs to resolve underlying NÇ sequences (nasal/voiced obstruent clusters remain intact, though Steinbergs provides no examples):

(28) Root-initial nasal substitution in OshiKwanyama
    /eːN+pati/   [eːmati]   "ribs"
    /oN+pote/   [omote]   "good-for-nothing"
    /oN+tana/   [onana]   "calf"

A straightforward analysis of OshiKwanyama is obtained under the assumptions of the present study. As in Indonesian, root-internal nasal substitution can be ruled out by a root-specific ranking of LINEARITY above *NÇ, while root-initial substitution is permitted because the general LINEARITY constraint is dominated by *NÇ. However, unlike Indonesian, IDENT[OBSVCE] is also ranked beneath *NÇ, so that postnasal voicing occurs root-internally. Also crucial here is the ranking of IDENT[OBSVCE] ≫ LIN, since the reverse ranking would result in post-nasal voicing everywhere, as can be verified in the following tableaux by comparing the violations incurred by candidates (29b) and (29c).

(29) Root-initial nasal substitution

Input: $N_1 \# T_2$	ROOT-LIN	*NÇ	IDENT[OBSVCE]	LIN
a. $N_1 \# T_2$		*!		
b. $N_1 \# D_2$			*!	
c. ☞ $\# N_{1,2}$				*

(30) Root-internal postnasal voicing

Input: N_1T_2	Root-Lin	*NÇ̥	Ident[ObsVce]	Lin
a. N_1T_2		*!		
b. ☞ N_1D_2			*	
c. $N_{1,2}$	*!			*

Since redundant-feature licensing cannot generate nasal substitution, it cannot express the OshiKwanyama conspiracy. This must be counted as a serious inadequacy, especially within Optimality Theory, in which output constraints play such a central role. For further evidence of conspiracies between NÇ̥ effects, drawn from Newton's (1972) study of Greek dialects, which pose similar problems for redundant-feature licensing, see Pater (1996).

5.3 Prenasal voicing

At least as problematic as the inability of redundant-feature licensing to generate nasal substitution is its ability to generate prenasal voicing. The result of supplying an input /TN/ cluster to exactly the same hierarchy that produces postnasal voicing is illustrated in (31):

(31) Prenasal voicing as redundant-feature licensing

Input: TN	License[Voice]	SonVoi	Faith

a.   TN
    │
  [voice]
	*!		

b. TN		*!	
c. DN \\/ ☞[voice]			*

With just the three constraints discussed thus far, all sonorants would be [voice]-linked to adjacent obstruents. Itô, Mester, and Padgett single out nasals as the only sonorant triggers of [voice] spread by introducing a set of constraints that have the effect of prohibiting linkage between obstruents and segments that are more sonorous than nasals (the NoLink constraints). However, both this solution, and the alternative of changing SonVoi to NasVoi (see Itô, Mester, and Padgett 1993, and the discussion in Itô, Mester, and Padgett 1995) would equally limit presonorant voicing to nasals. Though postnasal voicing is extremely widespread, there are no reported cases of regressive voicing triggered by nasals only. The progressive nature of nasal-obstruent voicing is particularly striking since more general forms of voicing assimilation tend to be regressive (Anderson 1979, Lombardi 1991, Mohanan 1993). This directional asymmetry, which is a fundamental property of postnasal voicing (hence the name), completely escapes the redundant-feature-licensing analysis.[19]

It is worth noting that the asymmetry of nasal-obstruent voicing also militates against a view of postnasal voicing as autosegmental spreading of [voice] (or copying of Sonorant Voice; see Rice 1993). If nasal[voice] can spread right, then why could it not spread left? One answer might involve claiming that rules only apply to repair an ill-formed configuration, and that *NÇ, but not *ÇN, defines a representation in need of repair. However, if spreading is itself not the motive force, but is only a response to an independent constraint, this essentially concedes the point that the locus of typological explanation here lies in the constraint system, rather than in the rule formalism.

5.4 Lyman's Law and redundant-feature licensing

While redundant-feature licensing fails to generalize to nasal substitution (or the other NÇ effects; see Pater 1996), it does generate the sonorant [voice] underspecification required for an OCP account of Lyman's Law in Yamato Japanese, and overcomes the ordering paradox between Lyman's Law and postnasal voicing first noted by Itô and Mester (1986). Here I will briefly discuss whether the Lyman's Law facts bear at all on an understanding of postnasal voicing.

Lyman's Law is a cooccurrence constraint that allows only one voiced obstruent per root. It can be analyzed in terms of an OCP-based restriction against adjacent [voice] features, provided that sonorants are unspecified for [voice] when this restriction applies. If postnasal voicing is viewed as the transmission of the nasal's [voice] feature to the obstruent, then Lyman's Law must derivationally precede postnasal voicing. The ordering paradox arises because the postnasal voiced obstruent is a target for Lyman's Law, which would lead one to believe that postnasal voicing occurs before, rather than after, Lyman's Law.

Redundant-feature licensing resolves this paradox by supplying a [voice] feature to sonorants only in the NC context. This is done by ranking LICENSE[VOICE] above SONVOI, so that when there is no adjacent obstruent licenser that would allow the satisfaction of both constraints, the satisfaction of LICENSE[VOICE] takes precedence.

(32) Underspecification of non-NC sonorants

Input: NV	LICENSE[VOICE]	SONVOI
a.　NV 　　| 　[VOICE]	*!	
b. ☞ NV		*

Without the adjacent obstruent as host for the parasitic licensing of [voice], the nasal without [voice] is optimal.

A *NC̥-based analysis of postnasal voicing, in contrast, is silent about the presence or absence of [voice] on sonorants. One result of this is that the OCP + underspecification account of Lyman's Law could be maintained by underspecifying all sonorants for [voice], including nasals in the NC̥ configuration, since *NC̥ would continue to demand a postnasal voiced obstruent, even if the nasal itself lacked [voice]. When postnasal voicing is attributed to a substantive output constraint like *NC̥, rather than to autosegmental feature propagation, the ordering paradox thus quietly vanishes.

On the other hand, because the *NC̥ analysis of postnasal voicing is completely independent of sonorant [voice] underspecification, we are free to contemplate alternative accounts of Lyman's Law. If temporary underspecification of noncontrastive features like sonorant [voice] were a typologically productive way of dealing with cooccurrence conditions and other phonological regularities, then the standard analysis would be secure. However, as Steriade (1995a) notes, no cases besides that of sonorant [voice] appear to exist. It is thus well worth considering alternatives that generalize to other phenomena, and avoid the proliferation of derivational stages that temporary underspecification requires. Extant accounts of Lyman's Law which make no appeal to temporary underspecification can be found in Rice (1993), Lombardi

(1995), Steriade (1995a), Itô and Mester (1996), and Alderete (1997); discussion of their relative generalizability would unfortunately take us too far afield. The crucial point here is that their very existence shows that dealing with each of Lyman's Law and postnasal voicing can, and probably should, be a separate undertaking.

In sum, the redundant-feature licensing and *NÇ̥ analyses of postnasal voicing extend to different phenomena: sonorant [voice] underspecification, and the NÇ̥ effects respectively. While the conspiracies examined here and in Pater (1996) firmly establish the need for a unified treatment of the NÇ̥ effects, neither empirical nor theoretical exigencies force an analytic consolidation of Lyman's Law and postnasal voicing.

6. Conclusions

I have argued that nasal substitution is best analyzed as fusion of a nasal and voiceless obstruent, driven by a phonotactic constraint against this sequence, *NÇ̥, which can also be satisfied by nasal deletion, denasalization, and postnasal voicing. The traditional analysis of nasal substitution, and the recent analysis of postnasal voicing in Itô, Mester, and Padgett (1995), were shown to capture both too much and too little, when cross-linguistic possibilities are taken into consideration. In contrast, the factorial typology predicted by the permutation of the ranking of *NÇ̥ and the faithfulness constraints is nearly completely fulfilled.

The fact that languages exercise a range of options in dealing with *NÇ̥ violations, along with the existence of conspiracies between these NÇ̥ effects, provides strong support for the Optimality Theoretic program of decoupling phonotactic constraints from faithfulness constraints, and allowing them to be freely ranked with respect to one another. However, the apparent lack of NÇ̥ epenthesis raises an intriguing question for future research: is it the case that every phonotactic constraint is satisfied in all of the ways predicted by the permutation of the rankings between it and the faithfulness constraints? Gaps in factorial typologies often serve as indications that constraints must be reformulated, but persistent links between marked configurations and the processes used to repair them would seem to force a more fundamental shift in theoretical assumptions. Either that, or we could settle for a theory of grammar that is in some respects only "exegetically adequate," as opposed to "explanatorily adequate," that is, we could rest content with having "made some progress in understanding the facts as they are, though not in the sense of showing that they could not be otherwise" (Anderson 1979: 18). Such resignation would be disappointing, though, in light of the strides that Optimality Theory has made toward predictive explanatory adequacy in many areas of phonology.

Finally, I would like to conclude by commenting on an issue that bears more directly on the main concern of this volume, that is, the nature of the interaction between phonology and morphology. The primary role of morpheme-specific faithfulness in McCarthy and Prince (1994b) and Urbanczyk (1996) is to explain prosodic influences on morphology that were formerly attributed to templates. In the present chapter, a root-specific constraint is used to account for an influence in the opposite direction: a morphological restriction on the phonotactically motivated process of nasal substitution. By keeping the phonotactic constraint general, and employing morphologically conditioned faithfulness constraints, we are able to straightforwardly capture the OshiKwanyama conspiracy, in which the way that *NC̥ is satisfied depends on the morphological context. This is counter to the usual approach to the morphological sensitivity of OCP effects, in which the morphological domain of the phonotactic constraint itself is stipulated (McCarthy 1986, Myers 1994). Significantly, cases like OshiKwanyama, in which there are different responses to a phonotactic constraint depending on the morphological environment, cannot be dealt with in Optimality Theory by proliferating domain-specific phonotactic constraints. Whatever the ranking of such specific phonotactic constraints might be, the lowest ranked faithfulness constraint will always be the one that is violated. It is to be expected that continued examination of the differences in empirical scope between these, as well as other approaches to morphological influences on phonology, should yield a clearer understanding of the principles underlying morphophonological processes.

Notes

1 This chapter has undergone substantial changes since it was originally presented in Utrecht. The comments of John Kingston, John McCarthy, and Donca Steriade have particularly helped to shape its present form. Thanks also to Abby Cohn, Edward Flemming, Bruce Hayes, Junko Itô, Takako Kawasaki, Jaye Padgett, Sharon Rose, Su Urbanczyk, Rachel Walker, and the participants in LING 751, University of Massachusetts, and the Rutgers/University of Massachusetts Joint Class Meeting, Spring

1995, for useful suggestions, and to Heather Goad and Glyne Piggott for their indispensable guidance. I would also like to acknowledge Choirul Djamhari for his help with the Indonesian data, and Lisa Travis for making it possible for me to work with him, as well as Jan Voskuil for his hospitality and assistance in securing many of the Austronesian materials during an all-too-short visit to Leiden. This research has been supported by SSHRCC fellowship no. 752-93-2773 to the author, and SSHRCC grant no. 410-92-0759 to Glyne Piggott.

2 Though the dialects of Malay spoken in Malaysia and Indonesia are distinct in some ways, unless noted otherwise the phenomena discussed here are common to both Bahasa Indonesia as described in Lapoliwa (1981), and Cohn and McCarthy (1994), amongst others, and the Johore dialect of Malay described in Onn (1980) and Teoh (1988). The Indonesian data cited are all from Lapoliwa (1981). Both Chamorro and Malagasy also display essentially the same pattern as that shown in (1), as do a number of other languages spoken in the Indonesian archipelago. The unspecified nasal in the underlying form of the /məN-/ prefix is employed only as a matter of convention, and does not imply any particular analysis of the assimilative behavior of the prefix.

3 I am grateful to John Kingston and Donca Steriade for very helpful discussion of the phonetic facts, though I hasten to claim sole responsibility for any errors of interpretation. See also Hayes (1995) for a somewhat different hypothesis about the phonetic grounding of *NÇ̥.

4 The discussion here abstracts from two other NÇ̥ effects: nasal devoicing and obstruent aspiration. These processes cannot be captured by the simple statement of *NÇ̥ in (3). It is conceivable that the articulatory or perceptual difficulties of postnasal voicelessness could be overcome by enhancement with aspiration and/or extension of the duration of voicelessness. However, a proper treatment of these phenomena would force a long digression from the central concerns of this chapter, since at least the following rather complex questions would have to be answered: what is the nature of the interaction between these processes: does devoicing result from aspiration, or vice versa (Herbert 1986, Nurse and Hinnebusch 1993)? Are voiceless nasals [–voice], or [+aspirated] (Lombardi 1991, Huffman 1994)? Are the voiceless nasals in fact even entirely voiceless (Maddieson and Ladefoged 1993: 262)? Related to the last question, are these processes categorical or more implementational in nature? Therefore, for present purposes I leave *NÇ̥ in its perhaps overly simple form.

5 In using LINEARITY to block fusion, I am adopting a suggestion of John McCarthy's (personal communication). While McCarthy and Prince (1995, this volume) have subsequently proposed a separate UNIFORMITY constraint for such cases (see also Gnanadesikan 1995), I have retained

LINEARITY because it is still not entirely clear that a separate constraint is in fact needed, and because LINEARITY has some interesting potential extensions in the featural domain, which are noted below in the text.

6 Here I am assuming that the input is made up of a linearly sequenced set of morphemes. It is not crucial to the analysis that this position be maintained, since it is only LINEARITY within the root that must be obeyed, and there are other ways of ruling out transmorphemic nasal substitution, such as through the use of DISJOINTNESS constraints (McCarthy and Prince 1995; also see note 7).

7 It should be noted that fusion is not free to occur between any two morphemes. Both the prefix+prefix and root+suffix boundaries are impermeable to nasal substitution (e.g., /məN+pər+besar/ [məmpərbesar] "to enlarge" and /məN+yakin+kan/ [məyakinkan] "to convince"). To encode this sort of morphological conditioning, constraints are needed to render particular morpheme boundaries opaque to fusion. In particular, McCarthy and Prince's (1995) DISJOINTNESS constraints, which require that the sets of correspondents (or exponents) of morphemes be nonoverlapping, could be recruited for this purpose.

8 See Itô and Mester's (1996) extension of this approach to Japanese Rendaku, in which a similar neighborhood constraint is proposed which does not require featural overlap.

9 Swahili nasal deletion is historically preceded by aspiration of the following voiceless consonant, which spread to the nasal, but there is no evidence for this intermediate stage in the other languages cited here (see Herbert 1986: 252, Nurse and Hinnebusch 1993: 168).

10 In discussing these African languages I follow, for ease of exposition, Herbert (1986) and Padgett (1994) in treating derived prenasalized stops as segmental sequences (cf. Piggott 1992, and Steriade 1993 for other views on prenasalization). It should be emphasized, though, that "segment" in Correspondence Theory might well be understood as the equivalent to what in feature-geometric terms is the root node and everything it dominates (i.e., a melodic element). Two root-node theories of prenasalized stops have been proposed by Piggott (1988), Rosenthall (1989), Trigo (1993), and, to some extent, Steriade (1993) and Piggott (1995).

11 One path to explanation may lie in the fact that NÇ sequences tend to be place assimilated, and thus resist epenthesis due to some version of geminate integrity. However, this explanation is difficult, if not impossible, to formalize in Optimality Theory (why should place assimilation have precedence over *NÇ?), and faces the empirical challenge that NÇ effects do occur in the absence of place assimilation in several languages.

12 In Toba Batak, the obstruents produced by denasalization fail to undergo the debuccalization that affects other obstruents in the same position.

Hayes (1986) attributes this to a type of geminate inalterability, with the double linking of a [-voice] feature spread from the following voiceless consonant inhibiting debuccalization. More plausibly, this is a case of avoidance of neutralization. That is, underlying nasals fail to go all the way to glottals so as to avoid neutralizing the distinction between them and underlying obstruents. See Flemming (1995) for discussion of the formal issues involved in setting up contrast-maintaining constraints; see also McCarthy (1993) and Kirchner (1995) for other approaches to chain shifts in Optimality Theory.

13 Mills does not comment on nasal-/s/ clusters, but as far as I can tell from Pelenkahu, Muthalib, and Sangi (1983), the same restriction holds as for the stops, since there are many examples of /-ss-/, but none of /-ns-/.

14 Since this was first written, Lombardi (1995) has found a "happy result" in one domain, while Alderete et al. (1996) find a "fatal flaw" in another. Needless to say, the issue is far from settled.

15 One could even imagine a hybrid theory. Features that display clear independence from segments, most prominently tones, might be subject to correspondence requirements, while those that do not would be targeted by identity.

16 There is no theoretical stance implicit in the representation of the geminated /t/ as a pair of segments. This representation is used because denasalization sometimes produces a nonassimilated segment (Kaingang and Toba Batak), and because the results in terms of correspondence and identity are the same if a single /t/ is used for a geminate. Different results in terms of LINEARITY might obtain depending on whether geminates were considered a single segment with a mora, or two segments with linked features. It should also be noted that these diagrams do not represent autosegmental mappings; rather, they illustrate the set-theoretic relationship between the input and output sets of segments.

17 This leaves a not-insignificant problem unresolved. How do we distinguish between nasalization of the voiceless stop, and nasal substitution? In terms of the constraints considered thus far, nasal substitution incurs all the violations that nasalization does, plus a LINEARITY violation that is avoided by nasalization. One possibly key difference is that in fusion, one of the underlying correspondents of the output nasal is a nasal, while in nasalization the second member of the cluster has as its sole correspondent a voiceless obstruent. I should also note here that Konjo nasalization is subject to considerable morphological conditioning. In fact, the prefix that causes nasalization has a homophonous counterpart that differs only in that it fails to nasalize the following voiceless obstruent.

18 These examples also demonstrate the well-known complication that /s/ becomes a palatal nasal under substitution. The apparent oddness of this alternation is somewhat tempered by the independent evidence from a

Javanese morpheme structure constraint that Austronesian /s/ is in fact itself phonologically palatal (Mester 1986). A related complication is that nasal substitution often fails to occur with a /c/ initial root (/c/ is variously described as a palatal stop or an alveo-palatal affricate); see Onn (1980: 62) for discussion.

19 See, however, Kawasaki (1995), in which redundant-feature licensing is supplemented by a principle of government that produces the required asymmetry in nasal-obstruent voicing.

References

Alderete, John. 1997. Dissimilation as local conjunction, in K. Kusumoto (ed.) *Proceedings of North East Linguistic Society* 27: 17–23.

Alderete, John, Jill Beckman, Laura Benua, Amalia Gnanadesikan, John J. McCarthy, and Suzanne Urbanczyk. 1996. Reduplication and segmental unmarkedness, ms. University of Massachusetts, Amherst, MA.

Anderson, Stephen R. 1979. On the subsequent development of the "standard theory" in phonology, in D. A. Dinnsen (ed.), *Current Approaches to Phonological Theory*, Bloomington, IN: Indiana University Press.

Archangeli, Diana, and Douglas Pulleyblank. 1995. *Grounded Phonology*. Cambridge, MA: MIT Press.

Beckman, Jill, Laura Walsh Dickey, and Suzanne Urbanczyk (eds.) 1995. *University of Massachusetts Occasional Papers* 18: *Papers in Optimality Theory*. Amherst, MA: Graduate Linguistic Student Association, University of Massachusetts, Amherst, MA.

Chomsky, Noam, and Morris Halle. 1968. *The Sound Pattern of English*, New York: Harper & Row.

Cohn, Abigail C. 1993. The status of nasalized continuants, in Huffman and Krakow (eds.), 329–68.

Cohn, Abigail C., and John J. McCarthy. 1994. Alignment and parallelism in Indonesian phonology, ms. Cornell University, Ithaca, NY, and University of Massachusetts, Amherst, MA.

Drachman, Gaberell, and Angeliki Malikouti-Drachman. 1973. Studies in the acquisition of Greek as a native language: I, Some preliminary findings on phonology, *Ohio State Working Papers in Linguistics* 15: 99–114.

Dziwirek, Katarzyna. 1989. Malagasy phonology and morphology, *Linguistic Notes from La Jolla* 15: 1–30.

Flemming, Edward. 1995. Perceptual features in phonology. Ph.D. dissertation, University of California, Los Angeles, CA.

Friberg, Timothy, and Barbara Friberg. 1991. Notes on Konjo phonology, in J. N. Sneddon (ed.) *Studies in Sulawesi Linguistics* Part 2. NUSA Linguistic Studies, Jakarta, Indonesia.

Givón, Talmy. 1970. *The Si-Luyana Language*, University of Zambia, Institute for Social Research, Communication 6.

Gnanadesikan, Amalia E. 1995. Markedness and faithfulness constraints in child phonology, ms. University of Massachusetts, Amherst, MA.

Goldsmith, John (ed.). 1995. *A Handbook of Phonological Theory*, Cambridge, MA: Basil Blackwell.

Halle, Morris and George N. Clements. 1983. *Problem Book in Phonology*, Cambridge, MA: MIT Press.

Hayes, Bruce. 1986. Assimilation as spreading in Toba Batak, *Linguistic Inquiry* 17: 467–99.

1995. A phonetically-driven, Optimality-Theoretic account of postnasal voicing. Handout from MIT colloquium, 28 July 1995.

Henry, Jules. 1948. The Kaingang language, *International Journal of American Linguistics* 14: 194–204.

Herbert, Robert K. 1986. *Language Universals, Markedness Theory, and Natural Phonetic Processes*, Berlin: Mouton de Gruyter.

Huffman, Marie K. 1993. Phonetic patterns of nasalization and implications for feature specification, in Huffman and Krakow (eds.), 303–27.

1994. Laryngeal specifications for the implementation of nasals. Handout of paper presented at the University of Delaware, Newark, DE, 14 November 1994.

Huffman, Marie K., and Rena A. Krakow (eds.). 1993. *Phonetics and Phonology 5: Nasals, Nasalization, and the Velum*, San Diego, CA: Academic Press.

Itô, Junko, and R. Armin Mester. 1986. The phonology of voicing in Japanese, *Linguistic Inquiry* 17: 49–73.

1996. Structural economy and OCP interactions in local domains, invited lecture, Western Conference on Linguistics.

Itô, Junko, R. Armin Mester, and Jaye Padgett. 1993. Licensing and redundancy: Underspecification Theory in Optimality Theory. Report no. LRC-93-07, Linguistics Research Center, University of California, Santa Cruz, CA.

1995. Licensing and underspecification in Optimality Theory, *Linguistic Inquiry* 26: 571–614.

Jun, Jongho. 1995. Perceptual and articulatory factors in Place Assimilation: an Optimality Theoretic approach. Ph.D. dissertation, University of California, Los Angeles, CA.

Kawasaki, Takako. 1995. Voicing and coda constraints, *McGill Working Papers in Linguistics* vol. 1, 22–45.

Kenstowicz, Michael, and Charles Kisseberth. 1979. *Generative Phonology: Description and Theory*, New York, NY: Academic Press.

Kiparsky, Paul. 1993. Blocking in nonderived environments, in S. Hargus and E. Kaisse (eds.), *Phonetics and Phonology 4: Studies in Lexical Phonology*, San Diego, CA: Academic Press, 277–313.

Kirchner, Robert. 1995. Contrastiveness is an epiphenomenon of constraint ranking, in *Proceedings of the Berkeley Linguistics Society*.

Kisseberth, Charles. 1970. On the functional unity of phonological rules, *Linguistic Inquiry* 1: 291–306.

Lamontagne, Greg, and Keren Rice. 1995. A correspondence account of coalescence, in Beckman *et al.* (eds.), 211–24.

Lapoliwa, Hans. 1981. *A Generative Approach to the Phonology of Bahasa Indonesia*. Canberra: Pacific Linguistics D 34.

Lombardi, Linda. 1991. Laryngeal features and laryngeal neutralization. Ph.D. dissertation, University of Massachusetts, Amherst, MA.

    1995. Why place and voice are different: constraint interactions and feature faithfulness in Optimality Theory, ms. University of Maryland, College Park, MD.

Maddieson, Ian. 1984. *Patterns of Sounds*, Cambridge University Press.

Maddieson, Ian, and Peter Ladefoged. 1993. Phonetics of partially nasal consonants, in Huffman and Krakow (eds.), 251–301.

McCarthy, John. J. 1986. OCP effects: gemination and antigemination, *Linguistic Inquiry* 17: 207–63.

    1993. The parallel advantage: containment, consistency, and alignment. Talk presented at Rutgers Optimality Workshop 1, Rutgers University, New Brunswick, NJ.

McCarthy, John J., and Alan S. Prince. 1993a. Prosodic Morphology I: constraint interaction and satisfaction, ms. University of Massachusetts, Amherst, MA and Rutgers University, New Brunswick, NJ.

    1993b. Generalized alignment, in G. E. Booij and J. van Marle (eds.), *Yearbook of Morphology 1993*, Dordrecht: Kluwer, 79–153.

    1994a. The emergence of the unmarked, *Proceedings of the North East Linguistic Society* 24, Amherst, MA: Graduate Linguistic Student Association, University of Massachusetts, 333–79.

    1994b. Prosodic Morphology: an overview, talks presented at the OTS/HIL Workshop on Prosodic Morphology, University of Utrecht.

    1995. Faithfulness and reduplicative identity, in Beckman *et al.* (eds.), 249–384.

    This volume. Faithfulness and identity in Prosodic Morphology.

Mester, R. Armin. 1986. Studies in tier structure. Ph.D. dissertation, University of Massachusetts, Amherst, MA.

Mills, Roger F. 1975. Proto South Sulawesi and Proto Austronesian phonology. Ph.D. dissertation, University of Michigan.

Mohanan, K. P. 1991. On the bases of radical underspecification, *Natural Language and Linguistic Theory* 9: 285–325.

    1993. Fields of attraction in phonology, in J. Goldsmith (ed.), *The Last Phonological Rule*, University of Chicago Press, 61–116.

Myers, Scott. 1994. OCP effects in Optimality Theory, ms. University of Texas, Austin, TX.

Newton, Brian. 1972. *The Generative Interpretation of Dialect: a Study of Modern Greek Phonology*, Cambridge University Press.

Nurse, Derek, and Thomas J. Hinnebusch. 1993. *Swahili and Sabaki: a Linguistic History*, Berkeley, CA: University of Los Angeles Press.

Odden, David, and Mary Odden. 1985. Ordered reduplication in Kíhehe, *Linguistic Inquiry* 16: 497–503.

Ohala, John J. and Manjari Ohala. 1991. Reply to commentators, *Phonetica* 48: 271–74.

1993. The phonetics of nasal phonology: theorems and data, in Huffman and Krakow (eds.), 225–49.

Onn, Farid M. 1980. *Aspects of Malay Phonology and Morphology*, Bangi: Universiti Kebangsaan Malaysia. [Published version of 1976 University of Illinois dissertation.]

Orr, Carolyn. 1962. Ecuador Quichua phonology, in B. Elson (ed.), *Studies in Ecuadorian Indian Languages*, Norman, Oklahoma: Summer Institute in Linguistics, 60–77.

Padgett, Jaye. 1995. Feature classes II. Handout of talk presented at the Holland Institute of Linguistics Phonology Conference, University of Amsterdam, January 1995.

Pater, Joe. 1995. On the nonuniformity of weight-to-stress and stress preservation effects in English, ms. McGill University, Montreal.

1996. *NC̩, Proceedings of the North East Linguistic Society* 26, 227–39.

Pelankahu, R. A., Abdul Muthalib, and M. Zain Sangi. 1983. *Struktur Bahasa Mandar*, Jakarta: Pusat Pembinaan dan Pengembangan Bahasa.

Piggott, Glyne L. 1988. Prenasalization and feature geometry, *Proceedings of the North East Linguistic Society* 19, 345–52.

1992. Variability in feature dependency: the case of nasality, *Natural Language and Linguistic Theory* 10: 33–77.

1993. The geometry of sonorant features, ms. McGill University, Montreal.

1995. Feature dependency in Optimality Theory: optimizing the phonology of sonorants, ms. McGill University, Montreal.

Poedjosoedarmo, Soepomo. 1982. *Javanese Influence on Indonesian*, Canberra: Pacific Linguistics D 38.

Prince, Alan S. and Paul Smolensky. 1993. Optimality Theory: constraint interaction in generative grammar, ms. Rutgers University, New Brunswick, NJ and University of Colorado, Boulder, CO.

Rice, Keren. 1993. A reexamination of the feature [sonorant]: the status of sonorant obstruents, *Language* 69: 308–44.

Rice, Keren, and Peter Avery. 1989. On the interaction between sonorancy and voicing, *Toronto Working Papers in Linguistics* 10: 65–82.

Rosenthall, Samuel. 1989. The phonology of nasal-obstruent sequences. Master's thesis, McGill University, Montreal.

Russell, Kevin. 1995. Morphemes and candidates in Optimality Theory, ms. University of Manitoba, Winnipeg.

Schadeberg, T. 1982. Nasalization in Umbundu, *Journal of African Languages and Linguistics* 4: 109–32.

Selkirk, Elisabeth. 1988. Dependency, place, and the notion "tier," ms. University of Massachusetts, Amherst, MA.

Smith, Neilson V. 1973. *The acquisition of phonology: a case study*, Cambridge University Press.

Stahlke, Herbert. 1976. Segment sequences and segmental fusion, *Studies in African Linguistics* 7: 44–63.

Steinbergs, Aleksandra. 1985. The role of MSCs in OshiKwanyama loan phonology, *Studies in African Linguistics* 16: 89–101.

Steriade, Donca. 1993. Closure, release, and nasal contours, in Huffman and Krakow (eds.), 401–70.

1995a. Underspecification and markedness, in J. Goldsmith (ed.), 114–74.

1995b. Positional neutralization. ms. University of California, Los Angeles, CA.

Teoh, Boon Seong. 1988. Aspects of Malay phonology – a non-linear approach. Ph.D. dissertation, University of Illinois, Urbana-Champaign, IL.

Topping, Donald M. 1969. A restatement of Chamorro phonology, *Anthropological Linguistics* 11: 62–77.

1973. *Chamorro Reference Grammar*, Honolulu, HI: University of Hawaii Press.

Trigo, R. Lorenza. 1993. The inherent structure of nasal segments, in Huffman and Krakow (eds.), 369–400.

Uhrbach, Amy. 1987. A formal analysis of reduplication and its interaction with phonological and morphological processes. Ph.D. dissertation, University of Texas, Austin, TX.

Urbanczyk, Suzanne. 1996. Patterns of reduplication in Lushootseed. Ph.D. dissertation, University of Massachusetts, Amherst, MA.

Vogel, Irene. 1976. Nasals and nasal assimilation patterns, in the acquisition of Chicano Spanish, *Papers and Reports in Child Language Development*, 201–14.

Wonderly, William. 1951. Zoque II, *International Journal of American Linguistics* 17: 105–23.

Ziervogel, D., P. J. Wetzel, and T. N. Makuya. 1972. *A Handbook of the Venda Language*, Pretoria: University of South Africa Press.

Zuckerman, Suzanne. 1972. The migratory habits of nasal consonants: a study in phonological universals. M. A. thesis, Ohio State University, Columbus, OH.

9 The prosodic base of the Hausa plural

Sam Rosenthall

1. Introduction

Hausa plural formation has associated with it a number of phonological phenomena called "root augmentations" (Newman 1972). These augmentations, shown in (1), range from gemination of the root-final consonant to broken plural patterns.

(1)	class	root	singular	plural	gloss
a.	-unaa	bak	bàkáa	bákkúnàa	"bow"
b.	-aaCee	birn	birnii	bíràanée	"city"
c.	-aa	tark	tárkóo	táràkkáa	"trap"

(1) shows examples of augmentation from three different plural classes. In the *-unaa* class, (1a), the root-final consonant is geminated in the plural, and in the *-aaCee* class, (1b), there is a broken plural pattern where the postvocalic consonants of the root are not adjacent in the plural. The *-aa* class in (1c) has a different type of broken plural pattern in which the postvocalic consonants of the root are separated by a short vowel and the root-final consonant is a geminate.

Root augmentation in the different plural classes is shown here to follow from the satisfaction of prosodic requirements on the base for the plural morpheme. The role of prosody in the analysis of Hausa plural formation is an illustration of McCarthy and Prince's (1990a) Prosodic Morphology Hypothesis which states that "templates are defined in terms of authentic units of prosody: mora (μ), syllable (σ), foot (F), prosodic word (W) and so on." The prosodic requirement in Hausa plural formation is that the plural must attach to a base that is equal to an iambic foot, but, as will be shown, the particular expansion of the iamb is subject to variation. The prosodic requirement is one of a number of constraints on the base of the Hausa plural. The various augmentations that

344

occur within a plural paradigm are the result of surface violations of constraints arising from constraint conflict. Using Prince and Smolensky's (1993) Optimality Theory, the Hausa plural is formed by best satisfying these conflicting constraints.

This chapter[1] proceeds as follows. Plural formation in four of the ten plural classes is discussed. According to Newman (1990), Hausa has twenty-eight plurals, which can be grouped into eight classes based on similar phonology and tonology.

(2) Hausa plural morpheme classes

$^+$=C is either the root-final consonant or a copy of the root-final consonant

*=C is a copy of the root-final consonant

**=add suffix and reduplicate penultimate syllable

a. -aaCee: H L H   b. -ai: L H

    -aayee   -ai
    -aaCee$^+$ -Cai*
    -aaCaa$^+$
    -aaCuu$^+$

c. -akii: L H   d. -aa: H L H

    -akii   -Caa*
    -akii**
    -anni

e. -ii: L H   f. -ooCii: H

    -ii   -ooCii*
    -uu
    -uu**

g. -unaa: H L   h. full reduplication

    -unaa   singular+singular
    -Cunaa*   root+e+root+e
    -ukaa   root+aa+root+ai
    -uwaa
    -ukaa**
    -uwaa**
    -unaa**
    -uCaa
    -uCaa**

Parsons (1975) notes that many common nouns have a number of different plurals, for example, [fìtíláa] "lamp" is pluralized as either [fìtìlúu] or [fítílóolíi]. Parsons also notes that levelling and reduction are beginning to occur and the -ooCii class is the largest and most productive. However, other plural formations are not obsolete since words borrowed from English, shown in (3), occur in most classes.

(3) a. kúrtùu   kúrtàatàa   "recruit"
    b. súlèe   súlúulúwàa   "shilling"
    c. fòotóo   fòotàaníi   "photo"
    d. šùu   šùwàašúwái   "shoe"

Some plural classes are quite small and the nouns share some semantic property. For example, the root+aa+root+ai class contains twenty or so nouns which are all bifurcated objects such as wings and heels, but note that the plural of "shoe," (3d), has been incorporated into this class.

The classes that are discussed here in sections 2, 3, 4, and 5 are -unaa, -aaCee, -ooCii, and -aa, respectively. Not all aspects of Hausa plural formation are discussed here, in particular, there is no analysis of reduplication (see Newman 1972, 1986a; Leben 1977a, b) or tone (see Newman 1986b). Furthermore, not all plural classes are included because classes like -akii and -ii do not have augmentation. These classes have predominantly polysyllabic roots.

(4) root   singular   plural   gloss
    tantabar   tàntabàraa   tàntabàrúu   "pigeon"
    jeemaag   jeemaagee   jeemaagúu   "fruit bat"
    kadangar   kadangaree   kadangarúu   "lizard"

The classes examined here, as seen in (1), all have monosyllabic roots. It will be shown that the fact that augmentation affects monosyllabic roots is not fortuitous since it is precisely these roots that are predicted to be affected by the Prosodic Morphology Hypothesis.

2. -*unaa* plurals

The -unaa plural class provides a rather straightforward case of prosodic requirements for the base. As shown in (5), the -unaa morpheme is simply suffixed to roots except roots that are CVC.[2] In this case, the root-final consonant surfaces as a geminate.

(5)		root	singular	plural	gloss
a.	CVC	bak	bàkáa	bákkúnàa	"bow"
		dam	dámìi	dámmúnàa	"bundle"
		cik	cíkìi	cíkkúnàa	"stomach"
b.	CVVC	jaak	jàakíi	jáakúnàa	"donkey"
		goor	gòoráa	góorúnàa	"gourd"
		kees	kéesòo	kéesúnàa	"matting"
c.	CVC$_i$C$_j$	barg	bàrgóo	bárgúnàa	"blanket"
		darn	dàrníi	dárnúkàa	"fence"
		karf	kàrfúu	kárfúnàa	"belt"
d.	CVC$_i$C$_i$	g^{w}agg	g^{w}ággòo	g^{w}ággúnàa	"baboon"

As proposed by Newman (1972), and adopted by all subsequent analyses (see Leben 1977a, b, Halle and Vergnaud 1980, Tuller 1981), the CVC roots are insufficient as a base for plural suffixation because they are too "small." In Newman's analysis, the base of the plural morpheme must be a heavy syllable (which other root types are), but CVC roots are light. They are made heavy by geminating the final consonant.

Newman's insight is easily translated into moraic phonology (McCarthy and Prince 1986, Hayes 1989). The CVC roots differ from the other types insofar as the CVC roots are monomoraic, but the other root types are all bimoraic which is equal to a heavy foot. CVVC roots are bimoraic since long vowels are underlyingly bimoraic (McCarthy and Prince 1986), the CVC$_i$C$_i$ roots are bimoraic since underlying geminates are prespecified by association to a mora (Inkelas and Cho 1993, Davis this volume), and the CVC$_i$C$_j$ roots are bimoraic by satisfaction of Weight-by-Position (Hayes 1989, Zec 1992). The surface forms of these roots in the plural are shown in (6).

(6) a. [jaa.ku.naa.]   b. [bar.gu.naa.]   c. [g^{w}ag.gu.naa.]

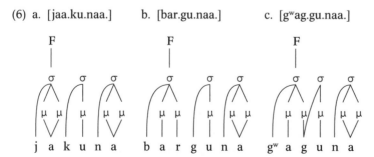

The absence of augmentation with the bimoraic roots in (6) means that these roots are suitable bases for the plural. The prosodic requirement on the base, in conformity to the Prosodic Morphology Hypothesis, can be characterized as a template that equals a bimoraic foot. As noted by McCarthy and Prince (1990a, b), the foot serves as the minimal word so another way to describe the base for *-unaa* plural formation is that *-unaa* must be suffixed to a minimal word.

The role of word minimality is evident from the augmentation that effects CVC roots. These roots, being monomoraic, are subminimal, but they must conform to the minimal word requirement of the base. This is achieved by satisfaction of a constraint called FOOTFORM (Prince and Smolensky 1993) which defines the shape of metrical constituents in either analyses of stress systems or morphological templates. FOOTFORM for the *-unaa* plural is equal to the bimoraic foot.

(7) *-unaa* base: FOOTFORM = H

Satisfaction of FOOTFORM manifests itself as a geminate. This is shown in (8) where there are two representations of the plural of /bak/. In (8a), *-unaa* is attached to a monomoraic base which violates FOOTFORM, but in (8b), on the other hand, *-unaa* is attached to a bimoraic base where the second mora of the base is linked to the root-final consonant, which is the representation of a geminate.

(8) a. *[ba.ku.naa.]   b. [bak.ku.naa.]

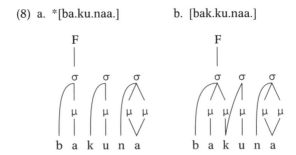

The augmentation of the CVC roots in the *-unaa* plural is accounted for by the requirement that a base must be a minimal word, which is defined through satisfaction of FOOTFORM. The CVVC and the CVC_iC_i roots in (6) do not have augmentations because these roots satisfy FOOTFORM since these roots are underlyingly bimoraic. The CVC_iC_j roots satisfy FOOTFORM by also satisfying Weight-by-Position; hence, the postvocalic consonant of the root is parsed moraically without augmentation.

The -*unaa* plural demonstrates the role of Prosodic Morphology in Hausa plural formation, but so far Optimality Theory has not been evoked because there has been no constraint conflict. The discussion of the -*aaCee* plurals in the next section demonstrates how the prosodic requirement of the base can interact with other well-formedness constraints.

3. -*aaCee* plurals

From looking at (9), the type of augmentation in the -*aaCee* plural is quite different from the -*unaa* plural. The CVC roots in (9) have a copy of the root-final consonant between the vowels of the plural morpheme and the CVC_iC_j roots have the postvocalic consonants separated by the vowels of the plural morpheme. These two root types have a broken plural pattern in contrast to the CVVC and the CVC_iC_i roots which have sound plurals with the vowels of the plural morpheme separated by [y].

(9)		root	singular	plural	gloss
a.	CVC	kar	káráa	káràarée	"corn stalk"
		ƙas	ƙásáa	ƙásàašée	"land"
		dam	dámóo	dámàamée	"land monitor"
b.	CVC_iC_j	birn	birnii	bíràanée	"city"
		kulk	kúlkíi	kúlàakée	"cudgel"
		kask	káskóo	kásàakée	"bowl"
c.	CVVC	beeb	béebée	béebàayée	"deaf mute"
		duul	dúulúu	dúulàayée	"basket"
		ɓuuz	ɓúuzúu	ɓúuzàayée	"camel trader"
d.	CVC_iC_i	gamm	gámmóo	gámmàayée	"head pad"
		hann	hánnúu	hánnàayée	"sleeve"
		tukk	túkkúu	túkkàayée	"plait of hair"

Looking at just the CVC and the CVC_iC_j roots, broken plurals have the canonical shape [CV.CVV.CVV.]. Following McCarthy and Prince's (1990a, b) analysis of broken plurals in Arabic (where it is proposed that plural formation involves an iambic (light^heavy) template, e.g., [{su.laa.}tiin]), a light^heavy iambic template can be extracted from the Hausa plural, that is, [{CV.CVV.}CVV]. From these plurals, it is proposed that the base for the -*aaCee* plural is a light^heavy iambic foot, which is a minimal word. As in the *-unaa* plural, word minimality is characterized by satisfaction of FOOTFORM.

(10) Base for *-aaCee*: FOOTFORM = L H

Plural formation for different root types, as shown below, involves the interaction of constraints. In this section, the constraints on the well-formedness of the base for the plural are ranked as defined by Optimality Theory.[3] Hence, surface violations of constraints occur. In particular, violations of FOOTFORM are crucial to account for the distribution of broken and sound plurals and so it is necessary to clarify what a violation of FOOTFORM is. FOOTFORM is interpreted here as a scalar constraint (see Prince and Smolensky 1993). Following Prince's (1990) analysis of metrical parsing, the maximal expansion of the iamb is preferred to other possible expansions, that is L H > {L L, H}. The preference for the maximal expansion of the iamb is used here for morphological templates as well so a surface violation of FOOTFORM means a submaximal iambic template is preferred. In accordance with Optimality Theory, different expansions of the iamb are simultaneously compared. This is at the heart of the distribution of broken and sound plurals. In brief, the sound plurals for CVVC and CVC_iC_i roots occur as a consequence of surface violations of FOOTFORM, that is, the L H template is not optimal. The discussion begins by first looking at broken plurals.

3.1 Broken plurals

3.1.1 CVC roots

Since FOOTFORM for the *-aaCee* plural is a L H iamb, a CVC root like /kar/ satisfies FOOTFORM as [karaa]. The problem now turns to the occurrence of the copy of the root-final consonant between the vowels of the plural. It is proposed that root-final consonant duplication arises as a result of satisfying a condition on the base of the plural that states that the base must have a final consonant. This condition on morphologically defined domains has been noted in other languages, notably Arabic (McCarthy and Prince 1990a, b) and English (McCarthy 1993). McCarthy (1993) calls this constraint FINAL-C, which prohibits a prosodic word from being vowel-final.

(11) FINAL-C
      *V]$_{PrWd}$

Satisfying both FOOTFORM and FINAL-C creates the base [karaar] and the syllabification of the plural [ka.raa.ree] is shown in (12).[4]

(12) [ka.raa.ree]

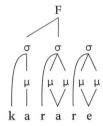

k a r a r e

3.1.2 CVC$_i$C$_j$ roots

The broken plurals of CVC$_i$C$_j$ roots in (9) satisfy the two constraints mentioned above, that is, the base is a L H iamb and the base ends with a consonant. For example, the plural [biraanee] has the base [biraan] as in (13b). The broken plural pattern, in fact, is the only way to satisfy both constraints on the base. If the segments of the root were parsed contiguously into the base of the plural as in (13a), the base for the plural would be a H foot and some consonant, [Δ], would separate the vowels of the plural morpheme.

(13) a. [bir.naa.Δee]   b. [bi.raa.nee]

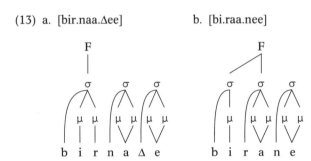

b i r n a Δ e   b i r a n e

The two candidates for the plural of /birn/ in (13) differ in two crucial respects alluded to above. (13a) is a sound plural where the segments of the root are contiguous in the base, but the base is a H foot. In (13b), the base is a L H foot but the segmental structure of the base is not equal to the root. The lack of segmental contiguity in the base of (13b) violates McCarthy and Prince's (1993a, 1994) CONTIGUITY, which states that segments are mapped contiguously into prosodically defined domains.

CONTIGUITY, as proposed by McCarthy and Prince (1994), concerns reduplication and ensures that "the portion of the base standing in correspondence forms a contiguous string as the correspondent of the reduplicant." CONTIGUITY here involves correspondence between morphological categories, namely the root and the base.

It is evident from (13) that FOOTFORM and CONTIGUITY conflict since they cannot be satisfied simultaneously. The satisfaction of FOOTFORM in (13b) compels a violation of CONTIGUITY and the satisfaction of CONTIGUITY in (13a) compels a base that is a submaximal iamb. Therefore, FOOTFORM dominates CONTIGUITY.[5]

(14) FOOTFORM ≫ CONTIGUITY: /birn + aa ee/

Candidate		FOOTFORM	CONTIGUITY
(13a)	[bir]naa∆ee	|H|!	
(13b) ☞	[biraan]ee	|L H|	*

The CVC_iC_j roots provide the first example of a constraint violation. The violation of CONTIGUITY is compelled by the satisfaction of FOOTFORM. The dominance of FOOTFORM, that is, the L H base, forces a broken plural. The broken plural pattern for CVC roots also occurs as a consequence of satisfying FOOTFORM. Root-final consonant duplication satisfies FINAL-C, although this is not considered a violation of CONTIGUITY.[6] The plural forms of the CVC roots in fact satisfy all relevant constraints. Constraint violation, as shown in the next section, is crucial in the account of plurals for CVVC and CVC_iC_j roots.

3.2 The sound plurals

The noticeable difference in the plurals of CVVC and CVC_iC_j roots in (9) is the [y] between the vowels of the plural morpheme. Of particular importance is the absence of root-final consonant duplication with these plurals, as there is with plurals of CVC roots. The [y] in (9c) and (9d) is proposed here to be the epenthetic [y] that resolves hiatus elsewhere in Hausa (Schuh 1989).

(15) shaa+ ar   shaayar   "to water"
     soo+ ayyaa   sooyayyaa   "mutual love"

Recall that root-final consonant duplication is related to satisfying FINAL-C thus making the [aa] part of the plural internal to the base. Since the CVVC and the CVC$_i$C$_i$ roots do not have final consonant duplication in their plural forms, the [aa] part of the plural cannot be internal to the base. In fact, there is complementary distribution between root-final consonant duplication and epenthesis. This can be seen by comparing the plural forms for /kar/ and /duul/.

(16) a. [karaar]ee   b. *[kar]aayee
     c. [duul]aayee   d. *[duulaal]ee

Since consonant duplication occurs to satisfy FINAL-C, which is a property of the base, epenthesis occurs to resolve hiatus outside the domain of the base. Epenthesis, therefore, cannot occur with a CVC root because the base, as shown in (16b), would be a L foot violating FOOT-FORM. For the CVVC root, consonant duplication and the internal [aa] in (16d) create a base that consists of two heavy syllables which also violates FOOTFORM.

The complementary distribution of consonant duplication and epenthesis is a consequence of the size of the base and follows from constraint interaction. FILL, Prince and Smolensky's constraint prohibiting empty positions, conflicts with FOOTFORM. This is evident from comparing (16c) and (16d). Satisfying FILL compels a non-iambic H H base in (16d). The base in (16c), where there is a surface violation of FILL, is actually the less preferred H iamb. Even though the H iamb is less preferred than a L H iamb, it is more harmonic than the non-iambic H H. FOOTFORM, therefore, dominates FILL.

(17) FOOTFORM ≫ FILL: /duul + aa ee/

Candidate	FOOTFORM	FILL
☞ [duul]aaΔee	|H|	*
[duulaal]ee	|H H|!	

The sound plurals occur because the H expansion of the iamb is most harmonic. This means that the H expansion must be preferred to the maximal L H expansion as well. To show this involves ranking other constraints. Since the roots with sound plurals are underlyingly bimoraic, a L H base would require leaving one of these moras unparsed. For example, the long vowel of the root /duul/ must be short on the surface as in *[{du<u>.laa.}lee.] for the first syllable of the foot to be light. The short-surface vowel in this candidate involves a violation of Parse-μ, which conflicts with FootForm since satisfying Parse-μ compels a less preferred iamb for the base. Since all moras are parsed, the plural cannot have a L H base, but rather it has a H base (and an epenthetic consonant). Hence Parse-μ dominates FootForm.

(18) Parse-μ ≫ FootForm: /duul + aa ee/

Candidate	Parse-μ	FootForm
☞ [duul]aaΔee		|H|
[du<u>laal]ee	*!	|L H|

The mix of broken and sound plurals in the -aaCee class occurs as a consequence of best satisfying the constraint rankings established so far. The composite ranking is shown in (19b).

(19) a. FootForm ≫ Contiguity   (14)
        FootForm ≫ Fill   (17)
        Parse-μ ≫ FootForm   (18)
    b. Parse-μ ≫ FootForm ≫ Contiguity, Fill

As shown in (20), this ranking accounts for the plurals of the different root types.

(20) a. FootForm ≫ Contiguity, Fill: /kar + aa ee/

Candidate	FootForm	Contiguity	Fill
[karr]aaΔee	|H|!		*
[kar]aaΔee	|L|!		*
☞ [karaar]ee	|L H|		

b. FootForm ≫ Contiguity, Fill: /birn + aa ee/

Candidate	FootForm	Contiguity	Fill
[birn]aaΔee	|H|!		*
☞ [biraan]ee	|L H|	*	

c. PARSE-μ ≫ FOOTFORM ≫ FILL: /duul + aa ee/

Candidate	PARSE-μ	FOOTFORM	FILL
[du<u>laal]ee	*!	|L H|	
☞ [duul]aaΔee		|H|	*
[duulaal]ee		|H H|!	

d. PARSE-μ ≫ FOOTFORM ≫ FILL: /gamm + aa ee/

Candidate	PARSE-μ	FOOTFORM	FILL
[ga<m>maam]ee	*!	|L H|	
☞ [gamm]aaΔee		|H|	*
[gammaam]ee		|H H|!	

CVC and CVC_iC_j roots, as illustrated in (20a) and (20b), have a broken plural because any other candidate expansion of the iamb violates FOOTFORM. For the CVC_iC_j roots, the CONTIGUITY violation is inconsequential. The sound plurals for the CVVC and the CVC_iC_j roots occur as a result of a H base for the plural. This is due to surface violations of FOOTFORM, that is, preferring a submaximal expansion of the iamb, under the duress to satisfy PARSE-μ.

One root type not discussed is roots with nasal-stop sequences which have sound plurals.

(21) root   singular   plural   gloss
     gunt   guntuu   guntaayee   "short person"
     bang   bangoo   bangaayee   "wall"
     gwant   gwantoo   gwantaayee   "village"

The sound plural pattern for this root type, as proposed by Tuller (1981), is related to the integrity of nasal-stop sequences. In Optimality Theoretic terms, the integrity of the sequence means that the sound plural [guntaayee] of /gunt/ is more harmonic than the broken plural [gunaatee] where the nasal-stop sequence is not adjacent. One way to account for the sound plurals in (21), proposed by Davis (this volume), is to claim that the nasals are underlyingly moraic. The integrity phenomenon follows since a broken plural would violate PARSE-μ. In (22), the mora associated with the nasal, $μ_n$, is unparsed.

(22) *[gu.naa.tee]

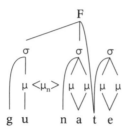

Since Parse-µ is ranked above FootForm, the sound plural is preferred. An alternative to underlying moraicity of the nasal is to say assimilation of the stop to the nasal is the most harmonic way of supplying place features for the nasal. These two views of nasal-stop integrity both have their merits, but the issue is not pursued here.

The combined Prosodic Morphology and Optimality Theoretic approach to root augmentation provides a unique way to capture the distribution of broken and sound plurals in the -aaCee plural class. Augmentation occurs only when the root is not a minimal word. This is in essence captured by Newman (1972) although it is stated in different terms. However, the procedural approach to account for the broken plural proposed by Newman is problematic. According to Newman, a CVC root like /kar/ becomes a suitable base for plural by gemination of the root-final consonant and then there is [aa] infixation, e.g., /kar/ → karr → [karaaree]. Although gemination makes the root the proper size, that is, a heavy syllable, problems emerge because CVC roots should neutralize with CVC_iC_i roots, which have sound plurals. In the proposal here, the base is a L H foot, not a heavy syllable. Therefore, there is no intermediate gemination. CVC roots and CVC_iC_i roots do not neutralize because only CVC roots can satisfy the L H base.

It is not an accident that CVVC and CVC_iC_i roots have sound plurals since these roots, which are underlyingly bimoraic, are minimal words. However, it is difficult to account for this within a theory in which all constraints must be satisfied at a particular level of representation. Without surface violations of constraints, there is no template that is satisfied by all root types. There would be a L H template for some roots and a H template for others and the condition on the distribution of the templates would be "the base is L H except when the root is equal to a minimal word." The Optimality Theoretic approach directly accounts for the distribution of broken and sound plurals through violations of FootForm. This allows for a single base, the L H iamb, which accounts for the broken plural pattern. The "except when a minimal word" fact follows since augmenting a bimoraic root creates a base that exceeds iambicity. Rather than exceed iambicity, the base is a H iamb, which is equivalent to the root.

4. -ooCii plural

The -ooCii plural, which is the most productive plural (Parsons 1975), differs significantly from the -unaa and the -aaCee plurals. As evident in (23), plural formation involves root-final consonant duplication for all root types.

(23)		root	singular	plural	gloss
	a. CVC	bar	báràa	báróoríi	"servant"
		cak	cákìi	cákóokíi	"cheque"
		taš	tášàa	tášóošíi	"station"
	b. CVC_iC_j	fark	fàrkáa	fárkóokíi	"paramour"
		hask	háskée	háskóokíi	"light"
		birk	bírkìi	birkóokíi	"brick"
	c. CVVC	taag	táagàa	táagóogíi	"window"
		taas	taasaa	táasóosíi	"bowl"
		ƙuus	ƙúusàa	ƙúusoošíi	"nail"
	d. CVC_iC_i	dall	dallaa	dállóolíi	
		hakk	hákkìi	hákkóokíi	"wage"
		fann	fánnìi	fánnóoníi	"subject"

Root-final consonant duplication, as discussed, satisfies Final-C. Recall in the analysis of -aaCee plurals, consonant duplication does not occur if the base exceeds iambicity. For consonant duplication to occur with CVVC and CVC_iC_i roots in the -ooCii class, iambicity must be irrelevant since the base in this case is H H, e.g., [{taa.soo.}sii.]. Therefore, the -ooCii base must be atemplatic: it is formed by the root plus /oo/. Since /oo/ is always part of the base, [y] epenthesis never occurs.

(24) a. [baroor]ii
     b. [hakkook]ii   *[hakk]ooyii

To summarize, the three plural morphemes discussed so far have the three different requirements on the base shown in (25).

(25) *-unaa*:   FootForm = H
    -aaCee: FootForm = L H
    -ooCii   atemplatic: base = root + /oo/

The bases for the *-unaa* and the *-aaCee* plurals are prosodically defined. For the *-unaa* plural, the base, as defined by FootForm, is a H foot and for the *-aaCee* plural, the base is a L H foot. Surface violations of FootForm account for the H base in the *-aaCee* plural. The *-ooCii* plural, in contrast, has an atemplatic base; hence, all roots exhibit the same augmentation as a result of satisfying Final-C.

5. *-aa* plural

The *-aa* plural shows the greatest variety of augmentation patterns. As shown in (26), no two root types have the same canonical surface shape in the plural.[7]

(26)		root	singular	plural	gloss
a.	CVC	tab	tábòo	tâbbáa	"scar"
		tud	túdùu	tûddáa	"high ground"
		kag	kágòo	kâggáa	"mud wall"
b.	CVVC	saas	sáašèe	sâssáa	"region"
		raas	ráašèe	râssáa	"branch"
		kaaɗ	káaɗòo	kâɗɗáa	"indigenous people"
c.	CVCC	tark	tárkóo	táràkkáa	"trap"
		kirz	kìrjíi	kírìzzáa	"chest"
		sird	sírdìi	sírìddáa	"saddle"

The CVC roots of this class, like the CVC roots in the *-unaa* class, augment by gemination of the root-final consonant and the CVCC roots have a broken plural pattern. Notice, however, that the broken plural pattern here contains a short vowel (that is a copy of the root vowel) and a geminate. This is different from the broken plural found in the *-aaCee* class. The CVVC roots in (26) augment by weight transfer, that is, the long vowel followed by a consonant, /VVC/, surfaces as a short vowel followed by a geminate, [VCC]. All plurals, however, have geminates of the root-final consonant.

The augmentations in the *-aa* plural involve satisfaction of a prosodically defined base which is proposed to be a L H foot. However, constraint interaction alone cannot be responsible for the surface forms in (26). The representation of the *-aa* plural morpheme also plays a critical role. It is proposed here that the *-aa* plural morpheme is a bipartite morpheme like the *-aaCee* and the *-ooCii* morphemes. The *-aa* morpheme, as shown in (27), contains an empty mora.

(27) μ   μ μ
        \/
        a

The empty mora is parsed at the right edge of the root, satisfying McCarthy and Prince's (1993a, b) ALIGN, which in this case is specifically ALIGN-R ([μ]_{af}, Rt). ALIGN is undominated and it is not included in the tableaux in the following discussion.

5.1 The CVC roots

Root-final consonant gemination with CVC roots is a consequence of the H iamb as the base for the plural in violation of FOOTFORM. The source of the geminate is the empty mora of the plural morpheme (shown as μ_p in (28)) associated to the root-final consonant of /tab/. The question, of course, is why the H base is preferred to (28b), the candidate with the L H base.[8]

(28) a. [tab.baa.]   b. [ta.bab.baa.]

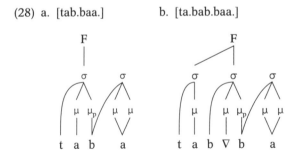

Looking at (28b), it also has a geminate for the same reason as (28a), but (28b) also contains an empty position, in violation of FILL-V, which is required to satisfy the L H foot. FOOTFORM and FILL-V clearly conflict since the satisfaction of the latter compels a violation of the former.

(29) FILL-V ≫ FOOTFORM: /tab +aa/

Candidate	FILL-V	FOOTFORM
(28a) ☞ [tabb]aa		|H|
(28b) [tabⱽbb]aa	*!	|L H|

Although the base for -*aa* plural is proposed to be L H, the H base is preferred under the duress of satisfying FILL-V.

5.2 The CVCC roots

Since the absence of a broken plural pattern for CVC roots is a consequence of FILL-V dominating FOOTFORM, the presence of the broken plural with CVCC roots must involve the violation of a high-ranking constraint in the sound plural candidate. Compare the candidate plural forms in (30).

(30) a. [sird.daa.]   b. [si.rid.daa.]   c. [sir.daa]

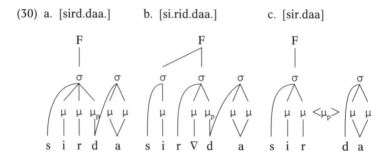

(30c) is nonharmonic since PARSE-μ dominates FOOTFORM, as already established.

(31) PARSE-μ ≫ FOOTFORM: /sird +aa/

Candidate	PARSE-μ	FOOTFORM
(30c) [sir]daa	*!	|H|
(30b) ☞ [sirⱽdd]aa		|L H|

A comparison of the candidates with faithfully parsed moras is more interesting. (30a) contains a trimoraic syllable since the vowel is underlyingly moraic, the postvocalic consonant is moraic through Weight-by-Position, and the root-final consonant is moraic through association to the mora of the plural morpheme. This trimoraic syllable violates the bimoraic size of Hausa syllables (cf. Leben 1980). This restriction is quite common and, as McCarthy and Prince (1986) note, the bimoraic maximum is a general constraint on syllable well-formedness. This constraint, called BıMax, conflicts with Fıll-V. This is evident in (30b) where the broken plural contains maximally bimoraic syllables and an empty position. Therefore, BıMax dominates Fıll-V.

(32) BıMax ≫ Fıll-V: /sird +aa/

Candidate	BıMax	Fıll-V
(30a) [sirdd]aa	*!	
(30b) ☞ [sirVdd]aa		*

The broken plural pattern in the -aa class is the maximal parse of moras and segments that satisfies BıMax and FootForm. The Fıll-V violation is inconsequential, which differs from the case of CVC roots where the Fıll-V violation is fatal.

5.3 The CVVC roots

The weight transfer exhibited by the CVVC roots, an augmentation not seen with other plurals, follows straightforwardly from the constraint rankings established so far. These rankings are summarized in (33).

(33) BıMax ≫ Fıll-V   (32)
     Fıll-V ≫ FootForm   (29)
     Parse-μ ≫ FootForm   (18)

One pair-wise ranking not established is between BıMax and Parse-μ. However, these constraints do conflict and can be used to account for closed-syllable shortening in Hausa (cf. Leben 1980, Schuh 1989).

(34) gidaa   "house"   gidan   "the house"
     riimii   "kapok tree"   riimin   "the kapok tree"
     tsuntsuu "bird"   tsuntsun "the bird"

Closed-syllable shortening occurs as a consequence of leaving a mora unparsed to preserve the bimoraic maximum of syllable weight. Hence BıMax dominates Parse-μ.

362   Sam Rosenthall

(35) BⅰMAX ≫ PARSE-μ: /gidaa+ n/

Candidate	BⅰMAX	PARSE-μ
gi.da:n.	*!	
☞ gi.da<:>n.		*

The combination of (33) and (35) is given in (36).

(36) BⅰMAX ≫ FILL-V, PARSE-μ ≫ FOOTFORM

To see how this ranking accounts for weight transfer with CVVC roots, consider the candidates for the plural of /saas/.

(37) a. [saas.saa.]   b. [sas.saa.]

c. [sa.sas.saa.]   d. [saa.sas.saa.]

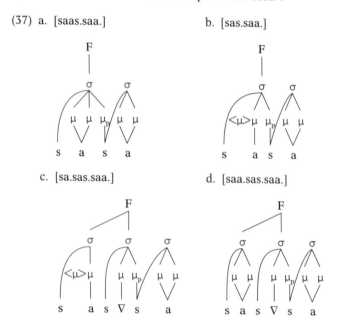

In (37), there are two sound-plural candidates and two broken-plural candidates. (37a) contains a parse of all segments and moras which leads to a BⅰMAX violation whereas (37b) contains a PARSE-μ violation and satisfies BⅰMAX. (37c) and (37d) are two broken-plural candidates that satisfy FINAL-C by a copy of the root-final consonant and have a FILL-V violation. (37c) also contains a PARSE-μ violation forced by satisfying the L H base. The base in (37d), on the other hand, is the non-iambic H H. In (38), it is shown how the constraint ranking in (36) predicts (37b) as the surface form.

(38) BiMax ≫ Fill-V, Parse-μ ≫ FootForm: /saas+ aa/

Candidate	BiMax	Fill-V	Parse-μ	Foot-Form
(37a) [saass]aa	*!			
(37c) [sa<a>sⱽss]aa		*	*!	|L H|
(37b) ☞ [sa<a>ss]aa			*	|H|
(37d) [saasⱽss]aa		*		|H H|!

The crucial comparison in (38) is between (37b) and (37d) because (37a) violates the undominated BiMax and (37c) violates two equally ranked constraints. The non-iambic base of (37d) is fatal because (37b) and (37d) tie with respect to higher ranking constraints.

Weight transfer, therefore, is the result of a H base for the plural morpheme that must include a parse of the empty mora of the plural morpheme. This ensures a geminate in the surface form of the *-aa* plural regardless of the root type. The short vowel in the surface form is a consequence of satisfying BiMax.

The surface forms for the other root types also follow from the ranking in (36).

(39) a. BiMax ≫ Fill-V, Parse-μ ≫ FootForm: /sird+ aa/

Candidate	BiMax	Fill-V	Parse-μ	FootForm
(30a) [sirdd]aa	*!			
(30c) [sir]daa			*	|H|!
(30b) ☞ [sirⱽdd]aa		*		|L H|

b. BiMax ≫ Fill-V, Parse-μ ≫ FootForm: /tab+ aa/

Candidate	BiMax	Fill-V	Parse-μ	FootForm
(28a) ☞ [tabb]aa				|H|
(28d) [tabⱽbb]aa		*!		|L H|

The broken plural pattern for CVCC roots is the result of the maximal expansion of the iamb. (39a), (30b) and (30c) violate equally ranked constraints. Therefore, the H expansion of the iamb is fatal for (30c). As for CVC roots, the H base in the output in (28c) follows from the FILL-V violation invoked by the L H base.

To summarize, the different augmentations associated with the -*aa* plural are the result of best satisfying conflicting constraints. The prosodic requirement is the L H iamb, but under duress of constraint satisfaction the base is the H iamb. All augmentations, including weight transfer of CVVC roots, are predicted by the constraint interaction.

6. Conclusion

Augmentations associated with some Hausa plural morphemes are accounted for by prosodically defining the base for the plural morpheme. In the -*aaCee* and the -*aa* classes the base is a L H iambic foot, which accounts for the broken plural patterns. The mixture of broken and sound plurals in the -*aaCee* class arises as a consequence of constraints that cannot be simultaneously satisfied. The sound plurals occur due to surface violations of the L H iambic foot for the base under the duress of satisfying higher ranking constraints. Likewise, the variety of augmentations in the -*aa* plural arise through violations of the L H base.

Prosodic Morphology and Optimality Theory capture the significant generalization concerning Hausa plural formation. Root augmentation crucially relies on a prosodically defined template as predicted by the Prosodic Morphology Hypothesis. However, the distribution of augmentation is accounted for by harmonic satisfaction of the prosodic requirement.

Notes

1 I thank John McCarthy who has provided many helpful comments and insights. Part of this chapter was written while I was at the School of Oriental and African Studies during 1994. From there, I wish to thank Judith Broadbent, Dick Hayward, and Phillip Jaggar for their comments and suggestions. I also want to thank the participants of the Workshop on Prosodic Morphology, Utrecht, June 1994. This research was supported by post-doctoral fellowship #752-93-0421 from the Social Science and Humanities Research Council of Canada.

2 The analysis here follows Newman (1972) and Halle and Vergnaud (1980) who propose Hausa plurals are formed by the root plus suffix. Alternative proposals by Burquest (1989) and McHugh (1993) claim that the plural is derived from the singular.

3 See McHugh (1993) and Borowsky (1995) for other Optimality Theoretic analyses of Hausa plural formation.
4 Following McCarthy (1993), the surface syllabification must contain an ambisyllabic parse to satisfy FINAL-C and ONSET simultaneously.
5 The base in all candidates is denoted by brackets.
6 Root-final consonant duplication might be considered a violation of a faithful correspondence between root and base and so it conceivably violates CONTIGUITY. Since FOOTFORM dominates CONTIGUITY, the analysis does not change if root-final consonant duplication is a CONTIGUITY violation.
7 I was unable to find CVC$_i$C$_i$ roots in this class.
8 It is worthwhile noting that (28b) is grammatical in some dialects (Parsons 1975).

References

Borowsky, Toni. 1995. Hausa plurals, in A. Traill and R. Vossen (eds.), *The Complete Linguist: Papers in Memory of Patrick Dickens*, Cologne: Koppe.
Burquest, Donald A. 1989. A note on Hausa plurals, *Studies in African Linguistics* 20: 265–78.
Davis, Stuart. This volume. On the moraic representation of underlying geminates: evidence from Prosodic Morphology.
Halle, Morris, and Jean-Roger Vergnaud. 1980. Three dimensional phonology, *Journal of Linguistic Research* 1: 83–105.
Hayes, Bruce. 1989. Compensatory lengthening in moraic phonology, *Linguistic Inquiry* 20: 253–306.
Inkelas, Sharon, and Young-mee Yu Cho. 1993. Inalterability as prespecification, *Language* 69: 529–74.
Leben, William R. 1977a. Doubling and reduplication in Hausa plurals, in A. Juilland (ed.), *Linguistic Studies Offered to Joseph Greenberg*, Saratoga, CA: Anma Libri.
  1977b. Parsing Hausa plurals, in P. Newman and R. M. Newman (eds.), *Papers in Chadic Linguistics*, Leiden: Afrika-Studiecentrum.
  1980. A metrical analysis of length, *Linguistic Inquiry* 11: 497–509.
McCarthy, John J. 1993. A case of surface constraint violation, *Canadian Journal of Linguistics* 38: 207–63.
McCarthy, John J., and Alan S. Prince. 1986. Prosodic Morphology, ms. University of Massachusetts, Amherst, MA and Brandeis University, Waltham, MA.
  1990a. Foot and word in Prosodic Morphology: the Arabic broken plural, *Natural Language and Linguistic Theory* 8: 209–83.

1990b. Prosodic Morphology and templatic morphology, in M. Eid and J. J. McCarthy (eds.), *Perspectives on Arabic Linguistics: Papers from the Second Symposium*, Amsterdam: Benjamins.

1993a. Prosodic Morphology I: constraint interaction and satisfaction, ms. University of Massachusetts, Amherst, MA and Rutgers University, New Brunswick, NJ.

1993b. Generalized alignment, in G. E. Booij and J. van Marle (eds.), *Yearbook of Morphology 1993*, Dordrecht: Kluwer, 79–153.

1994a. The emergence of the unmarked: Optimality in Prosodic Morphology, in M. Gonzàlez (ed.), *Proceedings of the North East Linguistic Society* 24; Amherst, MA: Graduate Linguistic Student Association, University of Massachusetts, 333–79.

1994b. Prosodic Morphology, in J. Goldsmith (ed.), *Handbook of Phonology*, Oxford: Basil Blackwell.

McHugh, Brian. 1993. Optimality Theory and Hausa plural nouns. Paper presented at the Rutgers Optimality Workshop, October 1993.

Newman, Paul. 1972. Syllable weight as a phonological variable, *Studies in African Linguistics* 3: 301–23.

1986a. Reduplicated nouns in Hausa, *Journal of African Languages and Linguistics* 8: 115–32.

1986b. Tone and affixation in Hausa, *Studies in African Linguistics* 17: 249–67.

Newman, Roxanna Ma. 1990. *An English-Hausa Dictionary*, New Haven, CT: Yale University Press.

Parsons, F. W. 1975. Hausa and Chadic, in J. and T. Bynon (eds.), *Hamito-Semitica*, The Hague: Mouton.

Prince, Alan S. 1990. Quantitative consequences of rhythmic organization, *Proceedings of the Chicago Linguistic Society* 26.

Prince, Alan S., and Paul Smolensky. 1993. Optimality Theory: constraint interaction in generative grammar, ms. Rutgers University, New Brunswick, NJ and University of Colorado, Boulder, CO.

Schuh, Russell G. 1989. Long vowels and diphthongs in Miya and Hausa, in P. Newman and R. D. Botne (eds.), *Current Approaches to African Linguistics* vol. 5, Dordrecht: Foris.

Tuller, Laurice. 1981. On nominal inflection in Hausa, *UCLA Occasional Papers in Linguistics* 4: 117–57.

Zec, Draga. 1992. Constraints on moraic structure. Paper presented at University of Massachusetts, Amherst, MA. 30 April 1992.

10   Prosodic optimality and prefixation in Polish

Grażyna Rowicka

1. Introduction

The present chapter[1] provides an account of vowel-zero alternations in prefixed words in Polish. I will propose a novel, prosodic analysis of vowels alternating with zero. The vowel-surfacing patterns provide evidence that prefixed words differ in terms of their prosodic structure. I will show that different prosodification is the result of the interaction between various well-formedness constraints demanding the alignment of prosodic and morphological categories. These constraints also determine the pattern of vowel surfacing in multiply prefixed verbs.

Several facts in Polish indicate that the prefix and its host stem do not generally belong to the same prosodic word (PrWd). Phonological processes whose domain is the PrWd have often been noted not to apply across the prefixal juncture. This is illustrated in the example of palatal assimilation in (1). In the words in the right-hand column the consonant [n] is palatalized to [ń] before the front vowel [e]. PrWd-internally in *bliźnie* (cf. (1a)) also the consonant preceding [n] is affected, due to palatal assimilation. As shown in (1b), however, palatal assimilation cannot apply across the prefixal juncture.

(1) Palatal assimilation (cf. Rowicka 1994)
  a. applicable PrWd-internally
     bli[zn]a   "scar"   bli[źń]e   "scar-LOC-SG"
     *bli[źń]e
  b. blocked across prefixal juncture
     [z=n]osić   "to bear-IMPERF."   [z=ń]eść   "to bear"
     *[ź=ń]eść
     where "=" marks the prefixal juncture

A number of other processes which exhibit such asymmetry are mentioned in Szpyra (1989). They indicate that the prefix is prosodically separate from the host stem which includes the morphological root and suffixes.

On the other hand, however, in a class of prefixed verbs the prefix and the stem constitute a single PrWd, as evidenced by vowel-zero alternations. In Polish an underlying *yer*, i.e., a vowel alternating with zero, surfaces as [e] only when followed by another *yer within the same PrWd*. Before any other vowel or PrWd-finally, *yers* do not show up. An example is given in (2).

(2) *Yer* surfacing and *yer* deletion
   a. X X → E ø   as in /cukXr+X/   cukiEr[2]   "sugar-NOM-SG"
   b. X V → ø V   as in /cukXr+u/   cukru   "sugar-GEN-SG"
   where "X" = an underlying *yer*
      "V" = any other vowel
      "E" = phonetic [e] derived from a *yer*[3]

The stem *yer* emerges as [e] before another *yer* in the inflectional ending, cf. (2a), but not before a "proper," i.e., nonalternating, vowel, (2b). Being PrWd-final, the *yer* of the inflectional ending in (2a) never surfaces itself.

If the prefix and its host stem do not belong to one PrWd, the prefix-final *yer* should never surface, just like the inflectional *yer* in (2a). However, this prediction turns out to be wrong. The prefix-final *yer does* surface if it is followed by another *yer* in the morphological root. A puzzling pattern is found in verbs with two *yer*-containing prefixes. Neither of the prefix *yers* surfaces if followed by a "proper" vowel in the root. However, before a *yer* in the root, the *yer* of the *first* prefix surfaces, while the one directly preceding the root does not. Examples are provided in (3).

(3) Vowel-zero alternations in singly prefixed verbs
   a. Roots without *yers*   b. Roots with *yers*
      z=nieść   "to bear"   zE=brać   "to collect"
      od=dać   "to give back"   odE=tchnąć "to relax"
   Vowel-zero alternations in doubly prefixed verbs
   c. Roots without *yers*   d. Roots with *yers*
      w=z=nieść   "to raise"   wE=z=brać   "to swell up"
      w=z=rosnąć "to grow up"   wE=s=tchnąć "to sigh"

In (3a) and (3c) prefixes precede roots with "proper" vowels, while in (3b) and (3d) they precede roots with non-surfacing *yers* /bXr/ and /dXch/. The evidence for the root *yers* comes from related forms (see (7) below). Prefix *yer* surfacing in the prefixed words in (3b) and (3d) shows that these items constitute single PrWds,[4] while the blocking of Palatal Assimilation in *znieść* in (3a) and *wznieść* in (3c) shows that those verbs are not single PrWds. This difference in the prosodic structure between groups of prefixed words calls for an explanation. Previous studies have failed to offer a satisfactory account. In particular, they could not predict correctly the *yer*-surfacing pattern in doubly prefixed words.

Before proposing a new analysis, I will present some more facts concerning vowel-zero alternations in Polish.

2. Preliminaries

2.1 Vowel-zero alternations

The phonological representation of *yers* has been a subject of heated debate in the literature. Since they are in a way only "potential" segments (i.e., phonetically realized only in some contexts), in non-linear studies *yers* have been analyzed as lacking some aspect of the multidimensional segmental structure that other vowels have. One interpretation may be that underlying *yers* have melodic specification, but lack a timing slot. Alternatively, they may have a skeletal position, but lack melodic specification. Both views have found their advocates (see e.g., Rubach 1985 and Bethin 1992 versus Spencer 1986, Gussmann 1997, Gussmann and Kaye 1993, and Szpyra 1992). Epenthetic analyses of *yers* have also been proposed (see, e.g., Czaykowska-Higgins 1988 and Gorecka 1988), but they have been shown to be untenable, e.g., by Bethin (1992), Szpyra (1992) and Gussmann and Kaye (1993). Accordingly, I adopt the view that *yers* are present underlyingly.

A simple pattern of *yer* surfacing and deletion has been illustrated in (2). Observe that a *yer* receives phonetic realization *only if* it is followed by another *yer*. The only context where a *single yer* surfaces is in derived imperfective (DI) verbs. Consider the examples below. A *yer* in the root remains silent in the primary verb (4b), but surfaces in the DI form of the same verb (4c), although it is followed by the DI /aj/ suffix and not by another *yer*. However, the phonetic reflex of such *yers* is different: it is [e] only when [r] follows (due to an independently motivated phono-tactic constraint in Polish) and otherwise [y].

(4) *Yer* surfacing in DI verbs

    a. Root   b. Primary verb   c. Derived imperfective

    /tXr/   wy=trzeć   wy=ciErać "to wipe out"

    /rXw/   po=rwać   po=rYwać "to kidnap"

Rowicka and van de Weijer (1994) offer an analysis according to which *yer* vocalization illustrated in (4) is forced by a prosodic-minimality condition on DI stems. The root and the DI suffix must form minimally a binary foot. To satisfy the condition, the root *yer* surfaces as *y*, i.e., the default vowel of Polish. However, such *yer* surfacing is unproductive and restricted to one morphological class.

Sequences of more than two *yers* also occur, for instance, in derivatives of the *yer*-containing diminutive suffix *-Ek*. Consider the following examples.

(5) *Yer* sequences in diminutives

    a. X X X   → E E ø

       /cukXr+Xk+X/   cukiErEk   "candy-NOM-SG"

       /cukXr+Xk+a/   cukiErka   "candy-GEN-SG"

    b. X X X X   → E E E ø

       /cukXr+Xk+Xk+X/   cukiErEczEk "candy-DIM-NOM-SG"

       /cukXr+Xk+Xk+a/   cukiErEczka "candy-DIM-GEN-SG"

(5b) gives an example of a double diminutive containing two suffixes *-Ek*. In both diminutives and double diminutives all *yers* in the sequence surface except for the last one.

Due to the great productivity of the diminutive suffix *-Ek*, the pattern of *yer* surfacing illustrated in (5) has been assumed by many phonologists to be representative of the behavior of *yer* sequences. Consider, however, the vowel-zero alternations below.[5]

(6) a. przeddziEń /przedXdXńX/ "the day before-NOM-SG"

    b. przedEdniu /przedXdXńu/ "the day before-LOC-SG"

(6a) contains a sequence of three *yers* of which only the one in the middle surfaces. In (6b) there are two *yers* of which the first turns up phonetically. The form in (6a) suggests that in a sequence of *yers* not more than *every other* one turns into [e]. Such a *yer*-surfacing paradigm is in fact in accord with the historical development of vowels alternating with zero in Slavic languages, known as "Havlik's Law."

The surfacing of every other *yer* is also argued to be the general pattern in present-day Polish by Gussmann (1997) and Gussmann and Kaye (1993). In their Government Phonology (GP) analyses *yers* are interpreted as empty syllabic nuclei. Apart from vowels alternating with zero, the presence of empty nuclei is assumed wherever consonants cannot otherwise be exhaustively syllabified according to the principles of GP. Therefore sequences of *yers* are postulated more often than in other frameworks. Such sequences behave as shown in (6). The pattern found in diminutives and illustrated in (5) is said to be restricted only to certain morphologically complex structures, where *yer* surfacing takes place in a sort of cyclic fashion.

In the present study I will follow GP analyses and assume that in the basic pattern a *yer* realized phonetically must always be followed by a silent one. The behavior of *yers* in diminutive nouns will not be considered here.

2.2 Yer surfacing in prefixes

Prefix *yers* surface only when followed by one of around thirty underived verbs.[6] Some examples, including those from (3), are given in (7).

(7) *Yer* surfacing in prefixes (cf. Szpyra 1989)

a. Root	b. Primary verb	c. Derived Imperfective	
/żXr/	podE=żreć	pod=żErać	"to eat up"
/tXr/	wE=trzeć	w=ciErać	"to rub in"
/pXch/	odE=pchnąć	od=pYchać	"to push away"
/rXw/	rozE=rwać	roz=rYwać	"to tear apart"
/bXr/	zE=brać	z=biErać	"to collect"
	wE=z=brać	w=z=biErać	"to swell up"
/dXch/	odE=tchnąć	od=dYchać	"to relax"
	wE=s=tchnąć	w=z=dYchać	"to sigh"

The roots of the verbs given in (7a) are all of a specific structure: consonant - *yer* - consonant. The evidence for the *yers* comes from DI forms of the same verbs, given in (7c). Prefix-*yer* surfacing is illustrated in (7b). The prosodic shape of prefixes does not seem to be relevant for the prefix-*yer* surfacing. *Yers* surface in monosyllabic *zE-* or *wE-*, as well as in bisyllabic *rozE-* or *odE-*. Of double prefixes, only one, *wEz-*, is of interest as containing *yers*. Others have only "proper" vowels.

From the facts presented here two basic questions arise which an adequate analysis should answer. First and foremost, how to account for the *yer* vocalization pattern, i.e., for no surfacing of single *yers*, for the surfacing of one *yer* in a sequence of two (as in singly prefixed verbs) and for the surfacing of always and only the first *yer* in a sequence of three (in doubly prefixed verbs)? Second, why do prefixed verbs containing the roots in (7a) prosodify as single PrWds, unlike prefixed verbs with other roots?

I will now proceed to develop an analysis within Optimality Theory, which theory facilitates new insights into the relationship between prosody and morphology.

3. Analysis

3.1 Prosodic status of yers

I adopt the view of *yers* as empty nuclei,[7] following the line of research done by, e.g., Spencer (1986), Piotrowski (1992), Gussmann (1997) and Gussmann and Kaye (1993). The discussion of evidence in favor of such a view deserves a separate study, and I will not go into details here. Let me point out one considerable advantage of such an analysis, namely, a fairly straightforward statement of Polish syllable structure.

Consider the syllabic structure of the nonprefixed verb *rwać* "to tear" given in (8). To indicate that the syllabic status of *yers* is not generally accepted the syllable node over the *yer* is bracketed.[8]

(8)

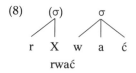

rwać

Under analyses according to which *yers* do not syllabify (they are invisible to syllabification or block it), the word begins with the consonant /r/ which cannot form one onset with the following /w/ and remains unsyllabified. To justify its appearance on the surface some *ad hoc* solution must be resorted to, such as linking the consonant directly to the PrWd node. On the other hand, in an approach where the *yer* is analyzed as a syllabic nucleus, the preceding [r] becomes its onset and is prosodically licensed on the level of the syllable. An analysis along these lines allows a large number of heavy consonantal clusters in Polish to syllabify in a straightforward manner.

However, *yer*-headed syllables do not have the same prosodic status as syllables with "proper" vowels in the nucleus. Postlexically, (nonsurfacing) *yers* are entirely ignored by stress feet. Lexically, *yers* do not seem either to count for the prosodic foot structure which incorporates "proper" vowels. Rowicka and van de Weijer's (1994) analysis points out that only vocalized *yers* may satisfy the binary foot requirement on DI verb stems. "Silent" *yers* apparently lack the prosodic weight that "proper" vowels have. I propose to capture this "weightlessness" of *yers* in terms of the absence of moras.

As evidenced by stress facts (see, e.g., Rubach and Booij 1985), "proper" vowels are grouped into trochees. Given no long-short distinction between vowels and the fact that postvocalic consonants have no effect on stress placement, Polish has generally been assumed to be weight-insensitive. However, under the "weightless" interpretation of *yers* put forward above, feet turn out to be sensitive to the presence versus absence of moras on syllabic nuclei. "Proper" vowels have one mora each and group into *moraic* trochees. Such feet are built on moras and therefore ignore moraless *yers*. The constraint Ft-Bin-μ demands that feet branch:

(9) Foot Binarity-μ (Ft-Bin-μ)
    Feet are binary on the level of the mora.

The above formulation is more specific than that adopted by Prince and Smolensky (1993). Their Ft-Bin constraint demands branchingness in terms of *either* moras *or* syllables. However, languages do not usually find a foot of two moras and one of two syllables equally good. Therefore I propose that *separate* constraints refer to the different levels of analysis, namely, Ft-Bin-μ and Ft-Bin-σ.

There are words in Polish of major lexical categories capable of bearing primary stress although they contain only one "proper" vowel (e.g., *zna* "(he) knows," *ma* "(he) has," or *zły* "angry"). The violation of

FT-BIN-μ in such cases may be due to the domination of the constraint PARSE-μ (Prince and Smolensky 1993), which demands parsing moras into feet. The ranking PARSE-μ ≫ FT-BIN-μ allows for nonbranching moraic feet.[9]

Observe that the alternating pattern of surfacing and nonsurfacing *yers* in a sequence is largely reminiscent of alternating strong and weak vowels in (stress) feet.[10] Sequences of *yers* also form some sort of binary left-headed groupings in which the head receives phonetic realization, while the dependent does not. Such groupings are strictly binary so that a single *yer* may not become the head of a nonbranching constituent and may not surface. The organization of *yer* groupings follows principles analogous to those governing foot well-formedness. I therefore propose to analyze them as a kind of foot structure. Parsing *yer*-headed syllables into feet cannot be triggered by PARSE-μ which affects other vowels, but by another constraint of the same family, PARSE-σ. Due to it, *yers* will be incorporated into *syllabic* feet. Strict binarity of such feet follows from the ranking FT-BIN-σ ≫ PARSE-σ. Note that, unlike FT-BIN-μ, the constraint FT-BIN-σ is never violated in Polish.

Parsing into syllabic feet triggers surfacing of some *yers*. The head of a *yer* foot receives prosodic weight as well as phonetic realization due to the prominence intrinsic to the strong metrical position.[11] The mora attributed to it will participate in the moraic foot structure. In this way "strong" *yers* seem to belong both to syllabic and moraic feet. However, what participates in the moraic foot structure is not a *yer* as such, but a mora associated with the head position (in a syllabic foot). It is thus not the case that one and the same nucleus can be parsed into two types of feet simultaneously, just as one vowel cannot be the nucleus of two different syllables. That is why a "proper" vowel cannot belong both to a moraic and a syllabic foot at the same time. Once it has been parsed into one kind of foot, it is no longer available for the other.

Under the ranking PARSE-σ ≫ PARSE-μ all syllables should be included in syllabic feet, irrespective of whether they have a mora, or not. The prediction is that the *yer*-surfacing pattern would depend on the configuration of syllables with "proper" vowels preceding or following sequences of *yer*-headed syllables. This is not the case in Polish, which points to the opposite ranking: PARSE-μ ≫ PARSE-σ. Given the latter hierarchy, moraic vowels will preferably be incorporated into moraic feet because syllabic feet parse syllable nodes, and not moras.[12]

The suggestion that more than one kind of foot may function within one language is not unprecedented in the literature. As observed by Prince and Smolensky (1993), some languages with weight-sensitive iambic-foot systems may, under certain conditions, allow for the formation of a weight-insensitive trochee. The analysis of Estonian in Prince (1980) points to moraic as well as syllabic trochees in its metrical system. Fikkert (1994) also shows that a weight-insensitive bisyllabic trochee is the first foot type found in the speech of children acquiring Dutch, which in its adult form is a weight-sensitive language.

The interpretation of *yers* as empty, weightless nuclei will be applied below in the analysis of the prosodic behavior of prefixed words in Polish.[13] To distinguish syllabic feet from moraic feet the former will be indicated by means of the superscript "σ" (F^σ).

3.2 ALIGN-RT

In what follows prefixes are analyzed as prosodic "proclitics" to the stem (cf. Booij 1996). The prosodic category containing a (pro)clitic and a PrWd will be referred to as a "clitic group," or CG (cf. Nespor and Vogel 1986). The structure of a prefixed word is represented in terms of prosodic bracketing in (10).

(10) $_{CG}$[Pref. $_{PrWd}$[Root + Suffix(es)]$_{PrWd}$]$_{CG}$

For the present analysis it is not essential whether the external prosodic category in (10) is labeled the CG or PrWd$_{max}$. It is, however, crucial that constraints on the well-formedness of the embedded PrWd may not *at the same time* refer to the external prosodic category containing it, which would often confuse well-formedness judgements.

Within OT the relationship between morphological and prosodic structure represented in (11) is expressed by the constraint ALIGN-RT.

(11) ALIGN-RT (ALIGN-L-ROOT in McCarthy and Prince 1993b)
Align (Root, Left, PrWd, Left)

ALIGN-RT requires that the left edge of every morphological root coincides with the left edge of a PrWd, disregarding preceding prefixes.

This gives the effect of rule blocking across the prefixal juncture, illustrated in (1b). In prefixed verbs which constitute single PrWds (cf. (3b) and (3d)), ALIGN-RT is violated. According to the assumptions of OT, constraint violation may only be forced by another, higher-ranked constraint. I will argue that in Polish ALIGN-RT is dominated by another constraint of the ALIGNMENT family, ALIGN-PRWD.

3.3 ALIGN-PRWD

ALIGN-PRWD (McCarthy and Prince 1993b) requires that the beginning of every PrWd should coincide with the beginning of a foot:

(12) ALIGN-PRWD
     Align (PrWd, Left, Foot, Left)

In the case of most prefixed words this constraint is satisfied. For instance, in the word *znieść*, (3a), the root begins with a syllable headed by a "proper" vowel which can be included in the foot structure, as shown in (13).

(13)   F
                          |
      $_{CG}$[zX $_{PrWd}$[nieść]$_{PrWd}$]$_{CG}$

                    znieść

In the example above, the foot begins at the edge of the root where the PrWd also starts.

Let us turn to words with the stems in (7a). Consider again the non-prefixed word *rwać* "to tear" whose prosodic structure is given below (cf. also (8) above).

(14)   F
                          |
      $_{PrWd}$[r X w a ć]$_{PrWd}$

                    rwać

The PrWd begins with a *yer*-headed syllable which is not parsed into a foot, hence ALIGN-PRWD is not satisfied. The constraint can be satisfied if the *yer* is parsed as the head of a non-branching syllabic foot (and as such it also participates in a moraic foot). The prosodic structure of such a candidate output is given in (15) below.

(15)   F

~PrWd~[r E w a ć]~PrWd~

           F^σ

       *rEwać

The above candidate output satisfies ALIGN-PRWD, but it contains a nonbranching syllabic foot which violates FT-BIN-σ. Under the constraint ranking ALIGN-PRWD ≫ FT-BIN-σ, the structure in (15) would be selected as optimal and all *yers* in PrWd-initial syllables in Polish should always be vocalized. Since this is not the case and *rEwać* is not the selected output, I conclude that the ranking is the opposite: FT-BIN-σ ≫ ALIGN-PRWD.

Consider now words where the stem like that in (14) is preceded by a *yer*-containing prefix, e.g., /zX=rXwać/ "to tear off." Such an input can be parsed as a CG [zX[rXwać]], analogically to *znieść* in (13). This parsing, corresponding to the phonetic form *[zrwac], will satisfy ALIGN-RT, but it will violate ALIGN-PRWD, just like its base verb [rXwać] (cf. (14)). The set of candidate outputs provided by the Generator will also include a parsing where the prefix and the stem are included in a single PrWd. The prosodic structure of such an output is given in (16).

(16)   F

~PrWd~[z E r X w a ć]~PrWd~

           F^σ

       zErwać

Since the latter output contains the prefix *yer* and the root *yer* in one domain, they can form a binary syllabic foot and the first *yer* surfaces. The candidate output in (16) violates ALIGN-RT but satisfies ALIGN-PRWD as well as FT-BIN-σ. It also corresponds to the actual form of the word "to tear off." I conclude that ALIGN-PRWD dominates ALIGN-RT in Polish: ALIGN-PRWD ≫ ALIGN-RT.

The tableau below shows the evaluation of a few candidate outputs of the inputs /rXwać/ and /zX=rXwać/ with respect to the constraints mentioned above. In the embedded prosodic structure the internal brackets "[...]" include a PrWd, while the external ones mark a CG.[14]

(17)   Evaluation tableau for some candidate outputs of /rXwać/ and /zX=rXwać/

Candidates	FT-BIN-σ	ALIGN-PRWD	ALIGN-RT
F | ☞ [rXwać]		*	
F ⋀ [rEwać] | Fσ	*!		
F | [zX[rXwać]]		*!	
F ⋀ ☞ [zErXwać] V Fσ			*
F ⋀ [zX[rEwać]] | Fσ	*!		

For the nonprefixed input, the first candidate *rwać* is selected although it violates ALIGN-PRWD because it satisfies higher-ranked FT-BIN-σ. The second candidate **rEwać* loses since it violates FT-BIN-σ. For the prefixed input, FT-BIN-σ rules out the third candidate **zrEwać*,

ALIGN-PRWD eliminates the first candidate *zrwać and the second candidate zErwać is selected.

3.4 Doubly prefixed words

The above analysis can be extended to doubly prefixed verbs. It predicts that, as in the case of singly prefixed words, the PrWd will be left-aligned with a prefix rather than the root if the root begins with a yer-headed syllable. However, more complex morphological structure of doubly prefixed words allows for numerous possible prosodic parsings and the constraints discussed so far do not suffice to make the right output selection.

Consider first a word where the root does not contain a yer: /wX= zX=nieść/ "to raise," (3c). To satisfy both ALIGN-PRWD and ALIGN-RT the root must be left-aligned with the PrWd in the selected output. However, these constraints alone cannot choose between two candidate outputs [wX[zX[nieść]]] and [wEzX[nieść]], of which only the first corresponds to the actual form wznieść. The candidates differ in the way prefixes are parsed: in the first one, every prefix is left-aligned with a CG. The requirement on such morphology-prosody correspondence can be expressed in terms of ALIGN-PREF, a constraint analogical to ALIGN-RT:

(18) ALIGN-PREF
     Align (Pref, Left, CG, Left)

ALIGN-PREF requires that the left edge of every prefix coincides with the left edge of a CG. The parsing [wX[zX[nieść]]] satisfies ALIGN-PREF, while [wEzX[nieść]] violates it because the prefix /zX/ is not left-aligned with a CG. ALIGN-PREF selects the former candidate as optimal.

As far as yer-containing roots are concerned, for both singly and doubly prefixed words the present analysis eliminates as nonoptimal candidate outputs where the root is left-aligned with the PrWd since they violate ALIGN-PRWD. For instance, for the input /wX=zX=bXrać/ "to swell up" the candidate output [wX[zX[bXrać]]], corresponding to *wzbrać, will be ruled out. In order to satisfy ALIGN-PRWD at least two yers must be included in one PrWd so that a syllabic foot can be formed. The head of this foot will also participate in the moraic foot structure. Consider two candidate outputs given in (19) below. In (19a) the PrWd is left-aligned with the first prefix and in (19b) with the second prefix. Both parsings satisfy ALIGN-PRWD as well as FT-BIN-σ, and both violate ALIGN-RT. They score differently with respect to ALIGN-PREF. (19a) violates the constraint twice because neither prefix is left-aligned with a CG, whereas (19b) violates it only once and therefore scores better.

(19) a.

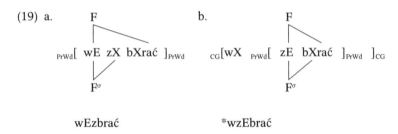

wEzbrać   *wzEbrać

It is, however, the parsing represented in (19a), and not the one in (19b), which corresponds to the selected output of the word "to swell up." The correct choice between candidates must therefore be due to another well-formedness constraint, ranked above ALIGN-PREF and not considered so far. I suggest that the constraint in question is ALIGN-STEM (ALIGN-L-STEM in McCarthy and Prince 1993b).

In many languages prefixes are always prosodified together with the root, and not procliticized to it as is usually the case in Polish. This is due to the high ranking of ALIGN-STEM which demands left-alignment between the morphological stem, including the root and all the prefixes,[15] and the PrWd:

(20) ALIGN-STEM
     Align (Stem, Left, PrWd, Left)

In Polish ALIGN-RT is ranked above ALIGN-STEM: the root, and not the stem, generally marks the beginning of a PrWd. However, in cases where the violation of ALIGN-RT is forced by the higher-ranked ALIGN-PRWD, ALIGN-STEM gets its chance to select the optimal output. Of the candidate parsings in (19) above, ALIGN-STEM favors (a) over (b) because in (19a) the whole stem with both prefixes is included within the same PrWd, while in (19b) the PrWd contains only part of this stem (with one prefix instead of two). For (19a) to be actually selected ALIGN-STEM must dominate ALIGN-PREF. I conclude that the ranking of the relevant constraints discussed above is the following:

FT BIN-σ ≫ ALIGN-PRWD ≫ ALIGN-RT ≫ ALIGN-STEM ≫ ALIGN-PREF

The interaction of the relevant constraints is illustrated in the two evaluation tableaux below. Tableau (21) evaluates some candidate outputs of prefixed words in which the root contains a "proper" vowel. For the singly prefixed word the first candidate output, *znieść*, is selected as optimal since it satisfies the three highest-ranked constraints. The second and the third candidates, *źnieść* (where palatal assimilation affects /z/ PrWd-internally) and *zEnieść*, lose because they violate ALIGN-PRWD and FT-BIN-σ, respectively. For the doubly prefixed word the second candidate output, *wźnieść* (where palatal assimilation is also applicable), is eliminated by ALIGN-PRWD, the fourth candidate, *wEźnieść*, is ruled out by ALIGN-RT and the fifth, *wEźEnieść*, violates fatally FT-BIN-σ. The third candidate, *wEznieść*, loses against the first candidate, *wznieść*, with respect to ALIGN-PREF.

Tableau (22) evaluates some candidate outputs of prefixed words with a *yer*-containing root. For the singly prefixed word the first candidate, *zbrać*, is ruled out by ALIGN-PRWD, the third by FT-BIN-σ, and the second candidate, *zEbrać*, is selected as the optimal. One of the losers, the third candidate output, happens to be phonetically identical to the actual DI form of the verb "to collect," *zbiErać*, but their prosodic structures are different. In the DI verb the *yer* is *not* the head of a (nonbranching) syllabic foot, and hence FT-BIN-σ is not violated. DI *yer* vocalization is due to a different mechanism than the surfacing of *yers* in foot-head position: the root *yer* is turned into the default vowel of Polish to satisfy the DI minimality condition (see Rowicka and van de Weijer 1994, and section 2.1 in this paper).

As far as the doubly prefixed words are concerned, the first candidate output, *wzbrać*, and the third are excluded by ALIGN-PRWD. The fourth candidate output, *wEzbiErać*, violates fatally FT-BIN-σ. The second candidate, *wzEbrać*, and the fifth, *wEzbrać*, score the same with respect to FT-BIN-σ, ALIGN-PRWD and ALIGN-RT, but the former loses because it violates ALIGN-STEM. The second candidate output is in fact phonetically indistinguishable from the selected output. However, the present analysis predicts that the parsing [wEzXbXrać] will be selected as optimal.[16]

(21) Evaluation tableau for some candidate outputs of /zX=nieść/ and /wX=zX=nieść/

Candidates	Ft-Bin-σ	Align-PrWd	Align-Rt	Align-Stem	Align-Pref
☞ F | [zX[nieść]]				*	
F | [zXnieść]		*!	*		*
F F | | [zE [nieść]] | F$^{\sigma}$	*!			*	
☞ F | [wX[zX [nieść]]]				*	
F | [wX[zXnieść]]		*!	*	*	*
F F | | [wEzX [nieść]] V F$^{\sigma}$				*	*!
F [wEzXnieść] V F$^{\sigma}$			*!		**
F F F | | | [wE [zE [nieść]]] | | F$^{\sigma}$ F$^{\sigma}$	*!*			*	

(22) Evaluation tableau for some candidate outputs of /zX=bXrać/ and /wX=zX=bXrać/

Candidates	FT-BIN-σ	ALIGN-PRWD	ALIGN-RT	ALIGN-STEM	ALIGN-PREF
F | [zX [bXrać]]		*!		*	
☞ F [zEbXrać] Fσ			*		*
F [zX [biErać]] Fσ	*!			*	
F | [wX[zX [bXrać]]]		*!		*	
F [wX [zEbXrać]] Fσ			*	*!	*
F F [wEzX[bXrać]] Fσ		*!		*	*
F F [wEzX[biErać]] Fσ Fσ	*!			*	*
☞ F [wEzXbXrać] Fσ			*		**

The candidate outputs which best satisfy the relevant constraints given in both tableaux correspond to the actual phonetic forms of the verbs *znieść*, *wznieść*, *wEbrać* and *wEzbrać*, which supports the preceding analysis.

Note that in order to arrive at correct results, violations of ALIGN-RT must be assessed in absolute, and not gradient, terms. With gradient assessment from among all candidates violating a constraint those are selected which disobey it minimally. Thus, [wX[zEbXrać]] would be selected over [wEzXbXrać] since in the first parsing ALIGN-RT is violated by two segments /zX/, while in the other it is violated by four segments /wX/ and /zX/. Given the principles of OT, the satisfaction or violation of lower-ranked constraints, such as ALIGN-STEM, would no longer be relevant. On the other hand, in the case of absolute assessment the degree of violation does not matter and the selection of the optimal candidate depends on the scores with respect to the immediately lower constraints.

One more candidate output of /wX=zX=bXrać/ which has not been included in tableau (22) deserves attention, namely **wzEbrać* [wXzE-bXrać]. It violates ALIGN-PRWD fatally since the syllabic foot is created on the second and third *yer* in the sequence, and not at the left edge of the PrWd. Recall, however, the *yer*-surfacing pattern in *przeddziEń* /przedXdXńX/, (6a), where the syllabic foot on the second and third *yer* is perfectly legitimate. The latter example indicates that in the default situation the formation of syllabic feet in Polish is right PrWd-edge oriented, which can be expressed in terms of an ALIGN-FOOT constraint (cf. McCarthy and Prince 1993a). The difference between the *yer*-surfacing patterns in *wEzbrać* and *przeddziEń*, which previous studies have overlooked, follows from the analysis developed in this paper. In the former word ALIGN-PRWD forces the surfacing of the first *yer* by demanding a foot PrWd-initially. In the latter word the constraint can be satisfied by the "proper" vowel in the initial syllable and the *yer* foot may be formed close to the right PrWd-edge. This adds another piece of evidence in favor of the account proposed here.

4. Conclusion

In this chapter I have proposed an OT analysis of *yer* surfacing in prefixed verbs in Polish. Such verbs have a different prosodic structure, depending on whether their root does or does not contain a *yer*. I have argued that the selection of different prosodic parsings follows from the interaction of requirements on the alignment between prosodic categories (foot, PrWd and CG) and morphological categories (root, stem and prefix). The default situation is that the root is left-aligned with the PrWd and with a foot, while prefixes are prosodified separately as proclitics. However, if the root begins with a *yer*-headed syllable, no foot can be formed at the left edge of the root. In this case the PrWd gets left-aligned with the stem (beginning with the leftmost prefix). If such a PrWd contains a sequence of (prefix and root) *yers*, some of these *yers* will surface.

As far as the pattern of *yer* surfacing is concerned, the facts addressed are: (i) a *yer* surfaces only when it is followed by a nonsurfacing *yer*, (ii) only *yer*-containing roots trigger *yer* surfacing in multiple prefixes, and (iii) in multiply prefixed verbs always and only the first *yer* in a sequence of three surfaces. I propose that *yers* are best interpreted as underlyingly empty and "weightless" nuclei. Sequences of *yers* are parsed into weight-insensitive bisyllabic feet. Heads of such feet surface and participate together with "proper" vowels in moraic foot structure. The location of *yer* feet can also be influenced by the prosodic alignment constraints. This is the case in doubly prefixed verbs with *yer*-containing roots. There a *yer* foot is formed on the first two *yers*, rather than on the last two, so that the whole PrWd begins with a syllable that can be footed.

Notes

1 I would like to thank Colin Ewen, Bożena Cetnarowska, Edmund Gussmann, Harry van der Hulst, Krisztina Polgárdi, Jeroen van de Weijer, the audience of the Prosodic Morphology Workshop in Utrecht, 1994, and the anonymous reviewers for their helpful discussions and comments. Any remaining errors are my own.
2 Orthographic *i* prevocalically denotes the palatalization of the preceding consonant. Palatalization in Polish, as independent of vowel-zero alternations, will not be treated here. For an analysis see Gussmann (1992).
3 Since not every phonetic [e] in Polish is a surface realization of a *yer*, vowels alternating with zero are capitalized.
4 In such words the context never arises for palatal assimilation or other PrWd-internal processes. Hence *yer* surfacing provides the only evidence about their prosodic structure.

5 The example below is a prefixed noun, lexicalized as a single PrWd. Pre-fixes do not normally prosodify together with nominal or adjectival stems (see note 6).

6 Except for a handful of lexicalizations, the alternations in question do not take place in prefixed verbs containing derived (denominal or de-adject-ival) stems nor in prefixed words of other categories (i.e., nouns, adject-ives, and adverbs). Cf. no prefix-*yer* surfacing in *rozkrwawić* "to (make) bleed heavily" before the nominal root /krXw/. In descriptive terms, a prefix may not be prosodified together with a grammatical category other than a verb. This issue will not be addressed here.

7 In the classical works of OT (Prince and Smolensky 1993, McCarthy and Prince 1993a, b) such empty nuclei are not allowed for: it is assumed that structurally present elements must also be realized phonetically. However, the view adopted here is also advocated in Harris (1994). He argues that it is not incompatible with the principles of OT, and the presence versus absence of empty nuclei in a language follows from constraint ranking.

8 The syllabic status of word-final consonants will not be addressed. In what follows they will be tentatively included in the coda of the preceding vowel.

9 The present analysis applies to *lexical* foot formation. No claims are made about the constraint ranking governing *postlexical* (stress) foot assign-ment in Polish.

10 These and other parallels between the behavior of empty nuclei and stress are addressed in van der Hulst and Rowicka (1997).

11 The relevant constraint can be seen as a mirror image of WEIGHT-TO-STRESS PRINCIPLE (Prince and Smolensky 1993). While WSP demands that prosodically heavy syllables are parsed into strong positions, the other constraint states that an element in a strong position in a foot is (inter-preted as) prosodically heavy. In the case of "weightless" vowels parsed as foot heads this means that they are treated as having a mora. The con-straint in question is never violated in Polish, i.e., whenever there is a sequence of *yers* which may form a syllabic foot, the one in the head posi-tion will surface.

12 For instance, for a sequence of a "proper" vowel and a *yer* more optimal is the parsing with a nonbranching moraic foot and unparsed *yer*-headed syl-lable than another parsing where both the "proper" vowel and the *yer* form a syllabic foot. The former parsing satisfies PARSE-μ and violates PARSE-σ, while the latter parsing satisfies PARSE-σ, but violates the higher-ranked PARSE-μ.

13 The interpretation of *yers* as empty nuclei is conceptually very close to Government Phonology (GP). However, the present account crucially differs in that,

(a) *yer* feet include *yers* only, while proper governing relations of GP hold between contentful and empty nuclei

(b) *yer* feet are left-headed, while Proper Government is right-headed

(c) the formation of *yer* feet is subject to soft, violable constraints, while GP is based on inviolable principles.

For an alternative analysis of vowel-zero alternations in a framework combining elements of GP and OT see Rowicka (forthcoming).

14 I do not adhere to the Strict Layer Hypothesis here and assume, noncrucially, that PrWds do not form CGs unless preceded by proclitics. However, the present analysis would arrive at the same results also given the opposite assumption.

15 As pointed out by an anonymous reviewer, this presupposes that the stem is a *nonrecursive* category: only the outermost morphological brackets qualify as stem brackets. This stipulation is not only necessary for the present analysis. If the stem were considered a recursive category, ALIGN-STEM could not select the optimal output for any multiply prefixed word. For instance, in the case of a doubly prefixed word the candidate outputs $_{PrWd}$[Pref. Pref. Root]$_{PrWd}$ and $_{CG}$[Pref.$_{PrWd}$[Pref. Root]$_{PrWd}$]$_{CG}$ would score the same with respect to the constraint. In the first candidate the second prefix is not left-aligned with any prosodic category, while in the second candidate the first prefix is left-aligned with a CG, and not a PrWd. The first candidate could never be chosen as optimal.

16 Under the GP analysis (Gussmann and Kaye 1993), of three *yers* in one domain the second one would always have to surface. Therefore those authors have to argue that in words such as *wEzbrać* the two suffixes have been "lexicalized" to form one domain, separate from the root: [wEzX[bXrać]]. However, their account cannot explain (i) why such lexicalization affects all and only double prefixes before *yer*-containing roots, and not words like *wznieść*, and (ii) why lexicalization does not lead to including both prefixes and the root in one domain, while a single prefix plus the root are free to form one domain in words such as *zEbrać* [zEbXrać].

References

Bethin, C. Y. 1992. *Polish Syllables – The Role of Prosody in Phonology and Morphology*, Columbus, OH: Slavica Publishers.

Booij, G. E. 1996. Cliticization as prosodic integration: the case of Dutch, *The Linguistic Review* 13: 219–42.

Czaykowska-Higgins, E. 1988. Investigations into Polish morphology and phonology, Ph.D. dissertation, Massachusetts Institute of Technology.

Fikkert, P. J. M. 1994. On the acquisition of prosodic structure, Ph.D. dissertation, University of Leiden, *Holland Institute of Linguistics Dissertations* 6.

Gorecka, E. 1988. Epenthesis and the coda constraints in Polish, ms. Massachusetts Institute of Technology.

Gussmann, E. 1992. Back to front: non-linear palatalisation and vowels in Polish, in J. Fisiak and S. Puppel (eds.), *Phonological Investigations*, Amsterdam and Philadelphia: John Benjamins, 5–66.

1997. Govern or perish, in R. Hickey and S. Puppel (eds.), *A Festschrift for Jacek Fisiak on his 60th Birthday*, Berlin: Mouton-de Gruyter, 1291–300.

Gussmann, E., and J. Kaye. 1993. Polish notes from a Dubrovnik café: the yers, *SOAS Working Papers in Linguistics and Phonetics* 3: 427–62.

Harris, J. 1994. Codas, constraints and coda constraints. Paper presented at the Second Manchester Phonology Workshop.

Hulst, H. G. van der and G. J. Rowicka. 1997. On some parallels between (un)realised empty nuclei and (un)stressed syllables, in G. E. Booij and J. van de Weijer (eds.), *Phonology in Progress: Progress in Phonology*, Holland Institute of Linguistics Phonology Papers III. The Hague: Holland Academic Graphics. 125–49.

McCarthy, John J., and Alan S. Prince. 1993a. Generalized alignment, in G. E. Booij and J. van Marle (eds.), *Yearbook of Morphology 1993*, 79–153.

1993b. Prosodic Morphology I, ms. University of Massachusetts at Amherst, MA and Rutgers University, New Brunswick, NJ.

Nespor, M., and Irene Vogel (1986). *Prosodic Phonology*, Dordrecht: Foris.

Piotrowski, M. 1992. Polish yers and extrasyllabicity: an autosegmental account, in J. Fisiak and S. Puppel (eds.), *Phonological Investigations*, Amsterdam and Philadelphia: John Benjamins, 67–108.

Prince, Alan S. 1980. A metrical theory for Estonian quantity, *Linguistic Inquiry* 11: 511–62.

Prince, Alan S., and P. Smolensky. 1993. Optimality Theory: constraint interaction in Generative Grammar, ms. Rutgers University, New Brunswick, NJ and University of Colorado, Boulder, CO.

Rowicka, G. J. 1994. Polish palatal assimilation in prefixed words, in R. Bok-Bennema and C. Cremers (eds.), *Linguistics in the Netherlands 1994*, Amsterdam: Benjamins, 211–22.

Rowicka, G. J. Forthcoming. On ghost vowels: a strict CV approach, Ph.D. dissertation, HIL/Leiden University, The Hague: Holland Academic Graphics.

Rowicka, G. J., and J. M. van de Weijer. 1994. Prosodic constraints in the lexicon of Polish: the case of Derived Imperfectives, *The Linguistic Review* 11: 49–76.

Rubach, J. 1985. Abstract vowels in three-dimensional phonology: the yers, *The Linguistic Review* 5: 247–80.

Rubach, J., and G. E. Booij. 1985. A grid theory of stress in Polish, *Lingua* 66: 281–319.

Spencer, A. J. 1986. A non-linear analysis of vowel-zero alternations in Polish, *Journal of Linguistics* 22: 249–80.

Szpyra, J. 1989. *The Phonology-Morphology Interface: Cycles, Levels and Words*, London: Routledge.

1992. Ghost segments in nonlinear phonology: Polish yers, *Language* 68: 277–312.

11 Double reduplications in parallel

Suzanne Urbanczyk

1. Introduction

There are a number of questions which one asks of the interaction
between prosody and morphology. For example, where does reduplication occur in the grammar – before or after prosody; and can reduplicative morphemes be applied cyclically? This chapter[1] examines some of
these issues in the nonderivational or "parallelist" theory of constraint
interaction, Optimality Theory. A leading idea in Optimality Theory is
parallelism of constraint satisfaction (Prince and Smolensky 1993: section 2). In parallelist Optimality Theory (henceforth OT) only fully
formed candidates are generated and evaluated for goodness against the
entire constraint hierarchy. There are no intermediate stages. This chapter examines a number of issues that parallelism raises in forming words
with two reduplicative morphemes – doubly reduplicated words.

Like many other Salish languages, Northern Lushootseed (a dialect
group of Puget Salish) has words which are composed of two reduplicative morphemes. The interest of the Lushootseed data here is that one set
of double reduplications appears to require an intermediate stage.

(1) Lushootseed reduplication (Hess and Hilbert 1976, 2: 165)
   a. bədá?   "child, offspring"
   b. bí-bəda?   "small child"   DIMINUTIVE
   c. bəd-bədá?   "children"   DISTRIBUTIVE
   d. bí-bəd-bəda? "dolls; litter [of animals]"   DIM-DIST
   e. bí-bi-bəda? "young children"   DIST-DIM

The root is shown in (1a). In (1b) the DIMINUTIVE is $C_1í$- with a fixed
segment in its nucleus. In (1c) the DISTRIBUTIVE is a $C_1V_1C_2$-prefix
with the base vowel in its nucleus. The DIMINUTIVE and DISTRIBUTIVE

390

reduplicative morphemes can cooccur on a number of stems (Hess 1967; Broselow 1983). When the DIMINUTIVE precedes the DISTRIBUTIVE, as in (1d), the reduplicative affixes are the same as in the single reduplications: $C_1 i\text{-}C_1 V_1 C_2\text{-}$. However, when the DISTRIBUTIVE precedes the DIMINUTIVE, as in (1e), the pattern is: $C_1 i\text{-}C_1 i\text{-}$. The distributive affix is not its usual $C_1 V_1 C_2\text{-}$ shape. In fact, it is identical to the diminutive reduplicant, suggesting that the stem in (1e) is derived from the stem in (1b).

The *bí-bi-bədà?* pattern of double reduplication presents an interesting challenge to parallelist OT because of this cyclic effect. In order to account for these irregularities, Broselow (1983) proposes that reduplication is cyclic, and the extent of the copying can be restricted by morphological subjacency. Indeed, each theory of reduplication which has a copying procedure must invoke the cycle to get the correct shape and fixed segmentism in Lushootseed. Rather than requiring an intermediate stage, in OT the identity between the distributive and diminutive morphemes in *bí-bi-bədà?* will be shown to be an instance of overapplication of fixed segmentism in reduplication, similar to other identity effects analyzed by Wilbur (1973), and following the OT model proposed by McCarthy and Prince (this volume). By showing that parallelism may be maintained in the face of a process of word-formation which was necessarily cyclic, this study provides further support for the nonderivational nature of OT.

The chapter is organized as follows. Section 2 contains the analysis developed in Broselow (1983), illustrating why the cycle is necessary in double reduplications. The remainder of the chapter presents an OT analysis where no intermediate stage is required. Parallelism of constraint evaluation results in the correct size and fixed segmentism of all reduplicative affixes, regardless of the morphological composition of the word. Section 3 presents a discussion of parallelism in OT and lays out the basic framework for reduplication. In section 4 a comprehensive analysis of the diminutive and distributive patterns of reduplications is presented. Finally, section 5 shows that the constraint rankings obtained for the single reduplications also account for the double reduplications: nothing special need be said of the doubly reduplicated stems. I will also discuss what would be required of a serial analysis, arguing that the parallel approach is formally more simple than one involving intermediate stages.

2. Cyclicity and double reduplications

Broselow's (1983) investigations into Salish double reduplications led her to propose two features of multiply reduplicated words: cyclicity and subjacency. Cyclicity, a standard assumption of lexical phonology (Kiparsky 1982; Mohanan 1986), states that "each reduplication affix involves a new cycle in the lexicon" (Broselow 1983: 327). It rules out forms like (2a), in which the distributive morpheme incorrectly copies the segmental material of the root. Subjacency is nececessary because it "prevents the copying of phonemic material across two or more bounding nodes, where 'stem' is a bounding node for word-level rules" (Broselow 1983: 342). It rules out forms like (2b), in which the DISTRIBUTIVE copies segmental material which extends past the DIMINUTIVE. (The portion of the word which supplies the segmental content of the distributive is underlined below.)

(2) DISTRIBUTIVE-DIMINUTIVE (modified from Broselow 1983: 325)

	DIST	DIM	STEM	
	CVC	Ci	CVCVCVC	
a. *bəd-bi-bəda?	bəd	bi	bəda?	
b. *bib-bi-bəda?	bib	bi	bəda?	
c. bi-bi-bəda?	bi	bi	bəda?	"small children"

The attested form is (2c), obeying cyclicity and subjacency. The segments in the adjacent morpheme (DIM) and only those are copied in DIST reduplication.

Cyclicity and subjacency are both required to explain why the distributive is Cí in DIST-DIM stems. Given the structure of bíbibədà? in (3), the derivation proceeds as in (4) and (5).

(3) [word [stemDIST [stemDIM [stembədá?]]]]

The first cycle produces [stembədá?].

On the second cycle the diminutive Ci skeleton is prefixed. The quality of the diminutive vowel is represented as a prespecified melody in the lexicon (see Marantz 1982). The melody contained in the subjacent stem (bəda?) is copied and associated from left to right. Schwa is prevented from associating because of the priority of prespecified material. Finally, all unassociated melodemes are erased.

(4) DIM STEM

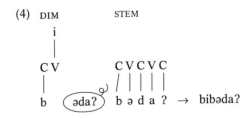

b əda? b ə d a ? → bibəda?

On the next cycle, the distributive CVC skeleton is prefixed. Subjacency ensures that only melodemes contained in the subjacent cycle (diminutive reduplication) are available for copy.

(5) DIST DIM STEM

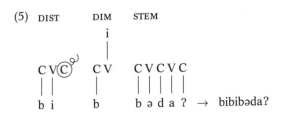

b i b b ə d a ? → bibibəda?

The melody *bi* is copied and associated. Because there are fewer melodemes than skeletal positions, a lone C slot remains unassociated and is erased at the end of the cycle.

Subjacency provides a principled explanation for the size alternation of the distributive affix. In DIM-DIST stems, the entire root is available for copy and the distributive is CVC. In DIST-DIM stems, only diminutive material is available for copy, hence the distributive is only bisegmental CV. While Broselow claims that subjacency is a general property of reduplication theory, in section 4 I will present evidence against subjacency as an account of the size alternation. Rather than providing a morphological analysis, I will present evidence that a general process of antigemination in Lushootseed is active in restricting the size of the distributive reduplicant.

In the copy and associate model that Broselow adopts, cyclicity is required in double reduplications because the reduplicant (the phonological exponent of a reduplicative affix) and the base (the string supplying the phonological content) must be adjacent. The following forms show that the distributive reduplicant must copy adjacent material. The adjacency requirement is particularly observable in stems which have a $C_1 i$- diminutive reduplicant.

(6) Double reduplications

    a. DIM-DIST: bí-bəd-bəda?   "dolls; litter [of animals]"

    b. DIST-DIM: bí-bi-bəda?   "young children"

In (a) the distributive is composed of the three segments to its immediate right. In (b) it is composed of the two segments (one of which is a fixed segment) to its immediate right. In this model of reduplication, the only way to achieve adjacency between reduplicant and base is to have cyclic application of segmental copying.

In fact, cyclicity is required to derive Lushootseed double reduplications in every theory of reduplication which has a process of copying: copy and associate (Marantz 1982), parafixation (Clements 1985; Mester 1986), and copy and trim (Steriade 1988). The following derivation, in which the stem *bəda?* is copied twice, shows that parallel affixation results in nonadjacency of the outermost reduplicant and its base.

(7) Parallel affixation

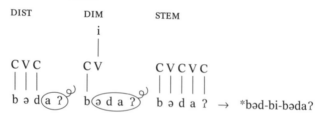

Nothing about copying theories of reduplication explains why parallel affixation cannot occur in Lushootseed. Thus each theory must invoke the cycle.

While in previous models, double reduplications must be formed cyclically, in OT they need not be. In OT, parallel affixation of both reduplicative morphemes can occur because reduplicant and base are adjacent in the output, and constraints which require identity between reduplicant and base are highly ranked for the DIST morpheme. In the next section I present an outline of the formal mechanism for reduplication in OT. In following sections I show that the shape and segmental content of both distributive alternants (CVC- and Cí-) result from general phonotactic constraints interacting with reduplicative constraints.

3. Parallelism in Optimality Theory

Parallelism can be many things. In OT, parallelism refers to a property of *Gen(erator)*, the operation that produces candidate output forms.

Only fully formed candidates are emitted (see Prince and Smolensky 1993: section 2 for details). These fully formed candidates are evaluated for well-formedness against the entire constraint hierarchy (the set of ranked constraints). Because the pairing of input and output involves no intermediate stages, this necessarily entails that there is no cycle in strict parallelist OT. To have a cycle would require an intermediate stage.

Two studies which provide evidence for separate levels or strata in OT are McCarthy and Prince (1993: appendix) and Kenstowicz (1994a). The motivation for distinct levels comes from constraint reranking. Note, however, that *Gen* still emits fully formed candidates at various stages. The different constraint rankings associated with separate strata is the hallmark of a serial derivation in OT. (See Benua (1995) for an account of identity effects in truncated words.)

The prediction that parallelism makes for doubly reduplicated stems is clear. If one constraint hierarchy can derive single and double reduplications, then both can be formed in parallel. If a separate constraint ranking is required for double reduplications, then there must be an intermediate stage.

The unique feature of reduplicative morphemes is that phonological invariance is defined by overall shape rather than segmental content, the segmental content being supplied by a base. McCarthy and Prince (1994a), in their Utrecht talks, outline two general mechanisms for deriving invariant shape and segmental dependency: Generalized Template Specification and Generalized Template Satisfaction. The need to generalize comes from the goal to eliminate as many reduplication-specific conditions from the grammar as possible. I outline first how reduplicative morphemes get variable segmentism, and then how shape invariance is achieved. The following echoes a more detailed discussion in McCarthy and Prince (this volume).

Reduplicative morphemes are represented in the input as abstract, phonologically empty RED_i, RED_j,..., where RED_i is specified only for morphological classification. The input is necessarily empty because the exact segmental content can only be determined by the base to which it is attached. The phonological exponent of RED_i is the output reduplicant string.

The segmental content of a reduplicant is achieved via a correspondence relation with a base, where base is defined as an adjacent string in the output (McCarthy and Prince 1993). For prefixing reduplication, the base is the string immediately to the right; for suffixing, it is to the left of the reduplicant. Correspondence is a relation pairing up strings of various types and is defined as follows.[2]

(8) Correspondence

Given two strings S_1 and S_2, related to one another by some linguistic process, *correspondence* is a function f from any subset of elements of S_1 to S_2. Any element α of S_1 and any element β of S_2 are *correspondents* of one another if α is the image of β under correspondence; that is, $\alpha=f(\beta)$. (McCarthy and Prince this volume)

Correspondence between base and reduplicant holds between output strings. It is similar in spirit to Wilbur's (1973) "mate" relation and replaces the inherently procedural operations of copying and association in obtaining segmental identity between base and reduplicant. Adjacency between base and reduplicant is obtained via the definition of base.

Gen is free to supply any string as the reduplicant, and identity between base and reduplicant is evaluated by a number of constraints which ensure goodness of correspondence. Faithfulness of reduplicant to base includes such properties as: whether the reduplicant begins or ends like its base, whether it reflects the same linear order as the base, whether it contains material not in the base, and whether it includes everything in the base. Two key faithfulness constraints are MAX and DEP: MAX ensures total copy and DEP bars all nonbase material. The definitions are provided below, where Domain refers to the set of correspondents in S_1 and Range refers to the set of correspondents in S_2; for reduplication S_1 is the base and S_2 is the reduplicant.

(9) MAX

Every element in S_1 has a correspondent in S_2. That is Domain(f)=S_1

DEP

Every element in S_2 has a correspondent in S_1. That is Range(f)=S_2

When MAX and DEP are obeyed, reduplication is total. Partial reduplication results when MAX is violated under compulsion of some higher ranked constraint(s).

The invariance associated with the shape of reduplicative morphemes has standardly been associated with a template of some form (Marantz 1982; McCarthy and Prince 1986, 1990). However, McCarthy and Prince (1994a: part 1) propose that the invariance need not be defined templatically.[3] Rather, it can be determined by the interaction of faithfulness constraints with general phono-constraints.

(10) Generalized template (McCarthy and Prince 1994a: part 1)
Templatic targets are determined by structural conditions, which, interacting through constraint ranking, properly characterize the desired invariance structure.

A central idea to generalized templates is that reduplicative morphemes need only be specified for morphological category, where MCat can be ROOT, AFX, or STEM (McCarthy and Prince 1994a: part 1). The shape invariance results from canonical morpheme shape emerging in reduplication, where the shape of reduplicants parallels the shape of morphemes in a language.

In addition to phono-constraints, Generalized Template Theory crucially requires constraints which refer to morphological and prosodic categories. These MCat/PCat constraints also serve to restrict the size of reduplicants. One such constraint proposed by McCarthy and Prince (1994b: part 1) is AFFI X$\leq$ σ.

(11) AFFI X$\leq$ σ The phonological exponent of an affix is no larger than a syllable.

Partial reduplication results because AFFI X$\leq$ σ dominates MAX.

The basic features of reduplication are summarized as RED being a phonologically empty morpheme, achieving its segmental content *via* correspondence with a base. Size restrictors and phono-constraints interact with MAX to achieve the invariant shape. Finally, something must be said about languages with multiple reduplicative morphemes.

Each reduplicative morpheme has its own correspondence relation. Because each reduplicative morpheme necessarily has a different shape, different conditions must figure into determining its invariance. As a consequence, each abstract RED$_i$ comes with an attendant set of faithfulness constraints. So, in doubly reduplicated words, the output will contain two reduplicants and two bases, evaluated by two RED$_i$-specific sets of faithfulness constraints. It is important to note that the ranking of the faithfulness constraints for distinct reduplicative morphemes is expected to differ.

Having introduced the basic assumptions and theoretical framework, I now turn to the analysis. First I present the single reduplications. Then I show that the rankings obtained for words with only one reduplicative morpheme also account for words with double reduplications. This result is expected under the strictest view of parallelism in OT.

4. Single reduplications

The complex and varied patterns of reduplication exhibited in Northern Lushootseed have been a topic of several studies (Haeberlin 1918; Hess 1966; Hess and Hilbert 1976; Broselow 1983; Broselow and McCarthy 1984; Bates 1986; Davis 1988; Kirkham 1992). The most recent reference on Lushootseed notes six distinct categories of reduplicative affix (Bates, Hess, and Hilbert 1994). Of these, diminutive and distributive are the most common and are the basis of this study.

4.1 Diminutive

Diminutive reduplication indicates smallness, diminished action, and endearment (Bates, Hess, and Hilbert 1994). It is characterized by the following patterns.

(12) Lushootseed Diminutive (BHH 94)[4]

a.	čáləs	"hand"	čá+čaləs	"little hand"
	hiw-il	"go ahead"	hi+hiwil	"go ahead a bit"
b.	č'λ'á?	"rock"	č'í+č'λ'á?	"little rock"
	təláw-il	"run"	tí+təlaw'-il	"jog"
	s-duukʷ	"knife"	s-dí+duukʷ	"small knife"
c.	s-dukʷ	"bad"	s-dú?+dukʷ	"riff-raff"
	súqʷ'a	"younger sibling"	sú?+suqʷ'a	"little younger sibling"
d.	buus	"four"	bí?+buus	"four little items"
	χəc-bid	"afraid"	χí?+χəc-bid	"a little afraid of it"

Stress always falls on the reduplicant (which is underlined). While there are four alternants, C_1V_1-, $C_1í$-, $C_1V_1?$-, and $C_1í?$-, Bates (1986) provides evidence that the basic alternant is C_1V_1-. First, Bates argues that the glottal stop in (12c) and (12d) is not a part of the reduplicative affix.[5] Thus we are left with C_1V_1- and $C_1í$-. Bates also observes that the choice between C_1V-, (12a) or (12c), and $C_1\acute{\imath}$-, (12b) or (12d), is entirely predictable: $C_1\acute{\imath}$- when the stem contains schwa, a long vowel, or begins with a consonant cluster, and C_1V- elsewhere.

The analysis requires two parts: first, specifying the morphological category of the diminutive, then determining the constraint interaction to derive the two predictable alternants. The diminutive is analyzed as an affix: RED-DIM=AFFI X^6 The two alternants, C_1V_1- and $C_1\acute{\imath}$-, have the same shape, but differ in the presence of a fixed segment. The basic shape is analyzed first, then the fixed segmentism. The fixed segmentism is only found with marked bases, and is analyzed as an instance of unmarked structure emerging in reduplication (McCarthy and Prince 1994b).

The CV- shape results because No-Coda (a constraint barring coda consonants: Prince and Smolensky 1993) dominates Max-Dim. The size restrictor Affi $X \leq \sigma$ keeps the reduplicant monosyllabic.

(13) Affi $X \leq \sigma \gg$ No-Coda $\gg$ Max-Dim

s-dim-čaləs	Affi $X \leq \sigma$	No-Coda	Max-Dim
a. ☞ čá- čaləs		*	***
b. čál-čaləs		**!	**
c. čálə-čaləs	*!	*	*

Candidate (a), the optimal form, obeys Affi $X \leq \sigma$ and has only one No-Coda violation. It is optimal even though it violates Max-Dim the most, but because of its low position in the hierarchy, the multiple violations of Max-Dim do not affect the outcome. Candidate (b) violates No-Coda twice, which proves fatal. Candidate (c) is suboptimal because it is bisyllabic. The correct shape is obtained because the correspondence constraint Max-Dim is subordinate to the size restrictor Affi $X \leq \sigma$ and the syllable-markedness constraint No-Coda.

The analysis of the $C\acute{\imath}$- alternant draws on the descriptive insights of Bates (1986: 11): "[f]orms take C_i- if CV- prefixation is prevented by independent principles." Essentially, when the base cannot provide an optimal nucleus for the reduplicant, i epenthesis results. The diminutive is $C\acute{\imath}$- under the following conditions: with cluster-initial roots, with roots which contain long vowels, and with roots whose initial vowel is schwa.

The fixed segmentism of the diminutive is not represented as a prespecified melody in the lexicon (McCarthy and Prince 1986, and others). Because the fixed segment is "epenthetic" (in the sense that it is not present in the base), all C_1i- alternants violate DEP-DIM, which bars nonbase material from the reduplicant.

(14) DEP

Every element of S_2 has a correspondent in S_1. That is Range(f)=S_2.

Noncorrespondence is compelled by a number of constraints, the general pattern falling under the ranking schema of the emergence of the unmarked (McCarthy and Prince 1994b).

(15) Emergence of the unmarked

Faithfulness$_{I/O}$ ≫ Phono-Constraint ≫ Faithfulness$_{B/R}$

Unmarked structure emerges in reduplication because a Phono-Constraint intervenes between input-output and base-reduplicant faithfulness. The logic of ranking is as follows (and will be demonstrated shortly). The cost of maintaining faithfulness of the input/output domain is that the output is marked with respect to the Phono-Constraint. Identity is maintained because the constraint against the marked structure is ranked lower (and can be violated). The cost of obeying the Phono-Constraint in the reduplicant is less than perfect identity. Because the markedness constraint is ranked higher than the requirement of reduplicative identity, the unmarked structure emerges in reduplication. Space limitations preclude a full analysis of the diminutive, so only the aspects relevant to base-reduplicant faithfulness will be presented in the following discussion. For further details see Urbanczyk (1996).

In cluster-initial roots, the reduplicant has only a simplex onset, while the base has a complex onset. The relevant Phono-Constraint is *COMPLEX.

(16) *COMPLEX (Prince and Smolensky 1993: 87)

No more than one C or V may associate to any syllable position node.

*COMPLEX ensures that the reduplicant has a simplex onset, but a further constraint is needed to rule out C_1V_1, in which the second consonant is skipped over to copy the base vowel. This segment-skipping pattern is attested in the Sanskrit perfective pattern: *pa-prath* "spread"

(Shaw 1994; Steriade 1988; Whitney 1889: section 590; McCarthy and Prince 1986). Lushootseed differs minimally from Sanskrit, because Sanskrit tolerates skipping while Lushootseed does not. The relevant faithfulness constraint is the No-Skipping portion of Contiguity.

(17) Contiguity (No-Skipping in B)
The portion of S_1 standing in correspondence forms a contiguous string, as does the correspondent portion of S_2. That is, Domain(f) is a single contiguous string.

The C_1i- pattern emerges because *Complex and No-Skipping are obeyed at the expense of Dep-Dim as the following tableau shows.

(18) *Complex, No-Skipping ≫ Dep-Dim

DIM-čλ'aʔ	*Complex	No-Skipping	Dep-Dim
a. c'λ'ác'λ'aʔ	**!		
b. c'áč'λ'aʔ	*	*!	
c. ☞ c'íč'λ'aʔ	*		*

The preceding ranking derives the Lushootseed pattern, while the reverse ranking (Dep dominating No-Skipping) derives the Sanskrit pattern.

The cluster-initial roots provide some evidence that the fixed segment does not have a correspondent in the base. If the fixed segment stood in correspondence with the base vowel, the reduplicant would violate No-Skipping. (See Urbanczyk 1996 for further arguments.) I now turn to the question of the quality of the fixed segment.

The fixed segment is i because it is the least marked nucleus under stress. The unmarkedness of i follows from two assumptions. i is specified with the feature [coronal] (Clements 1991), and because *Pl/Cor is universally low ranked, inserting [coronal] is more harmonic than inserting other place features. The "under stress" condition is important because, while schwa is the regular epenthetic vowel (Hess and Hilbert 1976; Broselow 1983; Bates 1986), it is marked when stressed. Recall that the diminutive is always stressed. Furthermore, the only time that schwa is stressed in Northern Lushootseed is when there are no full vowels in a word. Hess (1977) observes: stress falls on the first full vowel, or if the stem contains only schwas, then stress falls on the first schwa.[7] The Cí- reduplicant avoids stressing schwa because the unmarked vowel *i* can be made available in reduplication. The high vowel is the default under stress.

This idea that there is a different default vowel under stress also ties in to an explanation of why schwa-vowelled roots have the high vowel. Associating default vowel quality with stress (schwa is marked when stressed) is another way that marked structure is avoided in reduplication. Schwa is stressed only under duress, so with diminutive reduplication, stressed *i* is prefered over stressed *ə*.

Additional support for relating stress and vowel quality comes from the following cluster-initial and schwa-vowelled roots which would otherwise be exceptional. If stress is a determinant of whether the default vowel is schwa or *i*, then diminutives which do not have initial stress should have schwa in the nucleus.

(19) Diminutives with non-initial stress
    a. qsíʔ   "uncle"   qə+qsíʔ   "favorite uncle"
    b. ƛ'əl=ádiʔ "sound, noise" ƛ'ə+ƛ'əl=ádiʔ "little noise"

Here the fixed segment is schwa rather than *i*, but this is expected because stress does not fall on the diminutive. Presumably, these are cases of inherent stress overriding the regular pattern of initial stress. These data are supportive of a markedness constraint against stressed schwa. To motivate further such a constraint requires a brief excursus on the assignment of stress and the proposed Phono-Constraint *STRESSED-SCHWA.

First, let us examine some cross-linguistic evidence on markedness. The unstressability of schwa is common cross-linguistically. In addition to Northern Lushootseed, there are Dutch (Kager 1991), English, Eastern Cheremis (Hayes 1980), French (Selkirk 1977), Indonesian (Cohn 1989), and several languages discussed in Kenstowicz (1994b, Aljutor, Chukchee, Mari and Mordwin). The constraint *STRESSED-SCHWA is an informal way to capture the constraint against stressed schwa.[8] It is motivated by the observed tendency that if a language resists stressing a particular vowel, it is usually schwa.

Let us now consider how such a constraint-based approach may work for the basic stress pattern of Northern Lushootseed. The following ranking presents the basic interactions, ensuring that stress falls on the first full vowel, otherwise, stress falls on the first schwa. The prevalence of initial stress shows that feet are trochaic in Lushootseed. As their names imply, *Unstressed-V bars nonstressed full vowels, and *Stressed-Schwa bars stressed schwa. The alignment constraint ensures that feet are initial, where foot form is trochaic.

(20) *Unstressed-V ≫ Align-L(PrWd, Ft), *Stressed-Schwa

No ranking can be determined between Align-L(PrWd, Ft) and *Stressed-Schwa.

Diminutives of roots with schwa show that the preceding micro-hierarchy dominates Dep-Dim. The following tableau shows that this constraint ranking accounts for the fixed segment, initial stress, and secondary stress on a following full vowel.

(21) *Unstress-V ≫ Align-L, *Stress-Schwa ≫ Dep-Dim

DIM-bəda?	*Unstress-V	Align-L	*Stress-Schwa	Dep-Dim
a. ☞ bíbədà?				*
b. bə́bədà?			*!	
c. bəbədá?		*!		
d. bə́bəda?	*!		*	

The optimal candidate only violates Dep-Dim, while all the suboptimal candidates violate at least one of the higher-ranked constraints. The preceding tableau shows that the initial stress on diminutives follows the regular pattern of the language. Because Dep-Dim is low-ranking, a fixed segment occurs in the nucleus of the reduplicant. Once again the pattern is consistent with the ranking of the emergence of the unmarked, where high-ranking Dependence$_{I/O}$ is not indicated, *Stressed-Schwa being the intervening Phono-Constraint. Recall that even though it is marked, schwa is stressed in non-reduplicated stems.

The final forms to analyze are long-voweled roots. In this case, the relevant Phono-Constraint is No-Long-V, which prohibits long vowels.

(22) No-Long-V (Prince and Smolensky 1993; Rosenthall 1994)[9]

By having an epenthetic vowel, the diminutive can avoid having a long vowel, a marked structure linguistically. Assuming that the vowel /i/ is epenthetic also explains why a long vowel cannot be copied as short. While so far we have been analyzing this vowel as epenthetic, it is quite possible that it is a shortened version of the base vowel. However, it turns out that candidates with a short base vowel are marked as well.

Following Bates (1986), I analyze the failure to copy only a portion of the long vowel as a consequence of reduplicative transfer. Clements (1985) introduced the term "transfer" to refer to cases of reduplication which carry over aspects of syllable structure, such as vowel length and glide-hood, from base to affix (see also Levin 1983; McCarthy and Prince 1988; Steriade 1988). Transfer is formalized as a constraint on correspondence below, requiring faithful domination of moras.[10]

(23) TRANSFER $(S_1, S_2) = (B, R)$
If α (an integer) weight-bearing units dominate a segment in S_1, then α weight-bearing units dominate its correspondent in S_2.

Transfer ensures that the weight of a vowel (or geminate) remains constant in B and R.[11] The $C\acute{\imath}$- reduplicant trivially obeys TRANSFER because the long vowel in the base has no correspondent in the reduplicant.

(24) NO-LONG-V, TRANSFER ≫ DEP-DIM

s-dim-duuk^w	NO-LONG-V	TRANSFER	DEP-DIM
a. ☞ s-<u>dí</u>duuk^w	*		*
b. s-<u>dú</u>duuk^w	*	*!	
c. s-<u>dúu</u>duuk^w	*!*		

The optimal candidate (a) only contains a long vowel in the base and obeys TRANSFER at the expense of DEP-DIM. The suboptimal candidates incur a fatal violation of TRANSFER (b) and NO-LONG-V (c).

The preceding analysis shows that the size and fixed segmentism of the diminutive reduplicant are instances of unmarked structure emerging in reduplication.

(25) Diminutive summary ranking:
   a. Shape
      AFFIX ≤ σ, NOCODA ≫ MAX-DIM

b. Fixed segmentism
No-Skipping, Transfer, *Complex, No-Long-V ≫ Dep-Dim, Max-Dim
*Unstress-V ≫ Align-L(PrWd, Ft), *Stress-Schwa ≫ Dep-Dim, Max-Dim

The CV shape follows from the size restrictor Affi x≤ σ and NoCoda having precedence over total copy (Max-Dim). The appearance of the fixed segment may be described as "no copy is better than a bad copy." Unmarked structure emerges because of higher ranked Phono-Constraints (*Complex, *Stressed-Schwa, No-Long-V), but faithfulness also requires good correspondence as indicated by high-ranking No-Skipping and Transfer.

The correct analysis of fixed segmentism is significant to a parallel account of double reduplications because, as I will show, the diminutive faithfulness constraints are lower ranked than distributive ones. Double reduplications exploit this difference in ranking, resulting in the diminutive being less faithful to its base than the distributive in both single and double reduplications.

4.2 Distributive

Distributive reduplication indicates plurality and the distribution of items (Bates, Hess, and Hilbert 1994). The two productive patterns of the distributive are CVC- and CV-.[12] First let us examine the CVC- pattern exemplified below.

(26) Lushootseed distributive

a. saq$^{w\prime}$ "fly"   <u>sáq</u>$^{w\prime}$+saq$^{w\prime}$ "fly here and there"

    k'aw(a)   "chew (food)"   <u>k'áw</u>'+k'aw   "chewing"[13]

    dəš   "lean over"   <u>dəš</u>+dəš-ád   "set many things on their side"

b. d^{z}əX   "move"   <u>d^{z}əX</u>+d^{z}əX   "move household"

    d^{z}ək$^{w\prime}$ "travel"   <u>d^{z}ək$^{w\prime}$</u>+d^{z}ək$^{w\prime}$ "wander about continually"

    s-čətx^{w}əd   "bear"   s-<u>čət</u>+čətx^{w}əd   "bears"

In all cases the distributive is identical to the first CVC of the stem. Like the diminutive, the distributive follows the regular stress pattern of the language. However, unlike the diminutive, schwa can be stressed. This difference will be significant in the analysis of double reduplications.[14] The preceding pattern illustrates that the distributive is a CVC- prefix.

The CVC- shape results because MAX-DIST dominates NOCODA. The template is analyzed as affixal: RED-DIST=AFFI x Therefore, AFFI x≤ σ is active in restricting the size of the distributive reduplicant to a syllable.

(27) AFFI x≤ σ ≫ MAX-DIST ≫ NOCODA

	AFFI x≤ σ	MAX-DIST	NO-CODA
a. ☞ bədbədá?		**	**
b. bəbədá?		***!	*
c. bədabədá?	*!	*	*

Candidate (a) is selected as optimal. Candidate (b) fares the worst on MAX-DIST. Candidate (c) violates AFFI x≤ σ because it is disyllabic. With high ranking AFFI x≤ σ and MAX-DIST, the optimal shape of the distributive reduplicant is CVC.

A small number of forms have a CV- alternant: roots in which the first two consonants are identical. This pattern is significant to understanding the CV- alternant of the double reduplications. The following is an exhaustive list of stems with (almost) identical initial consonants and their distributive forms.

(28) Distributive: $C_1 = C_2$

    a. i. c'íc'al   "long feathers with thick stems"
           c'íc'íc'al-b   "sprouted wings"
      ii. t'ít'-əb   "bathe"
           t'ít'ít'-əb   "bathe for a while"
      iii. t'uc'-il   "fire a gun"
           t'út'c'-il   "shoot more than once"
      iv. wíw'su   "children; little"   [Southern Lushootseed]
           wíwiw'su   "little [plural]"
      v. ləlwá?səd   "sleeping platform"
           lələlwá?səd   "sleeping platforms"
    b.   lil   "far, far away"
           ?u-líllil-təb   "they were separated (from rest of group)"

In (a) there are five stems which have a CV- reduplicant. However, in (b) there is one stem with a CVC- reduplicant. The regular pattern for stems with identical initial consonants, then, is as in (a): only the first CV- of the root is copied.

A phonological analysis is required to explain why the second consonant does not reduplicate in (28a). A careful examination of the preceding stems, and segmentally similar forms in the *Lushootseed Dictionary*, shows that the identical consonants do not arise from reduplication. Because the forms are not reduplicated, failure to copy the second consonant cannot be due to subjacency as would be expected under Broselow's proposal. Recall that subjacency restricts the copying to the adjacent stem. The non-reduplicated stems are a copying domain. So a phonological analysis is required.

The failure to copy the second consonant in the distributive is analyzed as an instance of antigemination. If the distributive were the maximal $C_1V_1C_2$- prefix, the output would contain two adjacent identical consonants.

(29) Unattested distributive forms
  i. *c'ic'c'ic'al-b
  ii. *t'it't'it'-əb
  iii. *t'uc't'uc'-il
  iv. *wiw'wiw'su
  v. *ləlləlwaʔsəd

Antigemination accounts for all cases of a CV- distributive reduplicant. Thus, high-ranked phonological constraints prevent the maximal CVC- distributive affix from occurring whenever the first two consonants of a stem are identical.

Broselow (1983: 326) suggests that a process of antigemination would explain why the distributive is CV- in the DIST-DIM stems. With distributive affixation, the entire diminutive-stem melody is copied. Melodemes are associated to the CVC affix. The form is then subject to a rule of antigemination.

(30) DIST   DIM STEM

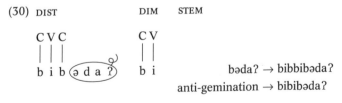

              bəda? → bibbibəda?
          anti-gemination → bibibəda?

While antigemination accounts for the DIST-TIM pattern of reduplication, Broselow maintains the subjacency analysis. She cites the form in (28b), with the CVC- shape, as evidence against an antigemination rule. As stated above, subjacency cannot derive the CV- pattern of single reduplications in (28a). I can find no explanation for why both consonants reduplicate in (28b), but will adopt the antigemination analysis based on language-internal evidence.

A large amount of evidence supports a general process of antigemination in Lushootseed. Hess (1967: 7) notes that identical stops reduce to a single stop. Snyder (1968: 22) also notes the loss of an identical consonant at morpheme junctures. An examination of the medial clusters in the recently expanded corpus (Bates, Hess, and Hilbert 1994) shows that geminates are extremely rare, limited to: $g^w g^w$, qq, and ll. Of the handful of words found with geminates, two have alternate pronunciations which avoid the geminate.

(31) Medial geminates
    a. ʔúdəgʷ=gwił ~ ʔúdəgʷ=ił   "middle of canoe"
       λ'əlla? ~ λ'ála?   "after a while"
    b. dxʷ-yəq=qíd-əb   "Speak up!"
       ʔu-lílil-təb   "they were separated (from
                               rest of group)"

Even when there are identical consonants as in (a), they are avoided by deletion. The virtual lack of geminates provides strong evidence that antigemination accounts for the CV- distributive.

Two constraints rule out geminate structures: the Obligatory Contour Principle (OCP) and NoLink. The OCP (Leben 1973; Goldsmith 1976; McCarthy 1986) rules out adjacent identical consonants:

(32) Obligatory Contour Principle
    At the melodic level, adjacent identical elements are prohibited

NoLink rules out linked structures (Selkirk 1984).[15]

(33) NoLink

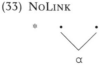

Gemination satisfies the OCP by linking identical melodemes, but it violates NoLink. Nowhere in the phonology of Lushootseed is there evidence of linking between adjacent consonants.[16] Antigemination satisfies both the OCP and NoLink: there is only one segment and it is not doubly linked.

High ranking OCP and NoLink compel violation of Max-Dist. The following tableau shows that Max-Dist is violated in order to satisfy the OCP and NoLink.

(34) OCP, NoLink ≫ Max-Dist

		OCP	NoLink	Max-Dist
a.	c'ic'c'ic'al	*!		**
b.	c'ic'c'ic'al $\vee$		*!	**
c. ☞	c'ic'ic'al			***

Candidates (a) and (b) fare the best on Max-Dist. However, (a) violates the OCP and (b) violates NoLink. The optimal candidate obeys the OCP and NoLink at the expense of Max-Dist.

External evidence for antigemination at the reduplicant/base boundary comes from a similar pattern of reduplication in Rotuman, an Austronesian language. Churchward (1940: 103) observes that if reduplication "results in two identical consonants coming together, the two coalesce into one." Observe the data below:

(35) Rotuman reduplication (Churchward 1940: 103)
    a. karkarā   <u>kar</u>karkarā   "to snore"
       ŋarue   <u>ŋar</u>ŋarue   "to work"
    b. čɔči   <u>čɔ</u>čɔči   "to shave"
       kokokā   <u>ko</u>kokā   "to cackle"

In (a) we see the regular pattern is CVC. However in (b), when the first two consonants of the stem are identical, antigemination results in a CV- reduplicant.[17] Thus cross-linguistic evidence supports the OCP as an active constraint in limiting the size of a reduplicant.

To summarize, the distributive reduplicant is CVC- because Max-Dist dominates No-Coda. The CV- alternant results because high-ranking constraints barring geminates rule out the CVC- reduplicant in stems with initial identical consonants.

(36) Distributive summary ranking

OCP, NoLink, Affi x≤ σ ≫ Max-Dist ≫ No-Coda

Each of the reduplicative morphemes has been formed in parallel. The input contains the abstract morpheme DIST or DIM, and the output contains a well-formed reduplicant. The overall shape and the presence or absence of fixed segmentism are derived by constraint interaction, according to the assumptions outlined in section 2. In the following section, I will combine the rankings obtained thus far and show that words with two reduplicative morphemes in the input can also be derived in parallel.

5. Double reduplications

There are two patterns of double reduplications with diminutive and distributive affixes.[18] As noted at the outset, the distributive and diminutive affixes may cooccur in either order, producing DIST-DIM and DIM-DIST stems. Some examples of both possible orders are provided below.

(37) Lushootseed double reduplications

    a. DIM-DIST

        bí-bəd-bəda?   "dolls, litter [of baby animals]"

        sá -sxʷ-saxʷəb   "legs partly covered"[19]

    b. DIST-DIM

        bí-bi-bəda?   "small children"

        sdí-di-duukʷ   "small knives"

        č'í-č'i-č'ʎ'a?   "gravel"

The DIST-DIM stems are the most productive. (This is probably the result of the unusual semantics of forming diminutive-distributives.) In the DIM-DIST stems (a), the size and vowel quality of R_{DIM} and R_{DIST} are identical to those observed in single reduplications: $C_1 i$ and $C_1 VC_2$. However, in the DIST-DIM stems in (b), there are three irregularities. The distributive reduplicant does not have the expected shape or segmentism; it is $C_1 i$ rather than $C_1 VC_2$. As noted in section 4.2, in single reduplications the distributive maintains schwa, even when stressed. Also, the nucleus of the diminutive reduplicant is i even though it is not stressed. Recall that when the diminutive is unstressed, the nucleus is schwa.

It turns out that the preceding patterns are the result of the distributive reduplicant being more faithful to its base than the diminutive. The ranking of distributive faithfulness over diminutive faithfulness (which is derived from the analysis of the single reduplications) results in the correct shape and fixed segmentism for all reduplication patterns.

In a parallel analysis both reduplicative morphemes are affixed and candidate outputs are evaluated against the constraint hierarchy. The input contains the abstract morphemes DIST and DIM, affixed in an order consistent with the lexical semantics of the word. In the candidate output forms, each reduplicative morpheme has its own reduplicant and base. It is fairly simple to recognize the reduplicants in the output, but is a matter of some delicacy to determine what portion of the output functions as the base for each morpheme. Recall that for prefixing reduplication, the base is the string immediately following the reduplicant. So, in DIST-DIM stems, the base for the distributive consists of any segments following it; this includes the string comprising the diminutive reduplicant plus stem. The base for the diminutive will be the following stem material. Likewise, in DIM-DIST stems, with the diminutive as the initial reduplicant, its base will contain the following distributive plus stem.

The following representations identify the correspondence relations for DIM-DIST and DIST-DIM stems. Correspondents are indexed with numbers for the diminutive morpheme and with lower case letters for the distributive morpheme. Bases are underlined.

(38) R-B correspondents

    a. DIM-DIST

		$\mathrm{RED}_{\mathrm{DIM}}$⁻	$\mathrm{RED}_{\mathrm{DIST}}$⁻	bəda?
input:				
output:		bi	bəd	bəda?
DIM	$R_{\mathrm{DIM}}/\underline{B}_{\mathrm{DIM}}$	1	<u>123</u>	<u>45678</u>
DIST	$R_{\mathrm{DIST}}/\underline{B}_{\mathrm{DIST}}$		abc	<u>abcde</u>

    b. DIST-DIM

		$\mathrm{RED}_{\mathrm{DIST}}$⁻	$\mathrm{RED}_{\mathrm{DIM}}$⁻	bəda?
input:				
output:		bi	bi	bəda?
DIST	$R_{\mathrm{DIST}}/\underline{B}_{\mathrm{DIST}}$	ab	<u>ab</u>	<u>cdefg</u>
DIM	$R_{\mathrm{DIM}}/\underline{B}_{\mathrm{DIM}}$		1	<u>12345</u>

Comparing the distributive correspondence relations in (a) and (b) shows that the distributive reduplicant only contains base segments. On the other hand, in the diminutive correspondence relations in (a) and (b), the reduplicants contain nonbase segments.

To preview the analysis: regardless of affix order, the diminutive reduplicant violates DEP-DIM, and the distributive reduplicant obeys DEP-DIST. This is an important result. The fact that one reduplicative morpheme obeys a faithfulness constraint while another one violates it provides evidence for separate correspondence functions for individual reduplicative morphemes. Further, the identity between reduplicants in DIST-DIM stems is the result of maintaining identity between distributive base and reduplicant.

As predicted by parallelism, the representations in (38) are the optimal candidates when evaluated against the entire constraint hierarchy. The shape and fixed segmentism in the output are consistent with the constraint rankings established for single reduplications. In all cases the output obeys distributive faithfulness at the expense of diminutive faithfulness. Let us first examine shape and then fixed segmentism.

5.1 Shape

Constraints interact with MAX to determine the size of the reduplicants. By transitivity of constraint ranking (MAX-DIST ≫ NO-CODA and NO-CODA ≫ MAX-DIM) we arrive at the following hierarchy.

(39) OCP/NOLINK[20] ≫ MAX-DIST ≫ NO-CODA ≫ MAX-DIM

The syllable-structure constraint which distinguishes the shape of the distributive and diminutive reduplicants (presence versus absence of a coda) intervenes between MAX-DIST and MAX-DIM.

In the single reduplications, the basic shapes of the diminutive and distributive are C_1V- and C_1VC_2-. For the double reduplications there are four candidate shapes to be compared: C_1V-C_1VC_2-, C_1VC_2-C_1VC_2-, C_1VC_1-C_1V-,[21] and C_1V-C_1V-. In both DIST-DIM and DIM-DIST stems, the optimal candidate obeys the OCP/NOLINK; it violates MAX-DIST and NO-CODA only minimally, and fares poorly on MAX-DIM.

The optimal shape of the reduplicants in DIST-DIM stems is C_1V-C_1V-. In the following tableau the vowel quality is held constant, but the shape varies among the candidates.

(40) DIST-DIM

DIST-DIM-bəda?	OCP/ NOLINK	MAX- DIST	NO-CODA	MAX- DIM
a. bí-bid-bəda?		******!	**	***
b. bíd-bid-bəda?		*****	***!	***
c. bíb-bi-bəda?	*!	****	**	****
d. ☞ bí-bi-bəda?		****	*	****

Candidate (d) best satisfies the constraint hierarchy. Candidate (a) violates MAX-DIST worse than others. The distributive reduplicant is *bi*, its base *bidbəda?*. Candidate (b) violates NO-CODA more than minimally, and candidate (c) fatally violates the OCP/NoLINK. In the optimal candidate, minimizing MAX-DIST violations leads to greater MAX-DIM violation (but MAX-DIM is irrelevant).

The comparison of candidates (a) and (d) shows a remarkable effect of parallelism. Candidate (a) is suboptimal because of MAX-DIST, and yet (a) and (d) differ in the size of the diminutive reduplicant. The correct size of the diminutive reduplicant is achieved by a higher-ranked constraint which does not directly evaluate diminutive correspondence. An interaction exists because the distributive base contains the diminutive reduplicant. In a serial derivation, the interaction between MAX-DIST and the size of the diminutive reduplicant is unexplainable. In a parallel derivation one expects high-ranking constraints to exert an effect over the entire word.

As a point of logic, a serial derivation would not need to explain such an interaction. The optimal diminutive form would be derived, and would serve as the input for distributive reduplication. A potential problem facing the serial account is that the input to distributive formation, *bíbədà?*, contains structure that would need to be erased. First, primary stress, but not secondary stress, would need to be reassigned. Second, in order for there not to be an interaction of the type seen in the preceding tableau, the correspondence relation between the diminutive reduplicant and base would also need to be erased. Otherwise *Gen* could change the exponence of the diminutive morpheme, and an interaction between MAX-DIST and the diminutive reduplicant would occur. These two changes to the diminutive stem are unnecessary complications to the grammar, given that parallelism derives the correct forms. While the serial account would not need to explain the interaction between MAX-DIST and the diminutive reduplicant, it would need to explain why the relation between reduplicant and base is obliterated between levels. A further problem is that there is no evidence for intermediate stages, because the constraint rankings do not differ. Serialism would also posit an intermediate stage for DIM-DIST stems, where the input to diminutive is the distributive stem *bədbədá?*.

The optimal shape of the reduplicants in DIM-DIST stems is C_1V-C_1VC_2-, which also follows from the constraint ranking established for single reduplications.

(41) DIM-DIST

DIM-DIST-bəda?	OCP/ NoLink	Max- Dist	No-Coda	Max- Dim
a. ☞ <u>bí-bəd</u>-bəda?		**	**	******
b. <u>bíd-bəd</u>-bəda?		**	***!	*****
c. <u>bíb-bə</u>-bəda?	*!	***	**	****
d. <u>bí-bə</u>-bəda?		***!	*	******

Candidate (a) best satisfies the constraint hierarchy. The suboptimal candidates incur fatal violations of No-Coda (b), OCP/NoLink (c), and Max-Dist (d).

Regardless of affix order, the four candidate shapes can be winnowed down to two, based on purely phonological grounds. Candidates with C_1VC_2-C_1VC_2 shape incur a fatal violation of No-Coda. Candidates with C_1VC_1-C_1V shape incur a fatal violation of OCP/NoLink. Of the two remaining candidate shapes, C_1V-C_1V and C_1V-C_1VC_2, both share the property that the initial reduplicant has the shape C_1V. Selection of the optimal candidate thus rests on selecting the correct shape for the second reduplicant.

The optimal reduplicant shapes obey Max-Dist at the expense of Max-Dim. An interaction occurs because the base of the outer reduplicant contains the segments of the inner reduplicant: there is a direct relationship between the size of reduplicants and bases. When DIST is outermost, its base contains diminutive material. Here, obeying Max-Dist coincides with minimizing the size of the distributive base, reducing the size of the diminutive reduplicant. A smaller diminutive reduplicant incurs more Max-Dim violations. So the optimal DIST-DIM stem is C_1V-C_1V-, with a smaller diminutive reduplicant. When DIM is outermost, its base contains distributive material. Obeying Max-Dist results in increasing the size of the distributive reduplicant; its base remains constant. A larger distributive reduplicant coincides with a larger diminutive base and a greater number of Max-Dim violations, making the optimal DIM-DIST candidate C_1V-C_1VC_2-.

The correct shapes of the reduplicative morphemes can be derived in parallel, regardless of the order of reduplicative affixes. Nothing special need be said about words with multiple reduplicative affixes. The only requirement is that the input have the correct morphological structure. Everything else follows from the constraint ranking independently required for single reduplications. Having established that shape can be derived in parallel I now turn to fixed segmentism.

5.2 Fixed segmentism

Recall that fixed segmentism results in a violation of DEPENDENCE. In order to derive the correct pattern of fixed segmentism we must establish an overall ranking of the different Dependence constraints for diminutive and distributive morphemes. I will limit the discussion to the stems which contain schwa vowels.

In the analysis of the diminutive, I established that the Phono-Constraint *STRESSED-SCHWA dominates DEP-DIM. Recall that the difference between diminutive and distributive was that the distributive reduplicant tolerated stressed schwas. However, no ranking between DEP-DIST and *STRESSED-SCHWA was provided because, as mentioned in note 14 in section 3.2, the crucial candidate *bid-bada? also violates CONTIGUITY-DIST. Therefore, the ranking of DEP-DIST and *STRESSED-SCHWA cannot be determined. However, when the distributive reduplicant is CV- (as in the DIST-DIM stems), CONTIGUITY is trivially obeyed, establishing the following ranking:

(42) DEP-DIST, *STRESSED-ə ≫ DEP-DIM

It is important to keep in mind that the addition of the distributive morpheme will not affect initial stress.[22] So, in the following discussion, stress remains on the initial syllable in accordance with ALIGN(PrWd, L, Ft, L).

Because we are only examining roots with schwa, there are two vowel qualities to consider: the root vowel ə or the fixed segment i. Freely generating all relevant candidates produces four possible vowel melodies for the double reduplications: ə-ə, i-ə, ə-i, and i-i. The optimal candidate will obey DEP-DIST and *STRESSED-SCHWA, faring poorly on DEP-DIM. The prediction is that for all stems, the distributive reduplicant will only contain base material and the diminutive will always contain non-base material.

The optimal shape for DIST-DIM stems is C_1V-C_1V as I have already established. In the following tableau the shape is held constant, but the vowel quality varies among the candidates.

(43) DIST-DIM

DIST-DIM-Root	DEP-DIST	*STRESSED-SCHWA	DEP-DIM
a. bə́-bə-bəda?		*!	
b. bí-bə-bəda?	*!		
c. bə́-bi-bəda?	*!	*!	*
d. ☞ bí-bi-bəda?			*

Candidate (d) is the optimal form. It only violates DEP-DIM. The distributive reduplicant is *bi*; its base *bibəda?*. DEP-DIM is violated because the diminutive reduplicant is *bi*, containing a segment not in its base *bəda?*. The suboptimal candidates violate *STRESSED-SCHWA (a), DEP-DIST (b), or all three constraints (c). Once again, distributive faithfulness is maintained over diminutive faithfulness.

The preceding tableau illustrates that DEP-DIST dominates DEP-DIM. A valid ranking argument obtains because all candidates obey CONTIGUITY-DIST. The ranking is determined by comparing candidates (b) and (d) repeated in the tableau below.

(44) DEP-DIST ≫ DEP-DIM

DIST-DIM-Root	DEP-DIST	DEP-DIM
b. bí-bə-bəda?	*!	
d. ☞ bí-bi-bəda?		*

In the optimal candidate, every segment of the distributive has a correspondent in its base. Higher ranking DEP-DIST compels violation of DEP-DIM, resulting in identity between the distributive and its base, which contains the diminutive reduplicant. This identity effect explains why the diminutive has the fixed segment even though it is not stressed.

The identity between the distributive and diminutive reduplicant is an instance of overapplication of fixed segmentism (as pointed out to me by Laura Walsh Dickey). Overapplication occurs when a phonological alternation applies in both base and copy, even though the trigger is present in only one string (Wilbur 1973; Kiparsky 1986; Mester 1986;

McCarthy and Prince this volume). A classic case of overapplication can be seen in the Indonesian nasal substitution below.

(45) Indonesian nasal substitution (Uhrbach 1987; McCarthy and Prince this volume)

pikir	məmikir	məmikir-mikir	"think (over)"
tari	mənari	mənari-nari	"dance (for joy)"
kira	məŋira	məŋira-ŋira	"approximately/to guess"

Overapplication results because identity is maintained between reduplicant and base. See McCarthy and Prince (this volume) for detailed discussion of reduplicative overapplication and Benua (1995) for overapplication in truncated words.

The ranking for overapplication of fixed segmentism in double reduplications shows remarkable parallels with the ranking established for overapplication in single reduplications (McCarthy and Prince this volume) and in truncated words (Benua 1995). The ranking schemata are presented below.

(46) Overapplication schemata
  a. Single reduplications (McCarthy and Prince this volume)
     BR-Faith, Phono-Constraint ≫ IO-Faith
  b. Truncated words (Benua 1995)
     BT-Faith, Phono-Constraint ≫ IO-Faith
  c. Double reduplications
     DEP-DIST, *STRESSED-SCHWA ≫ DEP-DIM

In all cases of overapplication, high-ranked reduplicative (and truncatory) faithfulness compels violation of lower-ranked base faithfulness. In single reduplications and truncated words, the faithfulness of the base is regulated by IO-correspondence, while in double reduplications, the faithfulness of the base is regulated by BR-correspondence.

In the DIST-DIM stems, initial stress compels the presence of a fixed segment. Because DEP-DIST is high ranking, it compels the presence of the fixed segment in its base, which contains the diminutive reduplicant.

The pattern of fixed segmentism in DIM-DIST stems also follows from the same ranking. Recall that the optimal shape is C_1V-C_1VC_2; again, only vowel quality varies among the candidates.

(47) DIM-DIST

DIM-DIST-Root	DEP-DIST	*STRESSED-SCHWA	DEP-DIM
a. bə́-bəd-bəda?		*!	
b. ☞ bí-bəd-bəda?			*
c. bə́-bid-bəda?	*!	*!	*
d. bí-bid-bəda?	*!		

Candidate (a) violates *STRESSED-SCHWA and candidates (c) and (d) violate DEP-DIST. Candidate (b) is optimal because R_{DIST} only contains base material ($R_{DIST}=bəd$; $B_{DIST}=bəda?$).

Overapplication does not apply in DIM-DIST stems because the diminutive base (the distributive reduplicant) has a stronger faithfulness requirement. The distributive must be faithful to its base, which is regulated by IO-Faith.

Regardless of affix order, the correct pattern of fixed segmentism is selected because the distributive maintains identity with its base, while the diminutive is always unfaithful to its base. High-ranking ALIGN(PrWd, L, Ft, L) and *STRESSED-SCHWA ensure that the initial reduplicant is always Cí. Thus the two vowel melodies to choose from are: *i-i* and *i-ə*. When the distributive is outermost (DIST-DIM), the identical vowel melody is optimal. Fixed segmentism overapplies. When the diminutive is outermost (DIM-DIST), the nonidentical vowel melody is optimal. There is normal application of fixed segmentism. In both DIST-DIM and DIM-DIST stems, obeying DEP-DIST results in violation of DEP-DIM.

5.3 Summary

I have shown that parallelism of constraint evaluation results in the correct shape and fixed segmentism in double reduplications. Previous accounts required cyclicity and subjacency. Subjacency is inappropriate to account for the CV- alternant in the DIST-DIM stems because a process of antigemination explains the pattern. Further, subjacency cannot account for the CV- alternants which occur with single reduplications. Cyclicity is not needed because with the advent of Correspondence Theory, reduplicant and base are necessarily adjacent in the output.[23] Recall that in Broselow's analysis cyclic reduplication ensured that the segmental content of the affix was obtained from an adjacent string. In addition, the identity effect, previously attributed to the cycle, is reanalyzed as an instance of overapplication.

The DIST-DIM pattern of double reduplication seemed to provide evidence for an intermediate stage in the derivation. A serial analysis would posit an intermediate stage in which DIM is affixed first. However, we saw that the distributive constraint exerts an influence over the diminutive shape and fixed segmentism.

One final point is that the constraint rankings for the two reduplicative affixes follow a pattern: the distributive R-B correspondence constraints dominate the diminutive ones. This is schematized as:

(48) DIST-Faith ≫ DIM-Faith

The distributive reduplicant is more faithful to its base than the diminutive: it contains more segments and contains only base material.

Two questions arise regarding the ranking in (48). The first is why the ranking should be as it is, and the second concerns encoding this relative ranking in the lexical entries of reduplicative affixes. The answer to both of these questions is the same if the distributive morpheme is a root reduplicant. Specifying the distributive template as $RED_{DIST}=ROOT$ rather than $RED_{DIST}=AFFI$ xproves to be an instance of the general schema:

(49) Meta-constraint on root and affix faithfulness (McCarthy and
      Prince 1994a; this volume)
      Root-faithfulness ≫ Affix-faithfulness (universally)

The fact that distributive correspondence dominates diminutive correspondence follows from the universal ranking in (49). McCarthy and Prince (this volume) propose that correspondence holds between input and output, as well as between base and reduplicant. If the distributive is a root and the diminutive is an affix, then the ranking in (48) is an instantiation of (49). The two faithfulness schemata refer to the same set of constraints, the only difference is that one measures I-O faithfulness and the other measures B-R faithfulness. (See McCarthy and Prince this volume for a discussion of other possible interactions between correspondence constraints.)

Analyzing the distributive template as a root proves to be an enterprise in its own right. Therefore I will just mention some of the issues which are raised by this proposal.

The first issue is to determine the constraints that characterize root shape. The analysis thus far assumes that the distributive is an affix, and therefore its syllable size obeys AFFI x≤ σ. While McCarthy and Prince (1994a) discuss several constraints on the shape of STEM and AFFI x it is more problematic to provide a uniform theory for roots. For example, it does not seem possible to reconcile concatenative morphological systems such as English with nonconcatenative morphological system like Arabic. A key issue is to determine the constraints on canonical root shape and how they affect the size of reduplicative affixes.

The second issue is to provide evidence that the distributive morpheme exhibits rootlike properties in Lushootseed. First, the canonical root shape in Lushootseed is CVC. Snyder (1968: 14) reports that sixty-eight percent of the seven hundred roots he collected are CVC and CəC (Southern Lushootseed). So, the distributive has the canonical root shape. Second, Broselow (1983: 337) proposes that the morphological structure of inherently reduplicated words like *pišpiš* "cat" is root+root.

(50)   stem

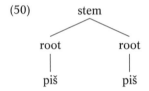

While a systematic study of inherently reduplicated words in Lushootseed has not yet been conducted, Broselow's proposal supports analyzing the distributive morpheme as a segmentally empty root. Third, the distributive exhibits the prosodic properties of roots. Two points are that, in posttonic position, both roots and distributives may have syncopated vowels, and both allow schwa to be stressed.

Further investigation is required to provide conclusive evidence that the distributive is a root. The proposal has the advantage that the faithfulness requirements of the distributive and diminutive follow a universal ranking schema. The individual properties of size and fixed segmentism follow from the universal ranking of root faithfulness over affix faithfulness.

6. Concluding remarks

The analysis of double reduplications in parallel has shown some striking results. Primarily, a pattern of reduplication which seemed to present evidence for an intermediate stage (DIST-DIM) actually shows that high-ranking reduplicative constraints exert an effect on unrelated reduplicative morphemes. This is quintessential parallelism. If the double reduplications were truly derived with an intermediate stage, a subsequent reduplicative morpheme could not disrupt the results of the first stage.

The patterns of Lushootseed double reduplication illustrate that in serial theories of reduplication (with an actual copy mechanism), the cycle is required to ensure that reduplicant and base are adjacent. In parallel OT, the adjacency of reduplicant and base in the output obviates the need for cyclicity.

Identity effects which had previously been attributed to the cycle are shown to be an instance of overapplication of fixed segmentism in double reduplications. When the morpheme with higher-ranked faithfulness requirements precedes the morpheme with lower-ranked faithfulness, identity is enforced. This pattern of overapplication shows striking parallels with identity effects in single reduplications and truncated words. It further shows that the crucial ranking is with RED-Faith dominating BASE-Faith. BASE-Faith can be regulated by IO-correspondence or BR-correspondence.

Finally, regardless of the morphological structure of the input, the constraint hierarchy (or grammar) of Lushootseed selects the correct candidates for all patterns of reduplication. Any alternations in size and fixed segmentism of the reduplicants follow from the interaction of general phonotactic constraints with reduplication specific constraints. This parallel analysis has been argued to be simpler than a serial account which would posit an unwarranted intermediate stage.

Notes

1 This ideas in this chapter were first developed while attending the University of Massachusetts. Since then, certain components of the analysis have been reworked and addressed more fully. I am grateful to John McCarthy for guiding me from the start of this research. For comments on an earlier draft, I would like to thank John Alderete, Jill Beckman, Mike Dickey, Joe Pater, Sharon Peperkamp, Sharon Rose, Lisa Selkirk, and Laura Walsh Dickey, as well as participants of the Correspondence Theory Seminar at University of Massachusetts (Spring 1995), and an anonymous reviewer. Special thanks to Laura Benua for many inspiring discussions. All errors

are my own. This work was supported in part by SSHRCC Doctoral Fellowship #752-92-0691.

2 Initially, correspondence related only reduplicant and base, however, recently it has been extended to input-output strings (McCarthy and Prince this volume) and truncated-base words (Benua 1995).

3 A similar idea has been proposed by Steriade (1988), who shows that templates can be composed of two conditions: one on phonological markedness and another on weight.

4 All data cited here are taken from Bates, Hess, and Hilbert (1994) *Lushootseed Dictionary*. Unless noted, all observations are of the Northern dialect group. The phoneme inventory of Lushootseed includes the following: /p, p′, t, t′, c, c′, č, č′, k, k′, kʷ, kʷ′, q, q′, qʷ, qʷ′, ʔ, ƛ′, b, d, dᶻ, j, g, gʷ, s, ɬ, š, xʷ, X, Xʷ, h, l, l′, y, y′, w, w′, i, ii, u, uu, a, aa, ə/. (The phonetic symbols follow those used in the *Lushootseed Dictionary* except that /X/ = /x̌/; /j/ = /ʧ/; /ƛ′/ = /ƛ̓/.) Following Salish convention, "=" indicates a lexical suffix; "–" indicates a fixed segmental affix; "+" indicates a reduplicative affix.

5 Bates (1986) analyzes the glottal stop as occuring postlexically, on open stressed syllables.

6 I will indicate the diminutive and distributive reduplicative constraints by suffixing the labels DIM and DIST respectively.

7 This predictable stress can be overridden by some inherently stressed suffixes. Prefixes are never stressed, providing evidence that the prosodic word coincides with the left edge of the root.

8 There are several approaches to formalizing *STRESSED-SCHWA. Language-internal evidence supports Kenstowicz's (1994b) sonority-based proposal, where prominence peaks are preferentially more sonorous vowels. Schwa is the least sonorous vowel, and makes the worst prominence peak. A second aspect of Kenstowicz's proposal is that sonorous vowels are marked when unstressed. In Lushootseed, /a/ is the only vowel that reduces to schwa when unstressed. Kenstowicz's proposal relates these two facts. Kager (1991) proposes that schwa is mora-less at early stages of syllabification (consistent with being mora-less in the input). Itô (personal communication) suggests that schwa cannot be stressed because the head of a stressed foot must be headed by a vowel feature. If schwa is placeless (and [Place] is the head of a segment as Itô and Mester 1993 propose), then schwa cannot be stressed because a headless vowel cannot head a stressed foot.

9 For a different conception of NO-LONG-V see Itô and Mester (this volume).

10 It is not clear whether TRANSFER should be generalized to include onset-hood and/or coda-hood. If so, the definition of TRANSFER can include onset-hood by including zero as a value for the variable.

11 TRANSFER bans shortening and lengthening of vowels. The definition of TRANSFER makes predictions about certain transfer effects. If a language has low-ranked TRANSFER then we predict that long vowels can shorten as well as short vowels lengthen. So far this prediction is borne out. For B-R correspondence, in Tagalog a long vowel shortens to accomodate a light-syllable template and a short vowel lengthens to accomodate a heavy-syllable template (Carrier-Duncan 1984). For I-O correspondence, in Luganda closed-syllable shortening is associated with some geminate forms, and compensatory lengthening accompanies glide formation (Clements 1986). For O-O correspondence of truncated forms, in Japanese Hypocoristic formation long vowels may shorten and short vowels may lengthen to accommodate the template (Poser 1990; Benua 1995).

12 Hess and Hilbert (1976: 2. 161) note that there are two irregular forms of the distributive which occur with high frequency words. A small set have the shape -VC$_2$-, and another small set have a C$_1$ə- affix.

13 Hess and Hilbert (1976: 2. 161) note that when the second consonant of the distributive is a sonorant, it is glottalized.

14 In the stems in (b) *STRESSED-SCHWA is violated and DEP-DIST is obeyed. The ranking between DEP-DIST and *STRESSED-SCHWA cannot be determined. While suboptimal *bid-bəda? violates DEP-DIST, it also violates both parts of CONTIGUITY (see McCarthy and Prince this volume). Correspondents in the base and reduplicant are discontiguous: only the consonants are in correspondence. Domain(f) is split: {b, d}, as is Range(f): {b, d}. A valid ranking argument cannot be obtained because CONTIGUITY (rather than DEPENDENCE) could compel violation of *STRESSED-SCHWA.

15 While Itô, Mester, and Padgett (1995) propose a family of NoLINK constraints, only the most general version is needed for the Lushootseed analysis.

16 In Lushootseed there is no assimilation between adjacent consonants. There are no nasals, and adjacent segments may differ in glottalization, voicing, and place. NoLINK is only violated between vowels. There are long vowels as well as a process of vowel harmony in a subset of transitive stems (e.g., bíx^{w}i-d "toss it, shake it" Bates, Hess, and Hilbert 94: 41).

17 Interestingly, Rotuman double reduplications are the same as the Lushootseed DIST-DIM stems.

(1) Rotuman double reduplications (Churchward 1940: 105)

toka	totoka	toktoka	tototoka	"to push against"
tuki	tutuki	tuktuki	tututuki	"to refrain"
?oro	?o?oro	?or?oro	?o?o?oro	"to tie or bind"

However, see Blevins (1994) who analyzes the CVCV pattern as a single bimoraic foot reduplicant.

18 A third reduplicative morpheme indicating "out of control" is also quite productive, and can occur with distributive or diminutive reduplication.

19 Syncope often accompanies reduplication (Hess 1966). The process is not entirely regular, but occurs most frequently between voiceless obstruents.

20 I will refer to the constraints OCP and NoLink as OCP/NoLink in order to economically examine the candidates with geminates and adjacent identical consonants. In the tableaux only one candidate, not two, will show violations of OCP/NoLink.

21 In the C_1VC_1-C_1V- pattern, the outer reduplicant contains two identical consonants because its base contains two identical consonants: base = $C_1VC_1V(C_2...)$. The base contains the inner reduplicant and the following stem. In strict prefixing reduplication, when a larger reduplicant precedes a smaller reduplicant, the larger reduplicant will always contain two identical consonants.

22 Forms like /bədbədá?/ are analyzed as having an initial foot that does not bear main stress. The initial foot satisfies Align-L(PrWd, Ft) and the lack of stress satisfies *Stressed-Schwa. For further details about Lushootseed prosody, see Urbanczyk (1996).

23 Adjacency of reduplicant and base is problematic for double reduplications with a reduplicative infix. The reduplicative infix is not part of the base, as the following dist-dim stems from Thompson (Interior Salish) show.

   (i) Thompson (Broselow 1983: 329)
      a. sil   "calico"
      b. sí-sil   dim
      c. sil-sil   dist
      d. sil-sí-sil dist-dim

It appears as if the segments of the diminutive affix (an infix) are skipped over in (id). This pattern also violates subjacency because the distributive contains segments from a nonadjacent stem. Broselow attributes the transparency of the diminutive to its status as an infix. She proposes that the diminutive attaches to a syllable (the locus of its attachment site is sensitive to stress) and does not produce a new stem, making it exempt from the subjacency condition. This pattern does not offer evidence for a serial derivation because it is not clear which stem has precedence (dim or dist) in forming double reduplications. Hewitt and Shaw (1995) propose that a similar pattern in St'at'imcets (Lillooet) results because of a correspondence relation between input and reduplicant for the plural morpheme (cognate with dist).

References

Bates, Dawn. 1986. An analysis of Lushootseed diminutive reduplication, *Proceedings of the Twelfth Annual Meeting of the Berkeley Linguistics Society*: 1–12.

Bates, Dawn, Thom Hess, and Vi Hilbert. 1994. *Lushootseed Dictionary*. Seattle, WA: University of Washington Press.

Benua, Laura. 1995. Identity effects in morphological truncation, in J. Beckman, S. Urbanczyk, and L. Walsh Dickey (eds.), *University of Massachusetts Occasional Papers in Linguistics* 18: *Papers in Optimality Theory*, Amherst, MA: Graduate Linguistic Student Association, University of Massachusetts.

Blevins, Juliette. 1994. The bimoraic foot in Rotuman phonology and morphology, *Oceanic Linguistics* 33.

Broselow, Ellen I. 1983. Subjacency in morphology: Salish double reduplications, *Natural Language and Linguistic Theory* 1: 317–46.

Broselow, Ellen I., and John J. McCarthy. 1984. A theory of internal reduplication, *Linguistic Review* 3: 25–88.

Carrier-Duncan, Jill. 1984. Some problems with prosodic accounts of reduplication, in M. Aronoff and R. T. Oehrle (eds.), *Language Sound Structure: Studies in Phonology presented to Morris Halle by his Teacher and Students*. Cambridge, MA: MIT Press, 260–86.

Churchward, C. Maxwell. 1940 [1978] *Rotuman Grammar and Dictionary*. Sidney: Australasian Medical Publishing Co. [Reprinted New York, NY: AMS Press.]

Clements, G. N. 1985. The problem of transfer in nonlinear morphology, *Cornell Working Papers in Linguistics* 7: 38–73.

1986. Compensatory lengthening and consonant gemination in Luganda, in L. Wetzels and E. Sezer (eds.), *Studies in Compensatory Lengthening*, Dordrecht: Foris, 37–77.

1993. Place of articulation in consonants and vowels: a unified theory, in B. Laks and A. Railland (eds.), *L'Architecture et la Géometrie des Représentations Phonologiques*. Paris: Editions du C.N.R.S.

Cohn, Abigail. 1989. Stress in Indonesian and bracketing paradoxes, *Natural Language and Linguistic Theory* 7: 167–216.

Davis, Stuart. 1988. On the nature of internal reduplication, *Theoretical Morphology*: 305–23.

Goldsmith, John. 1976. Autosegmental phonology, Ph.D. dissertation, Massachusetts Institute of Technology, Cambridge, MA.

Haeberlin, Herman K. 1918. Types of reduplication in the Salish dialects, *International Journal of American Linguistics* 1: 154–74.

Hayes, Bruce. 1980. A metrical theory of stress rules, Ph.D. dissertation, Massachusetts Institute of Technology, Cambridge, MA.

Hess, Thom. 1966. Snohomish chameleon morphology, *International Journal of American Linguistics* 32: 350–56.

1967. Snohomish grammatical structure, Ph.D. dissertation, University of Washington, Seattle, WA.

1977. Lushootseed dialects, *Anthropological Linguistics* 19: 403–419.

Hess, Thom, and Vi Hilbert. 1976. *Lushootseed 1 and 2*. Seattle, WA: Daybreak Press, United Indians of All Tribes Federation.

Hewitt, Mark, and Patricia Shaw. 1995. Cyclicity in OT: double reduplication in St'at'imcents, paper presented at the Tilburg conference on the Derivational Residue in Phonology, 6 October 1995.

Itô, Junko, and R. Armin Mester. 1993. Licensed segments and safe paths, *Canadian Journal of Linguistics* 38: 197–213.

This volume. Realignment.

Itô, Junko, R. Armin Mester, and Jaye Padgett. 1995. Licensing and underspecification in Optimality Theory, *Linguistic Inquiry* 26: 571–613.

Kager, René. 1991. Dutch schwa in moraic phonology, in M. Ziolkowski, M. Noske, and K. Deaton (eds.). *Papers from the 26th Regional Meeting of the Chicago Linguistic Society*, Part II. Chicago, IL: Chicago Linguistic Society, 241–55.

Kenstowicz, Michael. 1994a. Cyclic versus noncyclic constraint evaluation, *MIT Working Papers in Linguistics* 21: 11–42.

1994b. Sonority-driven stress, ms. Massachusetts Institute of Technology, Cambridge, MA.

Kiparsky, Paul. 1982. Lexical morphology and phonology, in Linguistic Society of Korea (ed.), *Linguistics in the Morning Calm*, Seoul: Hanshin Publishing Company, 3–91.

1986. The phonology of reduplication, ms. Stanford University, CA

Kirkham, Sandra. 1992. Reduplication in Lushootseed: a prosodic analysis, M.A. thesis, University of Victoria, Canada.

Leben, William. 1973. Suprasegmental phonology, Ph.D. dissertation, Massachusetts Institute of Technology, Cambridge, MA.

Levin, Juliette. 1983. Reduplication and prosodic structure, ms. Massachusetts Institute of Technology, Cambridge, MA.

Marantz, Alec. 1982. Re Reduplication, *Linguistic Inquiry* 13: 435–82.

McCarthy, John J. 1986. OCP effects: gemination and antigemination, *Linguistic Inquiry* 17: 207–63.

McCarthy, John J., and Alan S. Prince. 1986. Prosodic Morphology, ms. University of Massachusetts, Amherst, MA and Brandeis University, Waltham, MA.

1988. Quantitative transfer in reduplicative and templatic morphology, in Linguistic Society of Korea (ed.), *Linguistics in the Morning Calm*, vol. 2. Seoul: Hanshin Publishing Company, 3–35.

1990. Foot and word in Prosodic Morphology: the Arabic broken plural, *Natural Language and Linguistic Theory* 8: 209–83.

1993. Prosodic Morphology I: constraint interaction and satisfaction, ms. University of Massachusetts, Amherst, MA and Rutgers University, New Brunswick, NJ.

1994a. An overview of Prosodic Morphology: Parts I and II, handout of presentations at the Workshop on Prosodic Morphology, University of Utrecht, 1994.

1994b. The emergence of the unmarked: Optimality in Prosodic Morphology, in M. Gonzàlez (ed.), *Proceedings of the North East Linguistic Society* 24, Amherst, MA: Graduate Linguistic Student Association, University of Massachusetts, 333–79.

This volume. Faithfulness and reduplicative identity.

Mester, R. Armin. 1986. Studies in tier structure, Ph.D. dissertation, University of Massachusetts, Amherst, MA.

Mohanan, K. P. 1986. *The Theory of Lexical Phonology*. Dordrecht: D. Reidel Publishing Co.

Poser, William J. 1990. Evidence for foot structure in Japanese, *Language* 66, 78–105.

Prince, Alan S., and Paul Smolensky. 1993. Optimality Theory: constraint interaction in generative grammar, ms. Rutgers University, New Brunswick, NJ and University of Colorado, Boulder, CO.

Rosenthal, Samuel. 1994. Vowel/glide alternation in a theory of constraint interaction, Ph.D. dissertation, University of Massachusetts, Amherst, MA.

Selkirk, Elisabeth, O. 1977. The French foot: on the status of mute *e*, *Studies in French Linguistics* 1: 141–50.

1984. On the major class features and syllable theory, in M. Aronoff and R. T. Oehrle (eds.), *Language Sound Structure: Studies in Phonology presented to Morris Halle by his Teacher and Students*. Cambridge, MA: MIT Press, 107–36.

Shaw, Patricia A. 1994. Minimality and markedness. Handout of presentation at the Workshop on Prosodic Morphology, University of Utrecht, 1994.

Snyder, Warren. 1968. *Southern Puget Sound Salish: Phonology and Morphology*. Sacramento, CA: Sacramento Anthropological Society, Paper 8.

Steriade, Donca. 1988. Reduplication and syllable transfer in Sanskrit and elsewhere, *Phonology* 5: 73–155.

Uhrbach, Amy. 1987. A formal analysis of reduplication and its interaction with phonological and morphological processes, Ph.D. dissertation, University of Texas, Austin, TX.

Urbanczyk, Suzanne. 1994. Template violation in reduplication. Handout of presentation at the Workshop on Prosodic Morphology, University of Utrecht, 1994.

1996. Patterns of reduplication in Lushootseed, Ph.D. dissertation, University of Massachusetts, Amherst, MA.

Whitney, Dwight. 1889 [1973]. *Sanskrit Grammar*. [Thirteenth issue of the second edition.] Cambridge, MA: Harvard University Press.

Wilbur, Ronnie. 1973. The phonology of reduplication, Ph.D. dissertation, University of Illinois, Urbana-Champaign, IL.

Index of subjects

affixation
  base of 347–48
  degemination under 52
  discontinuous 5
  preservation (transfer) of weight
    52, 358
  verbal 63–64, 91–93
affixes 226, 232, 262, 266
  and faithfulness 277, 232
  reduplicative 226, 266
Alignment (Generalized) 163, 188,
    201–10
  and anchoring 222, 295
  crisp edge 208
  foot alignment 144, 263
  grid alignment 200–1, 213
  stem alignment 262, 380
  string alignment 200, 295
allomorphy
  allomorph selection 299
  prosodically governed 46, 49, 58,
    213, 344
association (mapping)
  and correspondence 228, 231, 291
  direction (left-to-right) 5, 10, 70,
    228, 392
  mapping of melody to template
    6–7, 10, 221–22, 392–93
  morpheme integrity 71
  Well-Formedness Condition 5–6,
    228
augmentation 65, 92–93, 344, 348,
    358

autosegmental phonology 2–5, 228,
    231, 242

catalexis 150, 180, 182
clitic group 375
coalescence (segmental fusion)
    231, 289, 296, 297, 313–17,
    321, 409
compounding 110, 253, 262
conspiracy 311, 327, 331
constraint (general) 220, 225–29,
    293–96
  articulatory basis of 312–13
  categorical versus gradient
    violation 196–97, 384
  ranking
    and cophonologies 138–39
    and cross-linguistic variation 62,
      67, 276, 318, 323, 334
    metacondition 232
    stringency relationship 284
    universal 319
  containment 26, 229–31, 298, 315,
    321
  contiguity 221
cophonology (sub-grammar)
    138–39, 142–55
copying (theory of reduplication) 10,
    14, 238–39, 253–58, 392–94
correspondence 24–25, 220–25, 314,
    321, 396
  constraints 225–29, 293–96
  definition of 223, 396

429

Index of constraints

Index of languages

Index of names

Agbayani, Brian 231
Akinlabi, Akinbiyi 221, 295, 296, 297
Alderete, John 222, 224, 227, 296, 297, 299, 300, 334, 338, 421
Anderson, Stephen 34, 239, 292, 332, 335
Archangeli, Diana 58, 71, 211, 230, 295, 296, 297, 298, 313
Aronoff, Mark 239, 286
Austin, Peter 221, 259, 264
Avery, Peter 324

Baković, Eric 246, 292, 296
Barker, Christopher 138, 143, 148, 149, 180, 181, 183
Bat-El, Outi 231
Bates, Dawn 398, 399, 401, 404, 405 408, 422, 423
Beckman, Jill 227, 230, 231, 296, 297, 421
Beckman, Mary 207, 297
Benson, Peter 239
Benson, T. G. 86
Benua, Laura 27, 223, 227, 231, 249, 292, 293, 296, 297, 395, 417, 421, 422, 423
Bessell, Nicola 296
Bethin, C. Y. 369
Blevins, Juliette 423
Bloomfield, Leonard 238, 239
Booij, Geert 373, 375
Borowsky, Toni 199, 365
Broadbent, Judith 364

Bromberger, Sylvain 243
Broselow, Ellen 391, 392, 393, 398, 401, 407, 408, 419, 420, 424
Buckley, Eugene 76, 85
Burquest, Donald 364
Burzio, Luigi 27, 188, 223, 231, 293, 296
Byarushengo, Ernest 122
Bye, Patrik 231

Cairns, Charles 297
Calabrese, Andrea 296
Carleton, Troi 90, 94, 108, 119, 121, 122, 231
Carlson, Kathryn 261, 296, 297
Carrier[-Duncan], Jill 234, 239, 423
Cetnarowska, Bożena 385
Chafe, Wallace 255
Charette, Monik 34
Chen, Su-I 231
Cho, Young-mee 60, 347
Chomsky, Noam 1, 3, 4, 6, 33, 229, 292, 324
Christaller, Rev. J. G. 234
Churchward, C. Maxwell 222, 409, 423
Clements, G. N. 2, 3, 27, 40, 201, 212, 227, 228, 242, 297, 310, 394, 401, 404, 423
Cohn, Abigail 188, 214, 296, 298, 314, 322, 327, 335, 336, 402
Cole, Jennifer 298
Colina, Sonia 261